I = information
T = refugee testimony
A = activity

CONTENTS

Why teach about refugees?

There are over 18 million refugees in today's world. They have escaped conflict and human rights abuses. Television has brought the experiences of refugees into everyone's sitting room. And the 1990s have seen an increased number of refugees fleeing to western Europe.

Most students are interested in, and often knowledgeable about the events that cause people to become refugees. Work about refugees enables school students to find out more about these current events. It also gives young people the opportunity to explore concepts such as human rights, justice, leaving home and being a newcomer. Such work should encourage students to develop empathy towards refugees and a commitment to justice. Ultimately the most important message is that refugees are ordinary people who have experienced extraordinary events.

Methodology

The information and activities in this book are aimed at 14-18 year old students, but not all the activities are suitable for use with younger students. Some activities can be used with students of all ages and abilities, other activities are more complex. All the activities can be used in schools, some can also be used in youth groups.

All the activities have teacher/leader instructions. Some activities also have student instructions. The student instructions may be photocopied if students are working collaboratively. Some of the activities can also be adapted for individual work.

The Curriculum

'Refugees: we left because we had to' can be used in many areas of the school curriculum. The information and activities in the book enable students to develop concepts and skills demanded in the National Curriculum and by examination boards. *'Refugees: we left because we had to'* is of particular relevance to the teaching of English, history, geography, religious education, sociology and social studies, integrated humanities, modern studies and personal and social education. The list below indicates the range of subjects for which the activities and information may be used.

English
Speaking and listening skills: Role play, presenting arguments, presenting information, negotiation.

Reading skills: reading and understanding non-fictional texts such as newspapers, autobiography, diaries, letters and leaflets.

Writing skills: writing to inform, writing to present arguments, writing stories and narrative.

History
'Refugees: we left because we had to' covers the following subject areas:

- The Huguenots
- Jewish migration in Victorian Britain
- The growth of multi-ethnic Britain 1880-1970
- The era of the Second World War
- The development of the United Nations and international humanitarian law
- The colonisation of Africa
- Post colonial Africa
- The Arab-Israeli conflict
- The Vietnam War
- Oral history

Geography
'Refugees: we left because we had to' examines poverty, migration and the impact of refugee movements on a host country.

Religious Education
'Refugees: we left because we had to' examines Jewish migration and looks at many contemporary moral issues such as:

- poverty
- war
- the arms trade
- social justice
- race and immigration issues
- responsibility to others.

Sociology/Social Studies
'Refugees: we left because we had to' examines race and immigration issues and pressure groups within a democratic society.

Integrated Humanities
'Refugees: we left because we had to' contains work which examines the concepts of:

- equality and inequality
- conflict and cooperation
- freedom and constraint
- justice and injustice
- pressure groups and political movements
- nationalism and internationalism
- poverty, wealth and welfare

'Refugees: we left because we had to' can also be used by teachers of politics and personal and social education.

Schools with refugee students

More and more British schools have refugee students, particularly those in Greater London. Teachers will obviously have to be sensitive to the needs of refugee children, particularly when initiating class projects on refugees.

Refugee children may have experienced great trauma in their home countries or during their escape. They may have seen members of their family injured, killed or arrested. Such horrific events cannot easily be discussed in classrooms.

Refugee children may also not want to talk about their home country or family circumstances because they are worried about family left at home, or because they feel that it might jeopardise their chances of staying in Britain, or eventually returning home. Refugee children may not want to discuss their circumstances because they do not want to feel different from other children. And they may feel embarrassed about the popular images of their home country. Some Somali children in British schools have felt unable to admit they were from Somalia because the only image their teachers and fellow pupils have of Somalia is that of famine and war.

But there are many ways of making refugee students feel secure, while at the same time increasing knowledge about their home countries. Displays about life in students' countries of origin are one way. Schools can also invite member of refugee communities to talk to students. All school work on refugees must seek to humanise those who flee, and to enable non-refugee students to feel empathy towards refugee students.

Work about why refugees flee their homes assumes greater importance at a time when hostility to refugees is increasing. Negative media coverage and the pejorative remarks of some politicians contribute to popular misconceptions about refugees. These misconceptions can affect the self-esteem of refugee students. It is essential that schools challenge such misinformation. All students must be prepared for life in a multi-ethnic democracy, of which refugees are a part.

CHAPTER ONE

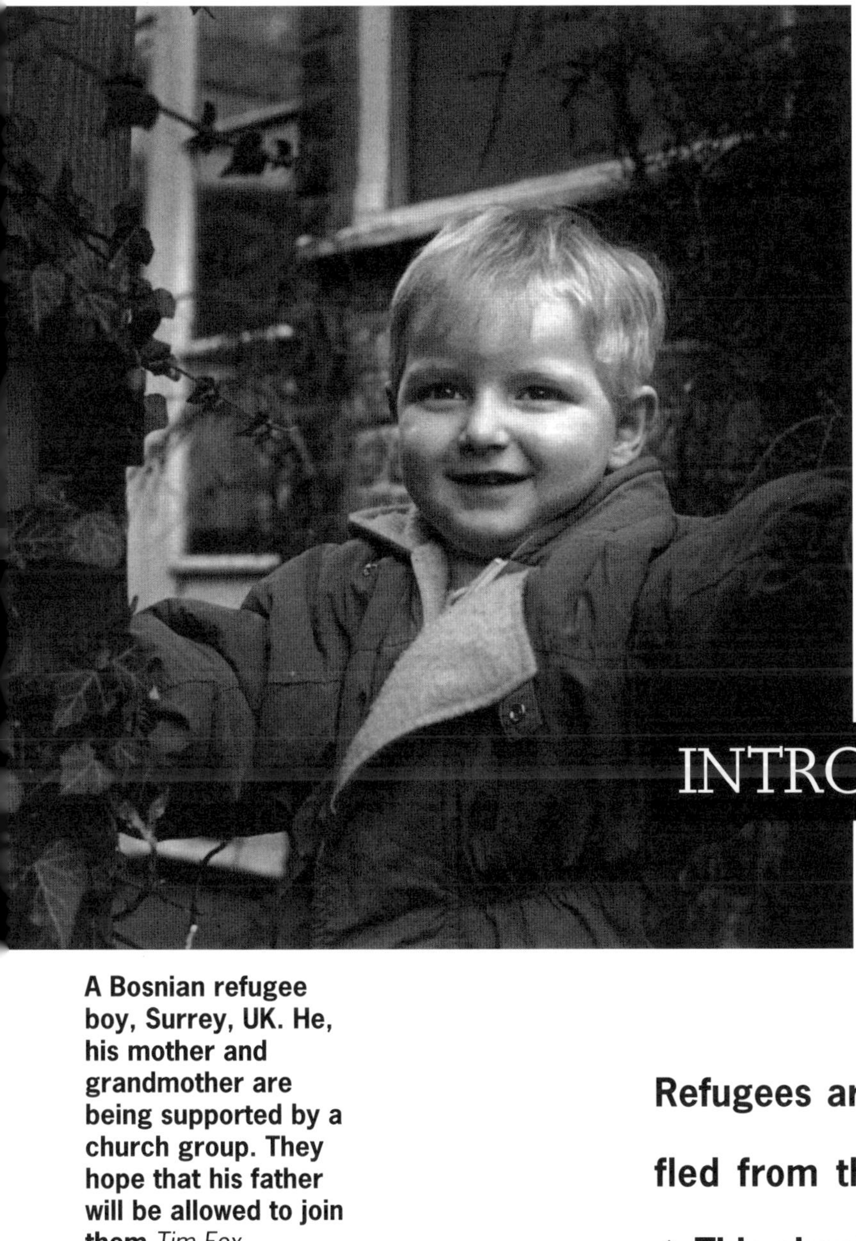

A Bosnian refugee boy, Surrey, UK. He, his mother and grandmother are being supported by a church group. They hope that his father will be allowed to join them *Tim Fox*

INTRODUCTION

Refugees are people who have fled from their homes in fear ◆ This chapter introduces word definitions, gives refugee statistics and describes some of the organisations that work with refugees.

Refugees: an issue for the 21st Century

Below are a cross-section of opinions about refugees. They were collected from students in a school in London. In pairs or in groups look at each statement and decide what you think about each opinion.

There are 18 million refugees in today's world. Another 25 million people are internally displaced within their own countries. There are more refugees now than at any other time in history. Most refugees are living in poor countries, in Africa and Asia. Many of them lack the basics of life: clean water, food and shelter.

The countries of Europe have again seen a rise in racism and nationalism. One aspect of this has been a change in the way that governments treat refugees. Since the mid-1980s it has become more difficult for refugees to reach safety in Europe. Refugees have also been made scapegoats by some politicians and the media. They have been blamed for causing social problems, such as unemployment and homelessness. Throughout Europe the general public has become more hostile to refugees.

The movement of refugees and their reception in new countries is one of the major political and moral issues facing today's world. The Refugee Council believes that it is important for young people to understand why people become refugees and the support refugees need when they are forced to move to a new country. With this knowledge young people can challenge some of the current misconceptions and prejudices about refugees. Young people can work to make their country and local community more welcoming to refugees. Finally, it is important to understand what governments and ordinary people can do to prevent people from becoming refugees. What do you think?

"It is up to politicians to sort out refugees."

"There are no refugees living near us or going to my school. It is not our problem."

"Refugees are ordinary people just like us. It could be me who was a refugee. So it is important that we find out about refugees and help them."

"We should all be welcoming to newcomers. It is not just refugees who move homes. You could be new in a school. If you were, you would want to be welcomed."

"Einstein was a refugee. Refugees often contribute things to their new country. It is important that we know things like that."

"Newspapers often give wrong information about refugees. So it is important to find out the truth."

"We should try to help people who are in difficulty or are less fortunate than ourselves."

"It isn't my fault that there are wars in other countries. So why should I bother about refugees?"

"Our country has sold weapons to countries at war. Often these weapons cause people to become refugees. We do have a link with refugees in other countries."

Brainstorming the word 'refugee'

Instructions

Time needed: 20 minutes

Thick colour marker pens and some large sheets of paper are needed.

Divide the students into groups of four or five. Each group should write down on the sheets any ideas that come into their minds when they hear the word 'refugee'.

When the papers are filled, pin them up. Are there any similarities between the sheets. Keep the sheets until you have found out more about refugees. You can return to them at a later date.

Why do people move?

Aims

To make participants aware that people move or migrate for many different reasons. Refugees are one group of people who migrate every year. They move involuntarily, because of fear.

Instructions

Time needed: 40 minutes

You will need some pens, a large sheet of paper, and some 'post-its'.

Divide the students up into groups of four and five. Each group should write on 'post-its' the reasons why people move their homes. Write down one reason on each 'post-it'. The group should all think about reasons why they and their family might have moved house. The group can also use the case study cards on page 10 to give ideas.

Then come together, and use all the 'post-its' to make a single list of why people might leave home. Sort out the reasons under two columns:

◆ Reasons why people move voluntarily

◆ Reasons why people move involuntarily (against their will)

Discussion points

◆ Why do people move involuntarily?

◆ Do refugees move voluntarily or against their will?

◆ Are there any other groups of people in the world who might move home involuntarily?

Participants can read the information sheet on page 11 after taking part in this activity. The class may want to discuss some of the points raised in the information sheet.

Migration

Aims

To help students understand the range of reasons that cause people to migrate.

Instructions

Time needed: 30 minutes

The cards should be prepared in advance. There should be enough sets of cards for each group. The students should be divided into groups of three. Each group should be given a set of cards. The students should be told that the aim of the activity is to examine the different reasons that cause people to migrate. The students should read through the cards and sort them into different groups according to the reasons that the people on the cards have had to move home.

The teacher or group leader can use the cards and the different methods of sorting them to prompt a discussion about forced and voluntary migration.

Ahmed moved from Morocco to France in 1989. He had just left school and there was very little work in the area where he lived. He decided to join his father who lives in Paris. He now works as a cleaner.

Tipu is Nepali and lived in a small village in eastern Nepal. During heavy rains in 199 there was a landslide near his house. The landslide was caused because the trees in the area had been cut and could no longer protect the soil. Tipu's house and most of his land were destroyed and now he has had to move to Katmandhu, the capital city, to find work as a porter for tourists.

Afia was born in Bangladesh. She and her family lived on a housing estate in London. Throughout 1989 a group of teenagers harassed the family. Her children were beaten when they came home from school and rubbish was put through the letter box. The family eventually decided to move to an area where there were more Bangladeshi families.

Helen lived in a small village in Cornwall until recently. In 1994 she moved home to study at a university in London.

Roisin is from Northern Ireland. She is Roman Catholic. In 1982 she married a Protestant and went to live with her new husband's parents in a part of Belfast where the population is Protestant. Roisin and her husband were sent threatening letters saying that Protestants and Catholics should not marry. They were continually harassed and decided to move to London.

Raju was born in a village in southern India. His family were not wealthy and their house did not have electricity or running water. He did very well at school and won a place at university in Delhi, the capital of India. Raju has decided to remain in Delhi as there are more job opportunities in the city.

Mahmut is a doctor and worked in a hospital in Turkey. He was active in politics and also campaigned for better health facilities for Kurdish people, a minority group in Turkey. In 1987 he was arrested and tortured, but later released. Fearing that this may happen again he came to Britain.

Leonardo is 14 years old and was born in Mozambique. The civil war in his country left him an orphan. His village was destroyed. Leonardo walked with other orphaned children to a nearby town. Here they were taken to a children's home where they are still living.

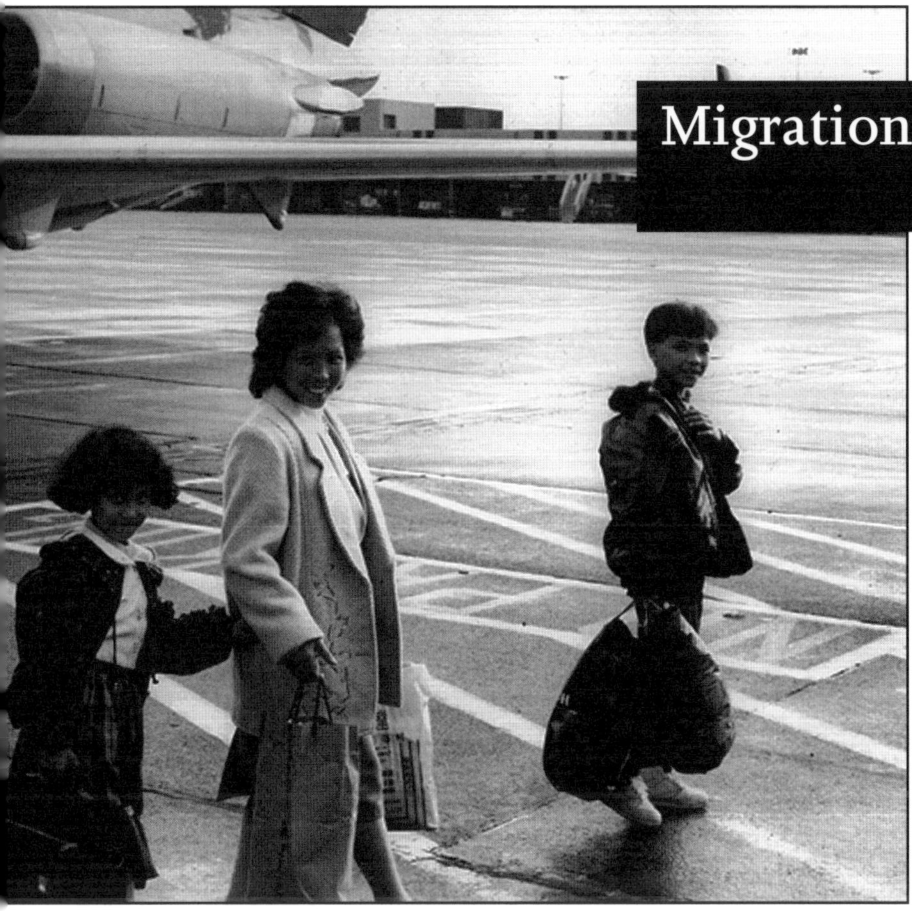

Migration

Vietnamese refugee family who have just arrived in Britain.
Howard Davies

The permanent movement of people from one place to another is called migration. People move for many different reasons. These can be divided into:

Push factors - things that push or force people to move from their homes to live in another place

Pull factors - things which attract people to a new place.

Push factors include:

- no work
- war
- threats to freedom
- threats to life
- no educational opportunities
- poverty
- hunger
- drought

Pull factors include:

- work
- safety
- good housing
- good schools
- food

Economic migrants have been pushed from their homes because of poverty. They may be pulled towards a new area by the promise of higher wages, work and better opportunities. In many cases economic migrants have left their homes voluntarily, although famine victims are forced to leave their homes against their will. Every year about 175 million people move home for economic reasons. In poor countries people move from the countryside to towns.

Refugees and internally displaced people have been pushed from their homes because of threats to their life or freedom. They are pulled to a new home by the promise of safety. They are involuntary migrants, having left their homes against their will. There are 18 million refugees in today's world and about 25 million internally displaced people.

Who is a refugee?

The word refugee is used in everyday speech, but under international law it has a precise meaning. A refugee is someone who has fled to another country and has been given refugee status by the government of the new country. To be given refugee status the government of the new country has to decide that the person has left his or her own country, or cannot return to it *'owing to a well-founded fear of being persecuted for reasons of race, religion, nationality, membership of a particular social group or political opinion'*.

There are 18 million refugees in the world.

An **asylum-seeker** is someone who has fled from his or her home country, and is seeking refugee status.

The definition of who is a refugee, and how countries are meant to treat asylum-seekers and refugees is outlined in international law, in the 1951 UN Convention and 1967 UN Protocol Relating to the Status of Refugees. Over 120 of the world's countries have signed these laws. It is the task of the United Nations High Commissioner for Refugees to ensure that countries respect these laws.

Other groups of people have fled from their homes in fear but are not recognised as refugees. They include:

Internally displaced people may have left their homes because of war or human rights abuses, but have not crossed an international border. There are about 25 million internally displaced people in the world.

De facto refugees are people who leave their country in fear, but do not apply for refugee status in their new country. Some people may flee from their homes and then move to another country where they live without permission. Other people may flee from their home country but be given permission to stay legally in another country, perhaps because they have relatives or work in that country.

People flee from homes and become refugees for many different reasons. The causes of refugee movements are:

◆ war between countries

◆ civil war

◆ the persecution of minority ethnic groups

◆ the persecution of religious groups

◆ the persecution of members of political organisations

◆ the persecution of people because they belong to a distinct social group, for example gay men and lesbians are persecuted in some countries. Women who refuse to wear veils are endangered in a few countries.

Somali refugee, Kenya *Howard Davies*

Aims

To draw participants attention to the varied experiences of refugees, and to develop empathy with refugees.

Instructions

Time needed: 30 minutes

Every group or pair needs a copy of the case studies so these will need to be prepared in advance. The participants will need to know who are refugees, and be familiar with the UN definition.

The students should be divided into groups of three. Everyone should receive a copy of the case studies. Explain to the participants that they have to decide whether each of the case studies fits the UN definition of a refugee. (A person who has left his/her own country, or is unable to return to it 'owing to a well-founded fear of being persecuted for reasons of race, religion, nationality, membership of a particular social group or political opinion').

The small groups should examine the case studies, and make a group decision on who fits the definition. The groups can them come together and compare their answers. Information is included on what happened to the people in real life.

Discussion points

◆ Was there anyone that all of the groups believed to be a refugee? Why?

◆ Was there anyone that all the groups believed was definitely not a refugee? Why?

◆ Which people did you disagree about whether they should be given refugee status or not?

◆ Were you surprised about what happened to them in real life?

◆ Why might they wish their names to be changed for use in this pack?

Who is a refugee?

Case studies

All six people below are real people whose testimonies have been collected by the Refugee Council. Their names have been changed.

Sami is a Turkish Kurd. He was a farmer in a village in eastern Turkey. In this part of the country most people belong to the Kurdish minority. Until recently Kurdish people were not allowed to speak their language in Turkey and suffered other forms of discrimination. There has been fighting between the Turkish army and Kurdish guerrillas, and many innocent people have been killed. Amnesty International has also criticised the Turkish government for detaining Kurds without trial and using torture on detainees. This part of eastern Turkey is also much poorer than the rest of the country.

Sami's family has suffered from continual harassment from the Turkish army during the last two years. Recently a Turkish soldier was killed by Kurdish guerrillas. Turkish soldiers arrived in Sami's village and arrested his brother, who they believe supported Kurdish guerrillas. The soldiers threatened to take more villagers if there was more trouble from the guerrillas. Sami believes that he is in danger, and has fled to Britain.

Siva is 17 years old and is a Sri Lankan Tamil. Until recently he lived in the town of Jaffna.

The Tamils are a minority group in Sri Lanka. Since 1948 they have suffered from discrimination and it has been more difficult for Tamils to enter university or get government jobs. Tired of waiting for political solutions, some Tamils have resorted to fighting for independence. Since 1983 a fierce war has raged in northern Sri Lanka between the Sri Lankan army and Tamil guerrillas. Jaffna has been under siege by the Sri Lankan army since 1990. There is no electricity in Jaffna, and basic foods and medicines are in very short supply. Many people are malnourished.

Siva and his family moved into Jaffna from an outlying village. The conditions under which they were forced to live caused them great stress. Siva's father used his last savings to pay for Siva to escape. In July 1993 Siva left Sri Lanka on a small boat bound for southern India. In Madras, India he bought an air ticket and a forged passport to enable him to come to Britain.

Amira is a Bosnian Muslim and has a Serbian husband. Until the war started in 1992 they lived in a village near Banja Luka, Bosnia. Amira and her husband teach in a secondary school. When the war started Amira and her family started receiving threats from Serbian extremists in the area. They were told that people in mixed marriages should leave the area.

Amira and her family decided to leave the village, and stay with her sister's family who live in Zagreb, Croatia. Soon after they left, their house was occupied by another family. Amira's sister's flat is very crowded. As both Amira and her husband are English teachers, they decided to come to Britain.

Augustina is 22 and is from Zaire. All political opposition is banned in Zaire and many opponents of the government have been detained. Until recently she was a student at the University of Lubumbashi. She and many of her friends were supporters of a banned political party and wanted Zaire to become a democracy.

One night policemen working for the president of Zaire came to the university. They arrested some students, including Augustina. She was taken to a detention centre in the forest. She did not know where she was being held. She was kept here for about one month, and beaten many times. She was then taken to another detention centre where she was held for several weeks. Her family then managed to pay a bribe for her to be released. Augustina escaped over the border to Zambia and then flew to London.

Hassan is from northern Somalia. He had just left university and started his first job as a civil servant. There was civil war in this part of the country for many years. It got worse in 1988. His home town was bombed and thousands of people were killed or injured. Hassan escaped to Ethiopia and lived in a camp for Somali refugees. Conditions in the camp were very hard, and there was not enough food or clean water. Hassan decided to leave the camp and travel to Addis Ababa, Ethiopia's capital city. Here he telephoned his uncle who lives in London. His uncle was able to lend Hassan the money to fly to London.

Ramon is from Colombia. He is 28 years old and worked as a lawyer in Colombia. During the day he worked for a firm of lawyers. In his spare time he gave his services to a human rights organisation which worked to monitor conditions in Colombia.

Ramon started to receive threatening telephone calls telling him to stop his work with the human rights organisation. He then received a letter saying that he would be killed. As many people who have worked for human rights organisations in Colombia have been killed, Ramon decided that he must leave the country. He flew to Britain.

What happened?

Sami was refused refugee status in Britain, but allowed to stay. He was given 'exceptional leave to remain'.

Siva was refused refugee status in Britain. He was told that although he suffered from persecution in Sri Lanka he could have sought refugee status in India. His lawyer made an appeal.

Amira is still waiting to hear if she will be given refugee status. She has been waiting for two years.

Augustina was asked for further evidence to support her application. She was asked to give information about the location of the detention camps in the forest. She could not supply the required information and she was refused refugee status. She is still in Britain, but does not know how much longer she will be allowed to stay.

Hassan was given refugee status.

Ramon was refused refugee status. His lawyer made an appeal but it was not successful. Ramon is thinking about leaving Britain and may go to Venezuela.

Refugees: myth or fact quiz

Aims

To highlight some of the misconceptions about refugees.

Instructions

Time needed: 45 minutes

The group should be divided into pairs. Each pair should be given a copy of the quiz sheet. After the pairs have written down the answers to the quiz the class should come together for a discussion. The quiz could also be used as a basis for a fundraising activity. Participants could be charged a small amount to answer the quiz and there could be a prize for the first set of correct answers.

Discussion points

- **Did any of the answers surprise you?**
- **Why?**

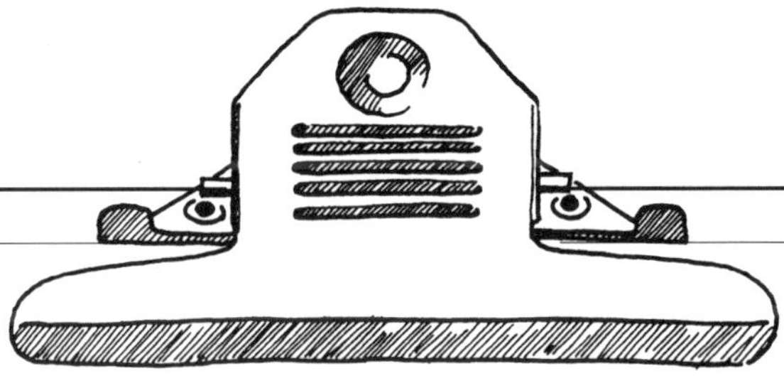

Quiz

In Britain there are a wide range of views about refugees. Some people have ideas and prejudices about refugees which are not based on fact. See how much you know about refugees!

1. Who are refugees? Give your own definition.

2. How many refugees are there in today's world? Are there:

☐ 3 ☐ 18 ☐ 39 ☐ 155

☐ 272 million?

3. Most of the world's refugees flee to rich European countries.

☐ True ☐ false?

4. Name three countries from which refugees are presently fleeing.

5. Refugees from former Yugoslavia are the largest refugee group in today's world.

☐ True ☐ false?

6. Wars cause people to flee as refugees. How many wars are being fought in today's world?
Is it:

☐ 9 ☐ 14 ☐ 28 ☐ 38 ☐ 52?

7. Over 125,000 asylum-seekers came to Britain in 1994.

☐ True ☐ false?

8. Refugees who arrive in Britain receive a lot of help when they first arrive.

☐ True ☐ false?

9. More people leave the United Kingdom every year than settle here as migrants or refugees.

☐ True ☐ false?

10. What links a roll of Andrex toilet paper and the paintings of Lucian Freud with Albert Einstein's theory of relativity?

(Answers are on page 27)

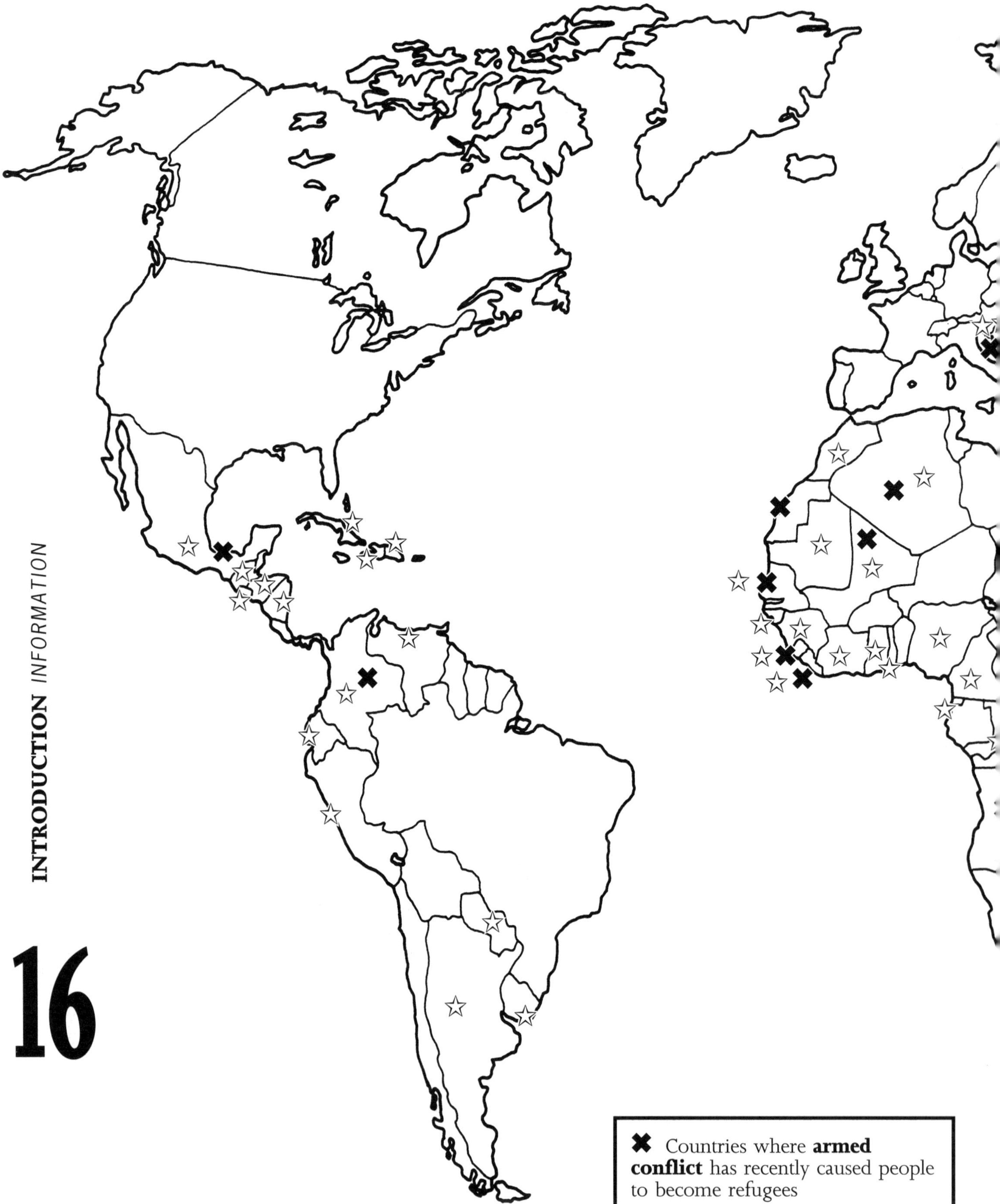

✖ Countries where **armed conflict** has recently caused people to become refugees

☆ Countries where **human rights abuses** have recently caused people to become refugees

Conflicts & human rights abuse 1995

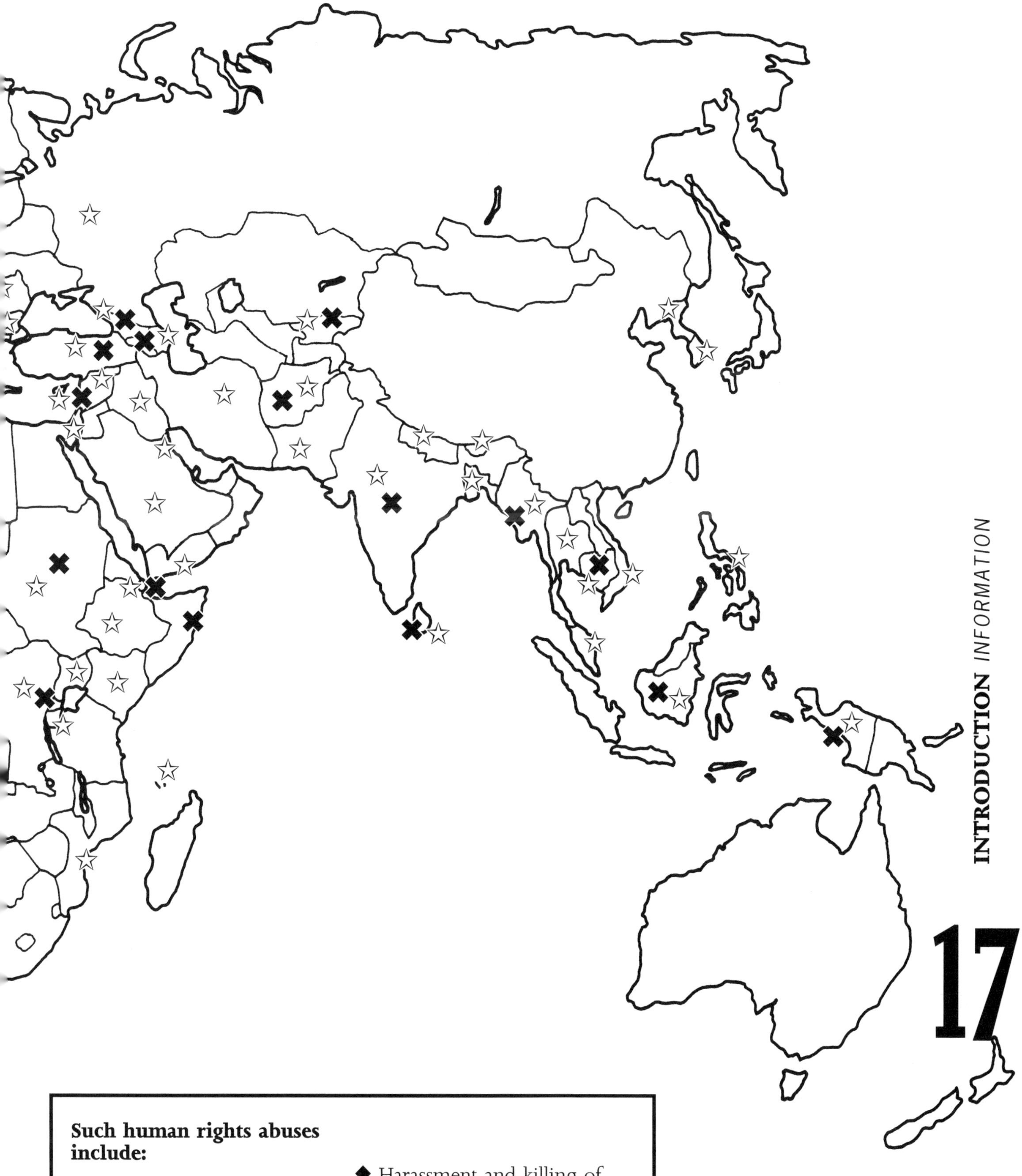

Such human rights abuses include:

◆ Harrassment of political opposition

◆ Extrajudicial executions

◆ Harassment and killing of ethnic and religious minorities

◆ Human rights abuse by armed guerrilla movements

Refugees in today's world

Source: Refugee Council and Amnesty International

People in exile

AFRICA

Angolans
There are 350,000 Angolan refugees living in neighbouring countries. Some 40,000 Angolans live in Europe and North America. Another 2,000,000 Angolans are internally displaced having fled civil war.

Burundis
There are 740,000 Burundi refugees in Rwanda, Zaire and Tanzania. Another 200,000 people are internally displaced having fled ethnic conflict between Hutu and Tutsi people.

Djiboutis
About 15,000 Djiboutis are living as refugees in Ethiopia. Another 130,000 people are internally displaced due to civil war.

Eritreans
There are 500,000 Eritrean refugees living in Sudan. The poverty of Eritrea prevents them from returning.

Kenyans
There are 300,000 internally displaced people in Kenya. They have fled ethnic conflict and human rights abuse.

Liberians
There are 865,000 Liberian refugees, mostly living in Guinea and the Ivory Coast. Another 1,450,000 people are internally displaced. The refugees began to flee after civil war started in 1989.

Malians
Some 87,000 Malian refugees are living in Mauritania and Algeria. Another 40,000 Malians are internally displaced. The refugees are ethnic Tuaregs who have fled fighting between Tuareg rebels and the Malian government.

Mauritanians
There are 80,000 Mauritanian refugees living in Senegal and Mali. The refugees are mostly of Black African origin who have been expelled from their home country on the basis of their ethnic group. The government of Mauritania is controlled by the Arabic-speaking population.

Mozambicans
About 100,000 Mozambicans remain as refugees in southern Africa. Another 800,000 people are still internally displaced after the civil war. In 1994 over 1,600,000 Mozambicans were helped to return home.

Rwandans
There are 2,000,000 Rwandan refugees living in Uganda, Burundi, Tanzania and Zaire. Another 1,800,000 Rwandans are internally displaced. The refugees have fled conflict between Tutsi and Hutu people.

Sahrawis
There are 165,000 Sahrawi refugees in Algeria. The refugees fled after the Moroccan occupation of Western Sahara.

Sierra Leoneans
There are 200,000 Sierra Leonean refugees living in neighbouring Guinea. Another 700,000 people are internally displaced. They have fled fighting in Sierra Leone.

Somalis
There are 600,000 Somali refugees living in camps in Kenya, Ethiopia, Djibouti and Yemen. About 40,000 Somali refugees live in Europe. The refugees have fled fighting which started in 1988.

Sudanese
There are 402,000 Sudanese refugees living in Kenya, Uganda, Ethiopia and in European countries. Additionally many Sudanese live in Egypt where they can stay without needing to register as refugees. The refugees have fled civil war and human rights abuse. Another 4,000,000 Sudanese are internally displaced.

Togolese
There are 150,000 Togolese refugees living in Benin and Ghana. Another 150,000 Togolese people are internally displaced. They have fled the human rights abuse of a repressive government.

Zaireans
There are 500,000 internally displaced people in Zaire after ethnic conflict in eastern and southern Zaire. Another 60,000 Zaireans have fled Zaire and are

Refugees in relation to total population of selected receiving country

Country/ territory	Number of refugees	Total population including refugees	Refugees as % of total population
Gaza Strip	644,000	700,000	92
West Bank	479,000	955,000	50
Jordan	1,850,000	3,800,000	48.7
Guinea	570,000	6,200,000	9.2
Armenia	290,000	3,600,000	8
Croatia	380,000	4,600,000	8.3
UK	230,000	56,700,000	0.4

living as refugees in neighbouring countries. About 40,000 Zairean refugees are living in western Europe.

ASIA AND THE MIDDLE EAST

Afghans
There are 2,400,000 Afghan refugees, mostly in Pakistan and Iran. They have fled fighting which started in 1979. Another 1,200,000 people are internally displaced.

Bangladeshis
There are 55,000 refugees from Bangladesh's Chittagong Hill Tracts living in India.

Bhutanese
There are 86,000 Bhutanese refugees living in Nepal. The refugees are ethnic Nepalis who have fled persecution.

Bidoons
The Bidoons are stateless Arab people lived in Kuwait. The Gulf War made them homeless. Some 120,000 Bidoons are now refugees in Iraq and another 120,000 Bidoons are stateless in Kuwait.

Burmese
There are 100,000 Burmese refugees living in Bangladesh and another 80,000 living in Thailand. Up to 1,000,000 internally displaced people may be living in Burma. The refugees have fled human rights violations and civil war.

Iraqis and Iraqi Kurds
There are 130,000 Iraqi refugees in Iran of whom 110,000 are Iraqi Kurds and 20,000 Shi'a Muslims and *Maadan* (Marsh Arabs). Over 80,000 Iraqis and Iraqi Kurds live as refugees in Europe and North America. There are 700,000 displaced people in Iraqi Kurdistan and Iraq. Most of them are Kurds.

Indians
There are 250,000 people who have been displaced by conflict in Kashmir.

Iranians
Some 300,000 Iranians have been forced to flee their country because of human rights abuses. The majority are living in India, Iraq, Europe and North America.

Lebanon
As well as Palestinian refugees some 200,000 Lebanese people are internally displaced.

Palestinians
There are 2,800,000 Palestinian refugees living in Syria, Lebanon, Jordan, Egypt, Iraq, the Gaza Strip and West Bank and other countries. They became refugees during wars in 1948/49 and in 1967. Others fled Kuwait after the Gulf War.

Sri Lankan Tamils
There are 420,000 refugees and 600,000 internally displaced people. The refugees have fled human rights abuse and civil war between Tamil guerrillas and the Sri Lankan army. About 170,000 Tamil refugees are living in India. Another 250,000 Tamil refugees are living in North American or European countries.

Tajiks
There are 20,000 Tajik refugees in Afghanistan. Another 500,000 people are internally displaced due to civil war.

Tibetans
There are 133,000 Tibetan refugees living in India and Nepal. They have been living in exile since China invaded Tibet in 1959.

Turkish Kurds
Some 20,000 Turkish Kurdish refugees are living in Iraqi Kurdistan and 220,000 Turkish Kurds live as refugees in western Europe. At least 800,000 Turkish Kurds have been displaced in eastern Turkey.

Vietnamese
International organisations still count 350,000 Vietnamese people as refugees as they still need protection and help. Over 1,000,000 people have left Vietnam since 1975.

EUROPE

Armenians
290,000 ethnic Armenian refugees have fled Azerbaijan since fighting between Armenia and Azerbaijan began in 1988.

Azeris
Some 230,000 ethnic Azeri refugees have fled from Armenia to Azerbaijan. Fighting between Armenian and Azerbaijan has displaced another 800,000 Azeri people.

Georgians
There are 186,000 Georgian refugees living in Russia. Another 250,000 Georgians are internally displaced. The refugees and displaced are Abkhazians, Georgians and Ossetians who have fled fighting and human rights abuses.

Russia
Some 150,000 Chechens and Russians were displaced by the conflict in Chechnya which began in 1995. Another 460,000 Russians are displaced within Russia after fleeing conflicts in the Caucasus and Tajikistan.

Refugees from Former Yugoslavia
There are 3,720,000 refugees and internally displaced people in the former Yugoslavia. The largest number are internally displaced in Bosnia-Hercegovina. There are another 570,000 refugees living in other European countries. The refugees have fled fighting and human rights abuse.

NORTH AND SOUTH AMERICA

Colombians
About 400,000 Colombians are internally displaced because of armed conflict and human rights abuse.

Guatemalans
There are 240,000 Guatemalan refugees living Mexico. Another 200,000 Guatemalans are internally displaced.

OTHER GROUPS

Another 1,700,000 people are refugees or in exile. They include Algerians, Ghanaians, Ivorians, Nigerians, Senegalese, South Africans, Ugandans, Cambodians, Indonesians (Achenese, East Timorese and West Papuans), Laotians, Cubans, Haitians, Hondurans, Salvadorians and Moldovans. Another 3,100,000 people are internally displaced.

Total No of Refugees in 1995
18,094,000

Total No of Internally Displaced People 24,700,000

The figures on refugee numbers include asylum-seekers, those granted refugee status and people living in refugee-like situations outside their home country. The figure only includes refugees who need legal protection or are in other ways vulnerable. It does not include people who fled their home country and are now permanently settled in a new country.

Sources: UNHCR, Refugee Council and the US Committee for Refugees.

Refugee numbers per continent

Africa
6,600,000

Asia & Middle East
6,600,000

Europe 4,300,000
(European Union countries 2,210,000)

North America
800,000

South America
50,000

Australasia
50,000

Numbers of asylum-seekers entering European Union countries 1994

Belgium	14,400
Denmark	6,700
Finland	800
France	26,000
Germany	127,200
Greece	1,300
Ireland	400
Italy	1,800
Luxembourg	200
Netherlands	52,600
Portugal	600
Spain	12,000
Sweden	18,600
United Kingdom	32,900

Using the statistical data

The above statistical data can be used in project work on refugees. Students can present the data in accessible forms to illustrate arguments. For example students can draw pie-charts or graphs to show the proportions of the world's refugees who are living in each continent.

Organisations that work with refugees

Afghan refugees, Pakistan
Howard Davies

Throughout the world many different organisations are working to support refugees. Some are large but most are small. Some work in many different countries, others in just one country. Here are some examples of organisations that work with refugees.

International organisations

Two United Nations organisations work with refugees. They are the United Nations High Commissioner for Refugees (UNHCR) and the United Nations Relief and Works Agency for Palestine Refugees in the Near East (UNRWA).

United Nations High Commissioner for Refugees - UNHCR

UNHCR was set up by the United Nations in 1951. Its headquarters are in Geneva, Switzerland and it has offices in more than 70 countries. UNHCR has three separate responsibilities:

◆ making sure that the governments of countries that have signed the 1951 UN Convention and 1967 Protocol Relating to the Status of Refugees treat asylum-seekers and refugees in a way that matches the requirements of international law.

◆ working with other organisations to make sure that aid reaches refugees.

◆ working for long-term solutions for refugees. UNHCR tries to help people return home if it becomes safe for them to do so. If this is impossible UNHCR helps people settle in a new country.

The British government gave £45 million to UNHCR in 1994.

United Nations Relief and Works Agency for Palestine Refugees in the Near East - UNRWA

The 1948 Arab-Israeli War and the 1967 Six Day War left many Palestinians as refugees. They are living in the West Bank, the Gaza Strip, Lebanon, Syria and Jordan. UNRWA began its work in 1950. It presently has its headquarters in Vienna, Austria, but UNRWA plans to move them to Gaza in the near future. UNRWA provides education, training and health-care to Palestinian refugees who live in the West Bank, Gaza, Lebanon, Syria and Jordan.

Other international organisations

Several other international organisations work with refugees. The United Nations Children's Fund sometimes works with refugee children. The International Committee for the Red Cross often works in war zones with refugees and displaced people.

Individual governments

Individual governments may work with refugee groups in their own countries. Here are some examples.

The Algerian government pays for food aid for the 165,000 Sahrawi refugees living in Algeria,

The British government has paid for reception centres and help for 4,000 Bosnian refugees who were given permission to stay in Britain for a limited period of time.

The Danish government provides funding to the Danish Refugee Council. The Danish Refugee Council, in turn, offers a wide range of services to asylum-seekers and refugees, including

- legal advice
- advice on housing, education, finding work and other matters
- Danish language classes.

Non-governmental organisations

Non-governmental organisations are not run by governments and are usually much smaller than international and government organisations. Usually they obtain their money from various sources including donations from members of the public.

There are over 300 non-governmental organisations working with refugees in Britain. They include overseas aid agencies, organisations that solely work with refugees in Britain, pressure groups and self-help groups.

Overseas aid agencies

Oxfam, CAFOD and the Save the Children Fund are three examples of overseas aid agencies. They are working with all the major refugee groups in today's world. Overseas agencies do receive small amounts of money from governments but for most of their work they rely on donations from members of the public.

Here is an example of the Save the Children Fund's work with Rwandan refugees.

The Save the Children Fund (SCF) is working with Rwandan refugees in Tanzania and Zaire and also with internally displaced people in Rwanda. In all three countries SCF is working with unaccompanied refugee children. These are children who are living by themselves. Sometimes they have been orphaned but more often they have been separated from their parents in the chaos of war. Over 100,000 Rwandan children are in this situation. SCF is helping trace the families of unaccompanied refugee children. Some 72 social workers are being employed to register information about the children and where they lost their families. The information is then put into a central computer. After the information has been put in the computer SCF can then begin to trace the families of unaccompanied children. This is a time consuming process.

In Rwanda SCF has set up a reception centre for unaccompanied children who are returning home from refugee camps in Zaire. Here the children receive food and medical care. Social workers then help them trace their families. SCF is also helping rebuild health centres inside Rwanda. Many health centres were damaged in the fighting in 1994. SCF is also providing resettlement packs to internally displaced Rwandans. The packs include items such as plastic sheeting for shelter, cooking pots, farm tools and seeds, to help them return to their homes.

SCF is assisting unaccompanied refugee children living in Zaire, providing shelter, food and healthcare.

SCF also works with refugee children in

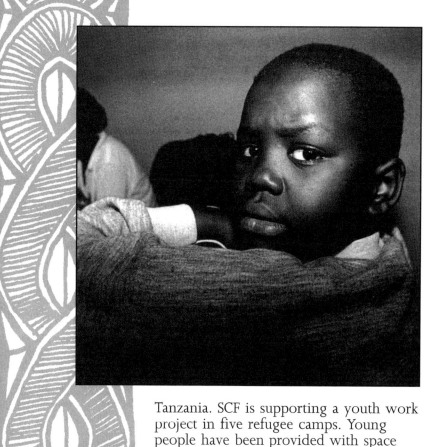

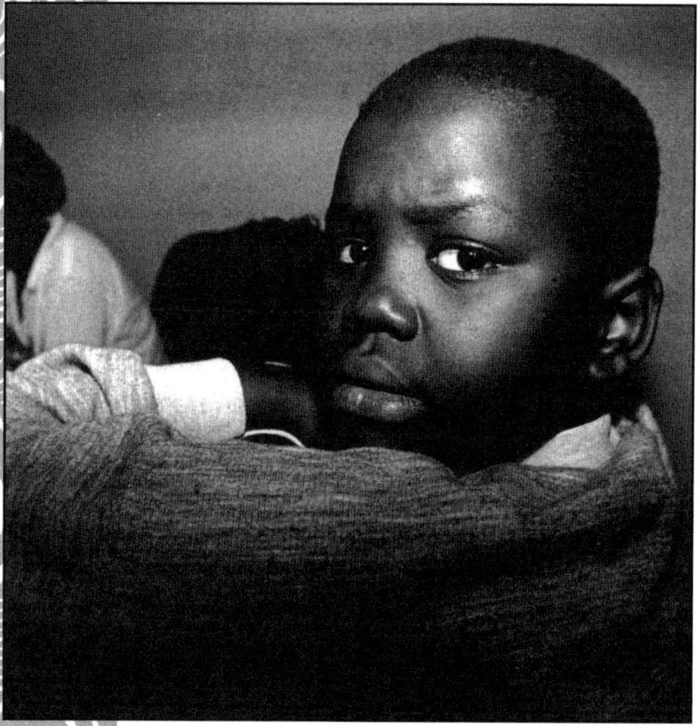

Tanzania. SCF is supporting a youth work project in five refugee camps. Young people have been provided with space and some equipment to organise activities such as music, football and volleyball.

British refugee agencies
These work with refugees of all nationalities. The Refugee Council is one example of such an organisation. On pages 25-26 is some information about its work.

Pressure groups

Pressure groups are important parts of a democratic society. A pressure group campaigns to defend the interests of its members or it can campaign for a certain cause. Most pressure groups concentrate on one issue. Pressure groups:

◆ build support with the public

◆ organise protest demonstrations and public meetings

◆ get their interests covered in the media

◆ lobby government and others in power

Some refugee organisations provide direct help to refugees but also act as a pressure group. For example the Refugee Council employs parliamentary lobbyists and press officers to do such work. Other examples of pressure groups that campaign for refugees are Amnesty International and the Minority Rights Group.

Self-help groups

A self-help group is an organisation founded by a certain group of people which works for its own members. Refugee community organisations are self-help groups. The Uganda Community Relief Association is one example of a self-help group.

There are over 7,000 recently arrived Ugandan refugees in Britain. They have fled the human rights abuses of successive Ugandan governments. Most Ugandan refugees who have come to Britain are highly qualified people who held good jobs in their home country. As English is the language used in Ugandan schools and universities almost all Ugandan refugees arrive in Britain speaking very good English. Unlike many other groups of refugees, Ugandans don't need extra help to learn English.

The Uganda Community Relief Association was founded by a small group of Ugandan refugees in 1984. Today it has offices in north London and employs seven full-time staff. The organisation also uses volunteers in its work.

The Uganda Community Relief Association offers a wide range of services to Ugandan refugees living in London. These include:

◆ immigration advice

◆ help in finding housing

◆ other advice and support to Ugandan refugees including advice on finding work, training and education and help in getting welfare benefits

◆ language classes in Luganda, Luo and Swahili for Ugandan children

◆ cultural activities such as music and art workshops

◆ advice on keeping healthy.

Uganda refugee boy, London. His father is in prison in Uganda.
Andrew North

THE REFUGEE COUNCIL
1
OFFICE
THE REFUGEE COUNCIL HELPS REFUGEES FROM MANY DIFFERENT COUNTRIES. ITS OFFICES ARE IN LONDON AND ABOUT 200 PEOPLE WORK AT THE REFUGEE COUNCIL
2
YOUR RIGHTS...
NEED ADVICE?...
HEALTH ISSUES...
SCHOOLING
THE REFUGEE COUNCIL GIVES ADVICE TO REFUGEES. IT EXPLAINS TO THEM HOW THEY CAN FIND A HOUSE AND A SCHOOL FOR THEIR CHILDREN.
3
THE REFUGEE COUNCIL TRAINS REFUGEES SO THEY WILL FIND IT EASIER TO FIND WORK.
4
IT GIVES HOMES TO SPECIAL GROUPS OF REFUGEES, SUCH AS THE ELDERLY OR REFUGEES WHO ARE ILL.

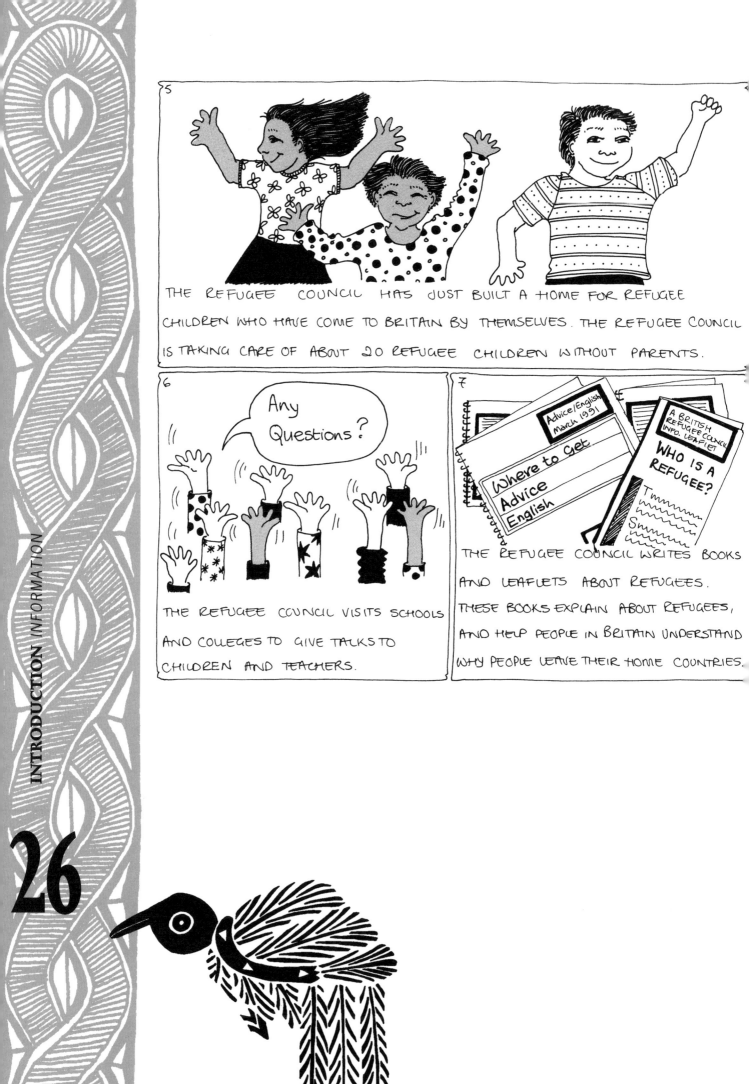

5
THE REFUGEE COUNCIL HAS JUST BUILT A HOME FOR REFUGEE CHILDREN WHO HAVE COME TO BRITAIN BY THEMSELVES. THE REFUGEE COUNCIL IS TAKING CARE OF ABOUT 20 REFUGEE CHILDREN WITHOUT PARENTS.
6
Any Questions?
THE REFUGEE COUNCIL VISITS SCHOOLS AND COLLEGES TO GIVE TALKS TO CHILDREN AND TEACHERS.
7
Advice/English March 1991
Where to Get Advice English
A BRITISH REFUGEE COUNCIL INFO. LEAFLET
WHO IS A REFUGEE?
THE REFUGEE COUNCIL WRITES BOOKS AND LEAFLETS ABOUT REFUGEES. THESE BOOKS EXPLAIN ABOUT REFUGEES, AND HELP PEOPLE IN BRITAIN UNDERSTAND WHY PEOPLE LEAVE THEIR HOME COUNTRIES.

Instructions

This activity can be done as a group activity or individually. The time needed to complete the activity will depend on how the activity is run.

The activity aims to make participants aware of the wide range of things with which refugee and human rights organisations are involved.

Students should be informed that they will be researching the activities of different organisations. Students should write to one or more organisation to find out about the different work they do with refugees.

Organisations that they could write to include:

Action Aid
Amnesty International
CAFOD
Christian Aid
Health Unlimited
Oxfam
Northern Refugee Centre
North East Refugee Services, Newcastle

Finding out about refugee organisations

Refugee Action
Refugee Council
Refugee Legal Centre
Refugee Studies Programme
Runneymede Trust
Save the Children Fund
Scottish Refugee Council
UNHCR
A local Race Equality Council
Refugee community organisations such as the Kurdish Information Centre, the Iranian Community Centre, the Tamil Refugee Action Group or the Uganda Community Relief Association.

An address list is provided at the end of this book.

Once students have received material back from organisations they can fill in the table overleaf. This can be used as basis for making comparisons between organisations.

Answers to Quiz on page 15

1. A refugee is someone who has 'a well-founded fear of being persecuted for reasons of race, religion, nationality, membership of a particular social group or political opinion.' This definition is taken from the 1951 UN Convention Relating to the Status of Refugees. The right answer should include words such as escaping from danger and persecution.

2. There are approximately 18 million refugees in today's world.

3. False. In 1994 some 295,500 refugees entered European Union countries. This compares with over two million refugees who fled from Rwanda alone in 1994. Most of the world's refugees live in poor countries in Africa, Asia and the Middle East.

4. Your answer could include Rwanda, Burundi, former Yugoslavia, Sri Lanka, Afghanistan and Sudan.

5. There are more Palestinian refugees than any other group of refugees. They number 2,800,000 people. Their numbers have increased since the Gulf War when they had to flee from Kuwait.

6. There are 28 conflicts which are presently causing people to become refugees in large numbers.

7. False. Some 32,900 people applied for political asylum in Britain in 1994. If the dependants of these people are taken into account this represents about 41,000 people.

8. False. Refugees who arrive in Britain receive very little extra help. They have to find housing, language classes and legal advice for themselves. This can be very difficult for a person who does not speak English or does not know his/her rights.

9. True. In 1992 11,000 more people left the UK than arrived to settle.

10. All three are contributions made by refugees. Andrex was founded by German Jewish refugees. They manufactured the first soft toilet paper in Britain in the 1930s. Lucian Freud and Albert Einstein were also refugees.

Name of organisation						
How many people work there?						
What type of things does the organisation do?						
Does the organisation just work with refugees, or does it work with other groups of people?						
Does the organisation work with refugees from a certain country or with refugees from different countries?						
Does the organisation fundraise for refugees?						
Does the organisation lobby on behalf of refugees?						
Does the organisation campaign about refugees?						
Is the organisation involved in public education and trying to change the public's views about refugees?						
Does the organisation give practical support to refugees? If so, what kind of things does it do?						
Is the organisation a non-governmental organisation?						
Is the organisation a self-help group?						
Does the organisation act as a pressure group?						

CHAPTER TWO

REFUGEES IN HISTORY

Elderly Polish refugees at a Refugee Council hostel

Throughout history people have been forced to flee. In the last 500 years more than one million refugees have arrived in Britain. Many of them have made enormous contributions to British life ◆ This chapter examines refugees of the past and raises questions about what can be learned from these events.

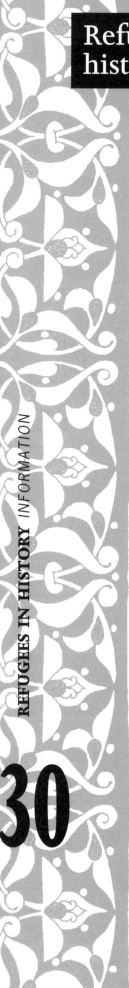

Refugees in ancient history

Seder night at Jewish Passover, London, 1920 *Jewish Museum, Finchley*

Throughout history, the idea of giving hospitality to people who are in danger has been seen as something that is good. Many religious books or works of literature describe stories of refugees who were forced to seek asylum. Here are some examples.

Ancient Greece

Oedipus, a hero of Greek mythology, freed the city of Thebes from the oppression of a monster called the Sphinx. As a reward, Oedipus was given the throne of Thebes and married Jocasta, the widow of the previous king. Oedipus and Jocasta ruled Thebes wisely, but Oedipus did not know that Jocasta was really his mother. Disaster soon struck, and Oedipus's life was threatened by his relatives, who wished to rule Thebes.

Oedipus fled to Athens and asked King Theseus for protection. Theseus, too, was a refugee during his youth. He was forced to hide from his enemies. Theseus was full of sympathy for Oedipus, and allowed him and his daughters to stay in Athens for the rest of their lives. Oedipus' story is told by Sophocles in his book *Oedipus at Colon.*

The Jewish tradition

The early history of the Jewish people contains many stories of refugees and exiles. The book of Exodus describes the escape of Jewish people from Egypt. The Egyptians so hated the Jews that the Pharoah (king) ordered that all Jewish baby boys be killed. One child escaped because his mother hid him in a basket by the river. An Egyptian princess found him and took care of him. His name was Moses. It was Moses who led the Jews out of exile in Egypt into the Land of Israel (then known as Canaan) about 3,250 years ago. Every year at Passover, Jewish people remember their journey from slavery and danger to freedom.

In 722 BC the Land of Israel was attacked by the Assyrian army. Jewish people were driven into exile. Later, in 586 BC the armies of Babylon (now in Iraq) attacked the area around Jerusalem, and destroyed the Temple. Some 10,000 Jewish families went into exile in Babylon. Babylon became a centre of Jewish learning. Today's Iranian, Iraqi, Kurdish and Georgian Jews are the descendants of Jewish people who stayed in Babylon.

The Christian tradition

Soon after the birth of the infant Jesus, Mary and Joseph were forced to flee with him to Egypt, to escape the persecution of King Herod. And in the famous scene from the Final Judgment, God blesses good people, saying …"I was a stranger and you took me into your homes." *(Matthew,* 25 *vv* 35)

The Muslim tradition

The Prophet Mohammed was also forced to flee from his home in Mecca. Mohammed started life as a poor shepherd in Mecca. It was at Mount Hira, near Mecca, that Mohammed received his prophecies from Allah. But Mohammed's beliefs were considered so dangerous and subversive that he and his followers were forced to flee from Mecca. They took refuge first in Abyssinia (Ethiopia) and then, in 622 AD, in the city of Medina. Mohammed's journey from Mecca to Medina is known as the *Hegira*.

As a consequence of Mohammed's journey, the Koran contains many references to the importance of welcoming strangers.

Activity

Students can carry out further research on the treatment of refugees in the ancient world. They might want to find out more about the stories mentioned above. Alternatively they might want to research other religious stories, for example, the Hindu story of Rama and Sita who had to flee from danger.

Refugees in Britain 1200-1970, a chronology

13th century Small numbers of Armenian merchants fled to Britain, escaping persecution in Ottoman Turkey. They settled in Plymouth and London.

1572 After large numbers of Protestants were killed in the St Bartholemew's Day Massacre, refugees from France fled to Britain and settled in London and towns in eastern England.

1560-1575 Dutch and Flemish Protestants fled the Spanish Netherlands and settled in towns in eastern England. With the French Protestants who arrived in the same period, some 50,000 refugees settled in England at this time.

1685 About 100,000 Huguenots - French Protestants - fled to Britain and Ireland.

1780-1900 Britain gave sanctuary to small numbers of refugees who had fled political upheavals in Europe. They included people who fled the French Revolution of 1789, the revolutions of 1848, or were political opponents of their governments. Famous people who fled to Britain as refugees included Karl Marx, Guiseppe Mazzini and Sun Yat Sen. Most of this group of refugees settled in London.

1870-1914 Over 200,000 eastern European Jewish refugees settled in Britain. They fled persecution in Russia, Russian Poland and Romania. Other Jews fled extreme poverty in Austrian Galicia. Most of the Jewish refugees settled in cities such as London, Leeds and Manchester.

1914-1918 Some 250,000 Belgian refugees fled to Britain, escaping fighting in the First World War. Almost all of them returned home in 1918.

1919-1921 Some 15,000 Russian opponents of the new communist government fled to Britain as refugees.

1936 About 5,000 Republican refugees from Spain (opponents of General Franco) settled in Britain.

1933-1939 Some 56,000 refugees from Nazi Germany, Austria and Czechoslovakia fled to Britain. Most of them were Jewish, although small numbers of political opponents of the Nazis sought safety in Britain. After the start of the Second World War it was almost impossible to escape from Germany or eastern Europe as a refugee.

1939-1945 About 100,000 refugees arrived in Britain, having fled the advancing German army. Most of this group of

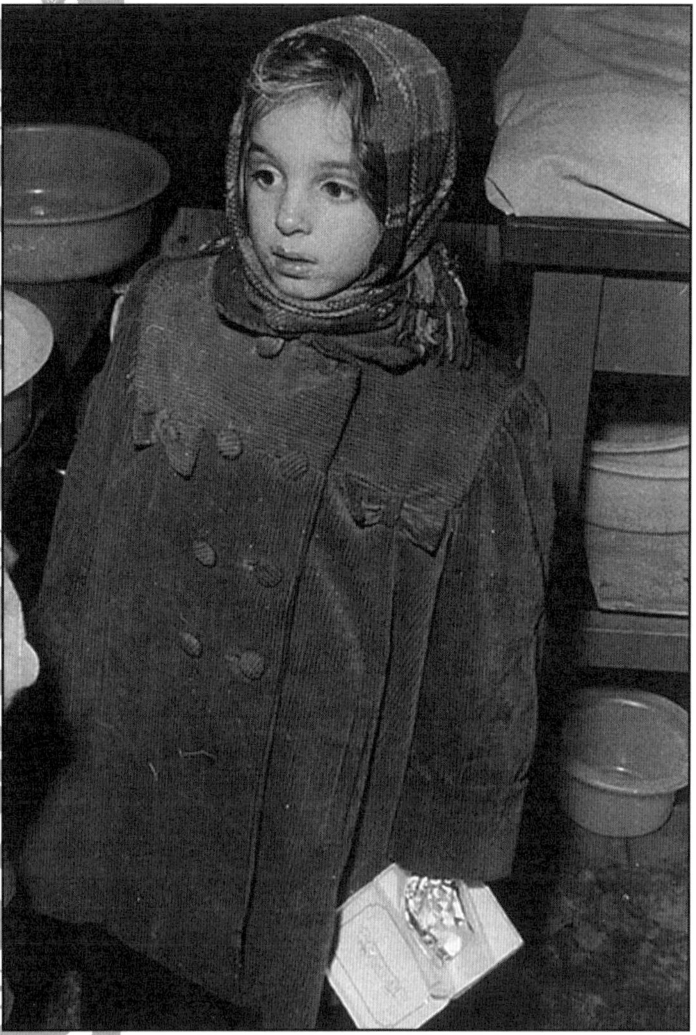

refugees were from Norway, Denmark, the Netherlands, Belgium and France. They returned home in 1945.

1939–1950 Some 250,000 Polish refugees settled permanently in Britain. They arrived during the Second World War, or came after 1945, as part of a group of soldiers who served with the British army. Other Polish people arrived from refugee camps in Europe, or fled the new communist government in Poland.

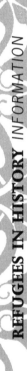

1945–60 Some 50,000 refugees from the Soviet Union, Romania, Czechoslovakia and Hungary arrived in Britain during this period. They formed two groups: those who found themselves in refugee camps at the end of the Second World War and did not want to return home, and those who were opponents of the new communist governments in eastern Europe and had to escape.

1956 After the Hungarian Uprising some 17,000 Hungarian refugees settled permanently in Britain.

1968 The Czechoslovak people were granted new freedoms by a more liberal communist government in 1968. But in August 1968 the Soviet Union and armies from other eastern European countries invaded Czechoslovakia. Thousands of refugees fled, and some 5,000 Czechoslovak refugees settled in Britain.

Leaving

But refugees have also fled from Britain and Ireland over the last 800 years. From 1100-1290 Jews were persecuted in Britain. Many were killed in massacres in Norwich, York and London. Others fled as refugees. All remaining Jews were expelled from Britain in 1290.

During the Reformation and Civil War refugees fled from Britain, mostly because of their religious beliefs. One large group were Roman Catholic Scots who fled to Poland in the 17th century. More recently, from 1968-1973 some 25,000 Irish nationalists from Northern Ireland fled to the Republic of Ireland to escape the violence of the Troubles.

Hungarian refugee, 1956 *UN*

BRITAINS FIRST REFUGEES

1.
THROUGHOUT HISTORY MANY DIFFERENT PEOPLE HAVE FLED TO ESCAPE PERSECUTION.
IN THE 1680's 100,000 HUGUENOT REFUGEES SETTLED IN BRITAIN.
2.
Arbour... Delahunt... Bygott.... Coutauld... Lefevre....
THE HUGUENOTS GAVE THE WORD 'REFUGEE' TO THE ENGLISH LANGUAGE.
3
DURING THE 18TH AND 19TH CENTURIES MANY WARS WERE FOUGHT IN EUROPE. IN FRANCE, POLAND AND OTHER COUNTRIES THERE WERE CHANGES OF GOVERNMENT. FOR MANY PEOPLE LIFE HAD BECOME DANGEROUS AND THEY HAD TO LEAVE THEIR HOMELANDS......
POLITICAL EXILES LEFT FRANCE, GERMANY, AUSTRIA, ITALY, POLAND, AND RUSSIA. MANY OF THEM CAME TO BRITAIN.
THE BRITISH GOVERNMENT DID NOT FORMALLY WELCOME THESE REFUGEES, BUT THE POLICE DID NOT BOTHER THEM. THEY WERE ALLOWED TO TRAVEL AND LIVE WHERE THEY PLEASED.
LONDON BECAME KNOWN AS A PLACE WHERE REFUGEES COULD FIND SAFETY. IN THE 1850's ABOUT 4,000 REFUGEES WERE LIVING IN LONDON....
Karl Marx
Prince Metternich
Giuseppe Mazzini

6. BETWEEN 1880 AND 1914 ABOUT 120,000 EASTERN EUROPEANS JEWS SETTLED IN BRITAIN. THEY HAD LEFT THEIR HOMES IN THE RUSSIAN EMPIRE, RUMANIA AND AUSTRIAN GALICIA.
KOVNO
VITEBSK
GERMANY
VILNA
MOSCOW
MOGILEV
GRODNO
MINSK
RUSSIA
CHERNIGOV
VOLHYNIA
KIEV
POLTAVA
AUSTRO-HUNGARY
PODOLIA
EKATERINOSLAV
KHERSON
BESSARABIA
RUMANIA
BLACKSEA
THE JEWISH PALE OF SETTLEMENT IN RUSSIA 1835–1917
7. THE JEWS WHO LEFT RUSSIA AND RUMANIA WERE REFUGEES. IN THESE COUNTRIES JEWS FACED THE VIOLENCE OF 'POGROMS'. POGROM IS THE RUSSIAN WORD FOR A RIOT.
YOUNG POGROM VICTIMS IN DNEPROPETROVSK IN THE UKRAINE
8.
JEWS FACED OTHER FORMS OF RELIGIOUS PERSECUTION IN RUSSIA. THEY FACED DISCRIMINATION IN EDUCATION, FORCED CONSCRIPTION INTO THE RUSSIAN ARMY, AND DISCRIMINATORY LAWS WHICH EXCLUDED THEM FROM CERTAIN JOBS AND FORCED THEM TO LIVE IN PARTICULAR PLACES.
9.
THE JEWISH REFUGEES WHO CAME TO BRITAIN WERE VERY POOR. ABOUT HALF OF THEM SETTLED IN WHITECHAPEL, THE POOREST PART OF LONDONS EAST END.
10.
WHITECHAPEL WAS AN AREA OF HIGH UNEMPLOYMENT AND BAD HOUSING. LANDLORDS DID NOT REPAIR HOMES, MANY HOUSES WERE DESTROYED TO MAKE WAY FOR RAILWAYS AND OFFICES. SOME EAST ENDERS RESENTED THE JEWISH REFUGEES. THEY MADE THE MISTAKE OF THINKING THE REFUGEES WERE TAKING THEIR JOBS AND HOUSING.

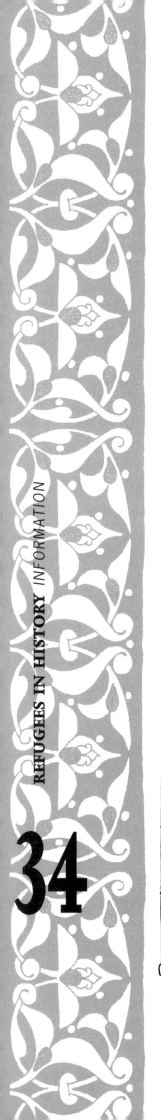

1.
IMMIGRATION SOON BECAME A POLITICAL SSUE. SOME M.P's, POOR EAST ENDERS AND RICHER JEWS OPPOSED THE UNLIMITED ENTRY OF POOR JEWISH REFUGEES FROM EASTERN EUROPE. POLITICIANS FELT THEY COULD WIN VOTES BY STOPPING EAST EUROPEAN JEWS ENTERING BRITAIN . . . .
12.
DURING THE YEARS 1900 ~ 1915 MAJOR GENERAL EVANS GORDON LED THE ANTI IMMIGRATION CAMPAIGN. HE ORGANIZED MEETINGS, MARCHES AND ALSO LEAFLETTING. HIS SUPPORTERS BROKE THE WINDOWS OF JEWISH HOMES AND CARRIED OUT VIOLENT ATTACKS...
13.
OPPOSE THE ALIENS ACT
NO TO ALL BIGOTS!
STOP THE RACISTS!
JEWISH EAST ENDERS AND SOME TRADE UNIONISTS AND POLITICIANS ORGANIZED THEIR OWN MEETINGS AND DEMONSTRATIONS TO OPPOSE MAJOR GENERAL EVANS GORDON AND HIS RACIST CAMPAIGN.
4.
HERE, HERE!!
GREAT IDEA!
MORE!
LOVE IT!
ALIENS ACT OF 1905
HOWEVER, AS A RESULT OF EVANS GORDONS CAMPAIGN THE BRITISH GOV'T PASSED THE ALIENS ACT IN 1905. THE ALIENS ACT COVERED ALL IMMIGRATION, INCLUDING ENTRY OF REFUGEES....
15.
TILBURY IMMIGRATION DESK
That's right! It's called a point of entry — but its not so for everyone!
16.
THE ALIENS ACT OF 1905 EXCLUDED THE IMMIGRANT WHO WAS SICK AND THOSE WHO MIGHT NOT BE ABLE TO SUPPORT THEMSELVES.
IN 1906 ABOUT 4% OF JEWISH IMMIGRANTS WERE REFUSED ENTRY TO BRITAIN...
THE JEWISH CHRONICLE CARRIED THE FOLLOWING REPORT IN 1907....
JEWISH CHRONICLE 25 OCT 1907
TWO REFUGEES REFUSED ENTRY....
SAMUEL JADWIG:
"THE IMMIGRANT WAS A DESERTER FROM THE RUSSIAN ARMY - A JUSTIFIABLE OFFENCE IN THE CASE OF A JEW WHOSE LIFE IN THE RUSSIAN ARMY IS MADE A VERITABLE PURGATORY. HE HAD ALSO SUFFERED FOR HIS POLITICAL ACTIONS. THE CHARGE OF BEING A REVOLUTIONIST HAS BEEN BROUGHT AGAINST HIM, AND HE WAS LIKEWISE ACCUSED OF HAVING STRUCK AN OFFICER. THIS LED TO IMPRISONMENT AND IMPRISONMENT LED TO ESCAPE — TO ENGLAND. HERE THEN WAS A TYPICAL CASE FOR THE CONSIDERATION TO BE ACCORDED TO REFUGEES. YET THIS MAN
JEWISH CHRONICLE 25 OCT 1907
WAS REJECTED. THE REASON FOR REJECTION OF JADWIG WAS THAT THE MAN WAS WITHOUT MEANS."
ITZIG FRIMSTEIN:
"ITZIG FRIMSTEIN ARRIVED IN LONDON FROM RUSSIA WITH HIS WIFE AND TWO CHILDREN. THEY CAME FROM A SMALL TOWN IN THE PODOLSKY GOVERNMENT WHERE THERE HAD BEEN THREATS AND WINDOW BREAKING. IN THEIR FEAR OF SOMETHING WORSE TO COME THEY RESOLVED TO LEAVE THE COUNTRY AND TO GO TO ENGLAND. THE ENTIRE FAMILY WAS EXCLUDED."

HE ALIENS ACT STATED THAT REFUGEES FLEEING PERSECUTION SHOULD BE LLOWED INTO BRITAIN. BUT THERE IS EVIDENCE THAT MANY GENUINE REFUGEES WERE REFUSED ENTRY.

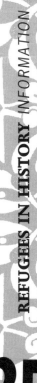

The Huguenots

The Huguenots were a refugee group who made enormous contributions to life in England and Northern Ireland. Today Huguenot industrics still survive in Britain.

There was a great deal of religious persecution in Europe in the 16th century. One such persecuted group were the Huguenots - French Protestants - who found themselves a minority in a Roman Catholic country. An earlier group of French Protestant refugees fled in 1572 after the St Bartholemew's Day Massacre. But in 1598 King Henry of France passed a law that was meant to guarantee religious minorities safety and freedom of worship. This law was called the Edict of Nantes. This helped the Huguenots feel safer.

By the mid 17th century the safety of the Huguenots was again under threat. Some of their churches were destroyed. In 1685 King Louis XIII repealed the Edict of Nantes. After this most Huguenots felt that they had no future in France. Between 200,000 and 250,000 refugees fled the country, mainly to the Netherlands and England.

Huguenot communities grew up in many parts of England and also in some towns in Ireland. The largest Huguenot community was to be found in Whitechapel, east London. Other towns with large Huguenot communities included Canterbury, Norwich, Ipswich, Dover, Rye, Southampton, Exeter, Dartmouth, Plymouth, Barnstaple, Bristol, Dublin and Derry.

The Huguenot refugees transformed the British and Irish clothing industry. They brought new skills, new dyes and new fabrics. In London many Huguenot refugees were employed in the silk weaving industry. By 1700 there may have been as many as 10,000 silk looms in the Whitechapel area in London. Courtauld's Textiles, a company which has survived to the present, was founded by Huguenot refugees. Other industries that employed Huguenots included fishing, market gardening, gun-making, silversmithing and papermaking. Huguenot refugees were also successful soldiers, lawyers and actors.

But as with other groups of refugees, not everyone welcomed Huguenot refugees. There was a great deal of anti-French feeling in 17th century England, and the Huguenots were French. Workers in the textile and clothing industry also felt that their livelihoods were threatened by the refugees. Throughout the reign of James I, the Company of Silkweavers protested about the 'multitude of aliens' engaged in their trade in England. There were also anti-refugee riots in 1675 and 1681. Huguenot refugees saw themselves stereotyped in books and drawings of the time. Other people however were more sympathetic to refugees. In particular many bishops urged their congregations to support them.

The Huguenots made a great contribution to life in Britain. Over 300 years later this can still be seen. And many people in Britain and Ireland have Huguenot ancestors.

Huguenot Silkweavers, Whitechapel London

Tracing the Huguenots

Students may wish to carry out research about the Huguenots. They could start by finding out who has Huguenot family names.

A local museum may have examples of Huguenot silver or other antiques.

Family names that may indicate Huguenot ancestors

Batchelor	Mitchell
Burgess	Oliver
Delamere	Parmenter
Devine	Reynolds

There may be Huguenot buildings, such as houses or Huguenot churches, in the neighbourhood that students could visit.

A local history library may be a good source of information about the Huguenots.

Eastern European Jews in Britain

Between 1870 and 1914 over 200,000 Jewish refugees from eastern Europe settled in Britain. They fled from Russia, Russian Poland, Austro-Hungary and Romania. At this time half of the Jewish population of these countries migrated. Nearly three million moved to the USA, Canada, Britain, Germany and France.

The reasons that people fled were complex. In Austro-Hungarian Galicia, Romania and Russia extreme poverty forced some Jewish people to leave their homes. Additionally in Romania, Russia and Russian Poland Jewish people were persecuted.

Life for Russian Jews was hardest of all. By 1870 about 5.4 million Jews lived in the Russian Empire. Russia was ruled by the Tsar, and there were no elections. Most Russian people lived in the country-side in great poverty. They were serfs, working on farms owned by a few rich families. Life for the serfs had not really changed in hundreds of years. Most Jewish people lived in small towns and villages called *shtetlach* (singular, *shtetl*). In the *shtetlach* Jewish people worked as potters, blacksmiths, rent collectors and farm workers.

In such conditions of poverty many Russian people were unhappy with the Tsar and the landowners. In order to divert attention from the real causes of poverty, the Russian government needed a scapegoat to blame. The scapegoat was the Jewish people. Jewish rent collectors were accused of extorting money from Russian peasants. The Russian Orthodox Church encouraged Russian peasants to think that Jewish people sacrificed Christian children so that their blood could be used to make Passover bread.

The governments of Catherine the Great (1762-1796) and Nicolas I (1825-1855) attempted to gain popularity by expelling Jews from certain parts of Russia. By

Jewish tailors in 19th century London *Jewish Museum, F nchley*

A

VOICE FROM THE ALIENS

About the Anti-Alien Resolution of the Cardiff Trade Union Congress.

WE, the organised Jewish workers of England, taking into consideration the Anti-Alien Resolution, and the uncomplimentary remarks of certain delegates about the Jewish workers specially, issue this leaflet, wherewith we hope to convince our English fellow workers of the untruthfulness, unreasonableness, and want of logic contained in the cry against the foreign worker in general, and against the Jewish worker in particular.

It is, and always has been, the policy of the ruling classes to attribute the sufferings and miseries of the masses (which are natural consequences of class rule and class exploitation) to all sorts of causes except the real ones. The cry against the foreigner is not merely peculiar to England; it is international. Everywhere he is the scapegoat for other's sins. Every class finds in him an enemy. So long as the Anti-Alien sentiment in this country was confined to politicians, wire-pullers, and to individual working men, we, the organised aliens, took no heed; but when this ill-founded sentiment has been officially expressed by the organised working men of England, then we believe that it is time to lift our voices and argue the matter out.

It has been proved by great political economists that a working man in a country where machinery is greatly developed produces in a day twice as many commodities as his daily wage enables him to consume.

Extract from a campaign leaflet against the 1905 Alien Act

1835 almost all Jews were confined to an area of Russia called the Pale of Settlement. Nicolas I introduced new military laws, after which thousands of Jewish boys were forcibly conscripted into the Russian army. If a young conscript survived, he often served for thirty or more years.

In 1881 Tsar Alexander II was assassinated by a political movement called *Narodnaya Volya*. Among the assassins was a young Jewish woman. To divert Russian people from this difficult situation, officials of the Tsar's government encouraged peasants to riot in many towns in the Pale of Settlement. Hundreds of Jewish people were killed in riots (usually called pogroms). After this, large numbers of Jewish refugees left Russia.

In May 1882 Tsar Alexander III passed the May Laws. Jewish people were not allowed to work on Sundays. They could not travel, and no Jew could own land, work or live in large parts of the Pale of Settlement. Further repression continued.

In 1896 Jews were prevented from selling alcohol (previously an important occupation). There were more pogroms.

Almost all Russian Jews spoke Yiddish as their first language. A Yiddish folksong of the 19th century laments conscription:

Trern gissen zikh in die gassn
In kinderishe blut ken men zikh vashn....
Kleine oifelekh resist men fun kheyder
M'tut zey on yevonishe kleider.
Unzere parneyssim, unzere rabbonim
Helfen noch zu optzugeben zey far yevonim.
Bei Zushe Rakover zeynen do zeibn bonim,
Un fun zey nit einer in yevonim.
Nor Leye die almones eintsike kind
Iz a kapore far keholishe zind.

Tears flow in the streets
One can wash oneself in children's blood...
Little doves are torn from school
And dressed up in non-Jewish clothes.
Our leaders and our rabbis
Even help disguise them as Gentiles.
Rich Zushe Rakover has seven sons
But not one puts on the uniform.
But Leah the widow's only child
Becomes a scapegoat for 'communal sin.'

Many Russian Jews were active in political groups that opposed the Tsar's government. Others fled as refugees. They made their way to the ports, and then bought boat tickets to Britain and North America. One woman who arrived in London in 1890 described what happened to her:

'It took eighteen months for my father to save up enough money to send for us...Every day he was worrying about us, and my mother was worrying about him. Of course, it was nothing like what happened later with the Germans, the terror and the killing. But at the time it was an awful experience. And today there are people with the same problems, aren't there?

Deciding what to take wasn't much of a problem because we had so little. We took some of the boxes and some linen - we didn't know what we were coming to.'

Jewish refugees in Whitechapel, East London

Most Jewish refugees settled in the East End of London, in an area previously settled by Huguenot refugees. Here it was easy to find work in the clothing industry, or making shoes, furniture or cigars. But housing conditions were poor, many Jewish refugees lived in overcrowded, insanitary conditions.

Whitechapel was a very lively place. Some Jewish people spent their time at the synagogue. Others were active in trade unions and political organisations. There were anarchists, socialists, communists and Zionists among the Jews of Whitechapel. Between 1880 and 1905 many Jewish political organisations worked to oppose new laws that would limit the entry of Jewish refugees.

Anti-immigration legislation

There was much opposition to the entry of eastern European Jewish refugees, just as there is opposition to the entry of refugees today. Newspapers started blaming Jewish refugees for causing housing shortages and unemployment. Jewish workers in the clothing industry were accused of undercutting wage rates. After 1888 the anti-immigration movement began to get more organised. Some Conservative MPs tried to introduce laws to limit immigration. In 1900, Major-General Evans Gordon, MP for Stepney in east London, formed the British Brothers League. This was a racist organisation which aimed to stop all Jewish immigration. The British Brothers League organised petitions and meetings. It also encouraged some of its members to attack Jewish people and their property and to riot.

By 1904, the British government decided it must act. It tried to pass anti-immigration legislation in 1904, but this was rejected after pressure from shipping companies. In 1905, the Aliens Act was passed by Parliament. Newly-arrived immigrants were subject to more complicated checks when they entered Britain. The immigration officer had power to reject people he considered to be undesirable. In 1906 some 38,527 'alien' boat passengers entered the UK. Of these, 931 were rejected immediately, 489 were rejected after appeal, and 360 were rejected due to poverty or disease.

Students

◆ **Read 'A Voice from the Aliens'. This was a political leaflet written in 1904 by Jewish trade unionists in Britain. What were the main points made in the leaflet?**

◆ **What similarities are there in the treatment of eastern European Jewish refugees in Britain and the treatment of refugees today?**

Refugees from Nazi-occupied Europe

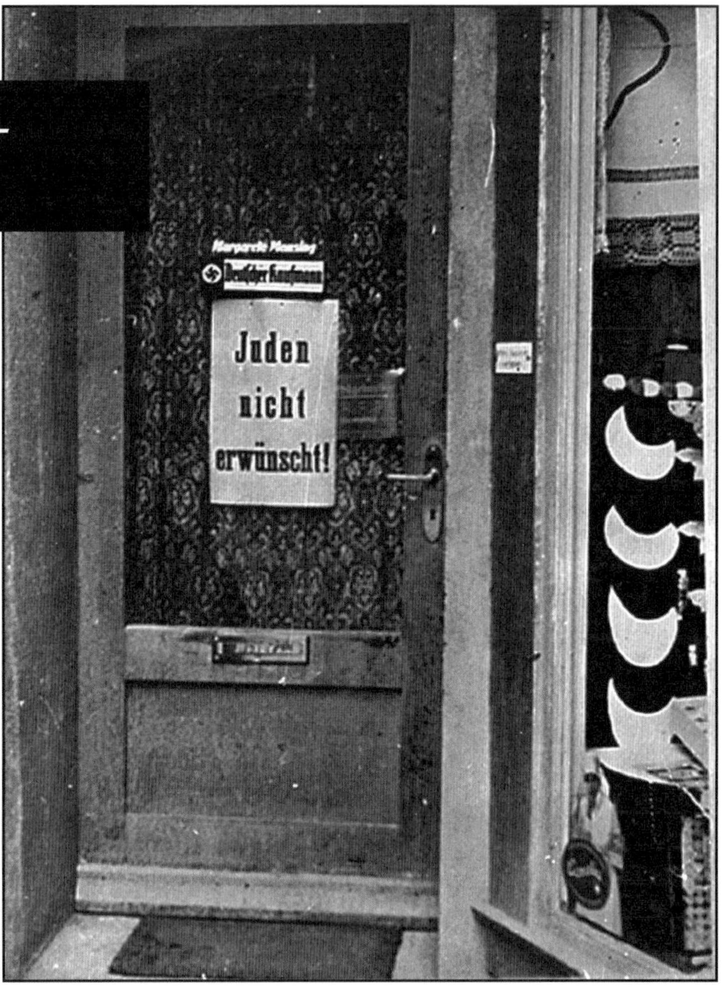

The sign reads 'Jews are not wanted here'. Germany, 1936
Wiener Library

Over 60,000,000 people became refugees during the Second World War. But one group of people, the Jews of Nazi-occupied Europe, were largely prevented from seeking asylum in safe countries.

Events in Nazi-occupied Europe – the causes of flight of refugees

1918 The end of the First World War. Germany is forced to pay compensation to Britain and France.

1920 The National Socialist (Nazi) Party is formed in Germany.

1923 The failure of the Munich Putsch. This is an attempt by Adolf Hitler and his supporters to take over the govern-ment in the German state of Bavaria. The Nazis fail and Hitler is given a prison sentence. It is during his time in prison that Hitler writes *Mein Kampf*. This book outlines Hitler's racial theories and his plans for Germany. Hitler believes certain races to be superior to others. Blond haired, blue-eyed 'Aryan' Germans are the 'master race' who would one day rule Europe. Other people, such as Poles and Russians, are 'sub-human'. Hitler plans to take their land and property and make them slaves to the Germans. Jews and Gypsies are 'non-human' and Hitler plans to kill them.

1928 Nazi party membership reaches 109,000. They get 2.6 per cent of the vote in elections to the Reichstag, the German parliament.

1930 The Nazis win 18.3 per cent of the vote in elections to the Reichstag.

July 1932 The Nazis receive 37 per cent of the vote in elections to the Reichstag. The combined vote of the Communist Party and the Social Democratic Party is greater, but these two parties cannot agree to form a united opposition to the Nazis. A further election in November 1932 does not produce a conclusive result.

January 1933 The political parties of the centre and right agree to accept Adolf Hitler as Chancellor (the head of govern-ment). Chancellor Hindenburg resigns,

Anti-Semitism

Anti-Semitism means discrimination against Jews. It is a form of racism. The Nazis did not invent anti-Semitism, but they revived something that had existed for centuries.

During the Middle Ages, Jews were persecuted by Christians. They were accused of killing Christ and of practising black magic. And in many countries only Jews were allowed to lend money for interest, so soon they were blamed for causing misery, by profiting from poor peasants who owed them money.

Anti-Semitism was revived in the 19th century, at the end of the Russian Empire. This was a time of great poverty and dissatisfaction. Rather than blame Russian landlords who charged high rents, the Tsar's government blamed Jewish rent-collectors. The Jews were made a scapegoat - a group who could easily be blamed for society's problems.

The Jews were also a convenient scapegoat for the Nazis. After the First World War, the German government had to pay large amounts of money to Britain and France as compensation. By the mid-1920s inflation was out of control. Bank savings became worthless overnight and many small businesses were ruined. Millions of workers lost their jobs. As there was no social security, people without work starved.

In these conditions, discontent spread. The Nazi Party offered simple solutions to Germany's problems. They built on old prejudices and blamed Jewish bankers for ruining the German economy.

The Nazis also believed that the Germans were a superior race; most other races were either destined to become slaves of the Germans, or to be exterminated. Jews, as well as Gypsies, were destined to be killed. Adolf Hitler's ideas about the German 'master race' restored national pride for a demoralised nation.

Anti-Semitic parties received support in other countries during the 1920s and 1930s, but not to the same extent as in Germany.

and Adolf Hitler becomes Chancellor on 30 January 1933.

April 1933 The first official boycott of Jewish shops. All Jewish enterprises have to be marked with signs. A law is passed to define who is 'Aryan' and laws are passed to enable 'undesirables' (Jews, Communists and trade unionists) to be sacked from the civil service. Universities and secondary schools are only allowed to accept 1.5 per cent Jewish students.

Refugee arriving in Britain, 1938
Wiener Library

1933 Random street violence carried out by Nazi supporters. This is directed against Jews and political opponents of the Nazis.

1934 More Jews are dismissed from the civil service, medical and legal professions, as it becomes necessary to be of 'Aryan' origin.

1935 The Nuremburg laws are passed, forbidding marriage and sexual relations between Jews and Germans.

1936 The more violent aspects of Nazi anti-Semitism are halted as Germany hosts the 1936 Olympic Games. Some refugees return to Germany.

1937 Throughout 1937 remaining Jewish businesses are seized by the Nazis.

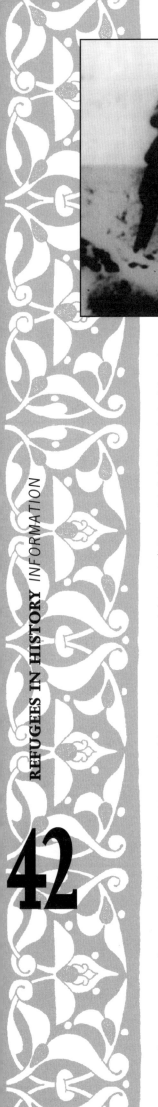

1938 All passports for Jews are stamped with the letter 'J'.

March 1938 *Anschluss*. Germany and Austria are unified. Some 183,000 Austrian Jews come under Nazi rule.

October 1938 Over 15,000 Jews of Polish nationality are expelled from Germany. They wait in camps on the Polish/German border.

9–10 November 1938 *Kristallnacht* (the Night of Broken Glass). Hirsch Grynzpan, a young Jew, assassinates Ernst vom Rath, a German diplomat, in Paris. The Nazis organise street rioting in response. Jewish homes, synagogues and shops are destroyed, 91 people are killed and over 20,000 are arrested.

15 November 1938 All remaining German Jewish children are expelled from school.

March 1939 The Nazis occupy all Czechoslovakia.

1 September 1939 Germany invades Poland. Britain and France declare war on Germany on 3 September 1939.

1940 Much of Europe is under German occupation. Some seven million Jews are living under German rule, mostly in Poland, Hungary and Czechoslovakia. About 250,000 Polish Jews manage to escape to the Soviet Union, but for most Jews and Gypsies, the escape route is sealed.

1941 Germany invades the Soviet Union. Special killing squads called *Einsatzgruppen* murder thousands of Soviet citizens after the German army advances.

Autumn 1941 Mobile gas vans are put into operation at Chelmno in Poland. From 1941-45 over 360,000 people, mostly Jews, are gassed. Only two people survive Chelmno.

20 January 1942 The Wannsee Conference is held in Berlin. It is for top Nazi officials. The plans for the 'final solution to the Jewish problem' are revealed. Jews are to be deported eastwards, to ghettos, and to be used as slave labourers. The ghettos would be systematically emptied as Jewish people are murdered in extermination camps.

1942 Extermination camps are opened at Auschwitz, Belzec, Majdanek, Sorbibor and Treblinka, in Nazi-occupied Poland.

26 March 1942 The first deportation to Auschwitz. During the next 32 months over four million Jews, Gypsies, Poles and Russians are gassed at Auschwitz. The victims come from all over Nazi-occupied Europe.

1943 There are Jewish uprisings in the Warsaw and Vilna ghettos. Several thousand Jews secretly join partisans who are fighting in the forests. There are also revolts in the labour and extermination camps in 1943 and 1944.

Late 1944 The Red Army pushes the Germans out of the Soviet Union and advances into eastern Poland.

October 1944 The last gassings at Auschwitz. The inmates of the slave labour and extermination camps are marched back towards Germany in the winter of 1944-45. Very few survive these death marches.

27 January 1945 Auschwitz is liberated by the Red Army. As the Allied armies advance across Europe, the full extent of the Nazi horror becomes obvious. Nearly six million Jewish people have been murdered in camps, and by *Einsatzgruppen*.

A member of an Einsatzgruppe shoots mother and child, Poland 1939.
Wiener Library

The fate of refugees escaping from the Nazis

February – April 1933 Over 1,000 refugees leave Nazi Germany, most of them teachers at colleges and universities. The leaders of Britain's Jewish community tell the British government that the Jewish community will meet all the expenses of incoming Jewish refugees. They hope that such a promise will result in the British government granting entry to more refugees.

End of 1933 Over 65,000 refugees have left Nazi Germany. As well as Jews, the refugees include political opponents of the Nazis. Most of them settle in France, but a small number flee to Britain and the USA. At this time most refugees find it fairly easy to come to Britain. Many organisations are set up to help them.

1934 Refugees leaving Germany have to pay a very high 'emigration' tax. This means that most refugees arriving in Britain have very little money.

The "Poor Refugees!"

Distressed Child: "Can't we be refugees too, Mummy?"

1935 The British government introduces visas for German citizens who want to enter Britain, her colonies or British-administered Palestine. It is almost impossible to get a visa unless the person concerned has an offer of a job. Refugee organisations help German doctors, university lecturers and teachers find jobs as domestic servants.

1935–37 Some 165,000 refugees leave Germany. About 43,000 flee to Palestine, 30,000 to Britain, others escape to France, the USA or the Netherlands.

A cartoon taken from an anti-refugee leaflet London, 1936. *Wiener Library*

In Britain public sympathy for the refugees decreases. Some politicians and newspapers are openly hostile to refugees.

'Once it was known that Britain offered sanctuary to all who cared to come, the floodgates would be opened, and we would be inundated by thousands seeking a home.' (Daily Mail, 1935).

The British Union of Fascists, a political party with views very similar to the Nazis, has 80,000 supporters by 1935. It has anti-Semitic policies and blames refugees, who are mostly Jewish, for taking away the jobs of 'British' workers.

1937 Jewish emigration to Palestine becomes a problem for the British government. The numbers of refugees settling in Palestine doubles in two years. Worried about their future, Palestinian Arabs protest. The British government decides to act. Britain needs to keep friendly relations with Arab governments in the Middle East, and to keep the Suez Canal open. Britain limits the number of Jewish refugees allowed to travel to Palestine. No more than 10,000 refugees will be allowed in over a five year period.

British ships patrol the Mediterranean Sea to stop refugee ships entering Palestine. Diplomatic pressure is put on the Greek and Yugoslav governments to stop refugees passing through these countries.

July 1938 An international conference about refugees from Germany and Austria is held at Evian in France. The conference cannot agree to a solution to resettle the refugees from these countries. The British government continues to prevent most refugees entering Britain or Palestine. Some sympathetic officials in the Foreign Office give a few refugees travel documents to enter Mauritius, British Honduras or British Guyana. Small numbers of refugees also travel to South American countries and Shanghai.

November 1938 After the *Kristallnacht* more Jewish refugees queue to get visas to leave Germany. In Britain there is an emergency debate in the House of Commons on the *Kristallnacht*. Britain decides to allow 10,000 unaccompanied refugee children to enter Britain. This is the *Kindertransporte* (the children's transport). Altogether 9,732 children from Germany, Austria and Czechoslovakia come to Britain. Most will never see their parents again.

September 1939 Britain declares war on Germany. Some 50,000 citizens of an enemy country are living in Britain as refugees. Some newspapers and politicians believe that the refugees are not loyal to Britain, and that it would be easy for German spies to live among the refugee community. A small number of refugees are interned in camps to protect 'national security.'

May 1940 After the Nazi invasion of the Netherlands, there is a public outcry in Britain about the dangers of 'enemy aliens' living in Britain. Some 27,000 refugees are interned in camps. Refugees are also deported to Canada and Australia.

Conditions in the camps are not luxurious. One particularly bad camp is Warth Mill in Lancashire. It is dirty and there is not enough bedding. The refugees go on hunger strike to try and improve camp conditions.

By May 1940 the numbers of refugees reaching Britain is very small. During the next five years less than 6,000 refugees escaping Nazi-occupied Europe manage to come to Britain.

August 1942 Evidence reaches Britain of the deportation of Jewish people to ghettos in Nazi-occupied Poland, and of the extermination of Jews at Chelmno and Auschwitz. On 17th December 1942 Anthony Eden, the Foreign Secretary, makes a public statement, on behalf of the War Cabinet. He describes conditions in the ghettos and how they are being emptied. But on 30 December 1942 Anthony Eden secretly tells the War Cabinet that Britain can only admit another 1,000-2,000 refugees.

Spring 1943 There is enormous public sympathy towards European Jews. Protest meetings are held. Many refugees are released from internment camps at this time. Public pressure also persuades the British government to hold an international conference about refugees. This is held in Bermuda in April 1943. It is unsuccessful because no country will agree to accept large numbers of refugees.

Autumn 1943 Public interest in refugees and the fate of European Jewry begins to fade.

Students

◆ **What is a scapegoat?**

◆ **Have you ever had a scapegoat in your school? What were they blamed for? Why do you think they were made a scapegoat?**

◆ **List individuals and groups of people in history who have been made scapegoats.**

Interview with Professor Ron Baker

Jewish refugee children on the train from Germany to Holland, 1938
Wiener Library

Ron Baker was born Rudi Aschheim in Berlin in 1932. At the age of six his family sent him to Holland to escape the Nazis. He came to Britain in May 1940, on the last 'Kindertransporte' (the children's transport). He was fostered by the Bakers, a Jewish family from Salford, Lancashire. Ron Baker has worked as a psychiatric nurse, social worker and university teacher.

'I was born in Berlin in 1932, the year before Hitler came to power. I left Germany in 1938. Because I was so young, I don't have many memories of life in Berlin. I can remember the Nazi rallies. As a child I stood on the balcony of our house. For such a young child, the rallies seemed exciting.

I can remember 'Kristallnacht'. I went with my father, on the Saturday, to the synagogue. The damage was as bad as portrayed. Pews were overturned and chandeliers smashed.

My parents were born in Poland, although they had lived in Germany for a long time. At first it was the Nazi policy to deport Polish Jews. When I was about five years old my father was deported to Tarnow in Poland. My mother, brother and I continued to live in Berlin. My father returned illegally one Friday to spend the Sabbath with us. The atmosphere at home was one of apprehension bordering on fear that my father would be discovered. I remember my mother very gravely telling me that if anyone asked for my father I was to say I had not seen him for a long time.

In the middle of the evening there was a knock on the door and my mother told me to open it. A smiling Gestapo officer stood there, impeccably dressed in his uniform. He quietly asked if my father was at home. I was terrified but said 'no'. He then asked quietly, almost gently, when I had last seen my father. I replied that I had not seen him for a long time. His smile remained constant. Surprisingly he neither asked for my mother, nor insisted on searching the house. He turned round and left.

Not long after, my mother sent my brother and me to Holland. My brother and I were separated when we got there and fostered by different families. We had very little contact over the next two years. I went to school in Holland and learnt to speak fluent Dutch.

When Hitler invaded Holland I was put on the last boat that left for England. That was in May 1940. As the Nazis invaded Holland, Jewish refugee children were herded together. We were escorted through the German firing line in the docks. We were put on a Chinese cargo boat. The memories of the boat were quite awful.

It was a boat of children, very few adults. There was a lot of fighting and bombing and we soon moved away from the quay. As the boat steamed out, we passed through bombing for two or three hours. Why the boat did not sink I do not know. It took a week for the boat to get to

Liverpool. We must have been a pathetic sight when we reached Liverpool.

On arrival in Liverpool we walked through the crowded streets to a reception hostel. Suddenly a woman darted out of the crowd and grabbed the first child she got hold of who happened to be me. She held me tightly, tears were streaming down her face, yet she was warm and smiling through them. Putting me down she pushed six pennies into my hand and went back into the crowd. Experience had taught me not to trust smiling people anymore and I was filled with confused feelings and intense anxiety.

We were housed in a church hall in Wigan for six months. We were looked after by volunteers. Although people were very kind, we couldn't actually communicate, as language was a problem. Gradually the appeal went out to foster refugee children and one by one the hall emptied. I remember being bundled into a car. I was picked up by this family called Baker. Overnight my name changed from Aschheim to Baker.

The next twelve months were difficult. I suffered nightmares and later the Bakers told me I sobbed myself to sleep for months. I was with the Bakers until 1947, when suddenly the International Red Cross tracing service linked me with my mother who had survived.

My mother escaped from Germany in 1941 and by a roundabout route got to Uruguay. She lived in dire poverty in Montevideo for five years. In 1947 she came to Israel via England.

The Bakers became very upset when they realised I had a mother. She stayed for three weeks. It was an odd time. To me she was a stranger. I was totally English. She went off to Israel. I did not see her until 1954. By this time I was playing a lot of table tennis and had been selected for the England team. I went to Israel for the 'Maccabi', an international Jewish sports competition. By this time my mother was married. After seeing her again we began to write to each other. My mother died in March 1988. She was 86.

My father and brother perished. At the end of the war I knew they had died and I was told they perished in Auschwitz, although I had no evidence of this.

When I was at university I happened to be in Manchester. At the time there was an exhibition on concentration camps. We decided to go and have a look at the exhibition. It was good and they had copies of all the Auschwitz documents. I began to leaf through them. I was looking for the name of Aschheim of course. I found the name of my father Michael Aschheim, and my brother's name Bernard Aschheim. I felt very sick, but I did not talk about this to anyone. It was not until about 1978 that I could talk about my refugee experience.

Very recently something incredible happened. When my mother died in Israel we had to go through her possessions. We found a letter from a lady in Holland saying a book had been written in which Bernard Aschheim had been featured. This woman gave a telephone number in Holland. When we got back to England my wife spoke to her and she said she would send the book. We got the book and it was translated. It mentioned my brother. He was seven years older than me.

My brother and a group of children were being trained as farmers to go to Palestine. When the Nazis invaded Holland seven of them tried to escape. They were caught by the Gestapo, on the Belgian border, and were eventually sent to Auschwitz. A monument was put up to the children in the village in Holland where they had lived. I hope to visit this monument soon.'

Why were Britain's doors closed to refugees?

Aims

The activity aims to help students decide why refugees were not allowed to escape to Britain, her colonies and British-administered Palestine between 1933 and 1945.

Instructions

Time needed: one hour.

Make copies of the cards (overleaf), students' instructions and the chronology about refugees in Nazi-occupied Europe. Cut up the cards. Each group of students needs a set of cards. Divide the class up into groups of three or four and give each group their instructions, a set of cards and the chronology.

Each group should try and decide the reasons that refugees were not allowed into Britain during the period 1933-45. The students should rank the cards in order of importance, starting with the most important reason for not allowing refugees to come to Britain, ending with the least important reason. The groups should come together, compare their answers, and examine the discussion points.

It is worth noting that this period of history is very controversial, and there are no right answers to the questions posed by the activity.

Discussion points

◆ What could ordinary British people have done to improve the situation for refugees stranded in Nazi-occupied Europe?

◆ What can we learn today from the way that refugees were treated in the period 1933-45?

Students

Read through the chronology of the period 1933-45. You are going to decide what were the reasons for the British government refusing entry to many refugees escaping Nazi-occupied Europe.

In your groups take turns to read out the statements on the cards. Then rank the cards in order of importance. Start with what the group thinks was the most important reason for keeping out refugees, and end with the least important reason. Write 1st, 2nd, 3rd etc on the cards.

The organisations that were formed to help refugees in Britain did not speak out against human rights abuses in Nazi-occupied Europe.

The British government only responded tc public pressure. There was not enough sympathy and pressure from the British public on the refugee issue.

The British government believed that all efforts had to be directed towards fighting the Germans. Helping refugees was a distraction from these aims.

If Jewish refugees were allowed to leave Europe they might eventually go to Palestine. This would cause unrest in Palestine and damage Britain's interests. U of the Suez Canal might be threatened.

Civil servants and diplomats who wanted to help refugees found it very complicated to get visas for them.

Powerful members of the British government were anti-Semitic and anti-communist. They did not care what happened to Jews and communists.

The British government feared that if it was seen to be too generous to refugees, there would be a flood of millions of Jews, Czechs, Poles and other refugees who would want to come to Britain.

The British government believed that people did not want a large number of refugees to settle in Britain or her colonie There would be racist riots.

There was no international organisation to protect human rights.

The British government did not think that the Nazis were murdering people. The accounts of the concentration camps were too horrific to believe.

Britain believed that the persecution of Jews was a purely German affair, and that the British government should not interfere.

The British government believed that refugees would be a financial burden. The would need housing and food.

The British government did not want refugees to come to Britain, as it would be easy for enemy spies to come with a group of refugees.

The British government believed that refugees would take 'British' people's jobs at a time when unemployment was high.

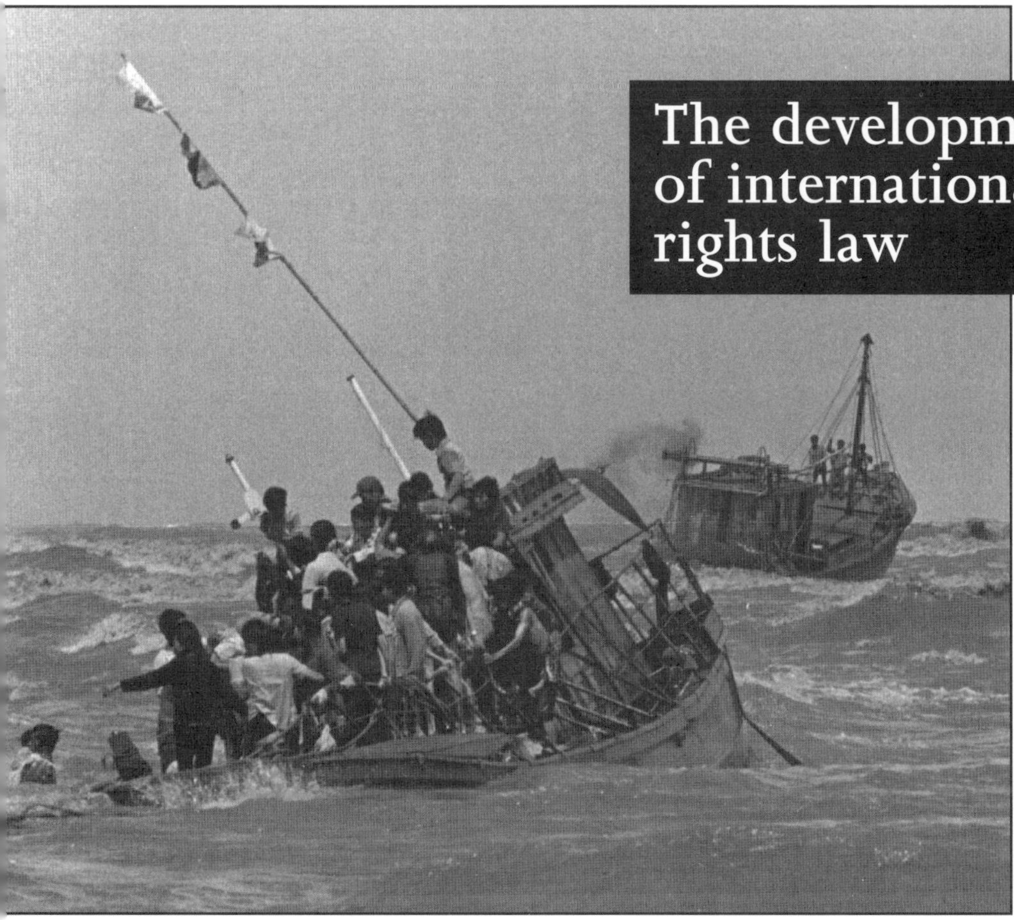

The development of international human rights law

A Vietnamese refugee boat 1980
UNHCR

The reasons that people leave their homes and become refugees are varied. Yet all refugees have one thing in common: their human rights are not being respected in their home country. But what is meant by a human right?

A right is something to which everyone is entitled. Rights that are laid down in law are called legal rights. Legal rights change as the laws of a country change. But not all laws are fair. People also have moral rights. Such rights reflect what is believed to be fair and just.

Human rights are universal moral rights. They apply to all people, at all times, and in all situations. Throughout history there have been both governments and individual people who have worked for human rights. The French Revolution of 1789 resulted in the passage of a constitution which included the Declaration of the Rights of Man. This stated the rights of French citizens, giving the right to personal freedom, property, security and freedom of speech.

After the horrors of the Second World War, representatives of 48 nations met, and wrote the Universal Declaration of Human Rights. This was passed by the United Nations General Assembly in 1948. There have been other international declarations about human rights such as the 1950 European Convention on Human Rights and more recently the 1989 Declaration on the Rights of the Child.

Sadly many countries continue to ignore the principles outlined in the Universal Declaration of Human Rights. For example Amnesty International, an organisation which campaigns for human rights, estimates that over 90 countries regularly torture prisoners.

Where human rights are not respected people are put in danger and some have to become refugees.

The Universal Declarat-ion of Human Rights

Instructions

Time needed: 30 minutes preparation time and about 60 minutes in the group.

Access to a photocopier is needed as well as scissors and envelopes.

On the following pages there is a simplified version of the statements in the Universal Declaration of Human Rights. This should be photocopied and cut up to make 30 'cards'. Put a set of cards in an envelope.

Divide the group up into fours.

The group is going to examine the Universal Declaration of Human Rights. Give each group an envelope with a set of cards in it. The groups should read through each card. They should take turns to do this. After each student has read a card, the group should decide whether they agree with what is written on it or not. Do they think what is stated on the card is a human right?

Make a group decision on this. Divide the cards into two piles:

◆ Human rights with which we agree.

◆ Statements which we don't think are human rights.

The groups should then come together.

Discussion points

◆ Which statements did everyone think were human rights?

◆ Were there any statements with which everyone disagreed?

◆ Now make a list of the main news stories on the television or radio. Which stories have resulted in a person or people losing their human rights?

Drawing up a charter for children's rights

Instructions

Time needed: 45 minutes

Pens and large sheets of paper are needed. Divide the class into groups of two or three. Explain about the Universal Declaration of Human Rights. Each group should then work to produce a charter for children's rights. Each group should decide on ten rights that all children everywhere should have. The charters should then be pinned up and compared. Obviously each charter will be different.

The teacher or group leader can discuss similarities and differences in the charters and then use the charters to produce one common charter.

Discussion point

◆ Do you think young refugees have all the rights listed in your charter?

The Universal Declaration of Human Rights in simple language

rticle 1 All people are born free and
ιual, and should behave with respect to
.ch other.

rticle 2 Everyone should have the
ghts outlined in the Universal
eclaration regardless of their race,
lour, sex, nationality, religion, political
pinion or social origin.

rticle 3 Everyone has a right to live in
eedom and safety.

rticle 4 No-one has a right to make
ople slaves.

ticle 5 No-one should be tortured or
nished in a cruel way.

ticle 6 The law must treat everyone as
ople, not objects.

ticle 7 Laws must not treat people
fferently because of their race, sex or
ay of life.

ticle 8 Everyone has a right to legal
otection if their rights are ignored.

Article 9 Nobody should be arrested, nor kept in prison or sent away from their country, without a just reason.

Article 10 Everyone is entitled to a fair and public trial if charged with an offence.

Article 11 If charged with an offence, a person should be considered innocent until it is proved that he or she is guilty.

Article 12 A person has a right to privacy. No-one has a right to say untrue and damaging things against another person.

Article 13 Everyone has a right to travel and live anywhere in their home country. A person also has the right to leave any country, including his or her own, and to return to it.

Article 14 People have the right to ask for asylum in another country, if they fear persecution. A person loses the right to ask for asylum if he or she has committed a serious non-political crime, and has not respected the Universal Declaration of Human Rights.

Article 15 Everyone has a right to a nationality.

Article 16 Every adult person has the right to marry and have children. Men and women have equal rights in marriage, and if they divorce. No-one should be forced to marry against his or her will.

Article 17 Everyone has the right to own property. No-one can take other people's possessions without a fair reason.

Article 18 Everyone has the right to think and believe in what they want, this includes the right to practice a religion.

Article 19 Everyone has the right to express their thoughts, whether by speaking or in writing.

Article 20 Everyone has the right to organise peaceful meetings, and to form groups. But no-one can be forced to join an organisation.

Article 21 Everyone has the right to take part in the government of his or her country, whether by voting or being an elected member of parliament. Fair elections should be held regularly, and everyone's vote is equal.

Article 22 Everyone has the right to social security. This includes shelter, health care and enough money with which to live.

Article 23 Everyone has the right to work. Wages should be fair and enable a family to live decently. Men and women should receive the same pay for doing the same work. A person has the right to join a trade union.

Article 24 Everyone has the right to reasonable working hours, rest and paid holidays.

Article 25 Everyone has the right to a decent standard of living. Those who cannot work should receive special help. A children, whether born outside marriage c not, have the same rights.

Article 26 Everyone has the right to educatior Primary education should be free and compul sory. A person should be able to continue his c her studies as far as he or she is able. Educatio should help people live with and respect othe people. Parents have the right to choose the kin of education that will be given to their child..

Article 27 Everyone has the right to join in cultural activities, and enjoy the arts. Anything that a person writes or invents should be protected and the person shoulc be able to benefit from its creation.

Article 28 For human rights to be protected there must be order and justice in the world.

Article 29 A person has responsibilities t other people. A person's rights and freedoms should be limited only so far as to protect the rights of other people.

Article 30 No government, group or person may ignore the rights set out in th Universal Declaration of Human Rights.

International laws to protect refugees

One of the human rights that was being discussed during the early part of the 20th century was the right to freedom of people who had been forced to flee from their homes. These people - refugees - needed to be protected from danger. As international human rights law began to develop so did international law to protect refugees.

Between 1912 and 1921 there were huge movements of people in Europe. During the Balkan Wars of 1912-1913 Greeks, Bulgarians and Turks fled from their homes. Soon afterwards thousands of Armenians and Assyrians living in the Ottoman Empire were uprooted and became refugees. The chaos of the First World War (1914-1918) made over six million people refugees.

Between 1917 and 1921 over 1,500,000 people became refugees in the Soviet Union. The fighting with Germany during the First World War caused many Russians and Ukrainians to flee their homes. Then in 1917 the Tsar was overthrown by the Bolsheviks. The Bolshevik-led Russian Revolution was opposed by some Russians who joined the White Russian army. Fighting between the Bolshevik Red Army and the White Russian army caused thousands of other people to flee their homes.

Ukrainian refugee, 1920 *Foto Klebig*

As a result of the Russian Revolution the League of Nations became concerned about the plight of refugees. (The League of Nations was an international organisation that worked like the United Nations does today. It ceased to exist in January 1946 when the United Nations was formed).

The League of Nations defined refugees as being people who were in danger if they returned to their home countries. In 1921 the League of Nations appointed Fridjof Nansen, the Norwegian explorer, as High Commissioner for Russian Refugees. Within a few years Nansen was asked to help other groups of refugees such as Greeks and Turks.

Nansen died in 1930. In the 1930s his organisation underwent many changes. Some of these changes were necessary to meet the needs of refugees escaping from the Spanish Civil War and Nazi Germany. By 1938 Nansen's organisation was called 'The Office of the High Commissioner for Refugees under the Protection of the League of Nations'. But the upheavals of the Second World War stopped this organisation from working effectively. It was replaced by a short-lived organisation called the United Nations Relief and Rehabilitation Organisation which helped refugees between 1943 and 1946. This organisation helped some of the 30 million refugees and displaced people who were homeless at the end of the Second World War.

When the United Nations replaced the League of Nations in 1946 it established a new body called the International Refugee Organisation. In 1951 the International Refugee Organisation handed over its responsibilities to a new body - the United Nations High Commissioner for Refugees (UNHCR). At the same time the United Nations General Assembly passed the UN Convention Relating to the Status of Refugees. This defined who were refugees.

A refugee is someone who has 'a well-founded fear of being persecuted for reasons of race, religion, nationality, membership of a particular social group or political opinion.'

The 1951 UN Convention Relating to the Status of Refugees also gave power to UNHCR to try to protect refugees from being returned to places where they would be in danger.

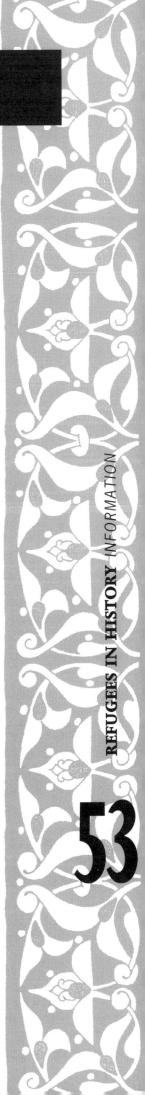

The Poles and the Hungarians

Hungarian refugee at Austrian border, 1956 *AP*

Between 1945 and 1970 most of the world's refugees left eastern Europe. The two largest groups were Poles and Hungarians. Many of them came to Britain.

Poles in Britain

Some 250,000 Polish refugees settled permanently in Britain. They entered Britain in five different migratory movements. The first group to arrive were Polish refugees who fled their homeland in September 1939, after the German invasion. About 440,000 people fled Poland at this time, of whom 60 per cent were Jewish. Of these refugees, some 2,000 entered Britain. Others made their way to France where a Polish government in exile was formed.

After France was invaded in 1940 over 30,000 Polish refugees fled to Britain. The Polish government in exile, led by General Sikorski, moved to London. Many of this group of Polish refugees became soldiers and airmen alongside British forces.

In September 1939, after Poland was invaded by Nazi Germany, it was divided between Germany and the Soviet Union. Some 1.8 million Polish citizens found themselves living in the Soviet Union where they were treated very badly. Nearly one million Poles were deported eastwards, to labour camps in Siberia. But in 1941, after the German invasion, the Soviet Union entered the Second World War. An agreement was signed between the Soviet Union and the Polish government in exile. The Polish government was allowed to organise an army made up of Poles who were living in the Soviet Union. That army was led by General Anders. The army of 220,000 people left the Soviet Union in March 1942 and started on an incredible journey across many countries. They travelled through Iran, Iraq, Jordan, Palestine and Egypt. In Egypt the army was organised into the Polish Second Corps who later fought with the British in Italy. In 1945, at the end of the Second World War, many of the soldiers who had fought in the Polish Second Corps came to Britain as refugees.

At the end of the Second World War many other Poles were living in refugee camps in Europe. Some of them were opponents of the new communist government in Poland, and did not want to return home. Others were from the Polish Ukraine which became part of the Soviet Union in 1945. Some 101,000 Polish refugees from refugee camps in Europe came as refugees to Britain between 1946 and 1950. Later another 14,000 Polish refugees entered Britain, as part of the European Volunteer Worker Scheme. This group of refugees was sent to work in key industries where labour was in short supply.

Most Polish refugees soon found work in all parts of Britain. They made great contributions to rebuilding the British economy after the Second World War. Industries which particularly benefited from the efforts of the Polish refugees included building, agriculture, coal mining, the hotel trade, the brick industry, iron and steel manufacture and the textile industry.

The Hungarians

Hungary was an ally of Nazi Germany in the Second World War, although in 1944 Germany invaded Hungary and murdered 300,000 Hungarian Jews. The Soviet Union freed Hungary from German rule in 1945. Communists became the largest single political party in elections held in 1947, and by 1949 controlled the country. Small numbers of refugees left

Rita's story

Rita was 26 years old when she joined General Anders' army in the Soviet Union. With the army she travelled through Iran, Iraq, Palestine, Egypt and finally to Italy where she was a nurse. She arrived in Britain in 1946. Her story was collected by the Ethnic Communities Oral History Project.

‘When the Russians invaded Lithuania, my father and I were arrested besides hundreds of others.... I was taken to Altaj in the middle of the Steppe region. We were told that this is where we were going to live and work. They directed me to a house where a young couple lived with a small son. I had a very small room, one table and a chair, there was no light there. There was no sanitation at all. Fuel was unobtainable so animal dung was mixed with straw and dried in the sun at the brick farm. It was called *kiziaki*, when burned it gave little heat but plenty of smoke. I worked in a workshop where we made uniforms for the army. Then I was transported to a barber shop; men called to serve in the army had to have their hair cut.

When General Sikorski signed an agreement with Stalin we were freed, an amnesty was announced on the radio. Then the winter came, each day it was colder and colder, we knew we would never survive the winter. There was one remedy, to go south where the Polish army was forming into units.

London (the Polish government in exile) decided to send us to Persia (Iran). We crossed the Caspian Sea in a very old ship. We met other Polish soldiers in tropical kit, how different we looked in our woolly dresses. We felt we were newly born, we were free after so many months of being suppressed, starved and living without hope.

The next stop was Egypt, then Italy where the fighting was in full swing. We all tried to do impossible tasks as we expected that this would be the last stage before we reached our homeland. But it wasn't to be - our country was sold down the river.

When we came to England we were disillusioned and knew we were destined to further wanderings. Some people returned to Poland to be arrested and imprisoned. Others went to Canada, Argentina or Australia. My husband and I toyed with the idea of going to Ecuador, we even started learning Spanish. I started work in a hairdressing business. Then we opened a delicatessen shop where we both worked together. The time came to retire and I hope to be in good health to see what other changes the future will bring.’

Hungary between 1946 and 1956.

In 1956 there were many demonstrations. These were caused by a split in the Communist Party between hardline communists and more liberal party members. For a while it looked possible that Hungary might return to democracy. But on 4 November 1956 a Soviet-led army invaded Hungary, and 3,000 people were killed. Over 200,000 people fled as refugees, most of them going to Austria and Yugoslavia.

Between November 1956 and January 1957 over 21,000 Hungarians entered Britain as refugees, including 400 unaccompanied refugee children. Some 4,000 refugees only stayed a few months, but most remained in Britain. Two organisations supported the newly arrived refugees: the National Coal Board and the British Council for Aid to Refugees. The National Coal Board housed Hungarian men and their families and found them work in coal mines. The British Council for Aid to Refugees set up temporary hostels before finding the Hungarian refugees work and a permanent home.

Refugees' contribution to life in Britain

Aims

The activity will increase students' understanding of the contribution that refugees have made to life in Britain and develop students' research skills.

Instructions

Time needed: at least three hours and homework. Students will need copies of the information sheet, large sheets of white paper, scissors, glue, paints or coloured pens.

The students are going to research local connections with refugees and produce a collage to show local links with refugees. The ideas on the information sheet can be used to stimulate ideas. Other places to find information include:

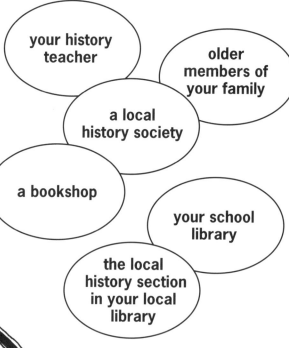

- **your history teacher**
- **older members of your family**
- **a local history society**
- **a bookshop**
- **your school library**
- **the local history section in your local library**

Refugees' contribution to life in Britain

Vietnamese restaurant owner *Howard Davies*

Britain has been receiving refugees for hundreds of years. Most refugees are ordinary people living ordinary lives. They may be longing to return home to their own country, but in the meantime get on with life in the place where they have settled. Refugees contribute to community life, as much as anyone else and, like most people's contributions, they are made quietly.

But some refugees or groups of refugees are famous for particular achievements.

During the 17th century over 100,000 Huguenot refugees settled in Britain. They regenerated economic life in southern England, draining the fens and building houses. Does your home town or city have any links with the Huguenots?

Some 16 Nobel Prizes have been won by refugees living in Britain, most of them in science and medicine. Famous refugee scientists include Albert Einstein, Sir Hans Krebs, Sir Ernst Chain, Charlotte Auerbach, Sir Walter Bodmer and Sir Rudolf Peierls. Can you find out about their scientific achievements?

Sigmund Freud, the psychoanalyst, was a refugee. He fled Vienna in 1938 and settled in London.

There have been many famous refugee painters. Lucian Freud is probably the best known British painter who was a refugee. See how many other artists you can find who were refugees.

Playwrights and novelists such as Bertold Brecht, Thomas Mann, Sousa Jamba and Franz Kafka were refugees. Many publishing companies such as Gollancz, Heinemann, Andre Deutsch, Thames and Hudson and Paul Hamlyn were founded by refugees.

Refugees have brought recipes to enrich our diet. The Huguenots brought oxtail soup to Britain. More recently refugees such as the Vietnamese and Turkish Kurds have set up restaurants.

Refugees have contributed to many of Britain's traditional industries. Some 30,000 Polish refugees were employed as coal miners by 1950. There have been many refugee industrialists such as Calouste Gulbenkian (Armenia), Minh To (Viet Nam) and Siegmund Warburg (Germany). Andrex - the first soft toilet paper in Britain - was manufactured by a firm founded by German Jewish refugees.

Refugees have particularly contributed to the fashion and textile industries. Courtaulds, the textile firm, was founded by Huguenot refugees. Many clothing firms in London are still owned by the descendants of eastern European Jewish refugees.

Refugees are involved in all types of music, as composers and performers, for example Hugh Masakela from South Africa.

Discussion point

◆ **In what ways do you think we can benefit from mixing with people from other cultures?**

Researching multi-ethnic Britain

Instructions

Time needed: 45 minutes. A greater length of time can be spent on this activity if desired.

Students will need access to local telephone directories, recent census data and, if available, a school language survey. Summaries of census data can be obtained from local libraries.

Students

You may be surprised at the numbers of people in Britain who were born abroad or who have ancestors who came from other nations. Two ways of studying this are to examine census data and to study people's family names.

The Census

A census is a government survey which is carried out to count the population and find out other facts. In Britain, a census is carried out every ten years. The census usually records a person's country of birth.

- Using your local census data find out what percentage of the population in your local authority was born outside Britain.

- List the five countries where most of the residents in your local authority were born.

- Using the census data and a school language survey, if available, can you find the names of countries where people might have fled as refugees?

Family names

Family names can also give an approximate guide to the ethnic origins of people in a given area. However some people change their names when they arrive in a new country, or have new names given to them by officials.

Using a telephone directory, select two pages where there are a reasonable number of different names. With a highlighting pen, mark all the names of people that you think may have families that have come from outside Britain. What percentage of names may originate from outside Britain?

Major second languages spoken in Camden primary & secondary schools, 1987

	Students
Bengali	1,270
Greek	378
Spanish	362
Chinese	288
Gujarati	208
Arabic	164
French	121
Turkish	115
Hebrew	282
Portuguese	233
Italian	216
Tagalog	90
Farsi	74
Polish	74

1981 Census Data & Borough Language Survey London Borough of Camden

Total population 161,098
Population born outside UK 48,300

Africa	**4813**
Algeria	52
Egypt	433
Ghana	365
Kenya	504
Libya	44
Malawi	35
Mauritius	172
Morocco	180
Nigeria	598
South Africa	1,170
Sierra Leone	83
Tanzania	226
Tunisia	35
Uganda	294
Zambia	115
Zimbabwe	220
Other African countries	287

North & South America	**2,234**
Barbados	204
Guyana	250
Jamaica	605
Trinidad & Tobago	332
Other Caribbean countries	683
South American countries	77

Asia	**10,606**
Bangladesh	1,282
Burma	72
China	308
Hong Kong	879
India	2,087
Iran	788
Israel	412
Japan	746
Malaysia	1,036
Pakistan	475
Philippines	802
Seychelles	17
Singapore	332
Sri Lanka	373
Vietnam	79
Other Asian countries	919

Europe & USSR	**29,975**
Austria	845
Belgium	187
Cyprus	1,837
Czechoslovakia	492
Denmark	214
Finland	120
France	865
Germany	2,193
Gibraltar	96
Greece	404
Hungary	394
Ireland	15,531
Italy	1,709
Malta	246
Netherlands	247
Norway	97
Poland	1,115
Portugal	881
Romania	119
Spain	1,320
Sweden	158
Switzerland	346
Turkey	314
USSR	681
Yugoslavia	217

CHAPTER THREE

REFUGEES IN TODAY'S WORLD

Displaced Somali woman
Hamish Wilson

Over 18,000,000 people are now refugees ◆ This chapter looks at the main refugee groups in today's world.

Angola

Angola has suffered from a war lasting nearly 35 years. Over 2 million people are internally displaced and 350,000 are refugees in neighbouring countries.

Howard Davies

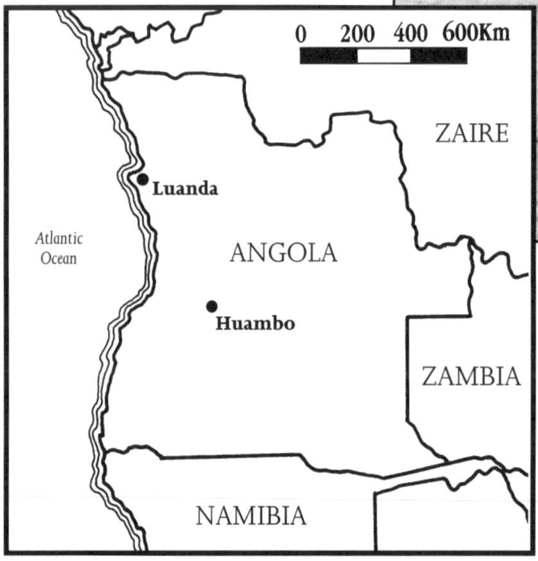

Population
11 million

Capital
Luanda

Economy
Most people in Angola depend on agriculture for their living. The main crops are maize, sugar cane, palms, coffee, cotton, sisal and vegetables. Angola is a fertile country, but fighting has prevented many people planting crops.

Angola has many natural resources and is potentially one of the richest countries in Africa. Over 90 per cent of the country's export earnings come from crude oil and petroleum products. There are also reserves of minerals such as gold, diamonds, iron and copper. But the war has disrupted all parts of the economy.

Ethnic groups
There are three main ethnic groups in Angola, and many smaller minorities. The largest ethnic group are the Ovimbundu. They speak Umbundu as their first language. Jonas Savimbi, UNITA leader, belongs to this group.

The Kimbundu and Kikongo are the other main ethnic groups.

Languages
The official language of Angola is Portuguese. The most important African language is Mbundu. Mbundu comprises two dialects: Umbundu, spoken by the Ovimbundu of central Angola, and Kimbundu spoken by the Kimbundu of northern Angola. Kikongo is spoken by about one million people living in northern Angola.

Events

Before the 13th century Angola was inhabited by Khoi San people. Migrants then moved south into Angola, displacing the Khoi San. The first Europeans arrived in Angola in 1482 when Diego Cao, a Portuguese explorer, reached the mouth of the River Congo. This expedition was the beginning of colonisation.

For over 300 years Portuguese colonisers made a great deal of money out of the slave trade. The Portuguese offered some Angolan ethnic groups money for the capture of slaves. As a result there was much internal conflict in Angola between those who were and were not recipients of Portuguese money. War and slavery reduced the population of Angola from 18 million in 1450 to about eight million people in 1850. The slaves were transported to North America, Brazil, Sao Tomé and Portugal. Nearly 50 per cent perished during the journey.

1850 The Portuguese control the coast of Angola, while the interior is controlled by Angolan traders and local lords. Slavery is still legal.

1884 The Berlin Conference grants Angola to the Portuguese. The boundaries are set in 1891.

1895–1921 A series of military campaigns gives Portugal control of the interior. The Portuguese are encouraged to settle in Angola to strengthen their presence. Some Angolans are given a missionary education, and then get jobs in commerce and government. They are known as the *assimilados* - assimilated Angolans.

1945–1960 Portuguese migration to Angola triples, the number of settlers reaches 350,000. Many of the Portuguese migrants are unable to read and write. The poorer settlers face direct competition with Angolans for jobs. It is the latter who lose out, and begin to agitate for independence, and an end to discrimination against Angolan people.

1956 The Popular Movement for the Liberation of Angola (MPLA) is founded, getting most of its support from the Kimbundu living around Luanda. It seeks an end to Portuguese rule. In the years that follow, other resistance movements are formed, including the Union for the Total Independence of Angola (UNITA) and the National Front for the Liberation of Angola (FNLA). UNITA draws most of its support from the Ovimbundu, and the FNLA from the Kikongo.

1961 The war of independence begins. MPLA fighters attack Luanda's prisons. At the same time Portuguese targets are attacked in north west Angola. The Portuguese army responds by bombing villages and using napalm. Over 60,000 refugees flee to Zaire.

1965 The war has forced 400,000 Angolan refugees into Zaire. Most settle in the border area.

1968 The war spreads south and refugees flee to Zambia.

1970s The MPLA, FNLA and UNITA continue to disagree with each other. More Angolans are killed in fighting between the three groups than are killed fighting the Portuguese. The super-powers worsen the conflict by arming different groups. The West backs UNITA, the Chinese back the FNLA and the Soviet Union backs the MPLA.

1974 A new government comes to power in Portugal. It announces it will leave its colonies. The three independence movements sign a ceasefire.

1975 The MPLA, FNLA and UNITA meet in Portugal and sign an agreement. But by March 1975 fighting breaks out between UNITA, the FNLA and the MPLA. The MPLA then establishes a government in Luanda. The FNLA and UNITA establish an alternative government in Huambo.

In late 1975 South African troops invade Angola. The South African government sees Angola as a potentially wealthy rival in southern Africa. The South African army comes within 200 kilometres of Luanda. Cuban troops arrive to support the MPLA, and together they manage to drive back the South Africans.

1976–1980 The US Congress stops

much military aid to UNITA. As a result UNITA is less active, and there is less fighting. The Angolan government is able to make improvements in healthcare and education.

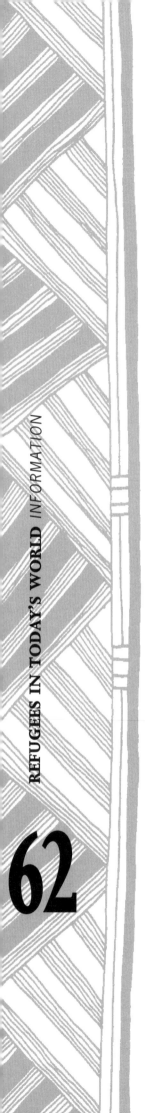

1980 Ronald Reagan, newly elected as President, promises more US military aid to UNITA. South Africa also increases aid to UNITA, and resumes bombing parts of southern Angola. Many economic targets such as railways and factories are destroyed.

1982–84 Refugees continue to flee to Zambia and Zaire. By 1984 over 600,000 people are internally displaced in Angola.

1984 Drought and the spread of civil war lead to severe food shortages.

1988 The US and African states put pressure on UNITA and the MPLA to negotiate a peace agreement. A ceasefire is signed in June, but fighting starts again in August. Both sides of the conflict are accused of human rights violations.

1989–1990 Over 400,000 Angolans are refugees in Zaire and Zambia. There is famine in rural areas.

1991 A peace agrement is signed by UNITA and the MPLA. A ceasefire is agreed, and the peace agreement is to be monitored by thc UN.

1992 General and presidential elections are held in September 1992. In the general election the MPLA secures 57 per cent of the vote, while UNITA receives 32 per cent. UN monitors declare the elections to be generally free and fair. But despite the international presence Jonas Savimbi, President of UNITA, refuses to recognise the result. UNITA soon reorganises its army and begins to seize towns and villages.

1993–94 The civil war worsens. Over two million people are internally displaced and over 350,000 are refugees in neighbouring countries.

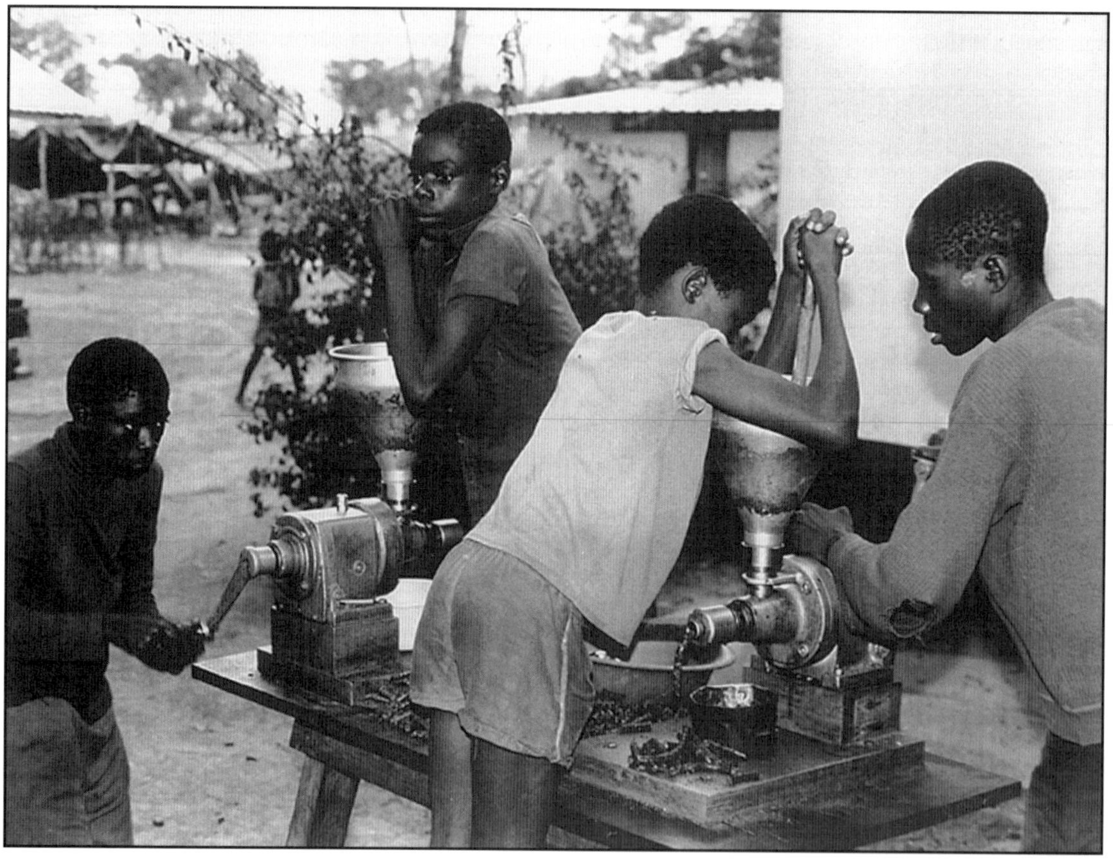

Angolan refugee camp
Constantia Treppe

Sousa Jamba's story

Sousa Jamba is a writer who fled from Angola in 1976. He now lives in London.

'I was born in 1966 at Dondi Mission in central Angola. My father was a school teacher who, with the help of Canadian missionaries, owned his own school. In 1972 my parents moved to Humabo, the main city in the central Angola highlands, where I started school.

In 1976, at the height of the first bout of the Angolan civil war, I fled with my sister Noemia to Zambia. My sister was married to an Angolan with Zambian roots and I lived in Zambia until 1985 when I went to join the UNITA guerrillas in the Angolan bush. I then worked as a reporter and translator for the UNITA news agency. My experiences of that part of Angola formed the background to *Patriots*, my first novel.

In 1986, aged 20, I came to Britain on a scholarship to study journalism. I was then given money by the Scottish Arts Council to work with school students in schools in south west Scotland. I am now living in London and my second novel, *A Lonely Devil*, was published in 1993.'

Here is an extract from 'Patriots', Sousa Jamba's first book. The book follows the life of Hosi Mbueti. As a boy Hosi fled Angola following the death of his parents, supporters of UNITA. Ten years later Hosi returns from exile in Zambia to join UNITA. He finds himself fighting against Osvaldo, his brother, who, many years before, chose to fight for the MPLA.

In the extract Hosi is still a boy, and still living in Angola. The civil war has just started.

'Valeriana Mbueti rushed off to the kitchen to get her sister some food. Aunt Laura turned to Hosi and said: 'It has come at last, Hosi.'
'What, Auntie?'
'The war.'
'What did I hear you say, Laura?' said Nathaniel Mbueti.
'The war. In Huambo people are killing each other. There was a time when we thought it would all end in Luanda. We were mistaken. It is now here.

Nataniel Mbueti ordered Hosi to go to bed. Hosi stalled for a while but a few fierce looks convinced him that his father meant business.

That night Hosi wondered what would happen next. There was talk of war everywhere. There were armed men everywhere. Children who had recently been playing mothers and fathers were now playing soldiers. They would divide themselves into three movements - UNITA, the MPLA and the FNLA - and then throw stones at each other. Hosi himself was a bit old for the game, and though the other children had tried to persuade him to play, he hadn't done so.

Hosi was worried, but not very worried. He knew there was nothing he could do to prevent the war, so at some point he began to enjoy the feeling that was spreading among the other children. Everyone wanted to have a uniform and a wooden AK47. Still, now and then he did wonder whether there would be a time when there were humans and dogs rotting in the streets.'

Family tracing

When war breaks out in a country it is easy to be parted from members of your family. Parents are often separated from their children or a husband may lose his wife. In such situations family tracing is very important. Organisations like the Red Cross and the Save the Children Fund are involved in family tracing. If family tracing is successful, divided families can be united.

Tracing can be divided into three different stages:

Identification and documentation involve listing the lost family members, interviewing the family about themselves and the way that they became separated.

Tracing is the process of looking for someone.

Reunification happens if tracing is successful. The family is brought together.

Different methods are used to trace a person. In some situations office-based tracing methods can be used. An advertisement can be placed in a newspaper, on a poster or on the radio. The advertisement will give details about the missing person. Red Cross tracing volunteers also trace people by travelling to different areas. This often involves difficult and uncomfortable journeys to remote areas.

A good tracer has many different skills. He or she will have a detailed knowledge about a particular area. The tracer also should be willing to travel widely, sometimes in difficult and dangerous conditions. A good tracer is also imaginative and uses lateral thinking. He/she uses deduction, guesswork, hypotheses and hunches to try and find where people might be. "That transit camp in the capital has a lot of people from the same area, let's ask there."

The Red Cross Tracing Service helps bring together close relatives who have been separated by armed conflict, political upheavals, natural or man-made disasters. The Tracing Service may also trace people on compassionate grounds, for example, people who were very close friends.

It is a free service and is in great demand. In 1993 the Red Cross Tracing Service received an average of 800 inquiries every day. It can take up to two years for a case to be examined.

Someone living in Britain who wishes to trace a relative has to refer to the Case Registry at British Red Cross headquarters. The enquirer has to fill in a tracing form giving information about the person being sought. The inquiry is recorded on a computer. The British Red Cross then has to decide whether to accept the tracing request. Sometimes, if a country is in crisis, the tracing service is suspended.

The tracing form is then sent to the Central Tracing Agency of the International Committee of the Red Cross (ICRC) in Geneva. It goes from there to one of the 60 different Red Cross national societies where volunteers do the search.

The Red Cross also runs the Family Message Service. This is often the only way for family members to keep in contact if they are separated by war and normal communications, such as post and telephones, have broken down. Family messages can also be sent to relatives who are in refugee or prisoner of war camps.

In Britain, a person wanting to send a message contacts their local Red Cross office and collects a family message form. They write the message and post the form to the British Red Cross headquarters in London. Only family news must be sent; no political or military information is allowed. The form is then sent on to a Red Cross society in the relevant country or to the ICRC in Geneva. The message service allows for a return message. Sometimes this brings very bad news. If this happens the Red Cross always delivers these messages in person. Tracing and the family message service have been very important in Angola.

Tracing a relative

Instructions

Time needed: 30 minutes

Copies of the tracing form and the information on family tracing are needed. Students can work in pairs and small groups.

Joaquim is a 22 year old Angolan man. In 1990 he became separated from his sister during the civil war. Both Joaquim and Jacinta had to leave their home town during the war. Their house was destroyed.

In 1993 Joaquim's aunt received a letter from Jacinta. She was a refugee in London. But since then the family has heard nothing from her. Letters sent to London have not been answered. Joaquim now wants to trace his sister.

The students are going to act as Red Cross staff. In groups they should work out a strategy to trace Jacinta.

Red Cross — National Headquarters

TRACING FORM

TO: RED CROSS — DATE: 25 August 1994
REF: 000001

SOUGHT PERSON	
1 Full Name (as used locally) - underline surname	Jacinta Paulo
2 Name at Birth	Jacinta Paulo
3 Father's Full Name (or head of family group)	Alphons Paulo
4 Mother's Full Name	Francisca Paulo
5 Date of Birth	26.5.71 — Sex: F — Marital Status **N/K**
6 Place of Birth	Huambo, Angola — Nationality Angolan
7 Country of origin	Angola
8 Profession/Occupation	Student
9 Name and Ages of Others with Sought Person	none
10 a) Last Known Address:	33 Acacia Road London SE15
b) Telephone No.	
11 Place and Date of Last News	address above 1993
12 Circumstances leading to the loss of contact	fighting in Huambo
ENQUIRER	
13 Full Name (Indicate Mr/Mrs/Miss)	Joaquim Paulo
14 Nationality	Angolan
15 Address	PO BOX 45231 Huambo Angola
16 Telephone No.	
17 Date and Place of Birth or Age	02.12.73
18 The Person to be traced is my	Sister
19 The media may be used if necessary for search	Yes

Burundi & Rwanda

Ethnic conflict between Tutsi and Hutu people over many years has forced millions of people to flee as refugees.

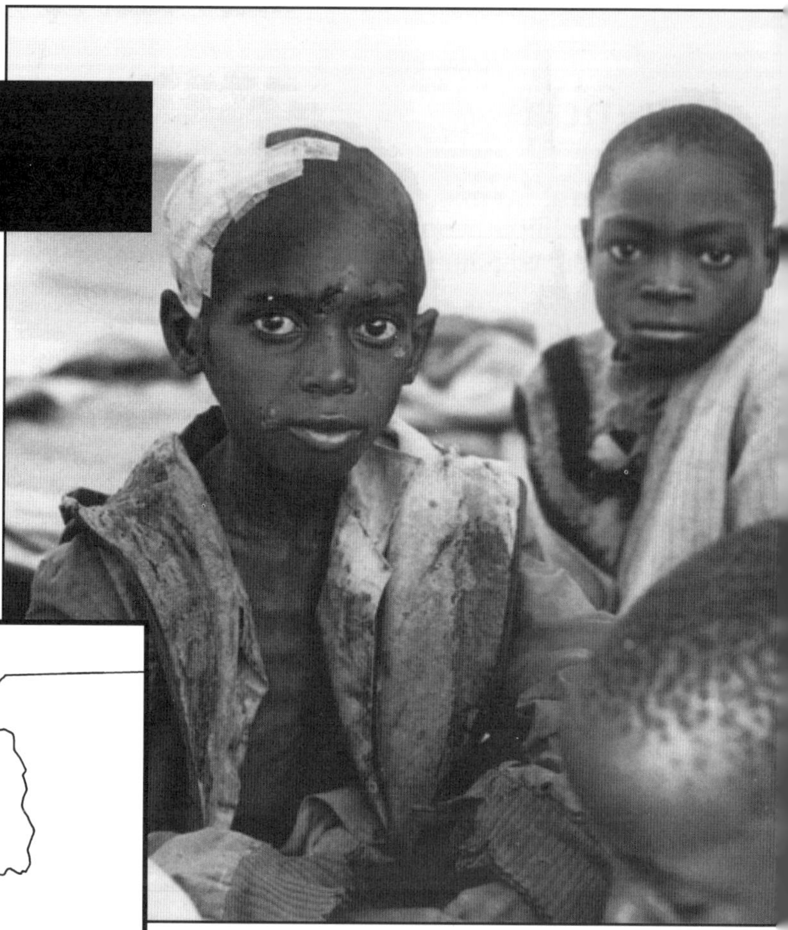

Orphaned Rwandan Tutsi refugee, Zaire 1994 *Howard Davies*

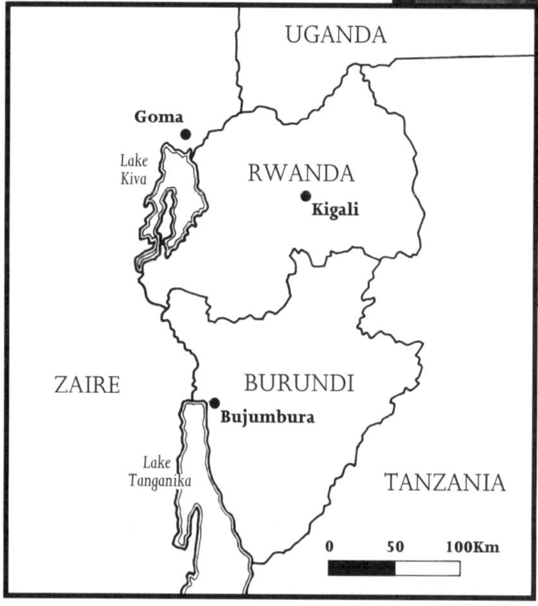

Burundi

Population
6 million

Capital
Bujumbura

Economy
Over 90 per cent of the population lives in the countryside and most people farm for a living. As in Rwanda, the main export is coffee.

Burundi has many of the same economic problems as Rwanda. The country has gone into debt because of a drop in the world price of coffee, its main export. As in Rwanda, Burundi is very densely populated. Farms are very small and many families cannot make a decent living from their land. Other problems are soil erosion and declining soil fertility. The declining quality of the soil reduces the yield of crops.

Burundi has a very poorly developed infrastructure. There are few roads and many people lack access to clean water.

Ethnic groups
As in neighbouring Rwanda, Burundi has experienced ethnic conflicts between the Tutsi and Hutu peoples for many years. There are three ethnic groups in Burundi. Most people are Hutu. The Hutu form 84 per cent of the population of Burundi. The Tutsi comprise 15 per cent of Rwanda's population. The Twa are pygmoid peoples who still live as hunter-gatherers in the forests. They make up less than one per cent of the population of Burundi.

Twa, Tutsi and Hutu also live in other central African countries; in Rwanda, Uganda and Zaire.

The conflict in Burundi is not solely an ethnic conflict. Economic, social, and political differences have contributed towards the tension and violence.

Languages
French is the official language. Rundi is spoken by most Burundis. This language is very closely related to Kinyarwanda, spoken in neighbouring Rwanda.

Rwanda

Population
About 4.5 million people now live in Rwanda. At least 500,000 people were murdered in 1994 and another 2 million Rwandans are refugees in neighbouring countries.

Capital
Kigali

Economy
Rwanda is a green and beautiful country and is sometimes called 'the land of a thousand hills'. Over 90 per cent of the population lives in the countryside and most people farm for a living. Rwanda's main export is coffee.

Despite being a fertile country, Rwanda has many economic problems. The country has gone into debt because of a drop in the world price of coffee, its main export. Rwanda is the most densely populated country in Africa. Farms are very small (most farms are under one hectare of land) and many families cannot make a decent living from their land. Other problems are soil erosion and declining soil fertility. The declining quality of the soil reduces the yield of crops.

Ethnic groups
Rwanda has experienced ethnic conflicts between the Tutsi and Hutu peoples for many years. There are three ethnic groups in Rwanda. Most people are Hutu. In 1993 the Hutu formed 90 per cent of the population of Rwanda, but now many have fled as refugees. The Tutsi make up about nine per cent of Rwanda's population. The Twa are pygmoid peoples and live as hunter-gatherers in the forests. They make up less than one per cent of the Rwandan population.

Twa, Tutsi and Hutu also live in other central African countries; in Burundi, Uganda and Zaire.

Newspapers have reported that the present conflict in Rwanda is ethnic. While it is true that most people who were killed in 1994 were Tutsi, there are political, economic and regional factors in today's conflict. Hutu who were opposed to the government of President Habyarimana were also killed. In the past there have also been economic inequalities between Hutu and Tutsi. From the 15th century until the late 1950s, Tutsi ruled most of Rwanda and held most of its wealth. Indeed some sociologists say that the differences between Hutu and Tutsi are not ethnic differences, but social and economic differences.

Languages
French and Kinyarwanda

Events

Burundi's first inhabitants were the Twa. They lived in the forests of Burundi and were hunter-gatherers.

1000–1500 AD New groups of people migrate to central Africa. They are the Hutu. They are farmers and clear much forest land for growing crops. Hutu people are ruled by local lords.

1600–1800 A new group of taller people migrate to central Africa from Sudan and Ethiopia. They are the Tutsi and are cattle-herding nomads. They soon emerge as the rulers. After the arrival of the Tutsi in Burundi, the country is ruled by a Tutsi king called the *mwami*, and a Tutsi princely class called the *ganwa*. The *mwami's* kingdom does not include Rwanda. Ordinary Tutsi and Hutu are in much the same position, and intermarriage between Tutsi and Hutu is common.

1894 The first European explorers arrive in Burundi. In the same year, European governments agree to divide central Africa among themselves. Burundi, along with today's Rwanda, becomes part of German East Africa. In order to bring the population of Burundi under control, the Germans give favours to a small number of wealthy Tutsi.

1916 During the First World War, Burundi is occupied by the Belgians who invade from neighbouring Belgian Congo.

1918 After Germany's defeat in the First World War, Belgium takes control of today's Rwanda and Burundi, under a

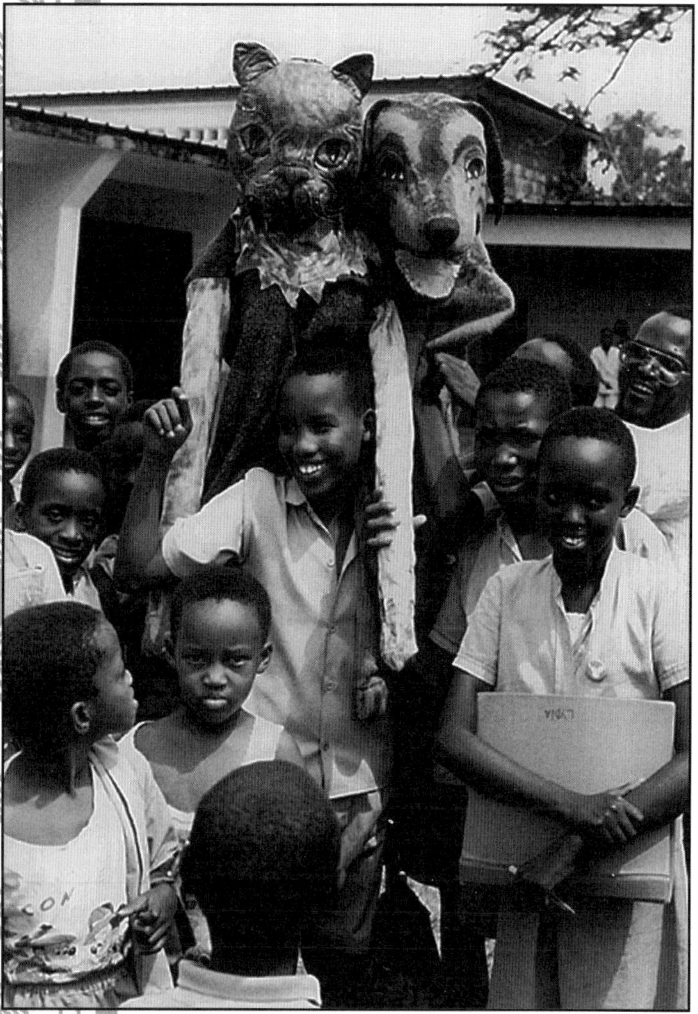

A conflict resolution project in Burundi *Howard Davies*

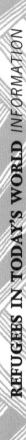

mandate from the League of Nations. The country is known as Ruanda-Urundi. The Belgians continue to favour a small Tutsi elite. The Belgians introduce identity cards and try to make the differences between Tutsi and Hutu greater.

1945–1948 After the creation of the UN, Ruanda-Urundi becomes a Belgian 'Trustee Territory'. The UN puts pressure on the Belgians to move Ruanda-Urundi towards democracy and independence. Burundi political parties begin to emerge. The two main parties are the UPRONA Party, led by Prince Louis Rwagasore and the Democratic Christian Party (PDC). In the years immediately after independence the UPRONA Party tries to unite Hutu and Tutsi.

1961 The Belgians decide to leave Ruanda-Urundi. Burundi and Rwanda move towards being separate states. In Burundi, elections are held in September 1961 to decide who will head the country's first government. The UPRONA Party wins, but two weeks later Prince Louis Rwagasore is murdered by agents of the PDC Party. His death leads to divisions within the UPRONA Party and the start of conflicts between Tutsi and Hutu.

1962 Burundi becomes an independent country, with the *mwami* as Head of State. The *mwami* tries to keep the peace in Burundi and gives equal amounts of political power to Tutsi and Hutu politicians.

1965 The newly-elected Prime Minister is murdered. He is a Hutu. This is followed by a political crisis and elections are held again. In these elections the Hutu are the winners, but despite their victory the *mwami* appoints a Tutsi prime minister. Many Hutu are angry about this and in October 1965 the Hutu dominated police force rebels and tries to take political power. They fail, and thousands of Hutu are murdered. Refugees flee to Rwanda and other neighbouring countries.

1966 There are two *coup d'etat* in Burundi. The latter results in the overthrow of the *mwami*. Burundi becomes a republic. Colonel Micombero, a Tutsi, becomes President. Most Hutu politicians and army officers are removed from their jobs.

1972 There is a Hutu rebellion against the Government. It is unsuccessful and the Hutu are not able to seize power. Following the rebellion, extremists in the Tutsi-dominated army murder at least 150,000 Hutu people. Another 300,000 Hutu flee to Rwanda, Zaire and Tanzania. Almost every Hutu is eliminated from the army. No-one is tried for the murders of 1972.

1976 Colonel Jean Baptiste Bagaza seizes power in another *coup d'etat*. He is also a Tutsi.

1982–84 Elections are held in 1982 and 1984, but Colonel Bagaza, now leader of the UPRONA party, is the only candidate in both elections.

1984–87 There are worsening human rights abuses in Burundi. Members of Hutu opposition groups and some church members are detained and tortured. Some Christian churches are denied freedom to worship.

1987 There is another military *coup d'etat*.

Major Pierre Buyoya becomes Burundi's new President. There are some improvements in human rights in Burundi, but most Hutu are still denied political power.

1988 There is further violence. The army kills at least 20,000 unarmed Hutu in towns in northern Burundi. Another 60,000 refugees flee to Rwanda. After this massacre, foreign governments put much pressure on the Burundi government. President Buyoya then decides that action must be taken to end the violence in Burundi. He appoints a Hutu prime minister and gives other government posts to Hutu. President Buyoya also sets up a National Commission to examine ways to prevent the violence.

1988–91 Burundi moves towards democracy. There is progress towards ending discrimination against the Hutu. A greater number of Hutu are able to go to university, more Hutu obtain jobs in the civil service and more Hutu obtain senior political posts. Many Hutu refugees also return to Burundi. But the army is still dominated by Tutsi and resists change.

1993 Elections are held in Burundi. Melchior Ndadaye beats Pierre Buyoya and becomes the new President. Ndadaye becomes Burundi's first Hutu President. But politicians fighting the election campaign exploit ethnic differences. Ndadaye leads the FRODEBU party. FRODEBU is seen as a Hutu party, while UPRONA is seen as a party that will defend Tutsi interests.

Although the FRODEBU party win the elections, the Tutsi-dominated army and those who support the UPRONA party are unwilling to give up the power they have held for many years. On 20 October 1993, army officers attack the President's palace. President Ndadaye is taken prisoner and killed the next day. The military *coup d'etat* is followed by violence. Supporters of UPRONA and many Tutsi are killed in revenge for the President's death. In other areas FRODEBU supporters and Hutu are killed by the army. Over 50,000 Hutu and Tutsi are murdered. Another 700,000 people, mostly Hutu, flee to Rwanda, Tanzania and Zaire. A large number of Tutsi and Hutu became internally displaced.

1994 The *coup d'etat* of October 1993 leaves Burundi without a government. In February 1994 a new government is formed, led by President Ntaryamira. Less than two months later he is dead, killed in an air crash with President Habyarimana of Rwanda. Since then there has been continued tension and violence, and Burundi may be drifting towards civil war. Parts of the army are not controlled by the government. Tutsi soldiers and Tutsi political extremists kill Hutu and members of FRODEBU. Armed Hutu extremists, helped by Hutu refugees living in neighbouring countries, kill Tutsi and members of UPRONA. Many Hutu switch their support from FRODEBU to more extreme Hutu parties.

The genocide and civil war in Rwanda causes increased tension in Burundi. Burundian Hutu refugees, living in Rwanda, are forced to return. Tutsi extremists kill some of the returning refugees. Those who return are joined by Rwandan Hutu refugees.

The new President is Sylvestre Ntibantunganya. He is a Hutu, but Tutsi and the UPRONA party hold more power in the new government.

1995 In March 1995 hundreds of people are killed in Bujumbura, the capital city. Burundi continues to be very tense. Ordinary Tutsi and Hutu do still live together in many parts of Burundi and there are some attempts at conflict resolution, but these have been small-scale. Over 200,000 Burundis are internally displaced; they include Tutsi and Hutu. Burundi is also host to 200,000 Rwandan refugees. Another 740,000 Burundis, mostly Hutu, are refugees in Zaire and Tanzania.

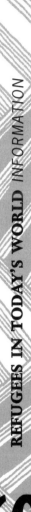

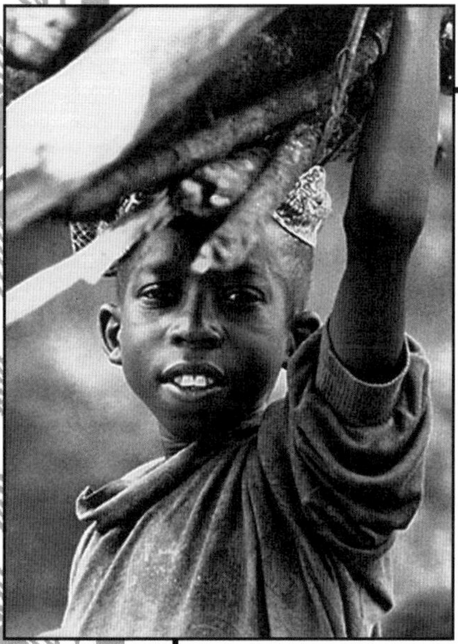

Renovat's story

Renovat is an 18 year old Tutsi from Lugazi, a village near Bujumbura in Burundi. Renovat and his family fled to a displaced person's camp in Bujumbura in 1993.

'After President Ndadaye was killed in October 1993, some of our neigh-bours started stealing our family's goats, cows and crops. One night people came with machetes and spears, so the family ran away with other neighbours. My grandparents were so old that they could not run and escape; they were killed and the houses were burned by people who were once my friends.

We arrived at Quartier Four camp after running 13 kilometres through the bush. Conditions in the camp are diff-icult; there is not enough water to drink or wash with, nor enough soap, clothes, blankets or sleeping mats. We are only able to eat once a day. My father is fortunate, he has been able to get some money by helping out in the office of a local vet.

Despite the risks my father decided to return to our village to see if it was safe enough to return with the whole family. He came back with the news that it was still too dangerous. But one of our Hutu neigh-bours had harvested our family's crops and was saving them for us so that we will have seeds to plant when we return. This kind-ness shows that not all our Hutu neighbours hate the Tutsi. Some are kind. It is the politicians who are causing the problems.

We are frightened of the FRODEBU Party, which is mainly Hutu. They speak of unity but they work in secret and after President Ndadaye was killed they encouraged the Hutu to rise up and kill members of the UPRONA Party whether they were Tutsi or Hutu. Me, I trust only the people of Burundi. We lived together and we will live together. I do not trust the politicians who cause the country's problems because they want good houses, cars and status. The people on the other hand are brothers and sisters; they want peace but everyone is afraid.'

Events

Rwanda's first inhabitants were the Twa. They lived in the forests of Rwanda and were hunter-gatherers. Twa still live in Rwanda, but today form less than one per cent of the population.

1000–1500 AD New groups of people migrate to central Africa. They are the Hutu. They are farmers and clear much forest land for growing crops. Hutu people are ruled by local lords.

1600–1800 A new group of taller people migrate to central Africa from Sudan and Ethiopia. They are the Tutsi and are cattle-herding nomads. They soon emerge as the rulers of much of Rwanda, apart from the north. This part of central Africa is ruled by Tutsi feudal chiefs. The Hutu have to provide free labour and crops to their Tutsi chiefs. In return the Hutu are allowed to graze their cattle on Tutsi land and are given military protection. There is also much intermarriage between Tutsi and Hutu.

1894 The first European explorers arrive in Rwanda. In the same year, European governments agree to divide central Africa among themselves. Rwanda, along with today's Burundi, becomes part of German East Africa. In order to bring the Hutu under control the Germans impose Tutsi chiefs on northern Rwanda. They favour the Tutsi in other ways - the Tutsi receive a European education and are used as administrators in the German colony. This reinforces the differences between Hutu and Tutsi.

1900–1910 French Catholic missionaries arrive in the region. The Roman Catholic Church also accepts the Tutsi as superior. This acts to reinforce differences between Hutu and Tutsi.

1911 There is a growing resentment in northern Rwanda towards the Tutsi, the Germans and the Roman Catholic Church. This leads to a short-lived violent uprising in part of northern Rwanda.

1916 During the First World War Rwanda is occupied by the Belgians who invade from the neighbouring Belgian Congo.

1918 After Germany's defeat in the First World War, the Belgians take control of today's Rwanda and Burundi under a mandate from the League of Nations. The country is known as Ruanda-Urundi. The Belgians continue to favour the Tutsi. The Tutsi are used as administrators. Hutu are removed from all positions of power in Ruanda-Urundi, and stopped from going on to study in higher education. The Belgians also introduce identity cards which state a person's ethnic group. The cards continue to be used throughout the 20th century, and have helped killers identify their victims.

1945 After the creation of the UN, Ruanda-Urundi becomes a Belgian 'Trustee Territory". The UN puts pressure on the Belgians to move Ruanda-Urundi towards independence.

1950–1960 Political parties begin to emerge in Ruanda-Urundi. They are organised along ethnic and regional lines. As the new parties begin to emerge, the Belgian rulers switch their support to the majority Hutu.

1959–1960 Hutu political leaders insist that there are major changes in Ruanda-Urundi. The Tutsi leaders resist. There is growing tension and then violence. The Hutu rebel against the Tutsi chiefs and then later the Belgian colonists and the wider Tutsi population. Over 10,000 Tutsi are killed and another 120,000 people flee to Uganda and other nearby countries. Many of the refugees remain in Uganda until the 1990s.

1961 The Belgians decide to leave Ruanda-Urundi. Rwanda and Burundi move towards becoming separate states. In Rwanda a referendum is held. It is decided to abolish the Tutsi monarchy and form a republic. Gregoire Kayibanda becomes the first president of Rwanda.

1962 Rwanda and Burundi become separate, independent states.

1963 Tutsi refugees living in Uganda

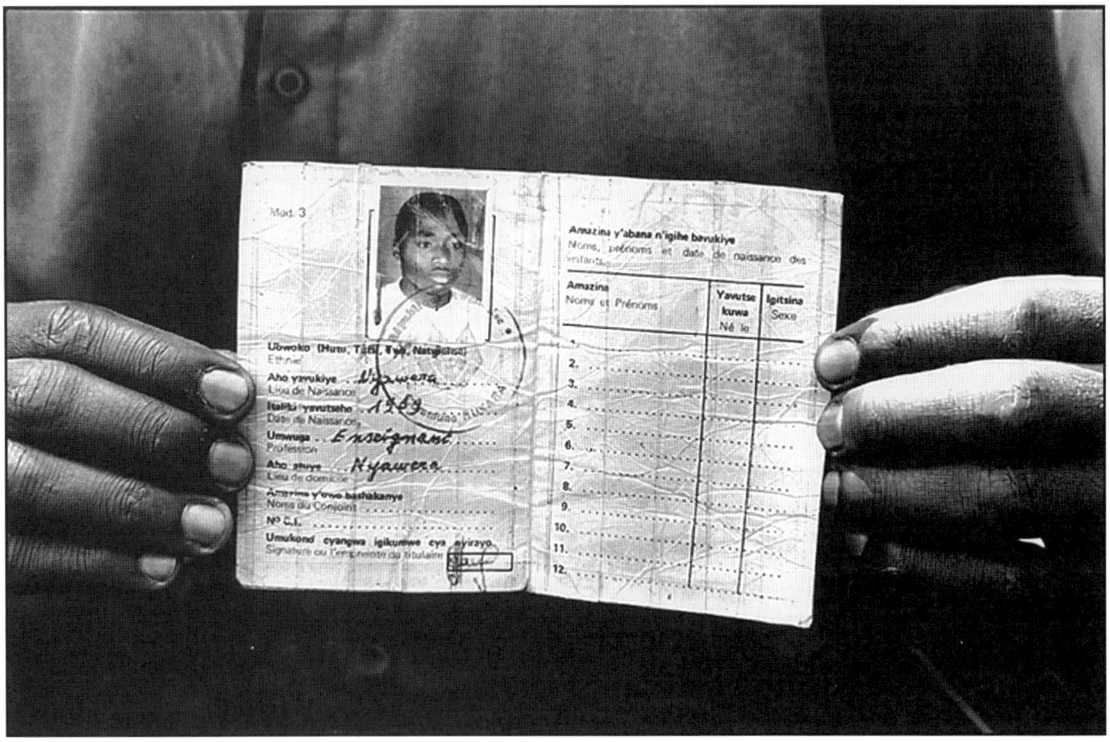

Identity card of Rwandan refugee
Howard Davies

and Burundi form terrorist organisations that attack Rwanda. These attacks cause the Hutu to fear that they will again be ruled by the Tutsi. Events in neighbouring Burundi justify these fears in the minds of many Hutu. The hatred between Hutu and Tutsi is kept alive. This erupts as violence in December 1963. Over 20,000 Tutsi are killed and another 150,000 Tutsi flee as refugees to Uganda and Burundi.

1969 Elections are held, and President Kayibanda is re-elected. All seats in the parliament are held by his Hutu-led party.

1972 There are widespread killings of Hutu in neighbouring Burundi. The killings lead to revenge attacks on Tutsi in Rwanda. At least 5,000 people, mostly Tutsi, are killed. In particular, school children are singled out for murder. The killings continue in 1973. There is widespread suspicion that Major General Juvenal Habyarimana, the army chief, is behind much of the unrest.

1973 Major-General Juvenal Habyarimana, a Hutu from northern Rwanda, leads a military *coup d'etat* and becomes President. All political parties are banned.

1975–1988 The National Revolutionary Movement for Development is founded. This is the only political party that is allowed. Elections are held in 1981 and 1985, with President Habyarimana always winning. Quotas are introduced for education and employment to try and make sure that all ethnic groups are treated fairly. There are also improvements in conditions for people living in rural areas. Many peasant farmers organise themselves into cooperatives, to plant trees, share tools and sell crops.

During this period there is growing conflict between Hutu from northern and southern Rwanda. Many Hutu from the south resent the power of the Hutu from President Habyarimana's northern homeland.

The Rwandan government also has difficult relations with neighbouring Uganda. Over 250,000 Tutsi refugees live in Uganda. Many of the refugees occupy high positions in the Ugandan army.

1989 World coffee prices fall. This reduces the income of small farmers. The country goes into debt and cannot afford to import food. A famine affects much of southern Rwanda and there is growing discontent, particularly in the south.

1990 President Habyarimana agrees to let political parties organise, and for Rwanda to have elections. But for Rwandan refugees in Uganda change has come too late. A force of over 5,000 Tutsi refugees attacks Rwanda from neighbouring Uganda. They call themselves the Rwandan Patriotic Front (RPF) and most of them are deserters from the Ugandan army. They are led by Major-General Fred Rwigyema, a formed Defence Minister in the Ugandan government. The RPF state that there must be more political reform in Rwanda and that President Habyarimana must go. After successes in the first weeks of fighting, the RPF are forced back by the Rwandan army, helped by French, Belgian and Zairean troops. The fighting kills over 100,000 people. Over 350,000 people are displaced by the conflict. Many Tutsi, fearing revenge attacks, flee to Uganda.

The RPF manages to hold on to a small strip of land along the border with Uganda. Here the fighting continues. In the rest of the country there is growing fear as the army takes greater control of policing the country.

1992–93 President Habyarimana is forced to give up much of his power. A new government is formed, with power shared between two moderate parties. But the *Comité pour la Defense de la Republique*, an extreme and racist Hutu Party, is excluded from power. In early 1993 supporters of this party respond by killing Tutsi and Hutu political opponents in northern Rwanda. The RPF then renews its activities. Many more Rwandans are killed and over 900,000 people are displaced. More refugees flee to Uganda and Burundi.

A ceasefire is agreed between the Rwandan government and the RPF and the UN sends a mission to Rwanda. A peace agreement is finally signed in Tanzania in July 1993.

1994 The peace agreement is not carried out. Many politicians, supported by Hutu extremists from northern Rwanda, resist the idea of sharing power with the Tutsi. They see all Tutsi as supporters of the RPF. Some politicians, plus radio stations and newspapers, also contribute towards anti-Tutsi feeling. The government begins to arm and train young Hutu men, forming them into militia known as the *interhamwe*. The government receives military aid from France.

On 6 April 1994 President Habyarimana of Rwanda and President Ntaryamira of Burundi are killed in an air crash in Kigali. The RPF are blamed. This gives a signal to the *interhamwe* to begin attacks on Tutsi and opposition Hutu. During the next two months over 500,000 people are murdered. Rwandans are killed by their neighbours and by people they trusted. Others flee as refugees to Burundi, Uganda and Tanzania.

As the massacre begins, the UN withdraws most of its military observers, saying that the peace agreement they were there to monitor is no longer valid.

In response to the massacres the Rwandan Patriotic Front invades the country. Over two million Hutu flee westwards to Zaire, fearing revenge attacks from the RPF. The refugees gather in camps around the towns of Goma and Bukavu. They have few possessions and no food. There is no clean water in Goma and conditions in the camps are soon horrific. Thousands of people die in an outbreak of cholera caused by a lack of sanitation and clean drinking water. The UN High Commissioner for Refugees and many other aid organisations are unprepared for such large numbers of refugees and it takes a long time to improve conditions in the refugee camps.

In response to the genocide and conditions in the refugee camps the UN sends troops. They help get clean water and food to refugees, but are months too late to prevent the genocide. The French government also sends an independent force to set up 'safe areas' for displaced Hutu in south west Rwanda. As France provided weapons to the government of President Habyarimana and the *interhamwe*, many Rwandans distrust its motives. They believe the French government wants to reinforce its influence in French-speaking Africa. The French leave Rwanda in August 1994.

By July the RPF has taken control of Kigali, the capital city. They form a new government. Although the government contains Hutu, real power lies with the Tutsi. There seems little hope of conflict resolution in Rwanda.

1995 Over 100,000 Rwandan children have been separated from their families during the last year. The Red Cross, the United Nations Children's Fund and the Save the Children Fund begin the long task of trying to trace the children's parents.

The *interhamwe* begin to regroup in the Zairean refugee camps. They try to prevent refugees from returning to Rwanda. Many human rights organisations fear that the *interhamwe* will form an army and invade Rwanda, leading to more killings and refugee movements.

There are growing human rights concerns in parts of Rwanda. The Tutsi-led army is accused of operating outside the control of the government. Soldiers also kill over 1,000 internally displaced Hutu.

Zaire starts to expel Hutu refugees. The Zairean government states that all Rwandan refugees must leave Zaire or be deported. A large number of Hutu living in Zaire, Uganda and Tanzania fear returning because they are afraid of revenge attacks. Other refugees do not want to return because they were actively involved in the killings in Rwanda.

There have been no trials of people accused of committing the killings of 1994 although many people are being held in Rwanda's overcrowded jails. Without trials of individual people, many people feel that all Hutu will be blamed for the genocide. Trials of those accused of murder seems necessary for conflict resolution in Rwanda.

In August 1995 Faustin Twagiramungu, Rwanda's Hutu Prime Minister, is sacked after criticising the army. This makes conflict resolution even more difficult.

Jacques Mutabazi's story

Technically Jacques Mutabazi is a refugee from Rwanda, but he prefers to be known as an Oxfam water engineer. He is now working at the Kahindu refugee camp in Zaire.

' I was living in Kigali and working there as an Oxfam water engineer, when the Rwandan President was killed on 6 April 1994. We were living in the town, near the Parliament House, but it soon became clear that it was very dangerous to stay there. We left in a great hurry. The day after we left, there were men shooting and the houses near mine were bombed. Although the bottom half of my house is still standing, the top half was dest-royed. But the most important thing for me is that my sons, my daughters and my wife have all been saved.

I fled to Goma and continued my work for Oxfam at the Kahindu refugee camp. This camp was created as an overflow for the other camps around Goma, where 800,000 refugees were living. When I arrived there the camp had not been prepared in any way. It was a jungle of swamps and wild plants. Nearby there was a polluted lake and some people were taking their water from that lake. As a result many people died from drinking contaminated water.

Oxfam's team of water engineers quickly got to work. We were soon able to provide clean drinking water for 85,000 people at Kahindu camp. Sanitation was established, including showers, latrines and washing areas. My main responsibility was building latrines, but health and hygiene education is just as important because refugees are not used to living in cramped conditions. When I travel through the camps, I can see that people are not used to being refugees. It is important that we quickly inform people about the need for sanitation.

I am separated from my family, they fled to Belgium at the start of the war, but I hope I will be reunited with them soon. It has been a long time since I last saw them. We hope to go back home, to Kigali, when things get better. At first, when I left the house, I thought that maybe in two weeks, or perhaps one month, there will be peace and we'll be able to go back home. Now I don't know when it will be. Hopefully soon.'

Genocide

The murder of 500,000 Tutsi and Hutu opposition in Rwanda is genocidal murder. This event is one of many cases of genocide in the 20th century. The events in Rwanda in 1994 pose many moral questions to all of us.

Genocide is the deliberate extermination of an ethnic, religious, political or national group. Three groups of people are involved in genocide. They are:

◆ the perpetrators

◆ the victims

◆ the bystanders.

In Rwanda the *interhamwe* were the perpetrators. They acted on the orders of the Government and army. The *interhamwe* were also, knowingly, provided with weapons by the French government.

In Rwanda the victims were Tutsi, and Hutu who opposed the policies of the government. Ordinary Hutu who tried to stop killings also risked their own murder.

In Rwanda there were many bystanders. There were Hutu who watched their neighbours being killed and did nothing. The UN and politicians in individual governments were also bystanders. The UN and politicians in individual governments knew what was happening in Rwanda, but they chose to do nothing. The television coverage of the murders in Rwanda meant that a far larger number of people were bystanders. Every person in the world who watched television news during the period April-June 1994 is a bystander to the genocide in Rwanda. Very few people then took any action such as writing to their MP or giving money to an aid organisation.

Genocide does not happen suddenly. There are many preconditions that must arise before a group of people become victims of genocide. These stages are:

◆ The victim group is stereotyped and defined as being 'different from the rest of society'. The rest of society readily believes that the victim group is different.

◆ The victim group may experience racial attacks and discrimination by ordinary people.

◆ The victim group loses many of its legal rights.

◆ The victim group is isolated from the rest of society.

◆ The victim group is dehumanised by politicians, the media and then by ordinary people. Ordinary people cease to see the victim group as being human beings just like them.

◆ There is a catalyst event which starts the genocide. This is a event which gives the perpetrators an excuse to carry out genocide.

◆ The perpetrators of genocide are led to believe that they are morally right in their actions. They continue to carry out the genocide.

Genocide in the 20th century

After the mass murders of Jews and Gypsies in the Second World War, the United Nations passed an international law to prevent future genocidal murders. This is known as the 1948 UN Convention on Genocide. To use this international law a UN member-state must challenge an offending country with evidence that shows that the offending country is deliberately inflicting on the group 'conditions of life calculated to bring about its destruction in whole or in part' (*1948 UN Convention on Genocide*). But this international law has rarely been used. There are many instances of genocide in the 20th century, both before and after the 1948 UN Convention on Genocide. In almost all cases the UN, individual governments and other bystanders did nothing.

It is sometimes difficult to decide when ethnic conflict becomes genocide, but the genocides of the 20th century must include:

Armenians in Turkey 1915–1920 Over 1,500,000 people were murdered.

Selected groups in the Soviet Union 1935–1953 Groups of people such as large peasant farmers were murdered by Stalin's government. It is difficult to estimate how many people were killed, but some people believe three million people were murdered at this time.

Jews of Europe 1939–45 Some six million Jewish people were murdered by the Nazis between 1939 and 1945.

Gypsies of Europe 1939–45 Over 200,000 Gypsies were murdered by the Nazis between 1939 and 1945.

Bangladeshis 1971 Between 1,500,000 and two million Bangladeshi people were murdered by the government of West Pakistan and its supporters during the 1971 War of Independence.

The Hutu of Burundi 1972 Some 150,000 Hutu were killed in revenge attacks following an unsuccessful *coup d'etat*.

Cambodians 1975–78 Between one and two million Cambodians were murdered by the Khmer Rouge government in Cambodia.

The East Timorese 1975 onwards Over 250,000 people have been killed by the Indonesian government who invaded East Timor in 1975.

Tigrayans and Ethiopians 1980 Over 250,000 people, mostly Eritreans and Tigrayans, were murdered by the Ethiopian government during the 'Red Terror'.

The Maya of Guatemala 1980 onwards At least 50,000 people have been killed and many more Maya Indians moved from their land.

The Kurds of Iraq 1980–88 Over 100,000 Kurdish people were killed by Saddam Hussein's Iraqi government and 500,000 people were forced to move.

The Nuba of Sudan 1990 onwards The Nuba mountains have been sealed off since 1990 and many Nuba people have been deliberately killed by government forces and militia.

Bosnian Muslims in Bosnia-Hercegovina 1992–1995 At least 100,000 Bosnian Muslims have been killed in a war where they have also been forced to leave their homes.

Rwandans 1994 Some 500,000 Tutsi and Hutu opponents of the government were murdered in two months of killing in 1994.

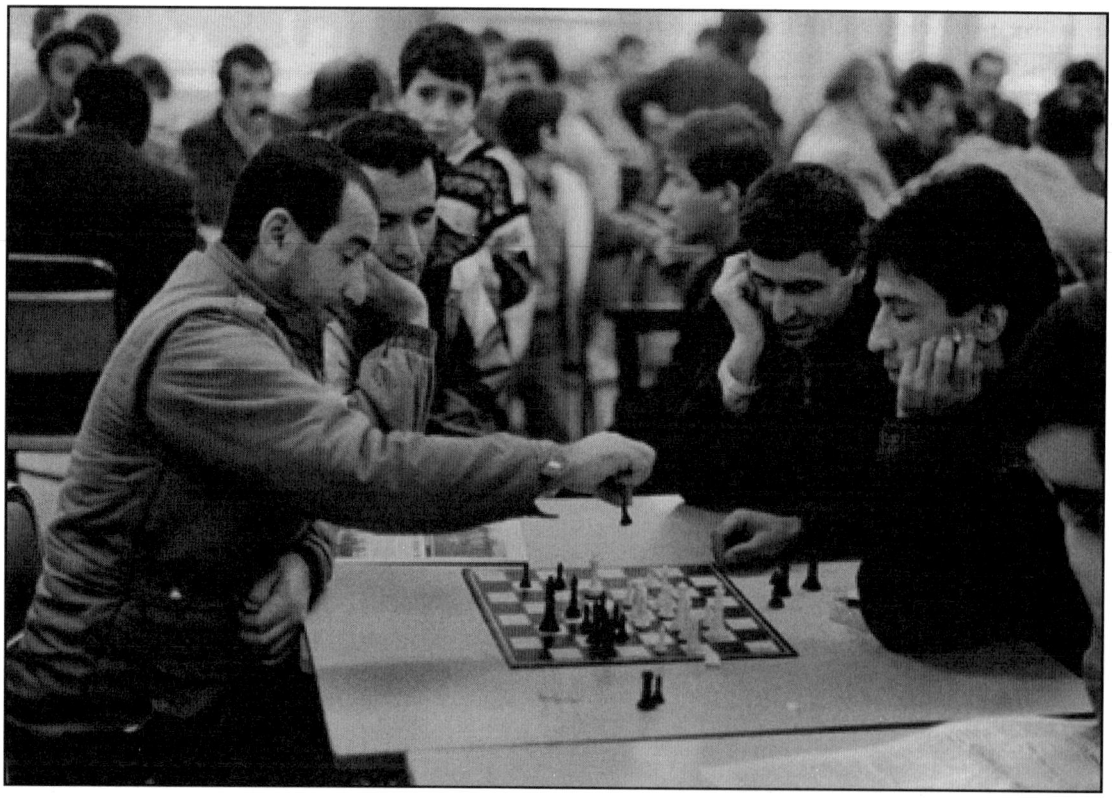

Kurdish refugees, London *Howard Davies*

Moral questions & genocide

Aim

To make students think about some of the moral questions surrounding the genocides in Burundi and Rwanda.

Instructions

Time needed: At least one hour to study the questions and then another hour for students to present the issues that they have examined.

All students should have copies of the background information on Burundi and Rwanda, and the background information on genocide. The teacher must introduce this work, perhaps by using television news footage or a television documentary about Rwanda.

Students should be divided into pairs. Each pair should be given one of the questions below. Each pair should prepare a five minute presentation that aims to answer the question they have been allocated.

Each pair should make its presentation, perhaps in a subsequent lesson.

The questions:

1. What were the causes of the genocide in Rwanda and Burundi?

2. How and why did the Rwandan government decide to exterminate the Tutsi?

3. How is it possible for a society to descend into such a level of barbarity?

4. Could genocide happen in Britain?

5. How should we judge the behaviour of people who saw their neighbours being killed and did nothing?

6. How should we judge our own behaviour after we saw the genocide on television and did nothing?

7. What should our government and the UN have done to prevent the genocide?

8. A number of those living in refugee camps in Zaire were actively involved in the genocide. Should aid agencies provide food to the refugee camps, knowing that they are also feeding people who have committed crimes against humanity?

9. How can there be reconciliation when such a large number of people on both sides have suffered and have lost relatives?

10. How can the world ensure that genocide will not happen again, either in Rwanda or elsewhere?

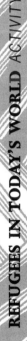

Eritrea

Over 500,000 Eritreans are refugees in the Sudan and in Europe and North America. Although peace has returned to Eritrea the poverty of the country is making it difficult for refugees to return.

Eritrean shepherd
Christian Aid/Mike Goldwater

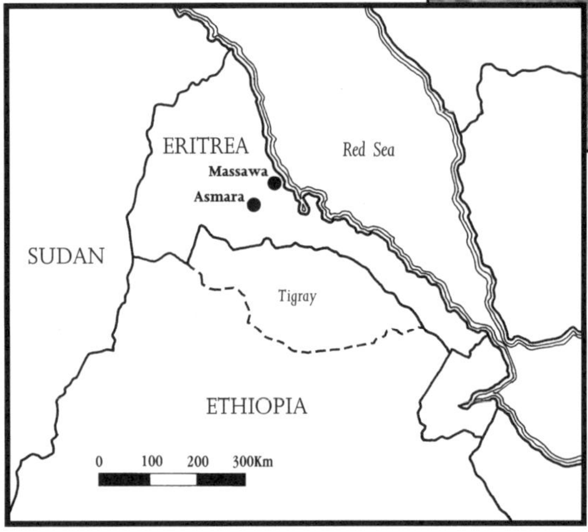

Population
3,500,000

Capital
Asmara

Languages
Tigrinya, Tigre and Arabic are the most widely spoken languages. English is the language in which school children are taught.

Events

Early history Ethiopia and Eritrea are the seat of ancient civilisations. The Kingdom of Axum came into existence in about 500BC. Around 300AD many people in Eritrea convert to Christianity.

Until the 19th century Eritrea was mostly ruled by local lords. Almost everyone was a peasant farmer, working on land owned by local nobles and landlords. The wealthier landlords took most of the crops and profits from the farms and there was very little investment in agriculture.

1871 Yohannes IV becomes Emperor of Ethiopia. He soon gains control of most of Ethiopia and Eritrea.

1870–1889 The Italians begin to show an interest in Ethiopia and Eritrea. They send an army to conquer this part of Africa. In 1889 Yohannes IV is killed in a battle against the Italians. Although he is killed, the Italians are defeated. They leave Ethiopia but remain in Eritrea. Eritrea becomes an Italian colony.

1930 In neighbouring Ethiopia, Ras Tafari becomes Emperor. He takes the name Haile Selassie.

Eritrea remains an Italian colony. By now over 60,000 Italian settlers are living in Eritrea. The Italians build roads, factories, a railway and a modern port at Massawa.

1935-36 Using Eritrea as a base, the Italians invade Ethiopia (then known as Abyssinia). By 1936 Eritrea and Ethiopia come under Italian rule.

1940-41 Britain declares war on Italy. The British army recruits Eritrean, Ethiopian and Somali soldiers. By 1941 the British have driven the Italians out of Eritrea and Ethiopia. Eritrea is ruled by a British military administration, but the Eritreans are promised independence.

1945 The British military administration in Eritrea finishes with the end of the Second World War. Eritrea and Ethiopia are then ruled as a British Protectorate. France, Britain, the USA and the Soviet Union have the task of deciding the future of Eritrea and Ethiopia. There are three options: independence for Eritrea, a federal state with regional government for Eritrea, or the complete union of Eritrea and Ethiopia.

Massawa, Eritrea's main port, is of military interest to USA and Britain. Haile Selassie, Emperor of Ethiopia, is friendly towards the USA and Britain. Both countries want Eritrea to become part of Ethiopia, so that Massawa remains in friendly hands.

After many meetings there is no agreement between France, Britain, the USA and the Soviet Union. Eventually the UN steps in, and recommends that Eritrea should become a federal state within Ethiopia. Eritrea should have its own parliament.

1952-1960 Eritrea and Ethiopia accept the UN plan for an independent, federal state. The UN agreement comes into operation. The Ethiopian government then ignores large parts of the UN plan. Eritrean factories are closed and moved to Ethiopia. Tigrinya and Arabic, languages spoken in Eritrea, are no longer taught in Eritrean schools. Eritrean political parties and trade unions are banned. The Ethiopian government begins to imprison its Eritrean opponents. By 1960 there are over 3,000 Eritrean political prisoners in Ethiopian jails.

At the same time any investment in Eritrea's agriculture, industry or infrastructure stops.

1961 Founding of the Eritrean Liberation Front, an Eritrean political party which fights to gain independence for Eritrea.

1962 The Ethiopian government manages to get a majority of its supporters elected to the Eritrean parliament. The parliament votes for complete unity between Eritrea and Ethiopia. The economic neglect of Eritrea continues.

1974 Famine hits large parts of Eritrea and Ethiopia. Haile Selassie's government collapses. A new military government, led by Colonel Mengistu, takes power. The Eritrean people hope that the new government will honour the 1952 UN plan and let Eritrea have its own parliament. But these hopes are short-lived. Colonel Mengistu's government draws support from many of the same people that supported Emperor Haile Selassie. The Ethiopian government continues to fight the Eritrean Liberation Front and the Eritrean People's Liberation Front (EPLF).

Colonel Mengistu's government - called the *Derg* - increases its spending on weapons. The Soviet Union gives military aid to Ethiopia. At the same time there is very little money spent on improving agriculture, education, health services and roads. Eritrea continues to be neglected.

1975 Fighting starts in other parts of Ethiopia. Tigrayan and Oromo people (ethnic groups within Ethiopia) form organisations that fight for justice and greater regional independence.

1977 The civil war worsens in Eritrea. At the same time the 'Red Terror' begins. Throughout Ethiopia over 250,000 people are murdered by government forces. Often the bodies of murdered people are left hanging or buried in mass graves.

The Red Terror and the worsening war cause 30 per cent of the population of Eritrea to flee from their homes. Some 250,000 Eritrean refugees flee to the Sudan.

The EPLF is now the main group fighting for independence in Eritrea. In late 1977 it makes many military gains and controls much of Eritrea. In the areas that it controls the EPLF sets up democratic local government and builds schools and clinics.

1978 The Red Terror continues throughout Ethiopia. The Ethiopian government attacks many Eritrean cities. Faced with a worsening conflict, thc EPLF decides to withdraw from the Eritrean cities that it controls.

1983–85 Two disastrous famines hit Eritrea and Ethiopia. Soil erosion and the continued lack of investment in agriculture have reduced farming to a subsistence level. When drought strikes in 1983 farmers cannot buy food. Nearly 300,000 people die and millions of Eritreans and Ethiopians walk to refugee camps. Food distribution is made difficult because of the war.

1987 Further famine hits Eritrea. This famine is made worse by the destruction of crops by swarms of locusts. The war in Eritrea makes it impossible to spray farmland to kill locusts. A large swarm of locusts can eat in one day as much grain as that which could feed 400,000 people for one year.

1988 The EPLF makes military gains in western and northern Eritrea.

1990 The EPLF captures Massawa, the Red Sea Port. The Ethiopian government bombs the city, destroying it. Asmara, and other towns held by the Ethiopian government are under nightly curfew and human rights violations continue.

Over 750,000 Eritrean refugees are now living in the Sudan. Some of the refugees live in cities like Khartoum, but most live in refugee camps in very bad conditions. Other Eritrean refugees are living in the Middle East, USA, UK, Germany, Italy and other European countries.

1991 The EPLF and other opposition groups in Ethiopia make military gains. The Ethiopian government collapses, and Eritrea declares independence. The EPLF forms a transitional government to rule the country until a referendum in 1993. A transitional government is also formed in Ethiopia and relations between Ethiopia and Eritrea are good.

Small numbers of refugees start to return from refugee camps in Sudan. The provisional government of Eritrea makes it a priority to help these refugees return, as most are living in very bad conditions. The returning refugees are given seeds, tools and food to help them come home, but most find their farms destroyed.

Refugees living in Germany are given financial help to enable them to return. Nevertheless it is difficult for many Eritrean families to go home because homes and farms have been destroyed and there is a shortage of jobs in Eritrea.

1993 A referendum is held so that the people of Eritrea can decide on their country's future. In April 1993 the majority of Eritreans vote for independence. In May 1993 Eritrea becomes Africa's newest country.

Betiel's story

Betiel is now in her early twenties. She came to Britain as a girl. When she wrote her account she was a student at South London College.

'Living in the village in Eritrea was like living in heaven. I know it sounds too good to be true, but I could tell you those were the happiest days of my life. However, the fairy tale did not continue. On September 29th my grandmother announced that we were leaving the village for good. She told us that we were going to Sudan to live with my parents. I had not seen them since they had left the country. Long before our family came to this village, we used to own a chemist's shop in Asmara, the capital city of Eritrea. However when the war between my country and Ethiopia got worse, my parents decided to help our soldiers by providing them with medicine. When the Ethiopian government found out that my parents were supplying medicine to their enemy, they burned the chemist's shop down and tried to kill them.

Even though I missed my parents very much, I did not want to leave the village and friends who I loved to go to Sudan. I cried and the little voice inside me screamed silently. But who would listen to a child, and who would understand how I felt?

On 30th September we were ready to leave. My grandmother had arranged everything we needed - the luggage and dry food. The time had come when I had to say goodbye to those people who I loved and admired; and believe me it was the hardest thing I ever did. That night we had dinner with my uncle's family. While we were having dinner, they were discussing where they were going to hire a camel and how we were going to get out of the village without the soldiers noticing us. I was quiet; I felt that my life was ruined and I blamed my parents. I blamed them for leaving me first, then taking me away from my friends. I was too selfish to notice that they were saving my life and giving me a better future.'

Betiel goes on to talk about what it is like for a young refugee in Britain.

'Most refugees arrive at their destination without any knowledge of the country's language, weather or culture. Their expectations are very high; they think all their problems are going to be solved when they get there. They find life different and extremely difficult. They feel confused, lonely, trapped and uncertain about their future. The main problem is the language and because of the language difficulty they can't express themselves or the circumstances they have faced. However, that is one factor; there are several other factors like religious or cultural barriers which divide the asylum-seeker and the provider. So refugees are driven to make their own community.

When you arrive in a European country such as Britain as a refugee, the last thing you need is an identity crisis. However, the older generation were brought up in strict discipline and a religious environment so they feel it is their duty to bring up the children in the same way. However, young people who left their country at a very early age find themselves in a dilemma - not knowing whether to follow their parents footsteps or let western society influence them.'

ኣብ ሃገረሰብ ምንባር ኣብ መንግስተ ሰማይ ከም ምንባር እዩ ኔሩ። እዚ ሓቂ'ዚ ዝተጋነነ ከም ዝመስል እፈልጥ። ግን እብለኩም ኣለኹ እዚ ግዜ'ዚ ኣብ ህይወተይ እቲ ብዝያዳ ዝተሓጎስኩሉ እዋን እዩ ኔሩ። ዝኾነ ኮይኑ ግን እዚ ሃገራዊ ኣይቀጸለን። ብ29 መስከረም ካብ ዓድና ንወጽእ ምዃንና ዓባየይ ትነግረና። ምስ ስድራይ ክንቅመጥ ንሱዳን ከምንኸይድ ትነግረ። ካብ ሃገርና ካብ ዝወጹ ርእየዮም ኣይፈልጦን። ናብ ሃገረሰብ ቅድሚ ምኻድና ኣብ ኣስመራ ፈርማሲ ኔሩና። ግን ኣብ መንጎ ሃገረይን ኢትዮጵያን ውግእ እንዳገደደ ምስ ከደ ስድራ ንተጋደልትና ኣፋዉስ ብምቕራብ (ምሃብ) ክተሓባበሩ መደቡ። ስድራይ ኣፋዉስ ብምሃብ ይተሓባበሩ ምህላዎም መንግስቲ ኢትዮጵያ ምስ ፈለጠ ነቲ ፋርማሲ ሓዊ ኣእትዩሉ ክቐትሎም ድማ ፈቲኑ። ንስድራ ብዙሕ ናፊቐ'ኺ እንተነበርኩ ንዓድናን ዘፍቅሮም መሓዙተይን ንድሕሪት ገዲፈ ንሱዳን ክኸይድ ኣይደልን ኔረ። ዓው ከይበልኩ ብውሽጠይ በኸየ። መን'ዩ ንቈልዓ ዝሰምዕA ከመይ ኢለ ከም ዝመጸኩ መንዩኸ ዝርድኦ፧

Betiel's story in **Tigrinya** *from the book 'Voices from Eritrea'.*

'Voices' and oral history

Betiel's story was collected for a project called 'Voices', run by an organisation called the Minority Rights Group. The Minority Rights Group worked with a group of refugee pupils in London schools. The refugee pupils wrote about important memories and events in their lives. Some of the young refugees wrote about their homelands. Others gave accounts of the events that caused them to become refugees and about their feelings about life in Britain.

Usually the refugee pupil's stories were written in their first language. The Minority Rights Group translated the stories into English and published them. There are seven books in the 'Voices' series. There are collections of refugee pupil's stories from Angola, Eritrea, Kurdistan, Somalia, Sudan, Uganda and Zaire.

For the refugee pupils who wrote the stories it has hugely increased their confidence. The seven books are now being used by other refugee pupils. They can read the stories in their first language and in English. For them it can be a great help to read about other young people who were in the same position as they are. The stories in the 'Voices' books also help all young people to become more aware about refugees.

The 'Voices' books are an example of oral history. Oral history is history with a difference. Instead of relying on text books and experts, it draws on the experiences of ordinary people, giving them a chance to record their lives for themselves. Oral history can:

◆ shed new light on well-known events

◆ build a more complete picture of a time, a subject or an area

◆ fill in gaps left out by other historians

◆ give a voice to ordinary people who are seldom heard.

Every person has a history and can participate in oral history projects.

Oral history is all about asking questions. An oral history project is often centred around a topic or event, such as childhood, moving home, the Second World War and so on. Oral history is used as a way of finding out more information. It involves:

◆ writing accounts of events that are important

◆ carrying out taped interviews

◆ collecting photographs, maps and ordinary objects

◆ collecting information about a family's history.

Oral history

Aims

To help students come up with their own definitions of oral history.

Instructions

Time needed: 30-40 minutes

Coloured pens, paper, copies of refugee testimonies and some standard history textbooks are needed. The students need an introduction from the teacher explaining that everyone has a history, but not everyone's history has been written down. This is where oral history comes in. The refugee testimonies and standard history textbooks can be used to illustrate the point that the teacher makes.

The students should then be divided into pairs. They should be asked to come up with their own definitions of oral history. They should write their definitions on sheets of plain paper. This should take 10-15 minutes. The definitions should be stuck on a board, and used to direct class discussion and further work on oral history.

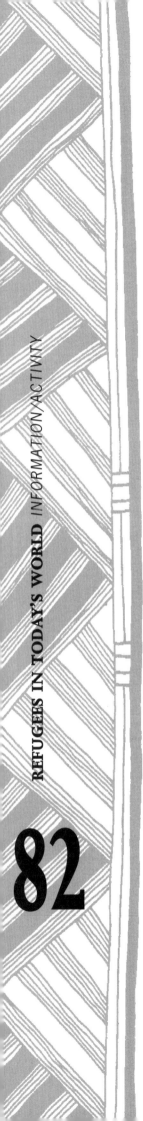

CR

Liberia & Sierra Leone

Liberia and Sierra Leone have suffered civil war that has forced thousands of people to flee their homes.

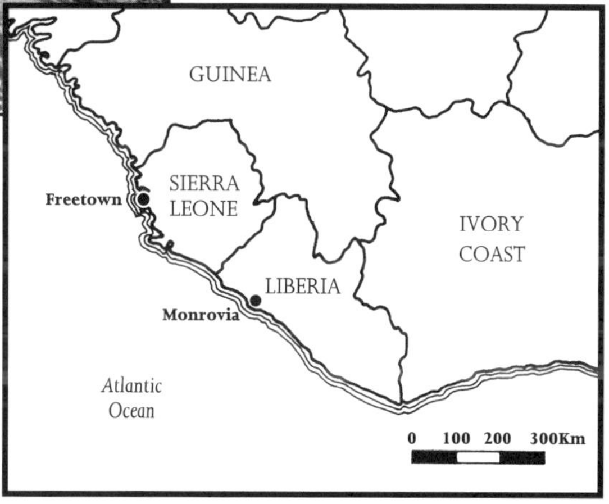

Liberia

Population
3 million

Capital
Monrovia

Economy
Most Liberians work in agriculture growing rubber, coffee, cocoa, rice and cassava. Liberia exports iron ore, diamonds and other minerals. The country also receives money from shipping. The wealth of the country is owned by a few people; this is one of the causes of the present conflict.

Ethnic groups
Americo-Liberians, who are descendants of freed African slaves from the USA, make up about 5 per cent of the population. This group dominate politics and own much of the country's wealth. There are 16 other ethnic groups living in Liberia, the largest being the Kpelle, Basse and Gio/Mano peoples. Today's fighting is partly an ethnic conflict.

Sierra Leone

Population
4.5 million

Capital
Freetown

Economy
About 71 per cent of Sierra Leoneans work in agriculture, growing rice, oil palms, cocoa, coffee, cassava and vegetables, and grazing cattle. Sierra Leone is a poor country despite its many natural resources which include gold, diamonds, iron ore and tropical timber. The diamond mines are owned by foreign companies and, like Liberia, the wealth of the country is owned by a small number of people. This, and government corruption, has meant that most Sierra Leoneans have not benefited from the country's natural resources.

Ethnic groups
The Temne and Mende are the two largest ethnic groups. The Krio are the descendants of freed African slaves returned from the West Indies by the British in the 19th century. There is also a Lebanese minority living in Freetown.

Languages
English is the official language. Most people speak Krio, which is based on English. Mende is another common language. Many other languages are spoken in Sierra Leone.

Events

During the 15th and 16th centuries Sudanic peoples from central Africa migrated to **Liberia** and integrated with local people. This part of Africa was ruled by many local chiefs.

1821 The first Americo-Liberians arrive in Liberia as a result of an American plan to settle former slaves from the USA in Africa. They are soon joined by other freed slaves.

1847 Liberia declares itself as an independent state. It is ruled by Americo-Liberians, but they have little control over the countryside. Ethnic groups living in the interior of Liberia resist rule by Americo-Liberians. The USA provides Liberia with some economic subsidies for the rest of the 19th century.

1915 The last resistance to Americo-Liberian rule is crushed. Few people from the interior of Liberia have a vote. The wealth and political power in Liberia is held by Americo-Liberians living in Monrovia.

1927 The Firestone Rubber Company, an American company, starts plantations in Liberia. Many Liberians find work on the rubber plantations, usually for very low wages and in poor conditions. From 1930-1950 the Liberian economy is very dependent upon the Firestone Rubber Company.

1944 William Tubman wins elections. He represents the True Whig Party. Although Liberia has a two chamber parliament and holds elections, all political power is held by the True Whig Party.

1971 President Tubman dies and is replaced by William Tolbert. But soon there is increasing resistance to the rule of the True Whig Party and the political dominance of Americo-Liberians. President Tolbert's government is also accused of corruption.

1978 An opposition party - the Progressive Alliance of Liberia - holds its first conference.

1979 There are riots, murders and looting after the government proposes to increase the price of rice.

1980 President Tolbert is killed in a military coup led by Sergeant Samuel Doe. Samuel Doe becomes President. All political parties are banned, although President Doe announces that Liberia will return to civilian rule.

1984-85 The ban on political parties is lifted and in 1985 elections are held. Samuel Doe wins the presidential election but there are widespread allegations of electoral fraud. After an attempted *coup d'etat* in 1985 those belonging to the Gio/Mano ethnic group are harassed and killed.

1986 Some opposition parties form a coalition to oppose the rule of Samuel Doe. Political opponents also face arrest. There is growing opposition to the rule of Samuel Doe.

1989 Fighting breaks out in north east Liberia between the Liberian army and a new opposition group called the National Patriotic Front of Liberia (NPFL). The NPFL is led by Charles Taylor. It quickly develops into an ethnic conflict between the Krahn, President Doe's ethnic group, and local Gio and Mano peoples. Over 150,000 people flee as refugees to Guinea and the Ivory Coast.

1990 NPFL guerrillas advance on Monrovia, the capital city. The NPFL and the Liberian army kill many civilians and are accused of severe human rights violations. Over 300,000 people are now refugees and another 500,000 internally displaced. The NPFL splits into two groups. Later, in 1990, they fight each other in and around Monrovia, the capital city.

Other West African states fear that the fighting in Liberia could destabilise the whole region. They attempt to call peace talks, but the NPFL refuse to attend. Later a peace-keeping force arrives, made up of soldiers from Nigeria, the Gambia, Sierra Leone, Ghana, Guinea and Togo. They soon become involved in the fighting.

Later in the year President Doe is captured by one of the rebel groups and

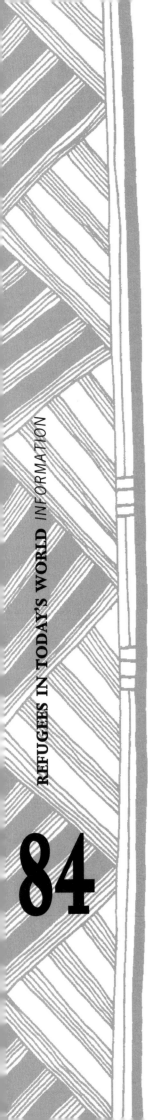

Emile's story

Emile Delano Cooper is 14 years old and lives with his family in Ghana. They fled from Liberia in 1990.

'I Emile Delano Cooper am dedicating this essay to the loving memory of all the innocent boys and girls who have died or continue to suffer in one form or another as a result of the senseless Liberian civil war which seems to be endless.

By African standards my family is not a very large one. It is composed of six persons: my father, my mother, a brother, two sisters and myself. I am the third child in my family.

Presently we are refugees in Ghana. Refugee is a word I never dreamed I would be called by! This proves that no-one knows what the future has in store.

Since the war began we have had many hard times. We have gone from sleeping in a decent home with warm beds and drinking cold water from the ice-box, to sleeping on the ground in the open air with mosquitos feasting on our blood and drinking unsafe water which causes us to get ill often.

Living as refugees is a painful pleasure. Painful because we have to work very hard sometimes. We depend on food rations from the UN and contributions from relatives and friends to keep us alive. A pleasure because we have learned the dignity of working with our hands. I could never have imagined myself working in a garden as a means of getting additional food. Now I am proudly doing it.'

is killed. After peace negotiations Dr Amos Sawyer becomes interim president of Liberia. In reality his government has very little control over the country. The interim government also has little control over its own army which continues to be accused of human rights violations.

1991 Liberia's conflict spills over into neighbouring Sierra Leone. The NPFL guerrillas invade Sierra Leone and civil war starts in that country. Some Liberian refugees are forced to return from Sierra Leone, even though it is still dangerous in their home country.

1992 The West African forces are accused of supporting groups opposed to the NPFL and arming them. Charles Taylor, the leader of the NPFL is very suspicious of the West African peace-keeping troops and this makes peace negotiations very difficult. Large numbers of ordinary Liberian people continue to be killed and flee as refugees.

1993–94 The UN attempts to find a peaceful solution to the conflict in Liberia. A ceasefire is announced between the NPFL, the Liberian government and ULIMO, another rebel group. All soldiers are meant to disarm Elections are meant to be held in 1994. But the elections do not take place and neither do the soldiers disarm.

New rebel groups enter the fighting. The conflict worsens in September 1994. The Liberian army and five larger rebel groups are involved in the fighting; the army and the rebel soldiers all act outside the control of their leaders and are accused of human rights abuses. As in neighbouring Sierra Leone, the Liberian army and all rebel groups use child soldiers.

1995 Liberian rebels attack the Ivory Coast. Fearing reprisals from their host country, Liberian refugees are forced to flee back into Liberia. Some 180,000 people have been killed since 1989. By the beginning of 1995 over 865,000 Liberians are refugees, mostly in Guinea and the Ivory Coast. Another 1,450,000 people are internally displaced.

Later in 1995 there are moves towards peace. Leaders of the main rebel group join a six-person collective presidency. A government is formed and elections are scheduled for 1996.

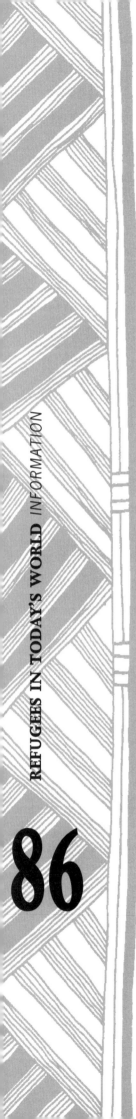

Events

During the 15th and 16th century Sudanic peoples from central Africa migrated to **Sierra Leone** and integrated with local people. This part of Africa was ruled by many local chiefs. Sierra Leone first attracted the attentions of European colonial powers in the 18th century. Slaves who had been freed or who had run away were transported to Sierra Leone by the British.

1808 The coast of today's Sierra Leone becomes a British colony. The population of Sierra Leone grows as the British take more freed slaves to the country. The descendants of the former slaves become the Krio.

1850–1900 Sierra Leone becomes a prosperous British colony, exporting palm oil and minerals. The Krio do well out of trade with Sierra Leone. They become important in politics and trade in all of Britain's west African colonies. At the end of the 19th century the British colonists move further inland, bringing the interior of Sierra Leone under their control.

1896 The boundaries of Sierra Leone are marked.

1898 The Temne and Mende people try to resist British rule. In particular they do not like the British tax system which forces them to pay a tax for their homes. Many people have to sell their small farms and leave their land to be able to pay the tax. The new landless then have to find work on British-owned plantations.

1930–1945 Sierra Leonean people first start to call for independence. The Krio are first to give their support to calls for independence. Later the Mende, Temne and other ethnic groups join in.

1951 As a result of the calls for independence Sierra Leonean people win more democratic rights. They are allowed to vote for their own government for the first time, although the country remains a British colony.

1961 Sierra Leone wins independence from Britain. Sir Milton Margai of the Sierra Leone People's Party become the first Prime Minister. When Sir Milton Margai dies in 1964 he is succeeded by his half-brother Sir Albert Margai. The economic situation deteriorates. People associated with the government are accused of smuggling diamonds out of the country.

1967 General elections are held. Dr Siaka Stevens, a trade unionist and leader of the All People's Congress appears to win. Initially Dr Siaka Stevens promises to improve the lot of the poor. But the results are challenged by those who control the country's wealth. The army takes over the government.

1968 Junior officers in the army seize power and Dr Siaka Stevens is invited to become Prime Minister.

1971 Sierra Leone becomes a republic and Dr Siaka Stevens is the first President.

1972–1976 Dr Siaka Steven's All People's Congress is the only party which contests elections in Sierra Leone. Other parties are suppressed. The economic situation in the country does not improve.

1977–78 Elections are held and are contested by opposition parties. The All People's Congress wins, but there is

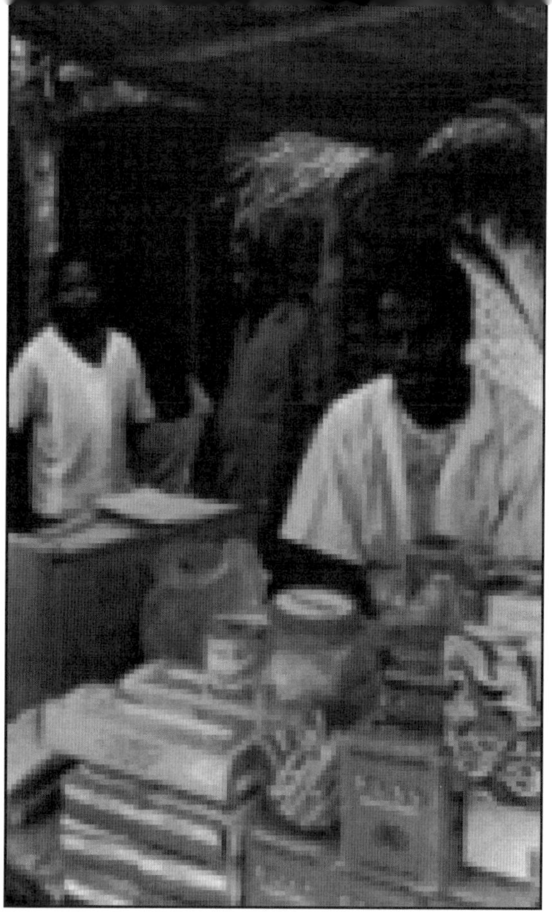

Sierra Leonian merchant
UNHCR

much violence during the elections. In 1978 Sierra Leone becomes a one party state. It becomes impossible for ordinary people to elect politicians who might change the country.

1981–84 Sierra Leone experiences severe economic problems and goes into debt. Food prices rise and as a result there are many demonstrations and riots in Freetown. Several government ministers are also accused of corruption, smuggling diamonds and gold out of the country and using public money as their own. In 1982 violence forces 4,000 refugees to flee to Liberia.

1985 President Siaka Stevens decides to step down. He is replaced by Major-General Joseph Momoh. Sierra Leone remains a one party state and opposition is not tolerated. President Momoh builds up the army so as to be able to suppress all opposition.

1986–1990 President Momoh's popularity declines, as he is unable to improve Sierra Leone's economy. At the same time Momoh builds up the army, but they are badly trained and ill-disciplined. There are continued demonstrations over food prices and against the one party state.

1990 Civil war begins in neighbouring Liberia. Sierra Leone sends troops to Liberia as part of the West African Peace Keeping Force (ECOWAS).

1991 Liberia's conflict spills over into Sierra Leone. Rebels belonging to the National Patriotic Front of Liberia advance into eastern Sierra Leone, partly to gain revenge over Sierra Leone's support for the ECOWAS force. Over 200,000 people become refugees by the end of 1991 and 150,000 people are internally displaced. Liberian refugees are also attacked by the Sierra Leonean army who blame them for causing conflict in Sierra Leone. Many Liberians return home, although the situation is still dangerous there. More and more Sierra Leoneans become involved in the fighting. A Sierra Leonean rebel group begins to emerge: the Revolutionary United Front led by Foday Sankoh. He aims to 'free the country of the government of Joseph Momoh'.

1992 President Momoh is overthrown in a military coup led by junior army officers. Captain Valentine Strasser becomes President at the age of 25. He promises to hold elections but this promise is not fulfilled. Political opponents of the new government face detention, torture or extrajudicial execution.

The new government states that it wishes to end the war but it is unsuccessful in doing this. The violence spreads throughout Sierra Leone and safety can only be found in Freetown. Both the rebels and soldiers in the Sierra Leonean army are accused of killing civilians in rural areas, and then looting their property.

1994–95 The war continues. A ceasefire is announced in December 1994 between the Revolutionary United Front rebels and the Sierra Leonean government, but this does not bring peace to the country.

1996 General elections are held in Sierra Leone, but the fighting continues. Over 200,000 people are refugees, mostly in Guinea and another 700,000 people are internally displaced.

The 'rebel' attacks on Sierra Leonean civilians involve members of the Revolutionary United Front, current or ex-Sierra Leonean soldiers and common criminals. Both the rebels and soldiers attack villages and small towns in rural areas. The attacks produce panic and people are forced to flee their homes in terror. Then their homes are looted by rebels or soldiers. Those who resist are killed.

The army, supported by some members of the Sierra Leonean government, are also accused of stealing gold and diamonds from mines in southern and eastern Sierra Leone. Most gold and diamonds are now being smuggled out of the country. Both soldiers and rebels continue to kill and loot, as it is an easy way of obtaining a living. As in Liberia, the fighting involves child soldiers who are often as young as 10.

Why do we fight?

Psychologists, anthropologists and philosophers have for many years studied why human beings are aggressive and fight wars. There are two opposing beliefs.

Some academics say that human beings are naturally aggressive. War and much violence is therefore unavoidable because it is a human instinct. To reach these conclusions human behaviour has been compared with animal behaviour. It is argued that all animals, including humans, have instincts to create territories and to defend them. Also all animals have instincts to attack other animals for food.

An opposing view is that animal and human behaviour is learned, rather than instinctive. Human beings learn to form themselves into groups. Human beings learn to be aggressive and to fight to defend the interests of their group. If aggression is learned behaviour, human beings should be capable of unlearning this behaviour and living in peace.

What do you think?

Sierra Leonean stories

Here are the testimonies of some Sierra Leonean refugees now living in London. They were collected at the Association for Sierra Leonean Refugees - a refugee community organisation based in London.

‘I was a soldier in Sierra Leone, fighting in the war against the rebels. Some rebel soldiers surrendered to us. A group of five of us were ordered to kill them. But I did not want to kill them because they had already surrendered. My colleagues detained five of us for refusing to kill the rebels.

As a result of refusing to carry out the order three of my friends were killed. Two of us managed to escape. But there is no place that is safe for us to hide as the army is looking for us. That is why I fled.’

‘I was a teacher in Sierra Leone and lived in the eastern part of the country. I am also a member of the People's Democratic Party. This party is now banned by the present government. I suffered a lot as a result of the fighting. As the situation got worse in Sierra Leone I came to learn that the government is concealing a lot of information about the war and human rights abuses. The realities of the war are hidden from the outside world. Many of those involved with opposition parties have been secretly killed.

I got caught up in some fighting along the highway and took the bold step of revealing what is happening to the press in Freetown. I appeared on the front page of one of the independent newspapers and because of this the government was hunting for me. I was threatened in Makeni, the town where I was staying. I knew then that the government was looking for me. My previous political links and the newspaper article meant that I was in danger. I decided to come to Britain.

I am waiting for the conditions to change in my country. Then I will go back home.’

Child soldiers

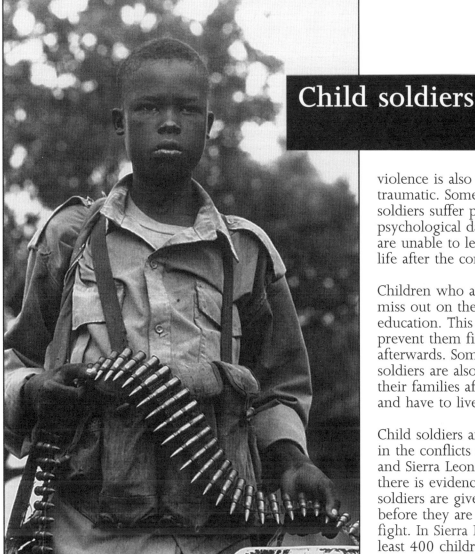

Child soldiers are young people under 18 who fight in wars. During the last ten years at least 200,000 young people have been involved in wars in different parts of the world. It is believed that there is an increased use of children and young people in wars. It is mostly boys who fight as child soldiers, but in some parts of the world girls are recruited too.

Sometimes children are forced to become soldiers. They might be taken out of their schools, or away from their villages. But frequently children join voluntarily. When a young person's school is destroyed, or when family and friends are involved in the conflict, fighting can seem attractive. It may seem better to become a soldier than to sit at home being frightened and helpless. Some children join so that they will receive food, clothing and shelter.

But fighting has major effects on children. They can be wounded and permanently disabled. Witnessing violence is also very traumatic. Some child soldiers suffer permanent psychological damage and are unable to lead a normal life after the conflict ends.

Children who are soldiers miss out on their education. This may prevent them finding work afterwards. Some child soldiers are also rejected by their families after a war and have to live alone.

Child soldiers are fighting in the conflicts in Liberia and Sierra Leone. In Liberia there is evidence that child soldiers are given drugs before they are sent to fight. In Sierra Leone at least 400 children are fighting in the Government's army. The youngest are eight years old. After six months training the children are sent to fight. One former child soldier said that children are "the bravest and most reckless of soldiers."

In Sierra Leone and Liberia children's organisations such as UNICEF are working to stop children being recruited to fight. They also support former child soldiers in rehabilitation centres. Here they receive food and shelter, education and training for employment. The former child soldiers also get counselling to help them overcome traumatic experiences. UNICEF tries to reunite child soldiers with their families.

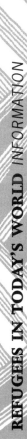

Countries where child soldiers are recruited to armies or guerrilla forces

Afghanistan	Mali
Angola	Sierra Leone
Burma	Somalia
Iraq	Sri Lanka
Lebanon	Sudan
Liberia	Former Yugoslavia

Child soldier, Sudan *Crispin Hughes/Panos Pictures*

War & the media

Aims

In some parts of the world, television, radio and newspapers are used to encourage young people to become soldiers. War is portrayed as being manly or glamorous. Viewers are encouraged to take sides. Television propaganda* has been used in Iraq and former Yugoslavia. In Sierra Leone and Liberia radio propaganda* has been used. This activity aims to help young people think about how television coverage of war affects them.

*

Propaganda is the use of the media to create certain actions or beliefs. Propaganda is used by all governments at times of crisis or war. Propaganda can include deliberate lies. Propaganda may also be a partial truth – things are concealed to give the impression that something else is happening.

Instructions

All students will need at least twenty copies of the survey.

The activity should be introduced. Students should be asked to monitor all the television programmes that they watch over a three day period, and to fill in the survey forms as they watch them.

After the three day period all students should write up their results. They can use graphs and pie charts to display their results. Alternatively, computers can be used to collate and analyse individual and class information.

Discussion Points

◆ Is war represented on television more than peace?

◆ How might television be used to encourage young people to join the army?

◆ Do you think girls react differently to war and violence on the television than boys?

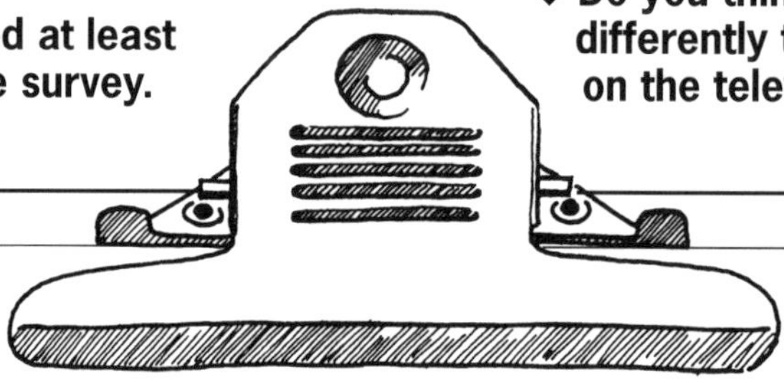

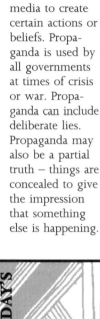

Survey on war and violence on television

Name of television programme.

....

What kind of programme was it?

News ☐
Documentary ☐
Drama/Film ☐
Children's TV ☐
Other (describe) ☐

....

How many times did violence occur on the programme? (Use a tally chart)

....

Did the programme portray war?

Yes ☐ No ☐

How was the violence portrayed?

Heroically ☐
As a terrible thing ☐
Neutrally ☐
Other (describe) ☐

....

How did the violence affect you?

I found it entertaining ☐
It excited me ☐
It frightened me ☐
I found the violence interesting and informative ☐
It made me angry ☐
It caused me to feel anxious and sad ☐
Other (describe) ☐

....

Did the portrayal of violence make you want to take any action?

Yes ☐ No ☐

If yes, describe what you wanted to do:

....

UNHCR

Mozambique

Many years of fighting left 900,000 Mozambicans dead and another 1,700,000 as refugees. The fighting stopped in 1992 and most of the refugees have returned. But Mozambique faces many problems in rebuilding the country.

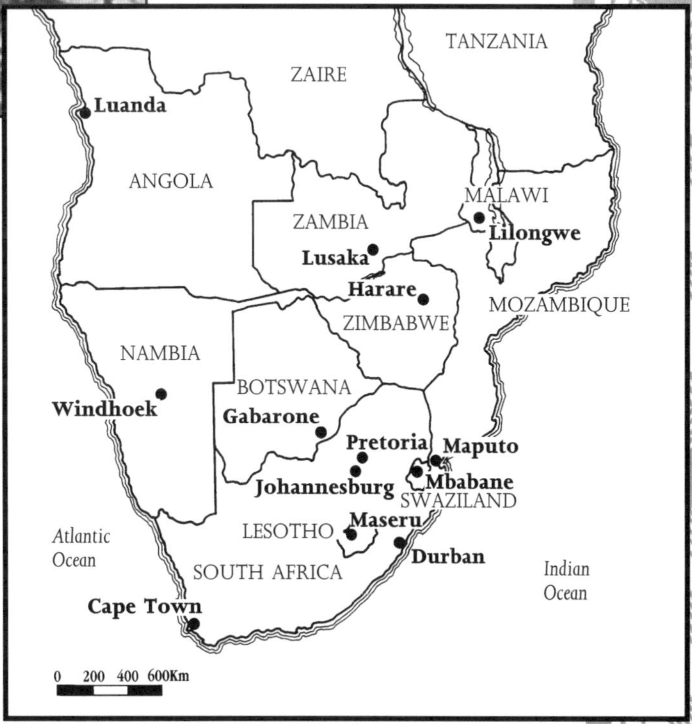

Population
17 million

Capital
Maputo

Languages
Portuguese is the official language. Many African languages are spoken by the different ethnic groups living in Mozambique. Macua Lomwe is the most widely spoken African language.

Events

Sixth century AD Arab and Asian merchants are the first foreign influence on Mozambique. They trade with the towns of the south and raid the north coast for slaves and ivory.

1498 Vasco da Gama, the Portuguese explorer, becomes the first European to reach the coast of Mozambique.

1572 The Portuguese send their first major military expedition to Mozambique. By the 17th century Portugal controls most coastal regions, but fails to gain control over the interior of Mozambique.

1884 The Berlin Conference draws up Mozambique's borders.

1891 One third of Mozambique's land is handed over to British companies. They establish large plantations that grow cash crops such as cotton, sugar, cashew nuts, sisal and tea. A tax system is introduced which forces Mozambican peasant farmers to work on the plantations in order to pay their taxes.

From the end of the 19th century the Portuguese stop Mozambique's industries from developing to ensure that the Portuguese have a market for their own industrial goods.

1926 Antonio Salazar becomes head of Portugal's fascist government. Portuguese people begin to settle in Mozambique.

1960 Discontent spreads among Mozambican workers. After a protest, more than 500 peasant farmers are killed by Portuguese troops.

1962 FRELIMO is founded. This Mozambican party hopes to win independence for the country.

1964 FRELIMO decides to abandon peaceful protest against Portuguese rule. The war to free Mozambique begins.

1970 Samora Machel is elected the new president of FRELIMO.

1973 The civil war in neighbouring Rhodesia (new Zimbabwe) worsens. Many Zimbabwean guerrillas flee to Mozambique. The Rhodesian and Portuguese secret services found an organisation called Renamo (sometimes called the MNR - Mozambique National Resistance). Renamo is not a political party, just an army of bandits. Renamo attacks Zimbabwean guerrilla bases in Mozambique.

1974 There is a revolution in Portugal. Dr Salazar's fascist dictatorship is replaced by an elected government. The new government decides Portugal should withdraw from its colonies.

1975 Mozambique wins its freedom from the Portuguese. Samora Machel becomes Mozambique's first president. Over 90 per cent of the Portuguese settlers leave. Policies to train workers and improve education and healthcare are introduced immediately. Education and training are a priority as Mozambique has very few skilled workers. There are only four Mozambican graduates in the whole country.

At independence Mozambique faces many economic problems. It is one of the poorest countries in the world.

1977–80 The Zimbabwean guerrilla movement is allowed to operate from Mozambique. Rhodesia increases its support for Renamo. Renamo also gets support from people who do not agree with FRELIMO and from wealthy Portuguese who used to live in Mozambique.

1980 Zimbabwe wins its independence and South Africa takes over as the main backer of Renamo.

1983 There is widespread drought in many parts of Mozambique. This leads to food shortages; due to the civil war it is difficult to transport food aid around the country. Over 100,000 people starve to death. Refugees flee to Malawi and Tanzania.

1984 South Africa and Mozambique sign a peace agreement. This is meant to guarantee peace and cooperation between the two countries but South Africa continues to give military aid to Renamo.

The civil war has reduced Mozambique to such chaos and poverty that some Mozambicans are forced to become Renamo bandits, to be able to steal what they cannot grow or buy.

1986 The fighting worsens. Over 25 per cent of all Mozambicans are refugees or internally displaced. Over 500,000 refugees flee to Malawi where they receive good treatment. In Malawi refugees are allowed to travel freely, farm land, work and attend school. Although welcome, the refugees face great poverty.

President Machel is killed in a mysterious air crash. Joachim Chissano becomes the new president.

1989 Over 1,300,000 people are refugees. Most of them are living in

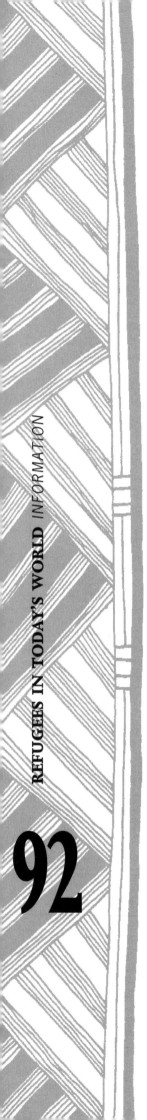

Malawi, placing great strain on this country which is also very poor. Another 4,000,000 people are internally displaced in Mozambique, living in the bush, in camps or in shanty towns. Not enough food aid reaches the refugees and internally displaced. Fighting continues in Mozambique.

1992 A peace agreement is signed between the Mozambican government and Renamo. The agreement will result in general elections and disarming of soldiers on both sides of the conflict. Rebels and government soldiers are to be integrated into ordinary life. Some former soldiers return to their family farms. Others attend training courses.

1993-1994 A repatriation programme starts to enable Mozambican refugees to return to their homes. Those who leave refugee camps are given food, seeds, farming tools, plastic sheets, blankets and buckets by UNHCR. These items will help people rebuild their lives. At the same time the Mozambican government receives money to rebuild schools, clinics, roads and wells. The repatriation programme costs £150 million. By the end of 1994 over 1,600,000 Mozambicans have returned home. But many people are still internally displaced - up to 800,000 people. They are living in camps and in shanty towns.

1994 There are general elections in Mozambique. President Chissano is reelected.

Paulino's & Farukh's stories

Conversations with teachers and pupils at Milange School, Zambezia Province, Mozambique. The school was destroyed in the civil war but has now been rebuilt with help from the Save the Children Fund. There are 650 pupils who are taught in two daily shifts by 12 teachers. The school has very few books, pens or chalk. Paulino Luciasse, the head teacher explains what life was like during the civil war.

'It was a very frightening time. You always had to sleep with your bags packed, in case you had to run. You never knew what was going to happen from one hour to the next.

Renamo rebels struck in September 1986 and the town was not freed for two years. The rebels targeted schools and clinics in their attempt to create terror and cripple the country.

The school was attacked at five in the morning so there were no children here. This was lucky. The Renamo rebels started firing into the town and everyone just ran. There was, however, nowhere to run to as the rebels had encircled the place. One of our teachers was killed - he fired in the air to alert his neighbours to the attack. Eleven schools in this area were destroyed by the rebels.

Behind the happy faces in my school are many sad stories. A lot of children here have been disturbed by the violence they have seen. As teachers we have to help the children come to terms with this and rebuild their lives. Many thousands of children became separated from their families during the war. It is now three years since the Peace Agreement was signed, but the lives of ordinary people take longer to restore than a handshake between leaders.

We are keeping a close eye on one little girl called Ana. She is eight years old and was found wandering in the shanty town. When questioned she said she had no mother or father. She had lost contact with her parents when she was five and had tagged along with another family and fled over the border into Malawi. When the family returned to Mozambique social workers found a foster family for Ana.

Now Ana's parents have turned up and she doesn't want to go back to them. She wants to live with the foster family and they want to keep her. She visits her family at weekends and is studying happily. But her parents are very upset.

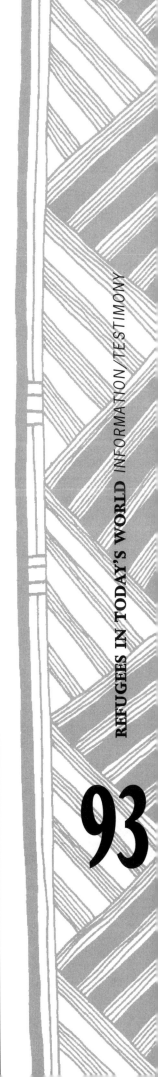

Returning refugees are joining our schools. They had a good standard of education in Malawi. But children who are coming here from areas held by Renamo have not been to school. It is very difficult to talk to these children, they are very reserved, very frightened and inarticulate. It takes them a long time to relax. After eight years of being displaced, they find a completely different situation.

Children from the Renamo areas always lived in fear. The rebels used them as porters. If the child couldn't carry the load he was killed. At night the children were tied up to stop them escaping.

Reconciliation is very important now. It is important to bury past hatreds. When people come from Renamo areas we try to accept them as our brothers because we know that they didn't have much choice. We know that people were forced to go with the Renamo rebels. Reconciliation is important if we want to see the peace continue.'

Farukh Julio aged 11 tells his story:

'I was three when my family fled into Malawi. My mother has stayed in Malawi but I came back to Mozambique with my stepfather.

I can still remember the war. I saw someone being killed and I remember that. Sometimes the cartridges were flying about everywhere. It was the ordinary people that got killed. War is very bad. We were all afraid of being killed at this time.

Since we came back home, we've had many problems because the fields were full of weeds and it was very difficult to clear the land and build new houses. When we went back our old houses were wrecked. We also found some people already living in our places. So we just went to another plot of land; there were no arguments.

We still don't have enough to eat, enough land to farm and enough clothes to wear. Here in school we have no books at all or all the other things that we need for school.'

Repatriation & reconstruction

Aims

The students are going to examine what is needed for refugees to be able to return to their home countries. Mozambique will be taken as a case study.

Instructions

Time needed: 45 minutes or more

The cards will need to be copied and prepared before the activity. Students will also need copies of the information about Mozambique.

Divide the students into groups of three. Each group is going to imagine that they are a Mozambican refugee family now living in a refugee camp in Malawi. The family now comprises a father, mother and two children. Before the war they were farmers in Mozambique. When Renamo attacked the family's village another two children got separated as people fled into the bush. They have not been seen since.

Each group should have a set of cards. The students should sort the cards into an order. Each group could decide what things are most important to enable the refugee family to return to Mozambique and which things are least important for return. Alternatively the cards could be sorted into two piles: short term needs to enable refugees to return and long term needs for return to Mozambique.

*

Repatriation means the return of people to their countries of origin. Sometimes refugees return by themselves. In other circumstances refugees return to their home country as part of a voluntary repatriation programme. This is usually organised by UNHCR. The refugees receive help to enable them to return.

Refugees and asylum-seekers can also be repatriated against their will. This is usually against international human rights law. Recently Sri Lankan Tamil refugees have been returned from India involuntarily. Human rights and refugee organisations protested against this.

A jerrycan for water	A hoe and scythe - tools you will need for your farm
A large canvas bag	A rebuilt school in your home village
News from relatives and friends who have returned that Mozambique is now safe	News that soldiers in Renamo and the Mozambican army have had their weapons taken away and are no longer fighting
A large sack of maize, some cooking oil, dried beans and salt	Training for you and your children on being aware of the dangers of landmines
Money - about £20	Blankets
Three loaves of bread	Plastic sheeting
Assurances from UNHCR that Mozambique is now safe	Some social workers to help you to trace your missing children
Seeds for planting on your farm	Wood - to help you rebuild your house
News heard on the BBC World ervice stating that your home area in Mozambique is now safe	Buses and lorries to take you home

The Sahrawis

In the area around Tindouf, Algeria, 165,000 Sahrawi refugees wait for a settlement to the conflict between Polisario and Morocco. Like many conflicts which involve refugees, its roots lie in colonial history.

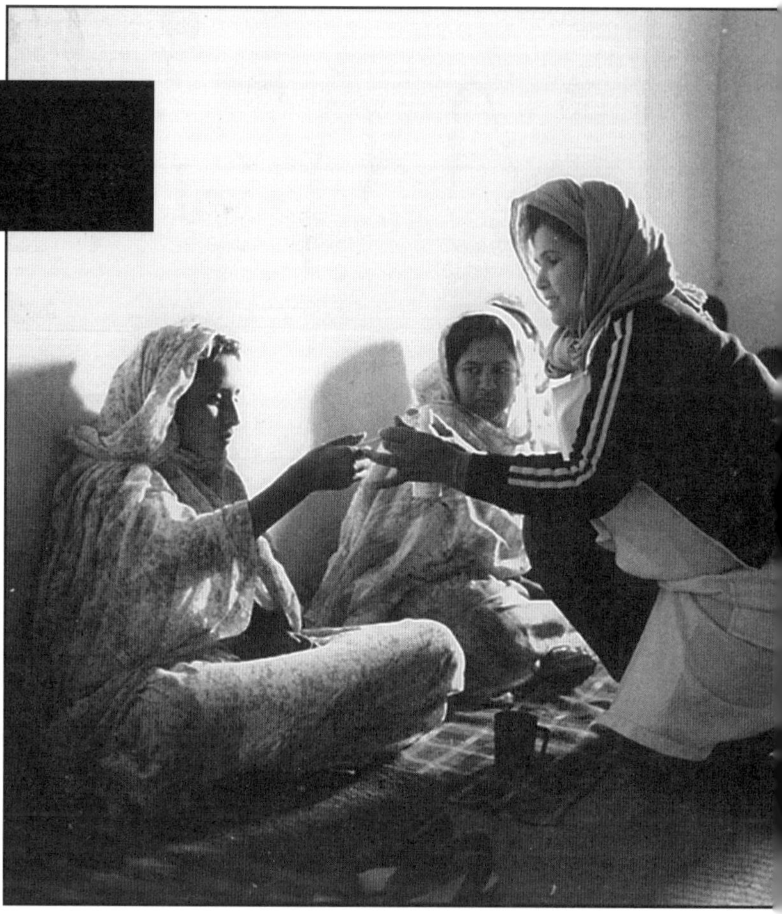

UNH

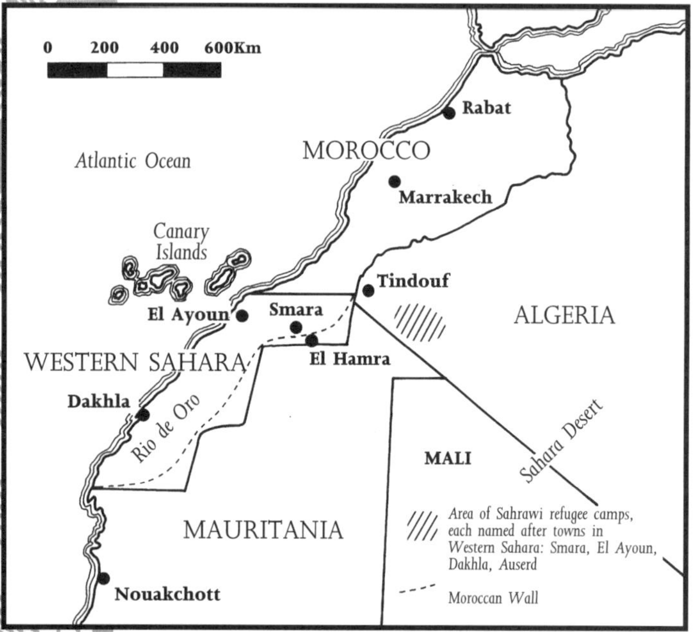

Events

Early history Berber tribes have lived in the area now known as Western Sahara since the first millennium BC. They practised pastoral nomadism - the camel was their key to survival. At a later date Berber tribes began to have contact with black Africans and Bedouin Arabs. Contact with Arabic culture ensured that the people of Western Sahara were converted to Islam by the 9th century AD.

The Sahrawi people are of mixed Bedouin Arab, Berber and black African descent. They speak a dialect of Arabic called Hassaniya.

15th century Spanish sea-farers raid and trade with the coastal areas of North Africa.

1884–1912 Spain loses her South American colonies and becomes interested in acquiring colonies closer to home. In 1884, as the European powers are carving up Africa at the Congress of Berlin, Spain proclaims a 'protectorate of the territories of Rio de Oro, Angra de Cintra and the Bay of the West'.

The borders of what becomes Spanish Sahara are drawn up in four successive French and Spanish treaties in 1886, 1900, 1904 and 1912. The territory is largely run by army officers from the Spanish Foreign Legion. Partly as a result of colonisation, Sahrawi nationalism and a distinct Sahrawi culture begin to evolve.

1936–1975 All dissent is ruthlessly suppressed in Spain and in Spanish territories during the rule of the military dictator, General Franco. A revolt in 1958 is the first challenge to Spanish rule in Spanish Sahara. French and Spanish troops put down the revolt with such violence that there are no more challenges to Spanish rule for ten years.

1966 To placate the UN, Spain promises that the Sahrawi people will eventually be allowed self-determination. But this promise is a sham: the discovery of rich mineral deposits makes Spanish Sahara a financially desirable colony. There are rich offshore fisheries and oil deposits, and unexploited sources of iron ore near the Algerian and Mauritanian borders. But it is the phosphate rock that is of greatest value. Phosphate is used to make fertiliser and it is thought that there are over 10 billion tons of phosphate reserves. This has the potential to make Spanish Sahara a very rich country.

After the discovery of mineral deposits both Morocco and Mauritania claim Spanish Sahara. Both countries base their claims on the extent of their 'rule' during medieval times.

1970 The Polisario Front (Frente Popular para la Liberacion de Saguia, El Hamra y Rio de Oro) is formed, to fight for independence from the Spanish. From the start Polisario seeks to gain independence through armed struggle. Between 1973 and 1975 Polisario carries out small-scale attacks on Spanish targets. At the same time it wins widespread support from the Sahrawi people.

1972–73 The Sahrawi cause begins to attract international attention. The UN General Assembly passes resolutions in support of the Sahrawi people. Soon after, General Franco announces that Spain will allow a referendum on self-determination to be held in Spanish Sahara. This announcement results in Morocco taking dramatic action. Spanish fishing boats are harassed and Morocco moves 20,000 soldiers to its border with Spanish Sahara.

October and November 1975 The International Court of Justice produces a report rejecting Moroccan and Mauritanian claims to Spanish Sahara. Within hours of publication of the report, King Hassan of Morocco announces that 350,000 volunteers will march across the border into Spanish Sahara. This stage-managed event is known as the Green March. It happens on 6 November 1975 and is designed to force Spain's hand.

As General Franco lies dying in Spain, Morocco moves troops into Spanish Sahara. Spain is in internal crisis, so war with Morocco is unlikely. Behind the scenes the Moroccan and Spanish governments have been meeting for some time. On 14 November 1975 Spain signs the Madrid Accords, dividing Spanish Sahara between its two neighbours.

January 1976 The last Spanish troops go, leaving Western Sahara in Moroccan and Mauritanian hands. But both occupiers underestimate the courage of the Sahrawis in resisting occupation.

Soon after, Polisario declares the birth of the Sahrawi Arab Democratic Republic. It is given the immediate support of Algeria. Polisario soon takes control of outlying settlements. In remote desert regions the Sahrawis hold both the Moroccan and Mauritanian army at bay.

Thousands of Sahrawi refugees flee to the desert and later to Algeria.

1978–79 The war proves too much for Mauritania's shaky government. After two *coup d'etat* Mauritania withdraws from Western Sahara. Morocco responds by claiming all of the country. But the Moroccan army cannot control the desert where Polisario has a network of hideouts.

1980 Morocco builds the 'Great Wall of the Sahara'. This formidable defence consists of a sandbank three metres high, fortified with minefields, barbed wire and observation points for troops. This brings the war to a stalemate; Morocco now controls the parts of Western Sahara enclosed by the wall.

1980s The war costs Morocco dearly. To keep 200,000 soldiers in Western Sahara consumes at least 40 per cent of Morocco's gross domestic product. This helps cause an economic crisis in Morocco. But for King Hassan to withdraw from Western Sahara will cause a dramatic loss of face for an already shaky monarchy.

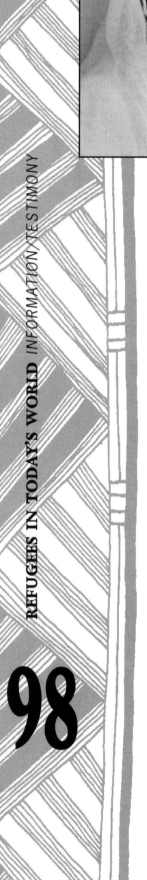

Hafsa Houd's story

Hafsa Houd, aged 53, lives in Tindouf, Algeria.

'I fled my home in Ouserd when the Moroccans invaded in 1975. We walked all the way to the camp, and when we arrived there was nothing. We started to work together so we could survive in this hostile environment.

My family followed me into exile a year later, and since then we have lived here. Life is very hard. In the winter it is cold and in the summer it is very hot. We have to constantly repair and replace our tents which only last three or four years. Sometimes there are not enough tents and families have to share their living space. This is how we are: we share everything, it is part of our culture.

We grow what food we can, and I help out in the garden when planting and harvesting is needed. There is still a problem with food supplies. Many of our children are ill due to the inadequate diet; my first grandchild goes to the clinic for regular check-ups, but there is still a shortage of medicines if he is ill.

I have benefitted from education. Like most women I could not read or write before I came to Tindouf. I attended classes. My children have also received a good education in the camps; this is important as education will help us when we return.

We are refugees. We are dependent on help from humanitarian organisations because we have been forced to live in the desert where no-one can survive without outside help. All I want is to be able to return home; that would be the best present from the international community.'

Morocco receives most of its military backing from France and the USA. Polisario's main supporter is the Algerian government. It supplies humanitarian aid to the refugees and arms Polisario. Algeria, however, would like a settlement of the conflict as it would like to build better relations with Morocco.

1988 Polisario and Morocco agree to a UN-supervised referendum and ceasefire. The referendum would give voters the choice between independence or integration with Morocco. But peace negotiations are complicated by Morocco's policy of settling its own citizens in Western Sahara. It is estimated that 170,000 settlers have arrived since 1980. Their position makes any referendum a problem. Morocco wishes to include the settlers and exclude the refugees in Algeria from any referendum. Polisario wishes to include the refugees and exclude the settlers.

1989 Peace talks break down and there is a worsening of the war.

1991 The UN starts to implement the peace plan. A ceasefire is agreed. The MINURSO mission (UN Mission for Referendum in Western Sahara) arrives in Western Sahara and starts to prepare for the referendum. But there are many disagreements about who is able to vote. The ceasefire breaks down in August 1991.

1992 The UN revives the peace process and the plans for the referendum.

1994 Severe floods in Algeria cause much damage to the Sahrawi camps. The UN starts to register people who are able to vote in the referendum. It is a slow process and the Moroccans are accused of delaying the registration.

1995 The referendum is planned for 1996.

SAHRAWIS

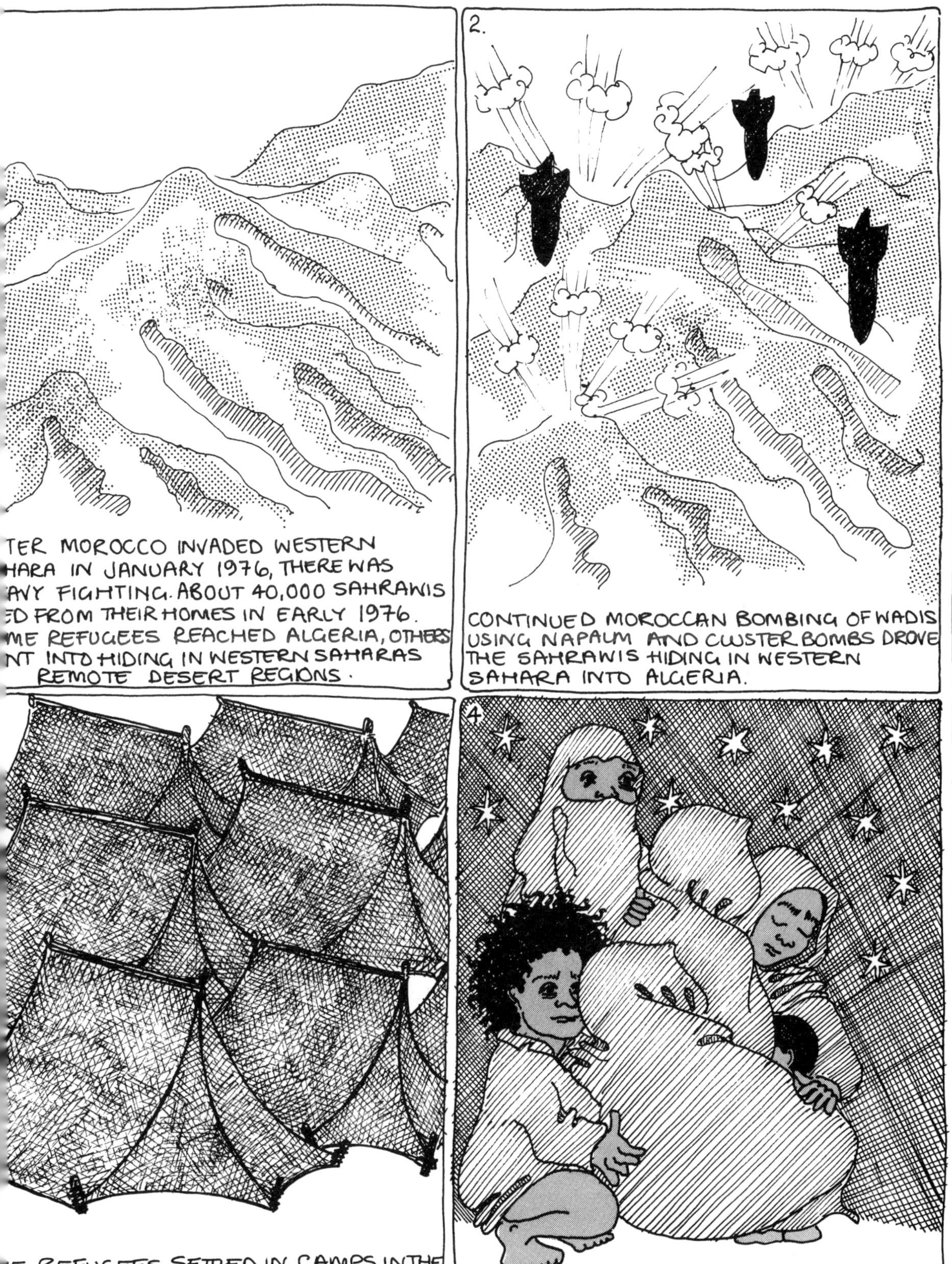
TER MOROCCO INVADED WESTERN
HARA IN JANUARY 1976, THERE WAS
AVY FIGHTING. ABOUT 40,000 SAHRAWIS
ED FROM THEIR HOMES IN EARLY 1976.
ME REFUGEES REACHED ALGERIA, OTHERS
NT INTO HIDING IN WESTERN SAHARAS
REMOTE DESERT REGIONS.
2.
CONTINUED MOROCCAN BOMBING OF WADIS
USING NAPALM AND CLUSTER BOMBS DROVE
THE SAHRAWIS HIDING IN WESTERN
SAHARA INTO ALGERIA.
E REFUGEES SETTLED IN CAMPS IN THE
NDOUF REGION OF ALGERIA. IN THE
ARLY DAYS CONDITIONS IN THE CAMPS
RE GRIM. THERE WAS NOT ENOUGH
FOOD AND WATER.
4
ON WINTER NIGHTS THE DESERT TEMPERATURE
DROPS BELOW FREEZING. IN THE FIRST
WINTER IN ALGERIA THE REFUGEES DID NOT
HAVE ENOUGH CLOTHES, BLANKETS OR TENTS.

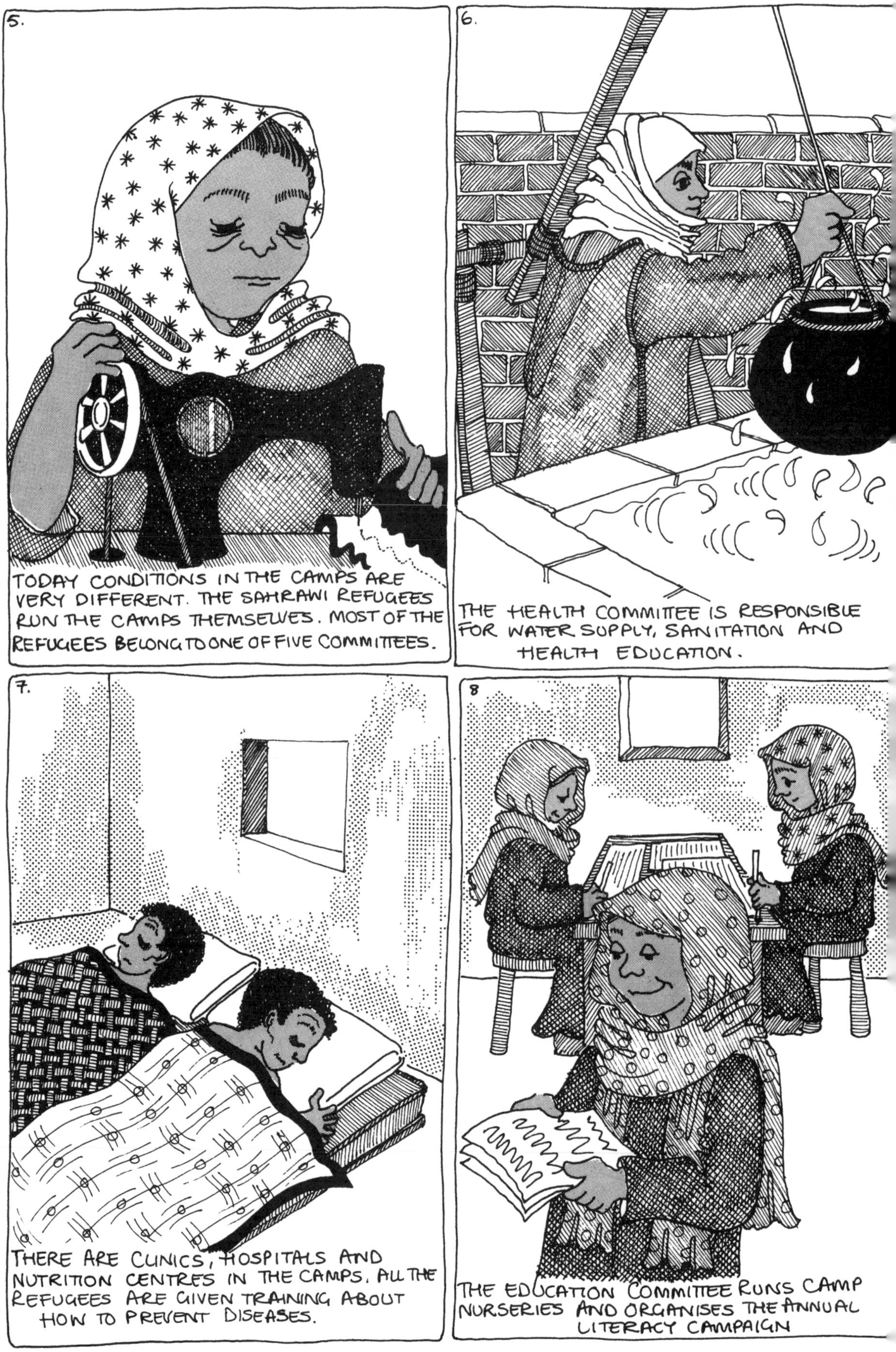
5.
TODAY CONDITIONS IN THE CAMPS ARE VERY DIFFERENT. THE SAHRAWI REFUGEES RUN THE CAMPS THEMSELVES. MOST OF THE REFUGEES BELONG TO ONE OF FIVE COMMITTEES.
6.
THE HEALTH COMMITTEE IS RESPONSIBLE FOR WATER SUPPLY, SANITATION AND HEALTH EDUCATION.
7.
THERE ARE CLINICS, HOSPITALS AND NUTRITION CENTRES IN THE CAMPS. ALL THE REFUGEES ARE GIVEN TRAINING ABOUT HOW TO PREVENT DISEASES.
8
THE EDUCATION COMMITTEE RUNS CAMP NURSERIES AND ORGANISES THE ANNUAL LITERACY CAMPAIGN

9.
WHILST SPAIN RULED, VERY FEW SAHRAWIS COULD READ OR WRITE. THERE WERE ONLY FOUR SAHRAWI GIRLS IN SECONDARY SCHOOLS. NOW IN THE CAMPS EVERY CHILD ATTENDS SCHOOL.
10.
THE PRODUCTION COMMITTEE RUNS WORKSHOPS THAT MAKE CLOTHES, SANDALS, REPAIR TENTS AND GROW VEGETABLES.
11.
THE SOCIAL AFFAIRS COMMITTEE REGISTERS BIRTHS, MARRIAGES AND DEATHS. IT ALSO ORGANISES SOCIAL EVENTS. ALTHOUGH LIFE IS STILL VERY HARD IN THE DESERT, THE SAHRAWI REFUGEES HAVE PUT A LOT OF EFFORT INTO EDUCATION, TRAINING AND HEALTH CARE. THEY BELIEVE THIS WILL HELP THEM PREPARE FOR THEIR RETURN TO WESTERN SAHARA IN FUTURE.

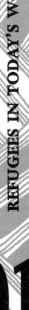

Refugee camps

The Sahrawis in Algeria are living in a refugee camp. Many other groups of refugees in the poorer countries of the world spend time in refugee camps. Most camps are located in border areas, near to where refugees entered their new country. They are not always safe places as refugee camps are often near to fighting.

Refugees who live in camps may not have access to sufficient clean water for drinking, cooking and washing. Getting enough food is another problem in refugee camps as they are often in isolated areas without good transport and food is a bulky product to transport. Shelter is another problem, particularly in areas that receive heavy rain or are cold at night.

Lack of firewood for cooking is another major problem in refugee camps. Often the trees around refugee camps are very quickly destroyed causing environmental damage.

Refugee camps are often very overcrowded places. Infectious diseases may spread quickly where people do not have clean water, sanitation and live very close together.

There are several different ways of providing clean water. If there are water-bearing rocks under the refugee camp a well can be drilled. Alternatively water can be collected from a lake or river, purified and then brought by tanker to a camp.

Food aid has to be planned carefully. The food provided should not need too much cooking or too much firewood will be needed. The food should be appropriate to local tastes - it is no good sending rice to people who have never eaten rice before. And food supplies to refugee camps must provide enough energy, protein, vitamins and minerals so that people stay healthy.

Many different organisations may work in a single refugee camp. They might include the local health and education departments and other people working for the host government. Staff from the United Nations High Commission for Refugee (UNHCR) and NGOs such as Oxfam and Save the Children may also work in refugee camps. It is very important that all the work to assist refugees is coordinated to ensure that all the needs of refugees are met. The UNHCR is usually responsible for coordinating emergency aid to refugees.

Refugee camps

Instructions

Time needed: 30 minutes

The cards should be prepared in advance. Students should be divided into pairs or small groups. Each group should be handed a role card and the needs cards. The groups should rank the needs cards in order of their priorities.

Role card

You have arrived in a refugee camp tired, hungry and frightened after escaping a massacre in your home town.

You had three children: a son aged 13, a daughter aged 11 and a baby of five months. You became separated from your two older children when you were fleeing from your home. The refugee camp has over 300,000 people living in it, and is located in a country where they speak a different language. Although warm in the day the nights can be very cold in this country.

There are lots of different things that you may require. Some of them you may need immediately. Using the 'needs cards' decide which are your ten priority needs.

Needs cards

cooking pots	toilets
cash	blankets
clean water	a warm jumper
social workers that trace missing children	a bucket
a radio	a passport
doctors and a clinic	a gun
a tent	an adult education class
food	wood and bricks to make a permanent house
firewood	a cow

Somalia

Continued fighting has displaced thousands of Somali people. Others have become refugees in east Africa and Europe.

Displaced Somali woman
Hamish Wilson

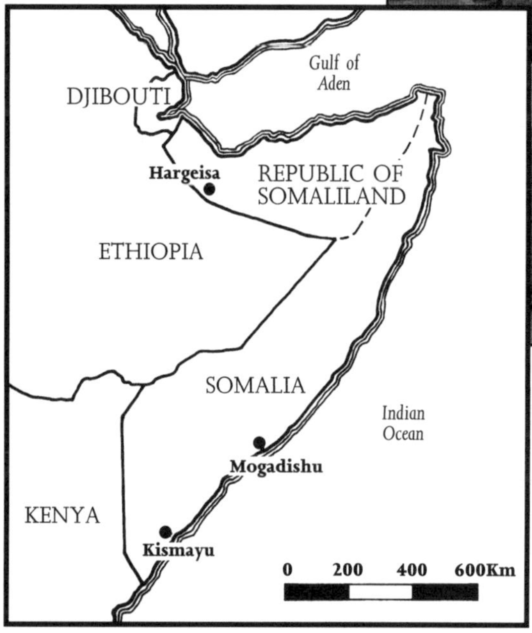

Population
7 million

Capital
Mogadishu

Economy
Most of Somalia is semi-desert with the exception of parts of southern Somalia where fruits and subsistence crops are grown. About 60 per cent of the population make their living from grazing sheep, cattle and camels. Most of the animals are exported to Saudi Arabia, to provide food for pilgrims attending the *Haj*.

In the 20th century payments from Somalis working abroad have become increasingly important. Since the beginning of the 20th century, Somali sailors have worked in the British merchant navy. Later some Somalis settled in parts of Britain, and today many Somalis are working in the Gulf States.

Ethnic groups
Most people living in Somalia and Somaliland are Somalis, and speak the Somali language. Somali people also live in Ethiopia, Djibouti and Kenya. There is a minority group called the Bravanese who live in the southern coastal towns and speak a dialect of Swahili called Brava.

Although almost all Somalis speak the same language and belong to the same ethnic group, Somali society is very divided. Somali society is divided into six clan families. Each clan family is divided up into clans, branches and family groups. A Somali owes personal allegiance to his or her clan and clan family. Clans and clan families have leaders called clan elders. Somalis often give support to different political groups on the basis of which clan they belong to.

Events

2000–1500 BC Archaeologists believe that Somali people have lived in the Horn of Africa for nearly 4,000 years. The ancient Egyptians know Somalia as the 'Land of Punt', meaning the land of frankincense. The Egyptians develop close trading links with the Somali towns and villages on the Red Sea coast.

900–1300 AD Somali nomads and traders convert to Islam. Somalia gradually emerges as a centre of trade.

19th century The country that is now Somalia begins to attract the attention of European colonisers. In 1884 the Berlin Conference divides up the African continent between various European powers. The northern part of Somalia becomes British Somaliland - a British colony. The Italians take control of southern Somalia.

Somali sailors join the British navy. At the end of the 19th century some Somali sailors make their homes in London, Cardiff, Liverpool and other British ports.

1897 The British are anxious to keep the support of neighbouring Ethiopia (then called Abyssinia). They give the Ogaden region of British Somaliland to the Ethiopians.

1899–1920 Sheikh Mohammed Abdilleh Hassan (called the Mad Mullah by the British) leads rebellions against the Ethiopians, British and Italians. Other Somalis join him in his call for an independent Somali country.

1939–45 Britain and Italy are on opposite sides during the Second World War. Many Somalis from British Somaliland join the British army. With their help Italian Somaliland is captured by the British in 1941.

1950–1960 Somalia is again divided. The Italians return to the south, with UN backing. The British continue to rule British Somaliland. At this time a greater number of Somalis begin to call for Somali unity and independence.

1960 British and Italian Somaliland win their independence and unite to form one country. But there are many problems for the new government. The country is very poor and the north and south have experienced different educational and administrative systems. Although almost all Somalis speak the same language and belong to the same ethnic group, there are deep political and clan divisions in the country. Many Somalis are also living outside Somalia, in Ethiopia, Djibouti and Kenya.

1969 The democratically elected Somali government loses public support. Somalia's president is murdered and a group of army officers seize power in a military coup. Major-General Mohammed Siad Barre becomes president and the country is ruled by an unelected body called the Supreme Revolutionary Council. Although the government is not democratic, President Siad Barre announces that Somalia will return to democracy and promises to improve the lives of ordinary people. In the next five years the Somali language is written down for the first time, and there is an educational campaign to help all Somalis learn to read and write.

1970 The Somali government is given increasing amounts of military aid by the Soviet Union. Soon it has one of the largest armies in Africa. In 1970 Somalia also suffers from a drought and severe food shortages. The government organises an efficient relief operation which stops large numbers of people dying of starvation.

1977 The Soviet military aid given to Somalia stops as the Soviet Union switches its support to the new Ethiopian government. In Somalia the USA steps into the shoes of the Soviet Union and gives military aid. Neither the Soviet Union or the USA contribute much to the economic development of Somalia.

War breaks out between Somalia and Ethiopia over the disputed Ogaden region. The Somali army fights with guerrillas of the Western Somalia Liberation Front. Many Somalis live in the Ogaden and President Siad Barre wants this area to join Somalia.

1978 Ethiopia wins back control of the disputed Ogaden region but the guerrilla war in this area continues until 1988.

An increase in world oil prices hits Somalia very badly and the country falls deeply into debt. The International Monetary Fund steps in to help Somalia out of its debts. It forces the Somali government to reduce its spending. Food subsidies are cut, causing hardship among town people who cannot grow their own food. Opposition to the rule of President Siad Barre begins to grow. Prompted by the discontent, one clan group tries to overthrow Siad Barre in a *coup d'etat*. But this fails, and President Siad Barre orders revenge attacks. Over 2,000 people are killed.

1982 Three opposition political parties are formed, including the Somali National Movement. All three parties soon resort to armed struggle to get rid of President Siad Barre. The civil war in Somalia starts. The fighting is worst in northern Somalia. Here the Somali National Movement is fighting the Somali government. Refugees flee from this area, going to camps in the Ogaden region of Ethiopia. Conditions in the refugee camps are very bad, and the Somali refugees do not receive enough food and water.

1988 After people living in northern towns are arrested and killed, the Somali National Movement launches military attacks to win towns in northern Somalia. The Somali government responds by destroying the northern towns of Burao and Hargeisa by shelling and bombing. Over 400,000 people flee as refugees. A few of the refugees flee to Britain, often joining relatives who have lived in Britain for many years.

1989 An increased number of the political opponents of the Somali government are imprisoned, tortured or killed, particularly in Mogadishu, the capital city.

1990 Opposition to the rule of Siad Barre grows rapidly throughout the country.

1991 Greater support for the opposition enables the United Somali Congress - another opposition group - to take control of Mogadishu. But the United Somali Congress splits into two groups almost immediately. Both groups are heavily armed with weapons from the USA and the Soviet Union. In other parts of the country political parties fail to unite and conflicts between the clans grow worse. The civil war is fought by different militias who have easy access to guns. Nearly one million people become refugees or are internally displaced.

In May 1991 the Somali National Movement declares independence in the north. The new country is called the Republic of Somaliland. There is very little fighting in the north. But the new country is not recognised by the UN and cannot get international aid to help it rebuild.

By the end of 1991 it is obvious that southern Somalia is facing severe food shortages as a result of drought and the disruption of farming caused by the war. But the UN does not respond.

1992 At the beginning of 1992 over four million Somalis are at risk of starvation. Food aid is very difficult to deliver to hungry people because of the fighting. Aid agencies have to pay protection money to the militias, to try and get food through. During 1992 about 500,000 Somalis die of starvation, including half of all children under five.

In December 1992 US troops land in Somalia in Operation Restore Hope. Food aid is delivered to starving people, but the US army is not successful in taking weapons off the militias.

1993 A UN peacekeeping force takes over from the US army. Fighting continues, mostly in Mogadishu and other towns in southern Somalia. The presence of the UN troops is opposed by many Somalis.

1995 The UN troops leave Somalia, even though there is still heavy fighting in the country. No transitional government or united leadership has emerged. In southern Somalia there have been some attempts by the UN to establish a legal system and to start schools running, but these are not well-established when the UN leave. Most ordinary Somalis survive by herding their cattle and trading. There are demonstrations, some led by Somali women, which call for an end to fighting. To the north, in Somaliland, there is greater peace.

Fatima's story

Fatima is a young Somali woman who is now living in London. Over 45,000 Somalis live in Britain. Most of them are refugees who have arrived since 1988. At the time she was interviewed Fatima was living in a bed and breakfast hotel in London. The interview was conducted through an interpreter.

'In January 1992 the fighting in Mogadishu got worse. It was then that my father realised that the army not only wanted power, but also to kill all members of our clan. My father decided to send us out, but there were army checkpoints all over the city. Only women could move around. The men were all targets and had to stay at home. We knew we had to get out or we would all be killed. So we managed to get to Jilib. Jilib is between Mogadishu and Kismayu. Here we waited for things to calm down, but nothing changed.

I tried to go back, but people were still being killed in Mogadishu. So I came back to Jilib. I saw so many people killed. Then the army started attacking people in the south of Somalia, near Kismayu. There was no food there, no shelter and no international help. There was nothing, so after two months we went to Nairobi, Kenya. I then sold some of my clothes to bribe Kenyan officials for a Kenyan visa. In Kenya the police would stop you in the streets and ask for your documents and would take you back to the border if you didn't have any. The police harassed women most of all. We suffered more in Kenya than we did in Kismayu. It was terrible.

My father spoke to my brother who lives in the USA. He told my brother how bad things were for us in Nairobi. My brother sent my father some money. But the money was not enough for all the family. It was decided that most of the family would go to Ethiopia. But I would go with my two children to my brother. With his money I bought a Kenyan passport and an American visa. I wanted to go anywhere in the world, anywhere away from the harassment in Kenya. I then bought a ticket to New York.

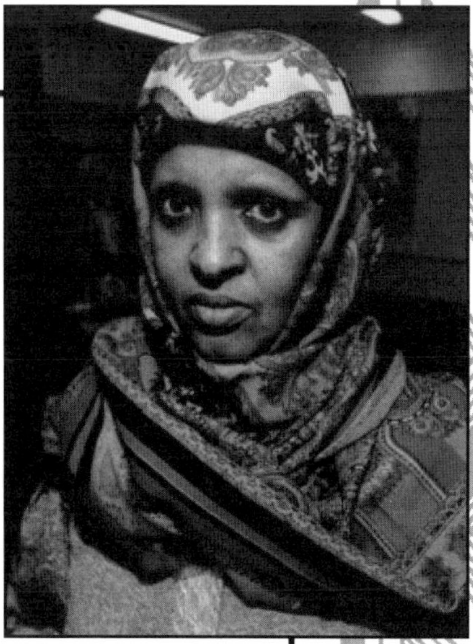

The plane passed through London. But when I was changing planes they discovered my forged passport. They told me I cannot go to New York. It was lucky I spoke Arabic, they got an Egyptian interpreter. He told me that as I had a forged passport they were going to send me back. If I didn't want to go back they would put me in jail here, he said. I was shocked. But I thought that jail in this country is still better than staying in Kenya. And so I decided to go to jail. Then my eldest son, who understood some Arabic, realised I was going to go to jail. He began to cry and my youngest son also began to cry. Suddenly the immigration officers changed their minds.

They took me for a medical check then to a bed and breakfast hotel some-where. I don't know where it was. That was for three days. Afterwards I was transferred here. I have been in Britain for seven months now.

The people are kind here. I have been through so much, at home and in Kenya. My main worry is the fate of my family back home. I hav not heard what has happened to those in Ethiopia. But my brother in Somalia was murdered. I received a letter to tell me, it was terrible.

I am also worried about my refugee status. I filled in the application forms, but I have heard nothing since then. I have been offered a house, but I have no furniture. If I don't move into this house I've been told that I won't get another place.'

Preventing refugee movements

Instructions

Time needed: one hour

The cards should be prepared in advance. The students will also need pens and paper, a copy of the information about Somalia and the information about preventing refugee movements. The students should be divided up into threes or fours and every group should be given a set of cards.

The students should first imagine that the year is 1982. They should rank the cards in order, starting with the most important thing that the UN could do to prevent people becoming refugees in Somalia.

The students should them imagine that the year is 1992. The students should rank the cards again, starting with the most important thing that the UN could do to prevent people becoming refugees in Somalia.

After the students have sorted the cards they should come together. A short time can be spent in comparing the students answers. The group can also discuss the points below.

Discussion points

◆ Do you think that the UN can take effective action to stop people becoming refugees?

◆ Do you think that the UN has a right to intervene in the affairs of individual countries?

◆ What are the benefits of intervening early in conflicts? What are the problems?

Students

During the last five years organisations that work with refugees have begun to think about ways that the UN and other bodies can prevent large numbers of people having to flee their homes as refugees. Most people now agree that large scale refugee movements can be prevented if the UN, individual governments and other organisations took action early enough. Unfortunately this rarely happens. It is usually left until large numbers of people start to flee their homes. By then it is much more difficult to do anything.

Although the most important step is for the opposing sides in a conflict to talk to each other, there are many actions which the UN can take to prevent people from becoming refugees. These actions are described on the cards.

Arms control -
trying to encourage individual countries not to sell arms to countries which are unstable or abuse human rights.

Arms control -
sending UN soldiers to take the weapons off groups who are fighting.

Economic sanctions -
not to give UN development aid to countries which abuse human rights, and encouraging individual countries to do the same.

Economic sanctions -
encouraging individual countries not to buy goods from countries which abuse human rights.

Diplomatic measures -
sending UN diplomats on visits to countries that abuse human rights, to explain that the UN is not pleased about what is happening and will take further action.

Protecting civilians -
sending UN soldiers to protect ordinary people from fighting.

Conflict resolution -
giving UN aid to small scale projects that work with ordinary people, bringing them together and helping them to resolve conflicts.

Conflict resolution -
helping the leaders of groups that are fighting to come together for peace talks.

Monitoring human rights -
sending UN human rights observers to countries where there is tension and human rights abuses. The human rights observers will be able to send news of human rights abuses to the outside world.

War crimes trials -
bringing people who commit human rights abuses before the International Court, to try them, and, if found guilty, to punish them.

Economic aid -
trying to ensure that poverty does not cause unrest. UN development aid can be given to help the poorest groups of people in a country.

Sudan

Human rights abuses and civil war in Southern Sudan have forced millions of Sudanese to flee from their homes

UNHCR

Population
28 million including four million internally displaced people

Capital
Khartoum

Economy
Sudan is an agricultural country and 62 per cent of all Sudanese work on farms. The main exports are cattle, cotton, sesame and gum arabic. The Nile Valley is the richest agricultural region and is the most densely populated. Southern Sudan is poorer and the civil war has disrupted the economy.

Ethnic groups
Sudan is an ethnically diverse country. About 40 per cent of the population identify themselves as Arabs and mostly live in northern Sudan. Non-Arab groups living in northern Sudan make up another 20 per cent of the population. They include the Nile Nubians who consider themselves to be the descendants of the people who lived in the ancient Kingdom of Nubia. The Nuba are another ethnic group living in northern Sudan. They have suffered terrible human rights abuse in recent years. Southern Sudanese form 30 per cent of the population. The people of southern Sudan identify themselves as black African. The main ethnic groups are the Dinka, Nuer, Shilluk, Azande and Bari. Longstanding conflicts exist between some of the different ethnic groups in southern Sudan, particularly the Nuer and Dinka who sometimes raid each other's cattle.

Since the Arab conquest in the 7th century there has been much mixing of the different ethnic groups.

Languages
Arabic is the official language of Sudan. Other languages include Beja, Dinka, Nuer and English.

Religion
Religious differences play a part in today's conflict. About 70 per cent of the population are Sunni Muslims, mostly living in northern Sudan. In recent years there has been a growth in Islamic fundamentalism in Sudan; the present Sudanese government gives support to fundamentalist groups. There have been some forced conversions of Christians and non-Muslims no longer have the same rights as Muslims. Hundreds of Coptic Christians, living in northern Sudan, have been dismissed from their jobs simply because they are Christian.

People living in southern Sudan are Christian or follow traditional beliefs.

Events

Sudan was called Kush by the ancient Egyptians and Nubia by the Greeks. It has come under the influence of many different cultures. In the 7th century Arab peoples moved south to conquer northern Sudan. At this time there were also small Nubian Christian kingdoms along the River Nile. After the Nubian peoples converted to Islam the Christian kingdoms were replaced by Muslim kingdoms.

1880s Africa is colonised by European powers and Britain becomes interested in Sudan. In 1889 an Anglo-Egyptian army defeats the Sudanese at the Battle of Omdurman. The two countries then jointly rule Sudan.

1920s The British move to separate Arab northern Sudan from the African south. The two parts of Sudan are ruled as separate provinces.

1930s and 1940s Northern Sudan begins a campaign for independence from the British. Many southern Sudanese, fearing they would be dominated by the north, are less keen to gain independence.

1956 Sudan wins its independence. Even before independence there is fighting between the Sudanese army and rebel soldiers in the south. The soldiers' rebellion grows into a bigger movement which fights for independence for southern Sudan.

1956–1972 Sudan experiences its first civil war which lasts for 16 years. The Sudanese government spends large sums of money on weapons to fight the civil war, and little on projects to help poor people. During the civil war thousands of people are killed and many more flee their homes as refugees. By 1972, over 700,000 Sudanese are internally displaced and another 200,000 people are refugees in Ethiopia, Uganda, Zaire and the Central African Republic.

In 1969 Colonel Jaafar Nimeiri seizes power in a *coup d'etat*.

In 1972 the civil war is ended after a peace agreement is signed in Addis Ababa. The peace agreement gives regional autonomy to southern Sudan.

1973–79 The world price of oil rises, followed by falls in the prices of some cash crops such as cotton. Sudan imports oil and one of its main exports is cotton. As a result the country begins to build up big debts. The economy is in crisis and eventually the International Monetary Fund is called in to help Sudan out of its debts. The International Monetary Fund makes the Sudanese government cut public spending, including subsidies on foods. This causes hardship in urban areas as those in towns have to buy their food. Ordinary people go on strike and join demonstrations to protest about the cost of food.

Other people living in northern Sudan start to give their support to Muslim fundamentalist organisations. They believe that God, and a religious government, will solve Sudan's economic crisis. President Nimeiri is eventually forced to include Muslim fundamentalists in his government. There is also growing dissatisfaction with the Sudanese government in southern Sudan.

1983 Soldiers in southern Sudan rebel again. They form the Sudanese People's Liberation Army (SPLA) to fight for

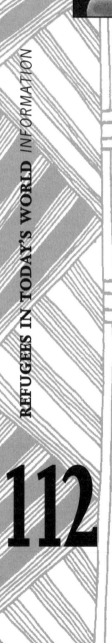

independence in southern Sudan. The conflict worsened later in 1983 after *shari'a* (Islamic laws) are introduced in the whole country. This causes much discontent in southern Sudan where few people are Muslims.

1984 Drought and civil war cause widespread famine in Sudan.

1985 Food prices increase and there are widespread demonstrations. The government of Colonel Nimeiri is overthrown. The new government abolishes *shari'a* laws and promises elections.

1986 A new government is formed after elections, led by Prime Minister Sadiq al Mahdi. But the civil war continues in southern Sudan. The SPLA is also accused of human rights abuses and this organisation keeps several southern Sudanese towns (with army bases) under siege, preventing food aid from reaching starving people.

1987–88 The civil war gets worse. In 1988 over 250,000 people starve to death in southern towns because both the Sudanese government and the SPLA prevent food aid from reaching the starving. Refugees flee to Ethiopia and Uganda and over one million people flee to Khartoum to escape famine and fighting. Most of them live in shanty towns at the edge of the capital city.

1989 There is *coup d'etat* and Brigadier Omar al Bashir becomes President of Sudan. He is supported by Muslim fundamentalists. Human rights abuses worsen including the detention of political opponents, executions, the banning of political parties and trade unions. A small number of people flee northern Sudan as refugees, escaping human rights violations.

1990 There is widespread famine in southern Sudan. The Nuba mountains, home of the Nuba people, are also sealed off by the Sudanese government. Nuba people have been murdered by the army and their villages destroyed.

1991 *Shari'a* - Islamic law - is introduced again in northern Sudan. A conflict also develops within the SPLA and its splits into two groups. One group is dominated by the Dinka people, and another group is dominated by Nuer people. In 1991 more than 5,000 Sudanese people are murdered in Bor, a town in southern Sudan, in fighting between the two southern Sudanese guerrilla groups.

1992 The Sudanese government expels more than 400,000 displaced people from the shanty towns around Khartoum. They are taken to the desert, and do not have access to enough water, food or shelter.

1993 The famine in southern Sudan worsens. Over 400,000 people are refugees in Kenya, Ethiopia, Uganda, Zaire and the Central African Republic. Four million people are internally displaced.

1994–95 Southern Sudanese camps for displaced people are bombed by the government. Unless a long-lasting peace settlement can be reached, millions of people will continue to flee from their homes to escape fighting and hunger.

Sudanese refugees in London *Howard Davies*

Chol Paul Guet's story

Chol was among a group of Sudanese boys who fled after Sudanese soldiers attacked his village. Chol is a Dinka. He, and thousands of other boys, walked hundreds of kilometres towards Ethiopia after they got separated from their families. Three years later he had to flee Ethiopia when there was a change of government. His story was collected by Sybella Wilkes who worked with the United Nations High Commission for Refugees in Kenya.

'It was something like an accident when I ran away from my village. We were playing at about five o'clock when these people, the soldiers came. We didn't know where we were going to, we just ran. The soldiers divided into two groups, one for the village and one for our herds of cattle. My brother helped me to run. We didn't know where my mother or father were, we didn't say goodbye. When there is shooting, when you hear "bang, bang bang" you don't think about your friend or your mother, you just run to save your life.

I didn't see the soldiers, I just heard the shooting, the screaming and the bombing that went "dum, dum, dum, dum" like this and killed many people. It all just happened, like an accident, and we ran without anything - nothing, no food, no clothes, nothing.

In the day the sun was hot and your feet burn. So we walked at night when it is cold, because then you don't say all the time "I want water, I want water." People died of hunger. I saw many dying. Even my friend died. There was no water, no food. When I saw my friend dying I carried on walking. You see, sometimes you can help, and then sometimes you can't.

After two months we came to the Anyak tribe who knew the way to Ethiopia. They helped us get fish and make dried fish. Not bad!

To go to Ethiopia, to the Panyido refugee camp, there was a big river we had to swim across. Many people drowned on the way. In Panyido we did not have food for two months, but at least there was peace.

I spent three years in Ethiopia and felt well. I went to school and lived with five other boys. Then the United Nations left and we had to run. You see the new president of Ethiopia did not want refugees. We couldn't do anything, what could we do? It was not our country.

So, we had to swim and then swim again. Some trucks took us from the border to Kapoeta town (in Sudan). It took two weeks. They gave us food, one hand like this, only one handful to last one week.

At Kapoeta, after three days the United Nations said 'Take them to Narus'. What was happening we didn't know. When we asked people, they said there was fighting and bombing and the soldiers might get us. In Narus (Sudan) we started building our schools and getting books, but we had to leave after only two months, because of more fighting. So we went to Kenya where we would be safe.

Now I live with other boys in Kakuma (Kenya). We cook for ourselves and build our own homes. I like playing basketball, but there is also football and school if you would like. I say, let us stay here where it is safe. In England you are safe, now let us stay here safely. Now we want to learn. One day I will be an engineer to build Sudan like the other countries in Africa.

I don't know whether my mother and father are dead or alive. I was nine when I left Sudan. I am 14 now. I am an oldie man now. My mother will not know me.'

Chol's story, and others like his, are published in 'One day we had to run', Evans Brothers, 2a Portman Mansions, Chiltern St, London W1, with UNHCR and Save the Children Fund.

Comparing your life with Chol's

Instructions:

Copy Chol's story and the chart which shows how he spends his day so that each student has a copy of the information. The students can work individually or in pairs.

Each student has to look at the information, copy the information on Chol's day on to the 24-hour clock and answer the two questions. The students should examine all aspects of Chol's life: his family, home, migration, education, aspirations and how he spends his day.

Discussion points

- **What similarities are there between Chol's life and yours?**

- **What differences are there between Chol's life and yours?**

Chol's school day

Chol lives in Kakuma refugee camp in Kenya. This is a very special refugee camp - out of 40,000 people nearly 25,000 are children. Most of the children are Sudanese boys under 15. There are two reasons for this. Many of these boys ran away to avoid being child soldiers. Other boys left for Kenya because they thought they would be able to attend school there.

The children live together in groups of five or six. They take turns to cook and collect water. Here is what happens on a typical school day.

6.00 Sunrise. Wake Up!

6.15 – 6.45 Wash and dress with my friends

6.45 – 7.15 Collect water

7.15 Eat some breakfast

7.30 Collect my things and walk to school.

8.00 – 13.00 School. We study English, maths, science and geography today. We also play football.

13.00 Come home. Cooking. I help make some bread for lunch. We eat together and then rest.

15.00 Homework.

16.00 Queue to collect some more water. Housework. I have to wash some clothes.

17.00 We all work together to prepare some food for later. Today we have beans, vegetables and bread. We cook on firewood.

17.30 Cooking done, one person looks after the fire. Now we can relax. We play football for a while.

18.00 It gets dark. There is no electricity where we live.

19.00 Supper and talking.

21.00 Sleep!

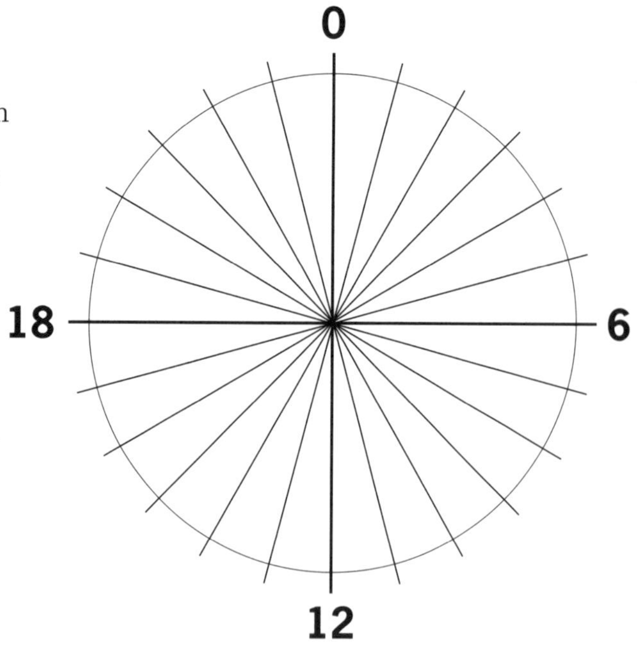

Zaire

Zaire has no democratic government. Human rights abuses and ethnic conflict have forced thousands of people to become refugees.

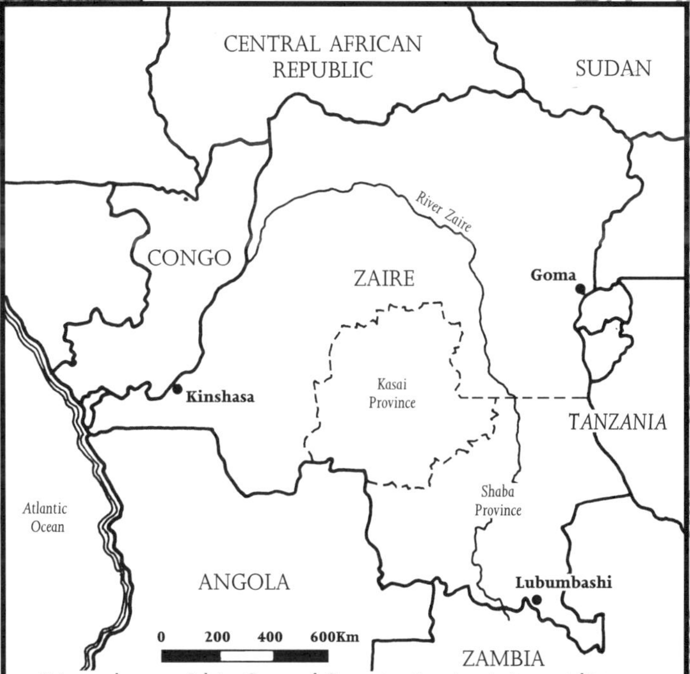

Zaire was known as Belgian Congo and Congo at various times in its recent history

Population
41 million

Capital
Kinshasa

Economy
About 68 per cent of people work in agriculture. Zaire's main exports are diamonds, copper, palm oil and coffee. The country is the world's largest producer of copper and has large reserves of other minerals such as tin and zinc, mostly in Shaba Province. There is also tropical rainforest in much of Zaire; it contains much valuable timber. Zaire could be a much more wealthy country, but government mismanagement has meant that the majority of people are very poor.

Ethnic groups
There are over 200 different ethnic groups in Zaire, speaking many different languages and dialects. The main ethnic groups are the Kikongo, Luba, Mongo, ethnic Rwandans and Bwaka.

There are ethnic conflicts in two parts of Zaire. In the mineral-rich Shaba Province there is conflict between Luba who originate in nearby Kasai Province and Luba and Lunda peoples from Shaba. During colonial times, Luba from Kasai Province were taken to work in the Shaba copper mines. Later, many Kasai Luba became successful as traders and owners of small businesses. This caused resentment among Shaba Luba. Conflict between the Shaba Luba and Kasai Luba has been encouraged by the present Zairean government, to distract people from the economic problems of the country. About 100,000 Kasai Luba have been forced to flee from Shaba.

Kivu Province in eastern Zaire is also a very tense area. It is home to one million ethnic Rwandans and another one million refugees from Rwanda and Burundi. Ethnic Rwandans started to

Zairean boys
UNHCR

move to Zaire in 1959 fleeing conflict in Rwanda. Soon after, other Rwandans migrated to find work. In Kivu many ethnic Rwandans have found success in trading and business, and are resented because of this. In 1992-1993 Rwandan businesses and shops were looted in Goma Province and ovcr 10,000 Rwandans killed. Another 200,000 people fled from their homes. The situation in this area has continued to be tense since the arrival of Rwandan and Burundian refugees in 1994-95.

Languages
French is the official language. The most widely spoken African languages are Kikongo, Tshiluba, Kiswahili and Lingala.

Events

The ancestors of today's Zairean people probably moved to this area about 1,500 years ago. Before colonisation Zaire was a collection of small states located along the River Congo. Information about Zaire reached Europe between 1840 and 1870 through the newspaper coverage of the expeditions of Dr David Livingstone and Henry Stanley. Henry Stanley's expeditions were financed by a Belgian trading company and he signed trading agreements with local leaders.

1884 The Berlin Conference draws up the borders of the Free State of Congo. The country is given as the personal property of the King of Belgium.

1908–1950 Congo becomes a Belgian colony. The Belgians exploit the country's timber and mineral resources but do very little to develop roads, schools, hospitals and local industries. African workers in mines and forests have to work in very poor conditions. The Belgians also brutally suppress all African political organisations who call for independence.

1955–57 African political parties are allowed to operate for the first time, but most of them draw their support from one ethnic group. Only the *Mouvement Nationale Congolaise*, led by Patrice Lumumba, is supported by people from different ethnic groups. In 1959 there is much violence after the police put down a peaceful political demonstration. King Badouin of Belgium promises independence to the people of the Belgian Congo, to try and stop further unrest.

1960 Congo wins its independence from the Belgians and Patrice Lumumba becomes the first Prime Minister. But within days the army revolts and Colonel Joseph-Desiré Mobutu seizes power. Later in the year there is a further crisis in Congo. Many people living in Shaba Province give support to political parties that want mineral-rich Shaba to become independent. Belgium gives support to the independence movement in Shaba (the Belgians are interested in the copper mines and other mineral resources). UN troops are later sent to the Congo to keep order.

1961 Colonel Mobutu gives political power to Joseph Kasavubu, who becomes Prime Minister. Patrice Lumumba is arrested by Kasavubu and handed over to Belgian mercenary soldiers in Shaba. They murder him.

1963–64 The independence movement in Shaba ends, but there is unrest in other parts of Zaire.

1965 Mobutu seizes power in a *coup d'etat* and declares himself President.

1970 Mobutu is elected President in an election where there is no opposition. Thousands of his opponents are arrested, tortured or killed. The *Mouvement Populaire de la Revolution*, a political party formed by Mobutu is the only legal party. Mobutu continues to receive support from the USA, Belgium and France. These governments see Mobutu as being anti-communist and an ally in southern Africa.

1971 The Democratic Republic of Congo is renamed the Republic of Zaire as part of the new government policy of adopting African names. President Mobutu becomes known as Mobutu Sese Seko. Place names are changed and people are encouraged to change their personal names.

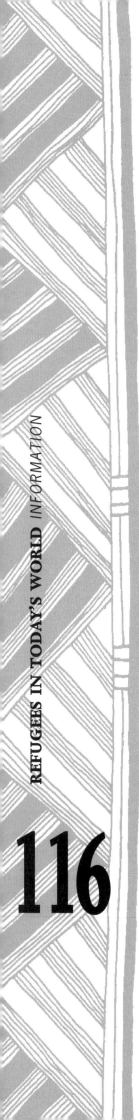

1977–78 Guerrillas fighting for the *Fronte Nationale de Liberation de Congo* invade Shaba Province in 1977 and 1978. They receive support from the Angolan government. Although the invasions are unsuccessful, large numbers of refugees are forced to flee to Zambia. Later in 1978 the Angolan and Zairean governments sign a peace agreement.

1982 A new political party is formed, called the *Union pour la Democratie et la Progrés Social* (UDPS). Its founders are arrested and sent to prison.

1983 Amnesty International publishes a report about human rights abuses in Zaire. The Zairean government is criticised for extrajudicial executions, the arrests of political opponents and the torture and ill-treatment of prisoners.

1984 There is further unrest in Shaba which is brutally put down by the army. President Mobutu is re-elected for a further seven years, in an election where there is no opposition.

1986 Another report from Amnesty International condemns further human rights abuses. Members of opposition parties are continually under the threat of arrest. Human rights organisations are finding it increasingly difficult to trace people who have been detained as they are usually held in secret detention camps. Amnesty International is also concerned about the violence used against those who take part in demonstrations.

1989 Students in Kinshasa and Lubumbashi demonstrate against price increases. Some 50 students are killed when the security services try to break up the demonstration. In this year there are also many arrests of UDPS members.

1990 President Mobutu announces some reforms, including the right to form political parties. But the human rights situation in Zaire does not improve. In May 1990 students at Lubumbashi University organise an anti-government demonstration. Later security forces enter the university. Students are taken from their beds. Between 50 and 150 students are murdered. Many others flee as refugees to Zambia and also to European countries such as Britain.

1991 Student demonstrations and UDPS meetings continue to be disrupted. In September 1991 the Zairean currency is devalued. This leads to huge rises in the price of food and other everyday items. The army riots and many shops and businesses are destroyed.

A group of politicians are appointed to help Zaire move towards democracy. This group is known as the National Conference. In October 1991 the National Conference appoints Etienne Tshisekedi, leader of the UDPS, as the new Prime Minister. But one month later Tshisekedi is sacked by Mobutu, and replaced by Mobutu's own candidate. This causes further riots and bloodshed. Tshisekedi refuses to resign and at the end of 1992 Zaire has two governments.

1992 Human rights abuses continue. There is also ethnic conflict in Shaba. Over 100,000 Kasai Luba are forced to flee their homes. Many people believe that the ethnic conflict is an attempt to divert attention from the economic problems in the country.

1993 Economic problems cause great hardship for ordinary people. Many town dwellers cannot afford to buy enough food. Inflation in Zaire is running at 7,000 per cent a year. A new 5,000,000 Zaire bank note is issued by President Mobutu. It is used to pay the army, but shop keepers refuse to accept it. The army riots and President Mobutu sends in his security forces. Over 1,000 people are killed. As the riots take place, the security forces also seek out and kill some opposition politicians.

In May and June 1993 ethnic Rwandans living in Kivu Province become the target of attack. Over 10,000 Rwandans are killed and another 200,000 people had to flee from their homes. There is also continued ethnic violence in Shaba Province.

1994 A new government is formed with a new Prime Minister. But the UDPS refuses to become part of the government. Eastern Zaire continues to be very tense as over one million refugees from Rwanda arrive there.

About 60,000 Zairean refugees are living in European countries, mostly in Britain, France, Belgium, Germany and Denmark.

Dido's story

Dido Natanbwe Lusamba is 35 years old. He is an art history graduate from the Academy of Fine Arts, Kinshasa, Zaire. He came to Denmark in 1984. He now runs Alfa Print in Copenhagen. He draws cartoons, paints and sculpts. He also directs videos and theatre.

'I grew up in Lubumbashi, a city in southern Zaire. I grew up with ethnic conflict being part of everyday life. In 1984 I had to flee the country after taking part in a student demonstration. I feared I would be arrested. Many people in Zaire have disappeared after being arrested, and are never seen again. And a student friend of mine was shot down on the same night that I fled.

My parents and nine brothers and sisters still live in Zaire. I have not seen them since 1984. But a recent letter from home informed me that the government soldiers have evicted my parents from their house, without any explanation or compensation. As a postmaster my father had lived there since 1967.

My first night in Denmark was spent in a very short child's bed. I was staying in a room at the Goldberg Refugee Centre with seven other refugees. All my new room mates were Iranians and they had never seen anyone from Zaire before or been close to a black man. They gave the child's bed to me! But we soon got to know each other better.

I spent six months in the refugee camp while the Danish government considered my case. We used our spare time in the refugee camp to write a play. With four Iranian actors, Iranian music and Danish everyday sounds we produced a mime. The audience was local people and after the performance everyone celebrated. I have also produced a cartoon book for adults. The book looks at the unrest between different ethnic groups in Zaire.

I get inspiration for new projects by being with other people. In my experience too, different cultures can get to understand each other by working on artistic or creative activities. One of my next projects will be to direct Danish and refugee school students from five primary schools in Copenhagen. They will be producing a play about human rights.'

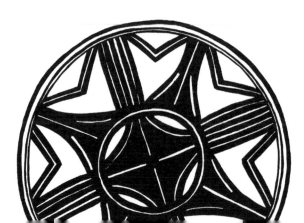

Collecting evidence of human rights abuses

Accurate, reliable evidence about human rights abuses in different countries is essential for organisations working to support refugees or to promote human rights.

The Refugee Legal Centre, an organisation that offers legal advice to asylum-seekers in Britain, needs to know the reasons that people have fled, and the human rights abuses in particular countries. The Refugee Legal Centre needs this information to help asylum-seekers in Britain prepare evidence of persecution.

The Refugee Council needs to know why refugees flee, the countries from which they have fled and the dangers they might face if returned. It needs this information to ensure that asylum-seekers are treated justly in this country. For example, in 1995 nearly all Nigerian asylum-seekers in Britain were refused refugee status, as the Home Office did not believe that Nigerians were being persecuted by their government. The Refugee Council gathered its own human rights information on Nigeria, and was able to challenge the policy of the Home Office.

Evidence about human rights abuses has to be accurate. How do organisations like Amnesty International, the Refugee Legal Centre and the Refugee Council collect their evidence?

Amnesty International

Amnesty International has a large research department, based in its international headquarters. Each researcher is responsible for an individual country, or a small number of countries. The researchers use a wide range of information sources to monitor events in a particular country. Information sources include:

◆ prisoners

◆ the relatives and friends of prisoners, or people who have disappeared or been killed

◆ the statements of people who have suffered or witnessed human rights abuses

◆ lawyers acting for people who have suffered human rights abuses

◆ religious organisations

◆ community organisations

◆ human rights groups within a particular country

◆ refugees who have fled a particular country

◆ people who have travelled in a particular country

◆ journalists who have covered events in a particular country

◆ independent diplomats

◆ newspapers, the radio and television reports

◆ human rights research missions to a particular country.

All the information that Amnesty International receives has to be checked very carefully. Where Amnesty International is dealing with allegations rather than established facts, it says so. If Amnesty International makes a mistake, it issues a correction immediately. Many other organisations, including the Refugee Council, rely on the accuracy of Amnesty International information. If Amnesty International is to lobby governments, its information has to be seen as independent and accurate.

Collecting evidence of human rights abuses in Zaire

Instructions

Time needed: 30 minutes

Each student needs a copy of the instructions and statements. Each pair needs a set of felt pens in three colours. Introduce the activity and talk about collecting reliable evidence. Then divide the students into pairs. Each pair should examine the statements, and answer the questions.

Students

British human rights researchers visited Zaire after students at a university in southern Zaire were shot during a demonstration on their campus. Other students were later arrested. The human rights researchers talked to many people. To be able to take further action, the researchers need clear evidence of human rights abuses.

Read the statements below and decide:

- **Which statements provide clear evidence of human rights abuse? Underline these in one colour.**
- **Which statements need further investigation? Underline these in a different colour.**
- **Which statements are not clear evidence? Underline these in a different colour.**

A student says that she heard shots fired during the demonstration.

An underground student newsletter reports that 100 students were arrested after the demonstration.

There is a long history of conflict between students and the Zairean government.

A university lecturer, now a refugee in London, reports that he has seen the body of a student taken away by soldiers after a demonstration

A priest living near the university says that the day after the demonstration some students told him that 150 students had disappeared from the campus.

A farmer finds two bodies buried on his land near the university campus. The bodies are of young men. Both bodies have gun shot wounds.

The mother of a student says that her son has not returned home for the holidays. Her son was active in a political group. The mother is very worried about her son.

A student gives an account of being dragged out of his bed by soldiers and taken to a detention camp in the forest. He is held in the camp for three days before being released. He does not know where the camp is located.

Another student reports that on the night of the arrest she heard shouting coming from a building on the campus.

The Zairean government denies to journalists that students were shot or arrested after the demonstration. The Zairean government says that the students made up the reports of a massacre to enable them to obtain refugee status in European countries.

A student alleges that she was tortured while she was held in a detention camp. She shows recent wounds on her back where she says she was beaten.

A Zairean soldier deserts from the army. He flees to Zambia and gives a human rights organisation an account of how soldiers were ordered to shoot student demonstrators.

Afghanistan

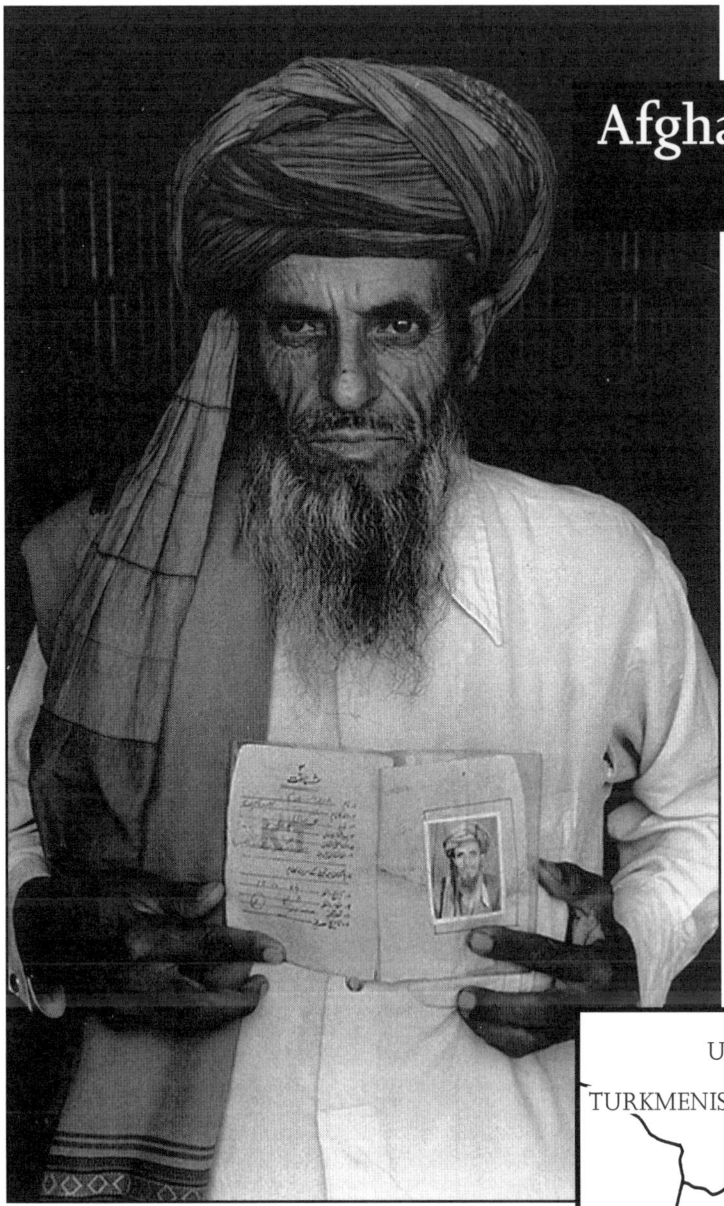

Howard Davies

Afghan refugees are still one of the largest groups in today's world. Some 2,400,000 people are refugees in Iran and Pakistan. Another 1,200,000 are internally displaced by fighting.

Population
16 million

Capital
Kabul

Economy
Afghanistan is a mountainous country. Most people work as farmers, keeping animals or growing wheat, fruit and vegetables. Some farmers also grow opium poppies for the drug's trade. Since 1979 fighting has disrupted the economy and today Afghanistan is one of the world's poorest countries.

Ethnic groups
Afghanistan is a multi-ethnic country. The main ethnic groups are the Pushtun tribes, Tadzhiks, Uzbeks, Turkomen and Hazara. The Pushtuns are the largest ethnic group and live in eastern Afghanistan as well as Pakistan.

Languages
Pushtu and Dari (Persian).

Events

The country that is now Afghanistan has been colonised by many different empires in the last 2,000 years.

From 1767 until 1973 Afghanistan was ruled by tribal leaders and kings. But although governments ruled from Kabul, the capital city, they never had much control over the countryside. Afghan people owe their loyalty first to their families and then to their tribal leaders. In the countryside little has changed in the last 500 years.

19th century At the end of the 19th century Afghanistan is squeezed between two more powerful empires. These are the Russian empire, and India, part of the British empire.

1893 Afghanistan's present borders are drawn. It becomes an independent buffer state, separating the British and Russian empires.

1919 A new government comes to power in Afghanistan and tries to modernise the country. It tries to abolish the wearing of veils for women. This so angers some Afghans that no Afghan government dares try further reforms until the 1950s.

1933 King Zaher Shah comes to the throne. The King introduces a new constitution for Afghanistan and political parties are made legal. Laws are passed that change land ownership and help poor farmers.

1973 King Zaher Shah is deposed. The King's cousin and former prime minister, Mohammed Daud, installs himself as president of a new republic. To start with the new government includes members of all political parties. As time goes by the government becomes less tolerant of opposition parties. Many leaders of opposition parties flee the country.

1978 Mohammed Daud is killed in a military coup. The People's Democratic Party of Afghanistan takes control. (The PDPA is the name of the communist party). The new communist government gets most of its support from people living in towns. It starts an ambitious programme to improve the lives of poor people. Laws are passed to redistribute land in favour of poor farmers. A major literacy campaign is planned.

Although the reforms sound good, they are hastily and insensitively carried out. Many people oppose the reforms. Some tribal leaders in the countryside use violence to stop the reforms being carried out.

1977 In the towns the PDPA becomes divided by bitter arguments. People who oppose the PDPA have to flee the country or are arrested or killed. From 1977-1980 over 200,000 refugees flee the country.

1979 Afghanistan's president is killed by some PDPA members and Hafizullah Amin becomes the new president. Human rights abuses get worse. At the same time the armed resistance to the

Afghan girls in Pakistan
UNHCR

Bahauddin's story

Bahauddin, his wife and three of their children arrived in London in May 1993. Nine months earlier they had fled from their home in Kabul, Afghanistan. They had 30 minutes to prepare for their journey after they were informed that their lives were in danger. Two of Bahauddin's daughters were out shopping at the time he was informed of the threat to his life. Bahauddin decided to save himself and the rest of his family and leave four year old Shafiqa and 10 year old Nooria behind.

'I was a clerical worker employed by the Afghan government at a security post. When Najibullah resigned the *mujahideen* entered Kabul. My wife and I were in definite danger.

One day in September 1992 a close friend of mine informed me that a group of *mujahideen* were searching for my wife and myself. When I heard the news I decided very quickly to take my family to a friend's house to hide from those trying to find me. But at that moment my two daughters were out shopping so I had to leave without them. I expected to return later to collect them.

Later the *mujahideen* came to my house. They expected to find me but only found my friend. He told them I had left with my family. But at this time my daughters returned back home and the *mujahideen* took my daughters for questioning.

I returned home and found my daughters had gone. But I had to leave Kabul. I took my family and hid with friends in Charikar Province. The fighting in Kabul and my work with the deposed government made it impossible for me to return.

We spent five months in hiding in Afghanistan. I then decided to go to Pakistan, to Karachi. We stayed there for several months. I tried to find out about my daughters. They had been released by the *mujahideen* and were being cared for by relatives in Afghanistan.

In Pakistan our lives were in danger again. We used all our savings to arrange flights and visas to come to London. We arrived here on 18th May 1993. Soon after Nooria and Shafiqa reached Pakistan.

I am very grateful to be in London, but my life is overshadowed by worries I have for my two daughters. They are staying in Pakistan with some of our Afghan relatives. My daughters depend on the good will of poor people, none of whom can provide for them for long periods. So the girls have moved twice making contact with us very difficult.

Nooria has sent letters to us every few months. A few days ago I received a tape from Nooria. She cried and asked to be united with us. Shafiqa has grown from a toddler to a small girl. I feel a lot of pressure. I will not be able to sleep peacefully until I have them with me again.'

Bahauddin and his family are still asylum-seekers in Britain. They have not received a decision enabling them to stay in Britain. As asylum-seekers they have no rights to bring their children to this country.

PDPA grows stronger. These fighters are known as *mujahideen*. By the end of the year the PDPA starts to lose control. On 27 December 1979 Soviet troops enter Afghanistan.

1980 After the Soviet invasion, the *mujahideen* grow more organised. They are supplied with arms by the USA, Saudi Arabia, France and Britain. The fighting gets worse and many more people flee as refugees.

1982 Over 3,300,000 refugees have fled to Pakistan and 2,850,000 to Iran. Nearly 3,000,000 Afghans have been forced to leave their own homes and find safety in other parts of Afghanistan. In Pakistan most of the refugees live in camps on the Afghanistan/Pakistan border. The refugees build their own homes out of mud. The United Nations High Commissioner for Refugees (UNHCR) and other aid organisations provide food, schools, clinics and employment training centres.

But despite these efforts life is very hard for refugees in Pakistan. Not all the refugees have ration books from UNHCR. Without a ration book a refugee cannot get food aid. The welcome from Pakistan is under increasing strain. Both refugees and local people cook with firewood. With nearly three million extra people in North West Pakistan, forests are quickly cut down. Afghan refugees also compete with local people for jobs and are often prepared to work for lower wages.

Many Afghan men in Pakistan return to Afghanistan to fight. In Pakistan the *mujahideen* are organised into seven political parties. These parties meet each other regularly and make up the Afghan Interim Government. But the seven groups hold very different political views and the Afghan Interim Government is not united.

In Iran, the refugees are welcomed at first. The *mujahideen* are seen as fighting a holy war against the godless communists. But like Pakistan, the welcome soon wears off and refugees are attacked in riots. In Iran the *mujahideen* support eight different political parties.

1986 The *mujahideen* control most of the countryside while the Afghan government and Soviet troops control the towns. Fighting is worst in rural areas. Over 25 per cent of Afghan villages are destroyed. Crops and farms are burned.

1989 Soviet troops withdraw from Afghanistan. The Soviet Union has lost many soldiers in the Afghan war and realises it cannot win. Everyone expects the Afghan government to fall within weeks of the departure of Soviet troops. But the Afghan government, led by President Najibullah, survives, partly because the *mujahideen* are not united in their opposition.

1989–1992 Fighting continues, especially around Kabul, Kandahar, Jalalabad and in parts of western Afghanistan.

1992 In early 1992, the *mujahideen* close in on Kabul and President Najibullah is overthrown. But the *mujahideen* are not able to form a replacement government and soon start to fight each other. The *mujahideen* have many weapons that they have stored so the fighting is very intense.

The *mujahideen* are organised into many different groups. They are divided along ethnic, religious, political and personal lines. Four main groups emerge. They are:

Hizb-i-Islami, led by Gulbuddin Hekmatyr. This group draws its support from the Pushtun and has a large stockpile of weapons.

Jamiat-Islami, led by President Rabbani and General Masoud. This groups draws support from people living in Kabul, and a wide range of others include Tadzhiks, ex-communists and people who believe in democracy.

General Dostam, whose forces draw support from the Uzbeks and other people who live in northern Afghanistan.

Hizb-i-Wahdat, which draws its support from Shi'a Muslims and holds control of central Afghanistan.

1993 President Rabbani is elected President. But he does not have the support of some of the other groups of *mujahideen*. There is no effective government in Afghanistan.

1992–95 Kabul is destroyed in the fighting between the different groups of *mujahideen*. Its people flee to refugee camps and the population drops from 2,000,000 to 500,000. There are no services in the city and most poor people cannot afford to buy enough food.

1995 A new political group emerges called the *Taleban*. They are fundamentalist Muslim students and they soon take control of large parts of Afghanistan. The *Taleban* and other *mujahideen* groups are accused of abusing human rights.

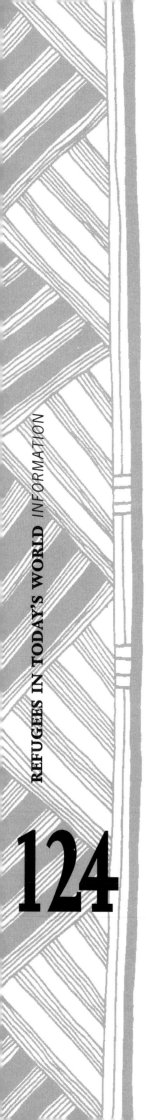

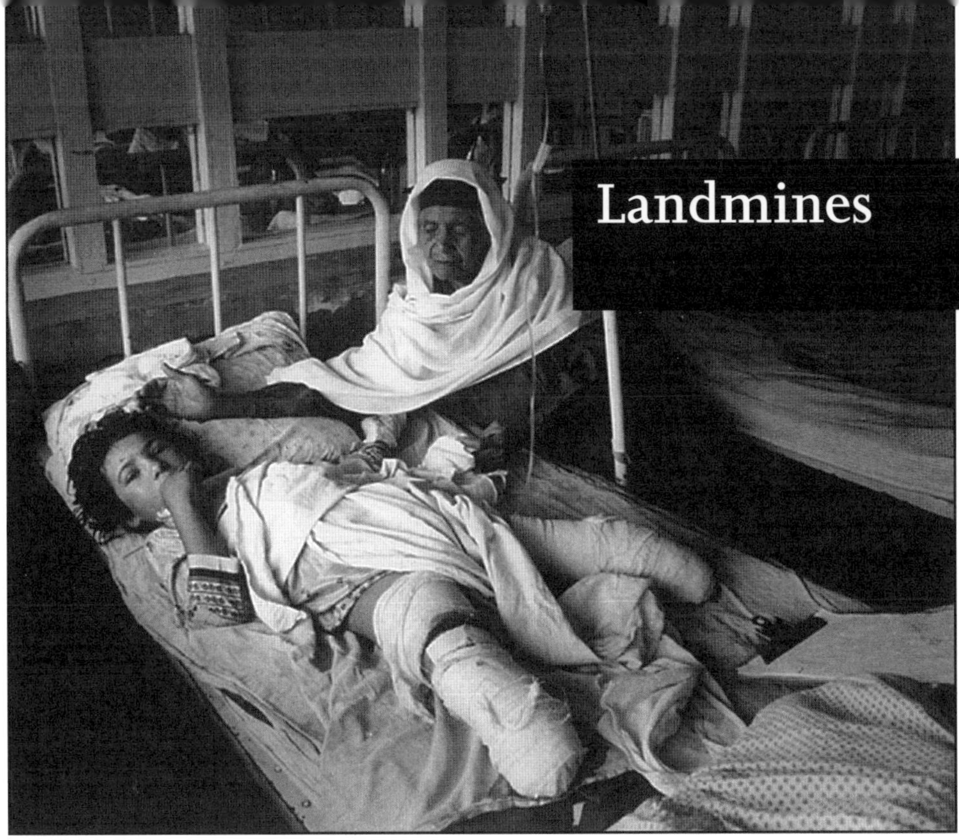

Landmines

A 12 year old Afghan girl who was injured by a landmine in Afghanistan
Howard Davies

Landmines are small explosive devices laid in the soil. They explode when a person treads on one. Most people who step on landmines lose a limb, but children are more likely to be killed. The UN Working Group on Mines estimate that 800 people die every month from mine-related injuries. Many more people lose their arms or legs.

There are over ten million mines laid in Afghanistan.

In Cambodia one person in 280 has lost limbs as a result of landmines.

In Angola one person in 470 have lost limbs as a result of landmines.

There are many different types of land-mine. Some landmines are meant to 'self-destruct' after a period of time. But self-destruct landmines do not always work properly and at least 10 per cent remain active.

Landmine injuries cause an enormous economic burden to a poor country. They remain active long after a war has finished. They create no-go areas and prevent refuges returning to their homes. Landmines prevent people from growing food or grazing animals in affected areas.

A landmine costs about 70p to manu-facture and lay. But it is an extremely lengthy process to remove them. It costs at least £200 to remove a landmine. Over 100 million landmines are still in place around the world. The worst affected countries are:

Afghanistan	Nicaragua
Angola	Rwanda
Cambodia	Somaliland
El Salvador	Sri Lanka
Ethiopia	Sudan
Iran	Uganda
Iraq	Vietnam
Kuwait	Western Sahara
Laos	Former Yugoslavia
Liberia	Zimbabwe
Mozambique	

Countries which produce or have recently produced landmines include:

Argentina	Israel
Austria	Italy
Belgium	Portugal
Chile	Russia
China	Spain
France	United Kingdom

The United Kingdom has not produced whole landmines for ten years. But it is producing parts for landmines and other explosive devices which can act like landmines.

The use of landmines is meant to be governed by international law. The 1980/81 UN Inhumane Weapons Con-vention was intended to stop landmines being used against civilians. But it failed to stop the production of mines. Belgium, Norway and Sweden have banned the production and export of landmines.

In 1994 the British government announced a ban on the export of landmines. This ban, however, did not include the export of self-destruct landmines.

Lobbying & campaigning

Aims

The activity aims to develop participants' knowledge of campaigning and lobbying. The group is going to be asked to run a campaign about landmines, asking for their production and export to be banned.

Instructions

Time needed: two hours

Information about landmines, campaigning and lobbying should be photocopied in advance. Pens and paper are also needed. As the activity develops other things may be required.

Divide the students into groups of four or five. Explain to them the purpose of the activity. Give them the information about landmines and campaigning. Tell them to organise a campaign to get the British government to ban the export of landmines.

Get the groups to design a campaign leaflet and then a strategy for campaigning. When the groups have finished, display their leaflets and get them to present their campaign strategies.

Students

Points to consider when lobbying:

◆ Lobbying means approaching people who hold power to get them to change laws or practices.

◆ You should first think about what you want to achieve. What laws or practices do you want to change?

◆ Who are you going to approach? Obviously your aims determine who you will approach. If you want to change things that are happening abroad you could write to the ambassador of that country. If you wish to change things in Britain you may want to lobby your MP or other people in power.

◆ What methods are you going to use? If you want to approach your local MP it is probably best to write to him or her. You could also invite your MP to your group.

Points to consider when campaigning:

◆ What do you aim to achieve in your campaign?

◆ Who is the target audience?

◆ What methods are you going to use? You must use methods that are appropriate to your audience. What are you going to ask people to do?

Points to consider when producing a leaflet:

◆ What do you wish to achieve?

◆ Who is the target audience? The audience will determine the look and feel of your leaflet, and you should use appropriate language for your target.

◆ What message do you wish to communicate? You should decide on the message you want to get over.

◆ What kind of images and pictures will you use to put across your message? Are they negative or positive images? Do they reinforce stereotypes?

The arms trade

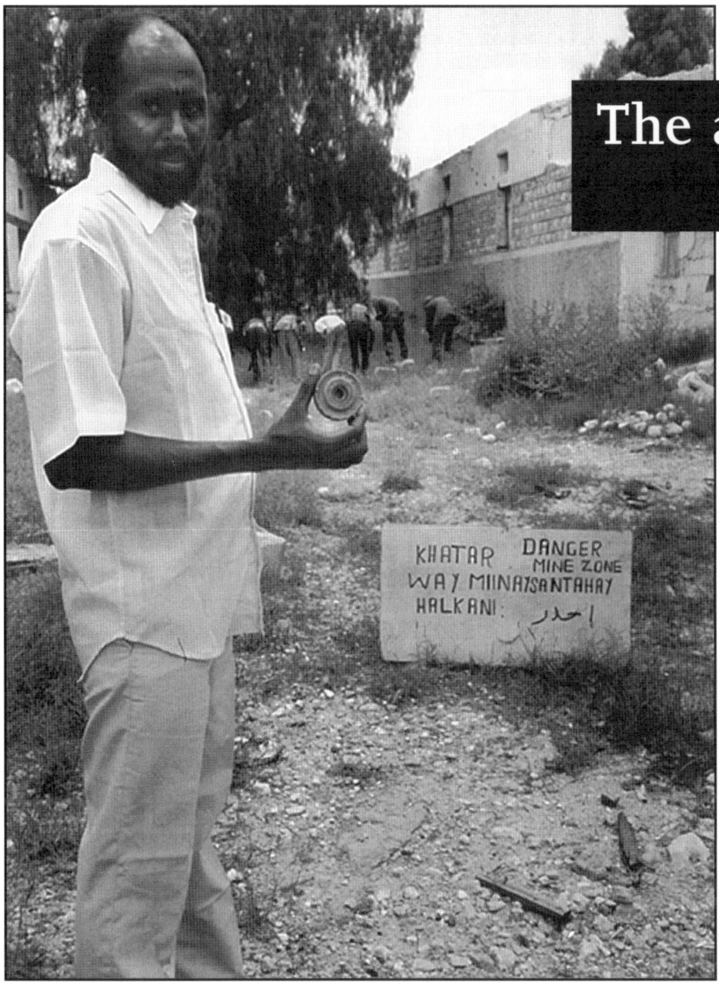

Removing landmines, Somalia *Hamish Wilson*

Landmines are just one military item sold to poor countries of the world. Many people believe that the arms trade worsens poverty and thus conflicts. The arms trade can eventually cause more people to become refugees. These are the arguments that organisations like Campaign Against the Arms Trade use in their work.

Poor countries spend money on their armed forces that could otherwise be spent on development projects to help poor people. Poverty causes discontent and can contribute to instability and conflicts. In 1993 the world's poor countries spent over £75 billion on their armed forces. Over £10 billion was spent on importing weapons from rich countries. The money to buy one British Aerospace Hawk fighter jet could be used to provide clean drinking water to 1,500,000 people.

The arms trade causes poor countries to go into debt. Throughout the 1970s poor countries borrowed money at low interest rates to be able to purchase arms. In the 1980s interest rates went up and some countries found they could not pay back their debts. If a country goes into debt it cannot use public money to help poor people. Food subsidies, education and health projects may have to be cut in a country facing debts. This can again lead to discontent and conflicts.

Second hand weapons are making conflicts worse in many poor countries. Since the collapse of the Soviet Union and the end of the Cold War, governments throughout Europe have been reducing the size of their armed forces. Many weapons from European weapons have been sold - to poor countries. The wars in Afghanistan, Liberia, Sierra Leone, Somalia and Sri Lanka are being fought with second hand weapons. These are all conflicts which are producing large numbers of refugees.

Arms sales can help governments that abuse human rights hang on to power. Many governments rule countries by force rather than consent. These governments rely on powerful security forces to keep their people in check. Powerful security forces have to be armed. Repressive governments kept in power by arms sales include Iraq,

Nigeria, Turkey, and Zaire. These are all countries from which political opponents have had to flee as refugees.

Arms sales can prolong international conflicts and heighten tensions that lead to war. For example the Iran/Iraq war of 1980-88 was partly caused by the massive arms buying by both countries during the 1970s. Other regional conflicts made worse by arms buying include North Korea and South Korea, Greece and Turkey, India and Pakistan and the Arab/Israeli conflict.

The arms trade

Instructions

Time needed: 30 minutes.

The students should be divided into pairs. Each group should be given the student instructions and statements.

Students

Many different countries have supplied weapons and landmines to the Afghan government and the mujahideen. Organisations like Campaign Against the Arms Trade believe that the sale of arms has made the Afghan war much worse. Not everyone agrees with their views about the arms trade. In pairs look at the statements below and see if you agree with them

◆ Britain should not sell arms to countries that are fighting wars. Arms sales only worsen conflicts, causing deaths, injuries and more refugees. Agree/Disagree

◆ Britain does not need to bother about which country or group buys its arms. The decision about using arms lies in the hands of the buyer, not the seller. Agree/Disagree

◆ Britain should not sell arms to countries that have bad records of human rights. Agree/Disagree

◆ Britain should be allowed to give military aid and sell arms to countries that are facing invasion or danger from other nations. Agree/Disagree

◆ If Britain stopped making arms, up to 625,000 people could lose their jobs and Britain would lose a valuable export. Agree/Disagree

◆ If Britain did not sell arms to countries at war, or with poor human rights records, other countries would still make the sales. Agree/Disagree

◆ The British government should be finding ways of making the British economy less dependent on the sale of arms. Agree/Disagree

Top 20 suppliers of major conventional weapons, 1990-94

1	USA	11	North Korea
2	USSR/Russia	12	Sweden
3	Germany	13	Yugoslavia
4	UK	14	Canada
5	France	15	Ukraine
6	China	16	Israel
7	Netherlands	17	Spain
8	Italy	18	Slovakia
9	Czechoslovakia/ Czech Republic	19	Brazil
		20	Norway
10	Switzerland		

Top 20 importers of major conventional weapons, 1990-94

1	Saudi Arabia	11	Pakistan
2	Japan	12	Iran
3	Turkey	13	China
4	Greece	14	Canada
5	India	15	Spain
6	Egypt	16	Thailand
7	Germany	17	South Korea
8	Taiwan	18	Kuwait
9	Afghanistan	19	Indonesia
10	Israel	20	UK

Source: Stockholm International Peace Research Institute Database

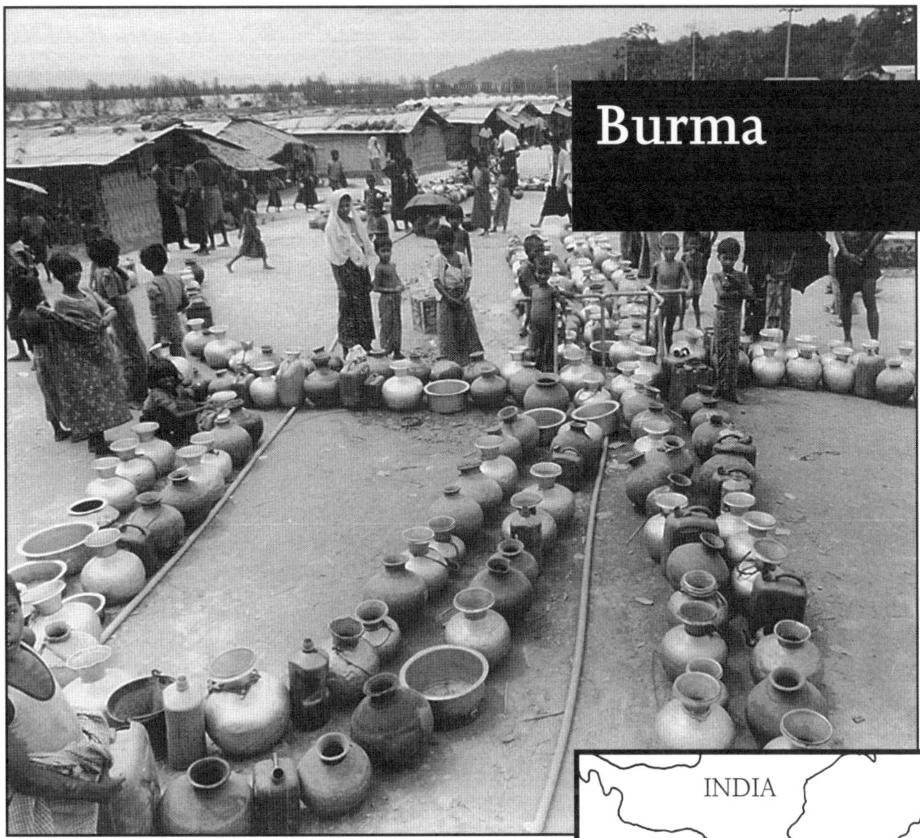

Burma

Human rights abuses have forced Burmese refugees to flee to Bangladesh and Thailand.

Burma is known officially as Myanmar.

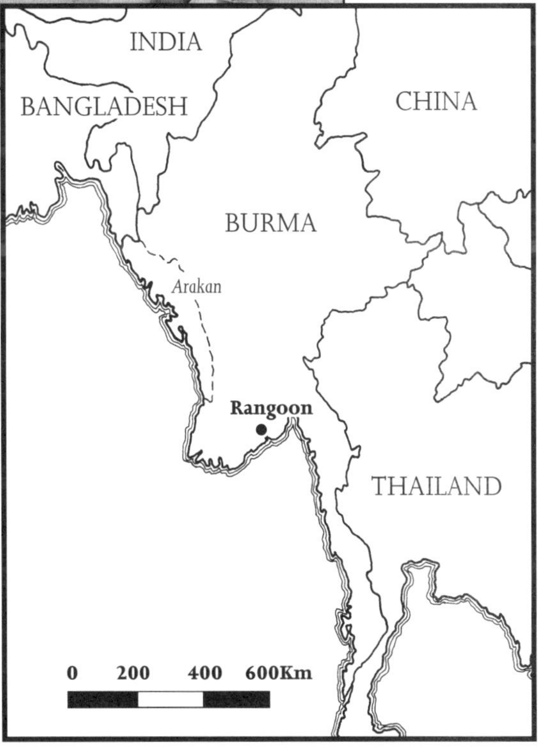

Population
43 million

Capital
Rangoon

Economy
About 65 per cent of Burma's population work on farms growing rice, maize and sugar cane. Burma's main exports are rice, rubber, teak, other tropical timbers, tobacco and gems. Burma has oil reserves that have not been exploited. Although it has many natural resources Burma is the sixth poorest country in the world. This is because there has been very little investment in Burma's infrastructure or industries since the 1960s. Burma's international isolation has also meant that the country has not been able to export many of its goods.

Ethnic groups
It is estimated that about 65 per cent of the population of Burma are ethnic Burmese. The rest of the population belong to ethnic minority groups. The main groups are:

The *Shan*, who make up 11 per cent of the population. Most Shan live in western Burma.

The *Karen*, who make up six per cent of the population. Most Karen live in south west Burma.

Burmese refugees in Bangladesh collect water *Howard Davies*

The *Arakanese*, who make up nine per cent of the population. They live in northern Burma, near the Bangladeshi border.

The *Kachin*, who make up four per cent of the population. They live in northern Burma near the Chinese border.

The *Mon*, who make up 2.5 per cent of the population.

There are other minorities living in Burma including the Chin, Chinese, Tamils and Bengalis.

Languages
It is estimated that there are over 100 languages and dialects in Burma. Burmese is the official language and is spoken by about 70 per cent of the population. Other languages include Karen, Shan, Chin and Mon.

Religion
Some 85 per cent of the population are Buddhist. There are also about 1.5 million Muslims, mostly living in Arakan. Many Karen, Chin and Kachin are Christian.

Events

Early writing indicates that there was an Arakan kingdom in today's Burma nearly 2,500 BC.

8th century AD There is a Mon kingdom in part of today's Burma. The Mon were Buddhists and had an advanced civilisation. It was through the Mon that the Burmese became Buddhist. The Mon alphabet is also adopted by the Burmese.

In the later part of the 8th century ethnic Burmese people enter northern Burma

1044 Burma becomes a united country with Pagan as a capital city. The culture of the Mon people dominates at this time.

1283-87 The central Asian Tartars invade Burma, assisted by Marco Polo. The Burmese kingdom collapses and the Tartars rule a large part of Burma. The Mon and Arakan people proclaim independence.

1301 The Tartars are defeated and leave Burma. For the next 300 years Burma is divided into many small kingdoms. The Shan control most of central Burma during this period. The Shan, Mon, Arakanese and Burmese are the dominant groups, and there are many wars between them after 1301.

17th century The British East India company begins to be interested in Burma's forest resources. The British sign agreements with local lords and start to exploit Burma's resources. The 17th century also sees conflict between the Burmese and the Mon.

1824-26 The Burmese fight three wars against the British.

1852-3 Lower Burma, including the city of Rangoon, becomes part of the British Empire.

1886 The remaining part of Burma becomes part of the British Empire. Burma is administered as a province of India. The Shan, Karen and Kachin states are administered as separate provinces. Many Indian civil servants settle in Burma.

1930s Burmese nationalism grows and many Burmese start to resent the British presence. The Burmese nationalists are led by Aung San. Students in the University of Rangoon riot and Indian settlers bear most of the anti-British feeling. Hundreds of Indians lose their lives in riots in 1930, 1931 and 1938.

1937 Burma is separated from India.

1940 Aung San flees to Japan.

1941 Japan enters the Second World War, on the side of the Axis Powers.

1942 The Japanese army enters Burma and the British are forced to retreat. As they retreat the British destroy towns, as part of a 'scorched earth' policy, designed to leave very little behind. Minority groups such as the Karen, Kachin and Chin stay loyal to the British and organise guerrilla groups against the Japanese. Aung San returns to Burma with the Japanese. He forms the Burma National Army.

1945 There is increasing tension between the Japanese and socialists within the Burma National Army. In March 1945 the Burma National Army declares war on the Japanese. With the help of the British, the Japanese are pushed out of Burma. But the Japanese army also uses scorched earth policies, and much of Burma's infrastructure is destroyed in the war.

1947 Aung San meets with the British to make arrangements for Burma's independence. Aung San has the support of the army, and has begun to win the confidence of Burma's minority groups. But Aung San and six of his cabinet ministers are assassinated in July 1947, before negotiations for independence are finished. U Nu steps in as leader. The Karen National Union is formed.

1948 Burma wins its independence from the British. U Nu is head of government, but he is unable to win the support of Burma's minority groups.

1949 The Karen rebel against Burmese rule. The Karen rebellion spreads to other groups - the Mon, Karennis and Kachins form their own guerrilla armies. There is a civil war in large parts of Burma.

1962 General Ne Win overthrows U Nu in a military coup. Ne Win states that the Communist party and minority groups are the enemies of Burma. He orders the army to intensify military attacks on minority groups. Ne Win also announces that Burma will follow 'the Burmese Way To Socialism'. Banks and trade are nationalised. Many small shopkeepers become unemployed, a large number of whom are Indian and Chinese minorities. Some 300,000 Indians and 100,000 Chinese leave Burma at this time. Military spending accounts for 40 per cent of the gross national product of Burma.

1974 The Burmese government brings in a new constitution. The Burmese Socialist Party Programme is the only legal party. There is no freedom of speech and opposition politicians flee the country or risk imprisonment. Burma's economy is in crisis.

1978-79 Over 200,000 Arakanese refugees (also know as the Rohingyas) flee from Burma to Bangladesh. But they are not welcome and the Bangladeshi government withholds food from them as a way of forcing them to leave. There is no international protest and 10,000 refugees die.

1984 The Burmese army attacks Karen-held areas in eastern Burma. Thousands of refugees are forced to flee into Thailand.

1987 Some 20,000 Burmese refugees are now living in Thailand. Most of them are living in refugee camps in the mountains along the Thai/Burmese border. Conditions in the camps are very hard and many refugees are malnourished or ill. The UN High Commissioner for Refugees does not have access to refugees living in the camps.

1988 There are many student-led demonstrations calling for democracy in Burma. A demonstration in Rangoon, held in August 1988, is the largest of these demonstrations. It seems that Burma is about to see a change of government. But in September 1988 there is a military coup, and General Saw Maung becomes head of government and head of the State Law and Order Restoration Council (SLORC). The SLORC arrests thousands of opponents and 10,000 people are killed by the army. Thousands of students and others who are involved with the pro-democracy movement flee to areas held by the minority groups. The students form an alliance with the Karen and other groups.

1989 The SLORC promises to hold elections. But human rights abuses worsen. All minority groups are treated as enemies and many villagers belonging to minority groups are forced to move. Over one million Burmese have become internally displaced. Civilians are also forced to become army porters, in very harsh conditions. Army porters are usually given very little to eat and made to carry very heavy loads. If they cannot do so, they are killed.

Aung San Suu Kyi, daughter of Aung San returns to Burma. She becomes leader of the National League for Democracy and soon gains widespread support. It seems that Aung San Suu Kyi's party will win the elections. But in July 1995 Aung San Suu Kyi is arrested. She is confined to her house.

1990 Elections are held in May 1990. Despite many difficulties in organising a campaign, the National League for Democracy wins 82 per cent of the seats. But the SLORC refuses to hand over power. Many MPs are arrested, others flee to Manerplaw, the headquarters of the Karen.

1991 Human rights abuses cause 270,000 Arakanese refugees to flee to southern Bangladesh. They flee from forced labour, the destruction of mosques and confiscation of their animals and crops. Burmese refugees (mostly Kachin)

UNHCR

Mi Mee Ong's story

Mi Mee Ong is from a village in Mon State, Burma. She belongs to the minority Mon ethnic group. She is 57 years old, and is married with seven children.

'I left my village 15 years ago. First we went to another village. Then when the Burmese army attacked Three Pagodas Pass six years ago we came into Thailand. We spent four years in Loh Loe camp then five months ago we moved back into Burma to Plat Hon Pai. The camp was about an hour's walk from the Thai border.

On July 21 1994 I was in the refugee camp. I saw the Burmese troops when they arrived at my house. They came inside, they cooked inside and they ate our food. They then arrested my son. Two of my sons were there, one ran away and they arrested the other. They wanted to arrest my husband but he was sick with a fever and he couldn't go. One soldier was going to beat him but another soldier said, "He's sick, don't beat him, don't take him." One of our neighbours was eating in our house and he was arrested too.

The soldiers fired a gun and ordered everyone to come out of their houses. Then they grabbed them by the hands, took them to the road and made them walk in front of them. The soldiers fired their guns. They arrested many people and then they left for another part of the camp.

There was still a soldier in my house who stayed to cook and eat. He told me to stay in the house and not to go outside. I stayed in front of the house but I couldn't see much. I saw army porters with soldiers around them. The soldiers cooked food, and gave the porters only a little rice to eat while the soldiers ate together. The soldier stayed in my house for more than two hours. When he left I saw people running from another part of the refugee camp. I went and hid under another house.

Soon more soldiers came. They ordered us all to leave and then they burnt our houses. They got kerosene from our lamps and put it on everything that burns. If they couldn't get the houses to burn they shot it with a flame throwing gun. When the soldiers had finished one house they would go on to the next. They stole things inside the houses and then burnt them.

When they came to my house I pleaded with the soldiers not to burn it. But a soldier said "I have to do it, it is the order of the commander." When the soldiers left I went to my house which was still burning. With a long bamboo stick I managed to save a couple of plates and one basin. That's all I could save. Afterwards I stayed near my house and sat down. That night we slept on the ground near our burnt houses. I was so angry with the soldiers and so depressed. They took my son and I had lost everything I had. I had been gathering things for my house for years and then I lost it all. I couldn't sleep that night, only sit there.

I was afraid the soldiers would come back. They said that they would come back. They said, "Next time we will burn the people." The next morning my daughter came and we decided to go back into Thailand. My husband walked very slowly with his stick and our youngest son came with us too. When we got here we stayed in a shelter with four other families. It is very hard to build another shelter because my husband is always sick.

My son managed to escape. He was taken by the Burmese army as a porter. They did not feed him properly and they threatened him with a knife.'

Testimony collected by the Karen Human Rights Group, Thailand.

are also living in China, in a cold, rainy, mountainous region.

1993 Aung San Suu Kyi wins the Nobel Peace Prize.

1995 Manerplaw, the headquarters of the Karen and the Burmese opposition, is captured in January 1995. Over 10,000 refugees flee to Thailand. Over 120,000 Arakanese refugees are returned from Bangladesh to Burma, under the supervision of the UN High Commissioner for Refugees. But many human rights organisations criticise this return as they feel that conditions for the returning refugees are not being monitored. Aung San Suu Kyi is released, but Buma has not returned to democracy.

'he Journey to afety Game

Aims

The game simulates the flight of two Burmese families from their home village into Bangladesh. The aim of the game is to get from the village at the start, across the border into the refugee camp in Bangladesh.

The families are fleeing the Burmese army who are forcing villagers to become porters for the army. They are trying to reach a refugee camp in Bangladesh, but have to travel through countryside in which landmines are scattered. Although fun to play, the game contains serious messages about the experiences of refugees fleeing conflicts.

Instructions

Time needed: one hour
The cards and the boards need to be prepared in advance.

1. The leader or class teacher should read out the aims of the game to the whole class.

2. The class should be split into groups of seven. Each group will need

one board
one set of make or break cards
one set of camp permit cards
one dice
six counters
one set of leader's instructions
two sets of instructions for the family teams (one for Family A and one for Family B)
30 small pieces of paper or card (15 pieces for each family team). It is a good idea to put 15 pieces of paper in an envelope, with a set of family instructions.

The game is a slightly adapted version of 'Run for your Life' published by CAFOD. CAFOD holds the copyright and this material is reproduced with their kind permission. *See* **Further Resources**.

3. Each group should elect a leader. The remaining six people should organise themselves into two family units - Family A and Family B.

4. The leader should hand out a set of family team instructions and 15 pieces of paper to each family team.

5. The leader should read through the leader's instructions.

6. After the board has been set up and Family A and Family B have decided what to take with them, the game can begin.

Leader's instructions

1. Each person throws the dice to see who goes first. The highest number goes first and so on.

2. Each person should throw the dice to move, having one throw per turn.

3. If a person lands on a LANDMINE square that person should throw the dice again to find out the extent of the damage. By reading from the Landmine Damage box below, find out the extent of the damage.

4. If a person lands on a MAKE OR BREAK square he or she should pick or a card from the top of the pile of Make or Break Cards. That person should

follow whatever the card says. The card should then be put at the bottom of the pile.

5. If a person lands on a CAMP PERMIT square he or she should be asked a question from the camp permit quiz. A correct answer should be rewarded with a camp permit. These will make it easier to cross the border near the refugee camp. The only other way to obtain a camp permit is to barter for one with another family.

6. All families must stop when they reach the BORDER GUARD square. They don't have to get an exact number on the dice.

If a person has a camp permit he/she can cross the border.

If a person has identification papers he/she can cross the border.

If a person has none of these he/she can try and sneak across the border by night. At the next turn he/she should throw a dice and take the 'night route'.

7. The game ends when everyone who is still alive has reached the refugee camp. The game leader should add up points to see how each family has scored.

10 points for the first person to arrive
5 points for the second person to arrive
3 points for the third person to arrive
1 point for the fourth person to arrive
1 point for every item brought safely to the camp

Take off 2 points for every person who has arrived sick or injured, as medical attention is difficult to obtain.

The winning family is the family with most points.

8. After the game has ended think about the discussion points as a whole group.

Discussion points

◆ What was the most difficult part of the journey?

◆ What was the least difficult part?

◆ What did you learn from the game about the experiences of refugees fleeing conflict?

◆ How do landmines threaten the lives of refugees?

Landmine damage

SHAKE ONE You are lucky. The landmine was a dud and did not go off.

TWO You were not at the centre of the blast but you received bad cuts and bruises to your face and arms. You can no longer carry more than three items. Discard any that you and your family cannot carry.

THREE All the possessions of the person who threw the dice are destroyed. You have also sustained a serious injury and need to pay for medical help. Does your family have any money or valuables to pay the doctor? If not, drop out of the game.

FOUR Your child is injured by a Russian-made 'butterfly' mine which looks like a toy and attracts the attention of children. You have to carry your child, so you must discard all your possessions.

FIVE You tread on a Chinese mine designed to maim rather than kill. You lose all your possessions. Your leg is badly injured and bleeds a lot. Does your family have any rope or cloth that you can tear to make a tourniquet? If not drop out of the game.

SIX The landmine you stood on was a nasty kind. It has killed you. Drop out of the game. The rest of your family must miss a turn as they have to bury you.

Camp Permit Quiz questions to be read by the leader

The correct answers are in *italics*.

1. How many refugees are there in today's world? Is it five million, *18 million,* **39 million or 134 million?**

2. Most of the world's refugees live in poor countries. *True* **or false?**

3. Most people fleeing dangerous situations do not make it to an international border. *True* **or false?**

4. Which three countries host large numbers of Burmese refugees. Is it *China*, **Malaysia, Russia, Japan,** *Bangladesh*, **India,** *Thailand* **or Indonesia?**

5. There are large numbers of Burmese refugees living in Britain. True or *false*.

6. How many landmines are scattered around the world. Is it 10 million, *100 million* **or 250 million.**

7. How many people are killed by landmines every month throughout the world. Is it 80, *800*, **8,000 or 18,000?**

8. Nine out of ten people killed by landmines are soldiers. True or *false*?

9. What is the most common activity people are doing when they are killed by landmines? Is it fighting in a war, clearing mines, grazing animals or *collecting firewood*?

10. Britain has never produced landmines. True or *false*?

CAMP PERMIT	**CAMP PERMIT**
CAMP PERMIT	**CAMP PERMIT**
CAMP PERMIT	**CAMP PERMIT**
CAMP PERMIT	**CAMP PERMIT**

Family team instructions

Each family comprises three people.

You have heard that the Burmese army is near to your village and is forcing all children and adults to become porters. You know that army porters die as conditions are so bad.

You decide to leave. You have five minutes to pack your bags. What would you take with you? As a family of three people you can take no more than 15 items. No person can carry more than five items.

As a family decide what you want to take from the list below. Write one item on each piece of paper, and divide them among you. You can repeat the items by writing them on more than one card, but no more than 15 items may be taken altogether.

a bag of rice

a calf

a small amount of money

some medicine for upset stomachs

a blanket

a water pot

a gold necklace

cooking oil

your dog

an old Koran belonging to your grandfather

identification papers

a jumper and shirt

a knife

a large piece of cloth

a radio

a cooking pot

a loaf of bread

a photograph of all your family

three school books

a piece of matting

a large, strong bag

a torch

spare batteries

some metal plates

some rope

a large piece of plastic sheet

some firewood

a walking stick

some lentils

matches

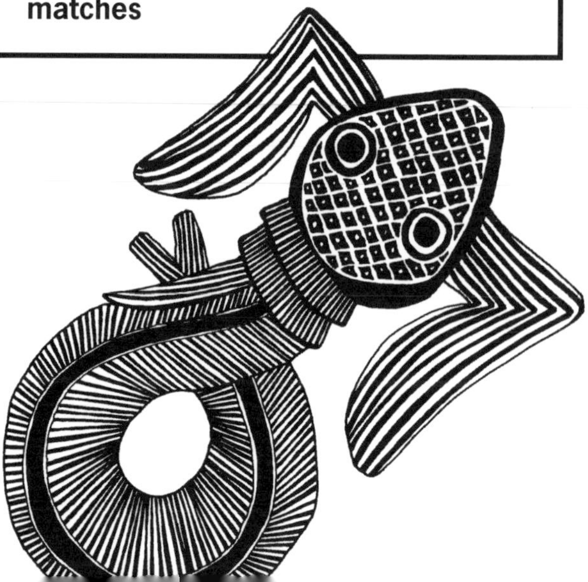

ake or Break
ıere is very heavy rain. In your hurry find shelter you drop something. What it?

Make or Break
Soldiers are looking for people from your village. Destroy any identification you have.

ake or Break
u pass a field full of tomatoes and other getables. Have meal. Throw again.

Make or Break
A lorry passes by on the bumpy track. A bag of rice falls off. Move on three spaces.

ake or Break
eavy rain again and no shelter in sight. n you make a shelter from the things u have? If not, miss a go.

Make or Break
You lose your way in an area that you know is landmined. Go back to the last LANDMINE square.

ake or Break
e United Nations has recognised that rmese refugees and internally displaced ople are in need of emergency aid. Go the next CAMP PERMIT square and try obtain a permit.

Make or Break
You hear shooting nearby. Hide and wait until night comes. Miss a turn.

ake or Break
lorry offers you a lift. Throw again.

Make or Break
You have blisters on your feet and a bad back. Have a day's rest. Miss a turn.

ake or Break
u lose your way. Miss two turns.

Make or Break
The rain stops and you can make better progress. Move on two squares.

ake or Break
meone you know has become an icial in the refugee camp. Move to the xt CAMP PERMIT square and try and t a permit.

Make or Break
Have you got any food left? If not, your family must stay put while one person goes to find some. Stay where you are until someone throws a 'three'.

ake or Break
u meet someone on the road who offers u money for one of your valuables. He ants a cooking pot or some metal plates. ill you sell anything?

Make or Break
You are hungry and spot a goat in the distance. If you can catch it with your rope and kill it with your knife, have another throw.

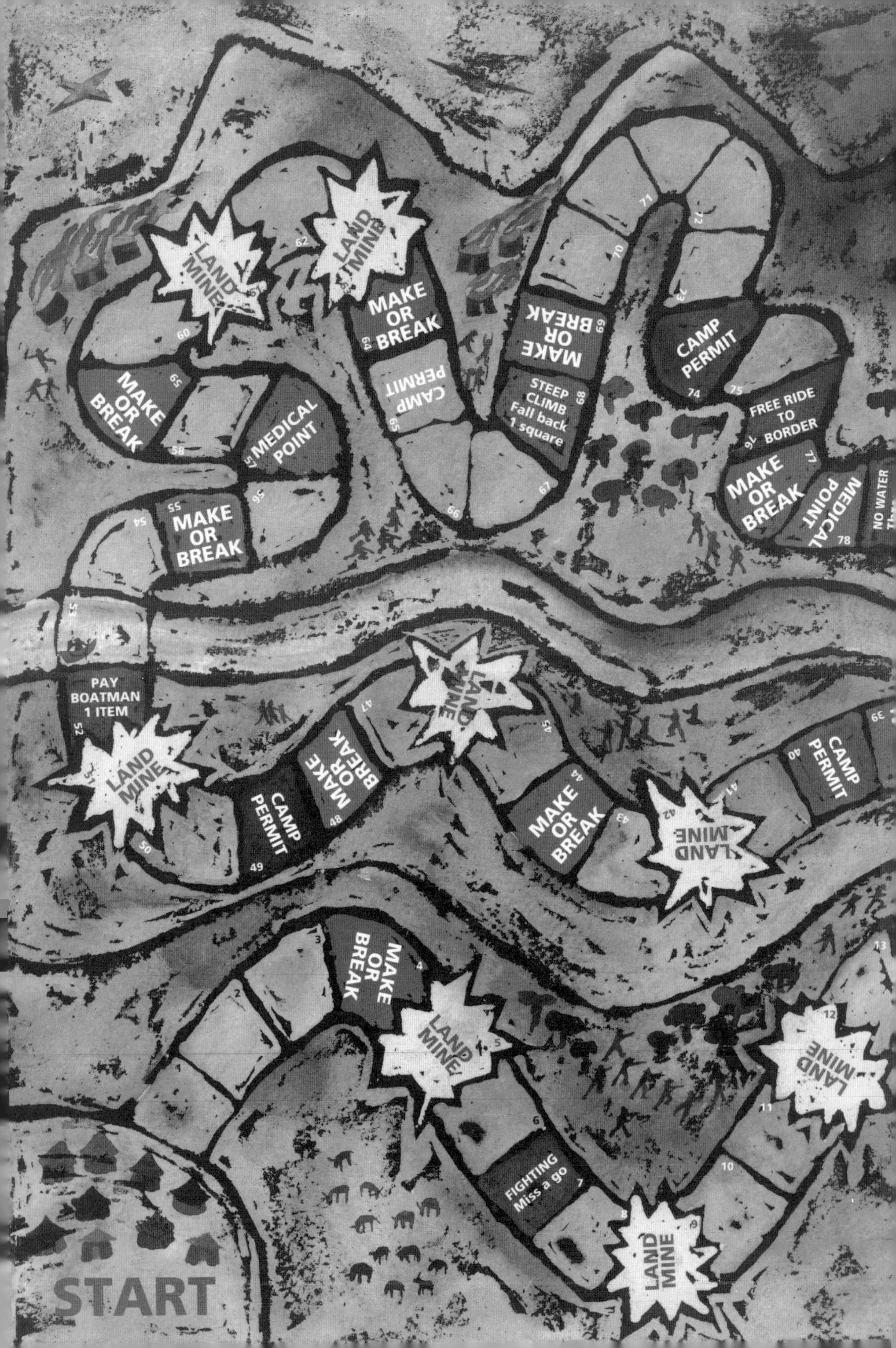
START
MAKE OR BREAK
LAND MINE
FIGHTING Miss a go
LAND MINE
LAND MINE
CAMP PERMIT
LAND MINE
MAKE OR BREAK
LAND MINE
MAKE OR BREAK
CAMP PERMIT
LAND MINE
PAY BOATMAN 1 ITEM
MAKE OR BREAK
MEDICAL POINT
MAKE OR BREAK
LAND MINE
LAND MINE
MAKE OR BREAK
CAMP PERMIT
STEEP CLIMB Fall back 1 square
MAKE OR BREAK
CAMP PERMIT
FREE RIDE TO BORDER
MAKE OR BREAK
MEDICAL POINT
NO WATER

REFUGEE CAMP
LAND MINE 95
96
94
93
LOSE YOUR WAY Go back 3 squares 91
90
LAND MINE 89
LAND MINE 92
88
87
LAND MINE 86
NIGHT ROUTE 85
BORDER 84
83
82
LAND MINE 81
MAKE OR 80
85
86
87
88
89
NO FOOD Throw a 5 to continue 90
91
92
MAKE OR BREAK CARD
MAKE OR BREAK 37
36
LAND MINE 35
34
MAKE OR BREAK 33
32
LAND MINE 31
30
29
LAND MINE 28
MAKE OR BREAK 27
26
CAMP PERMIT 25
MAKE OR BREAK 24
SHORT CUT Move 3 squares 23
22
LAND MINE 21
20
19
18
MAKE OR BREAK 17
16
15
14

Make or Break
Torrential rain washes landmines on to your path. Move to the next LANDMINE square.

Make or Break
Bandits attack. Lose all money, jewellery, radio or animals.

Make or Break
You find a stray goat. Take it with you.

Make or Break
You are attacked by bandits. You lose all the money you have.

Make or Break
You meet someone from your village. They tell you that your favourite aunt managed to escape and has reached the safety of Bangladesh. You are happy. Have an extra go.

Make or Break
You hear an aeroplane pass overhead. Run and hide in the forest. Miss a go.

Make or Break
Your youngest child wanders off while you are sleeping. Move back five spaces.

Make or Break
A lone soldiers stops you. At first you are scared, but he only wants money. If you have money or a gold necklace, give it to him. If not miss two goes.

Make or Break
You get malaria. Do you have any money to buy tablets? If not miss three goes.

Make or Break
You meet a family you helped earlier. They ask you to share their meal. Have a extra go.

Make or Break
You drink some dirty water and feel very sick. Do you have medicine for an upset stomach? If not, miss a go.

Make or Break
You meet a group of human rights research-ers and they offer you a lift in their Land Rover. Move to the next CAMP PERMIT square and try and get a camp permit.

Make or Break
You pass through a deserted village. Ther is a well. If you have a water pot, fill it u and move to the next blank square. If no just have a drink.

Make or Break
You meet someone who knows how to cross the river and get to the refugee camp. Move to the next CAMP PERMIT square and try and get a permit.

Make or Break
You have a very disturbing nightmare about being attacked by soldiers. It makes you feel anxious all next day. Miss a go.

Make or Break
You have run out of water. Your family must stay where they are until one perso goes to find some. Stay where you are until one person throws a 'six'.

The Kurds

Kurdish refugee in London *David Hoffman*

About 20 million people identify themselves as Kurds. They live in Armenia, Azerbaijan, Iran, Iraq, Syria and Turkey. The Kurds have been persecuted since the 1920s. Today there are about 400,000 Kurdish refugees in the Middle East and Europe and another 1,500,000 internally displaced Kurds.

Where the Kurds live

Most Kurds live in the mountains of the Caucasus, eastern Turkey, northern Iraq and north west Iran. Kurdish people have a strong cultural identity which is different from their Turkish, Arab or Iranian neighbours.

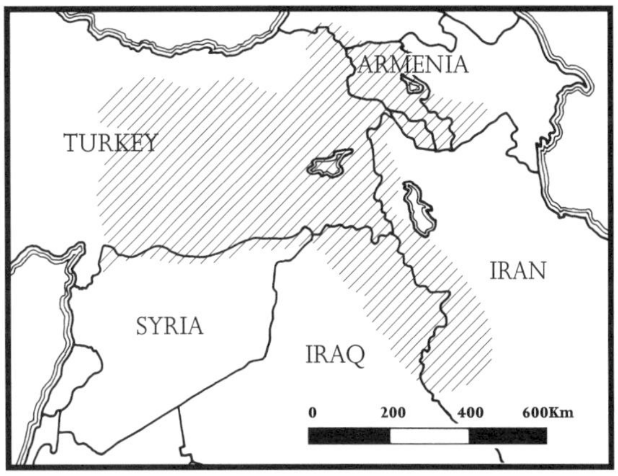

The origins of the Kurds are uncertain, but it is thought that they have lived in this region for at least 4,000 years. In the years before the First World War the Kurds lived under the control of the Ottoman and Persian Empires. When the Ottoman Empire was divided up at the end of the First World War the Kurds found themselves divided between five countries.

Country	No of Kurdish People	% of Population
Armenia & Azerbaijan	265,000	2
Iran	5,000,000	10
Iraq	3,900,000	23
Turkey	9,600,000	19
Syria	900,000	8

Kurdish refugees are living in Iran, Iraq and European countries such as Britain, Germany and Sweden.

Language

Most Kurds speak the Kurdish language - it is central to their identity as Kurds. The Kurdish language is most closely

Karen Robinson

related to Persian.

In Turkey it was forbidden to speak Kurdish from 1935 until 1991. It is now legal to speak Kurdish in Turkey, but the Kurdish language cannot be used in political speeches or in newspapers. As a result very few Turkish Kurds can read or write Kurdish. In Iran it was also forbidden to speak Kurdish for many years.

Events - Turkey

The Kurds mostly live in the mountainous parts of eastern Turkey. This part of the country is the poorest. There are fewer roads, schools and industries. Unemployment is much higher in Turkish Kurdistan than in the rest of Turkey. In rural areas most Kurds are farmers.

The Ottoman Empire The Kurds were ruled by the Ottoman Empire for 400 years. Kurdish nationalism began to develop in the 19th century and there were several revolts against Turkish rulers. It was at this time that the Turks began the deportation of Kurds. Whole villages were transferred to areas which were judged not to support the rebels.

During the early years of the 20th century the Kurds suffered at the hands of Turkish nationalists. In 1908 there was a *coup d'etat* in Turkey and the Ottoman Sultan was replaced by a more democratic government. The *coup d'etat* was led by the 'Young Turks' who were very nationalistic. Minority groups such as the Armenians and Kurds suffered in their hands. The new government denied that the Kurds formed a different ethnic group.

1918–1960 At the end of the First World War the Ottoman Empire was broken up. The Kurds hoped for an independent country. The Treaty of Sevres was signed in 1920 between Turkey and the Allied powers (including Britain). It promised autonomy for both Armenians and Kurds. But this never happened. In 1923 the Treaty of Lausanne was signed. The signatories included Britain, France, Italy, Japan, Romania, Serbia and Turkey. The Treaty of Lausanne divided the Kurds between five countries: Turkey, Iraq, Iran, Syria and the Soviet Union. The reaction of the Kurds was to rebel. Two rebellions in 1923 and 1927 were put down very harshly. At least 100,000 Kurds were killed. New laws were passed which forbade the use of the Kurdish language. All Kurdish schools, organisations and publications were also forbidden.

1960–1995 During the 1960s and 1970s Kurdish political parties were formed. Almost all of them called for political independence for Kurdish people. The best known party is called the PKK which uses guerrilla tactics against the Turkish state. The Turkish government has responded by arresting, torturing and killing all those Kurds who they suspect of supporting Kurdish political parties. The army often enters villages which it suspects of supporting PKK guerrillas. In order to try and frighten Kurdish villagers, men are often detained and tortured. Some are executed. Large numbers of Turkish soldiers are based in eastern Turkey.

Human rights groups in Turkey say that at least one million Kurds have been displaced. Amnesty International estimate that since 1980 some 250,000 Kurds have been tortured in prison. In 1980 over 15,000 Kurdish people have been killed in eastern Turkey.

In 1993 the PKK moved its military bases into Iraqi Kurdistan. The Turkish army has entered Iraqi Kurdistan on many occasions. In early 1995 the Turkish army invaded Iraqi Kurdistan in an attempt to crush the PKK guerrillas. Many innocent Kurds were killed in the fighting.

Refugees
Kurds have been leaving Turkey since the 1970s. Many live in Britain, Germany or Sweden. In 1989 there were local elections in the Maras region of Turkey. Kurds live in this area. One of the winners of the elections was a man who was suspected of organising a massacre of Kurds. After this many Kurds feared for their future and fled to countries such as Britain and Germany.

In 1994, after a worsening of the human rights situation in eastern Turkey, nearly 20,000 Turkish Kurds fled to Iraqi Kurdistan.

Iraq

Iraqi Kurds mostly live in the mountains of northern Iraq. Some Kurds are still nomadic farmers, following their grazing animals. Northern Iraq has rich oil reserves.

1923–1980 As in Turkey, Iraqi Kurds have long desired autonomy. In 1958 a group of Kurds, led by Mullah Mustafa Barzani, founded the Kurdish Democratic Party. It called for Kurdish autonomy in Iraq. This demand was rejected by the Iraqi government. After this Barzani returned to Iraqi Kurdistan and started a guerrilla war against the Iraqi government.

In 1974 the Iraqi government offered the Kurds some measure of autonomy. This was rejected and the civil war worsened. With military aid from Iran, and over 100,000 Kurdish fighters, Barzani launched a fierce attack against the Iraqi government. Over 250,000 refugees fled to Iran. In 1975 Iran signed an agreement with Iraq and withdrew its support for the Kurdish guerrillas. The Kurdish resistance collapsed.

The Iran–Iraq War 1980–88 During the Iran-Iraq War the Iranian government resumed its support for the Kurdish guerrillas. The Iraqi army was also tied down fighting the Iranians. The two main Kurdish guerrilla groups gained control of a large part of northern Iraq. Western countries, including Britain, supported the Iraqis during the Iran-Iraq war. Weapons that were manufactured in Britain were sold to Iraq. These weapons were used against the Kurds.

At the same time the Iraqi government tried to solve the Kurdish 'problem' by moving Kurds from northern Iraq and resettling them in the south. This did not happen peacefully and Amnesty International records forced evictions of Kurdish villagers and other human rights abuses. An estimated 500,000 Kurds were deported from their homes and many Kurdish villages were destroyed. It is believed that over 100,000 people were killed during this time.

From 1987 the Iraqi government began to use chemical weapons against the Kurds. In March 1988 6,000 Kurdish people were killed in a chemical weapons attack on the town of Halabja.

The Iran-Iraq War came to an end on 20 August 1988. During the next two weeks the Iraqi army drove Kurdish fighters out of the area under Kurdish control. The Iraqi army used saturation bombing and chemical weapons to do this. Over 450 Kurdish villages were destroyed at this time. Thousands of people were killed and 80,000 people fled as refugees to Iran and Turkey.

The Kurds and chemical weapons
Chemical weapons were certainly used against the Iraqi Kurds in August 1988 even though the Iraqi government has signed the 1925 Geneva Protocol on Chemical Weapons. This international law forbids the use of chemical weapons against other countries which have signed the law. It is unclear whether the 1925 Geneva Protocol on Chemical Weapons forbids a government to use chemical weapons against its own people.

In August 1988 the UN Security Council passed Resolution 620 which condemned Iraq's use of chemical weapons. Resolution 620 was passed just a few days after Iraq used chemical weapons on Kurdish villages. It called for appropriate sanctions to punish Iraq if chemical weapons were used again.

Mahmut's story

Mahmut is studying in a north London school. He is 13 years old.

'I am Kurdish. I speak Turkish and I understand Kurdish but I can't read or write them. I came to London from Turkey when I was eight. In Turkey we start school when we are seven so I didn't know much about school when I came to London.

I've been in six different schools in four years and lived in five different houses. Each time I changed schools I had to make new friends which was very hard. My little brother used to cry because it was so hard for him to get used to each new school. I used to get really hurt when other children teased me and made me look stupid because I didn't know English. When you're new you get picked on a lot. It sometimes happens even now.

We came to London because of the political situation in Turkey. People were always harassing and terrorising Kurdish people. I wish people understood more about refugees and had more respect for people's different backgrounds.

I interpret a lot at the doctor's, solicitor's, DSS and job centres. I don't take as much time off school for this as I used to. My mother is learning English and my brother can help now too.

I'd like to be an interpreter, a teacher in a junior school or a computer operator. I also want to travel to visit my relatives in Cyprus, France and Germany.'

There is evidence that the Iraqi government used gas on other Kurdish villages within two days of Resolution 620 being passed. The Iraqi government then denied that it had done so. No member of the UN Security Council took any action against Iraq. No government introduced economic sanctions against Iraq.

Failure to punish Iraq may encourage it, and other governments, to believe they can use chemical weapons against people and escape punishment.

1989–1995 In 1990 Iraq invaded Kuwait. In early 1991 the Gulf War started. A joint armed force backed by the UN and led by 500,000 US troops declared war on Iraq. Some 42,000 British troops were sent to the Gulf. The Iraqi government, led by Saddam Hussein withdrew from Kuwait in February 1991.

Following the defeat of the Iraqi army there was a widespread uprising in many parts of Iraq including Kurdistan. It was followed by massive Iraqi reprisals. The Iraqi army quickly overran the Kurds. Fearing what may happen to them next, some 1.5 million Kurds fled to Turkey and Iran. Thousands of Kurds died in the cold mountains at this time.

The Kurdish refugees began returning after the USA and other troops established a 'safe-haven' covering north east Kurdistan.

Kurdish leaders held talks with the Iraqi government in August 1991 but these soon broke down. In October 1991 the Iraqi government withdrew all troops, funds, and services from much of Iraqi Kurdistan. The Iraqis stopped all travel into Kurdistan.

The Iraqi Kurds have now set up their own government. A Kurdish parliament was elected in May 1992. But there are many problems facing the Iraqi Kurds. There has been fighting between the two largest Iraqi political parties. Iraqi Kurdistan is not a recognised country so it cannot get any aid from governments or the UN. The passage of basic supplies into Iraqi Kurdistan is dependent on the Turkish government. The Turks are opposed to any independent Kurdish state.

About 700,000 Iraqi Kurds are displaced in Iraqi Kurdistan having fled their homes in 1991. There are about 40,000 Kurdish refugees living in Iraq.

Personal responsibility to refugees

Aims

To help students reflect on personal responsibilities to refugees.

Instructions

Time needed: Students will have to do some prior preparation. At least 50 minutes is needed in a class or group.

Students should be given task one to complete before a lesson. The remaining tasks should be completed during the lesson in small groups.

Task one

Find out what responsibility means. You can:

- Ask your family
- Look it up in a dictionary
- Ask your teacher
- See what your friends think

Task two

You have some more ideas about what responsibility means. With the other members of your group compare the ideas that you have from task one. Then try and fill in the gaps on the diagram below.

Discussion point

- Does responsibility mean different things to different people? Why?

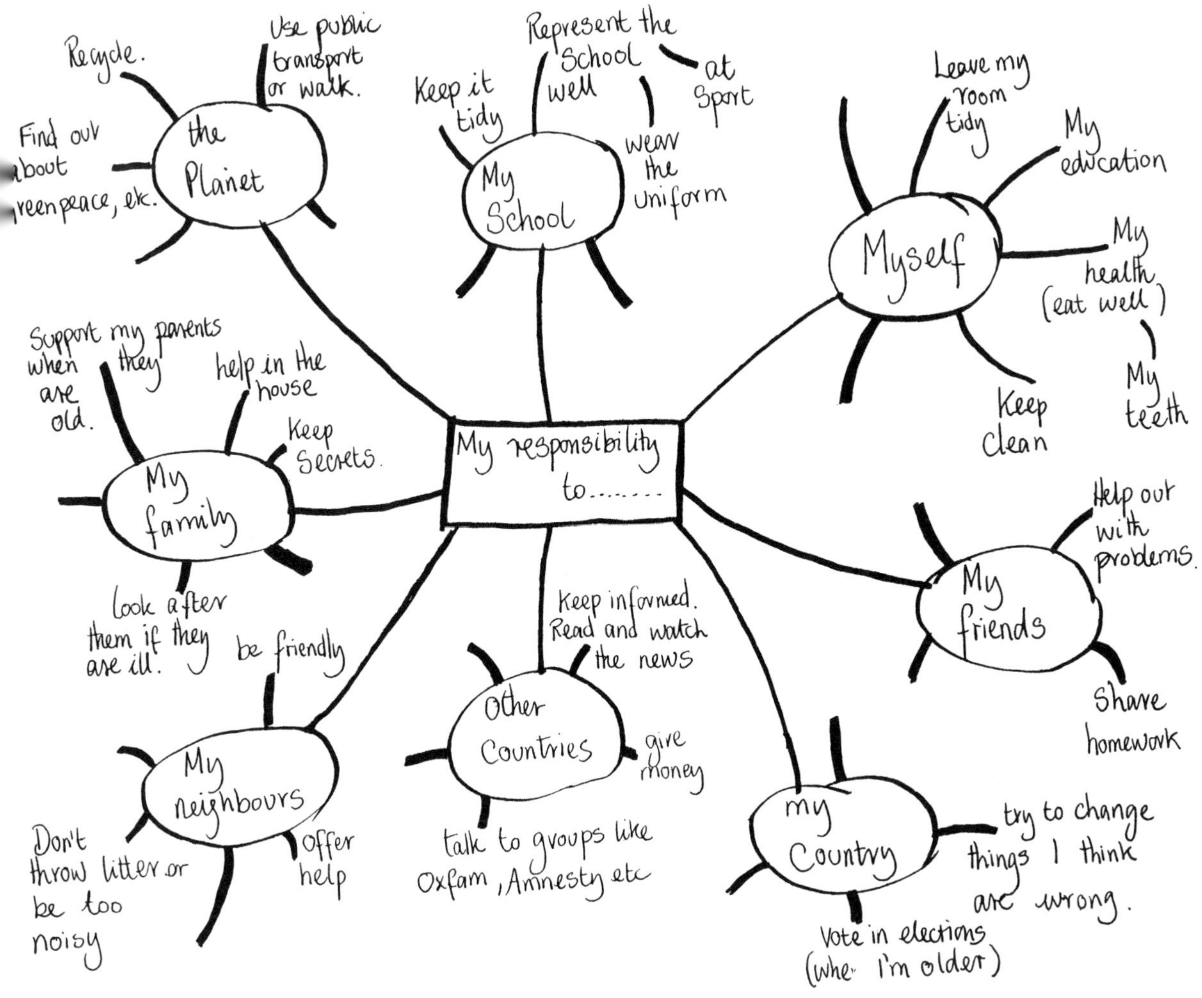

Task three

Read the background information on the Kurds. Think about the work that you have just completed about responsibility. Then look at the comments made in the speech bubbles. In your groups discuss what you think about each of the comments.

Write down whether you agreed with the comments or not, and your reasons.

'Kurdish refugees are not my problem'

'Someone else can help Kurdish refugees'

'It is up to politicians to sort out the problems facing the Kurds'

International links with the Kurds

Find out about Britain's links with the Kurds at different times in history:

- **Between 1920 and 1923**
- **During the Iran-Iraq War**
- **In 1988 when chemical weapons were used against the Kurds**
- **During the Gulf War**
- **In 1995 when Turkey invaded Iraqi Kurdistan**

Aim

To get students to debate Britain's links with the Kurdish conflict and about international responsibility and obligations.

Instructions

At least one hour is needed for this activity. Students will need the information above and also extra supporting inforamtion about the Kurds. 'Voices from Kurdistan' (Minority Rights Group) and 'The Kurds' (John King, Wayland) can be used, plus any press cuttings that have been saved.

Divide the group up into fours. Get them to research Britain's links with the Kurds at varying times in history.

Each group should then prepare arguments for a debate. Half of the groups should argue for the motion below, the other half against. The groups should elect one person to make a four minute presentation. The subject for the debate is

'The British government has a responsibility to help the Kurdish people'.

The Palestinians

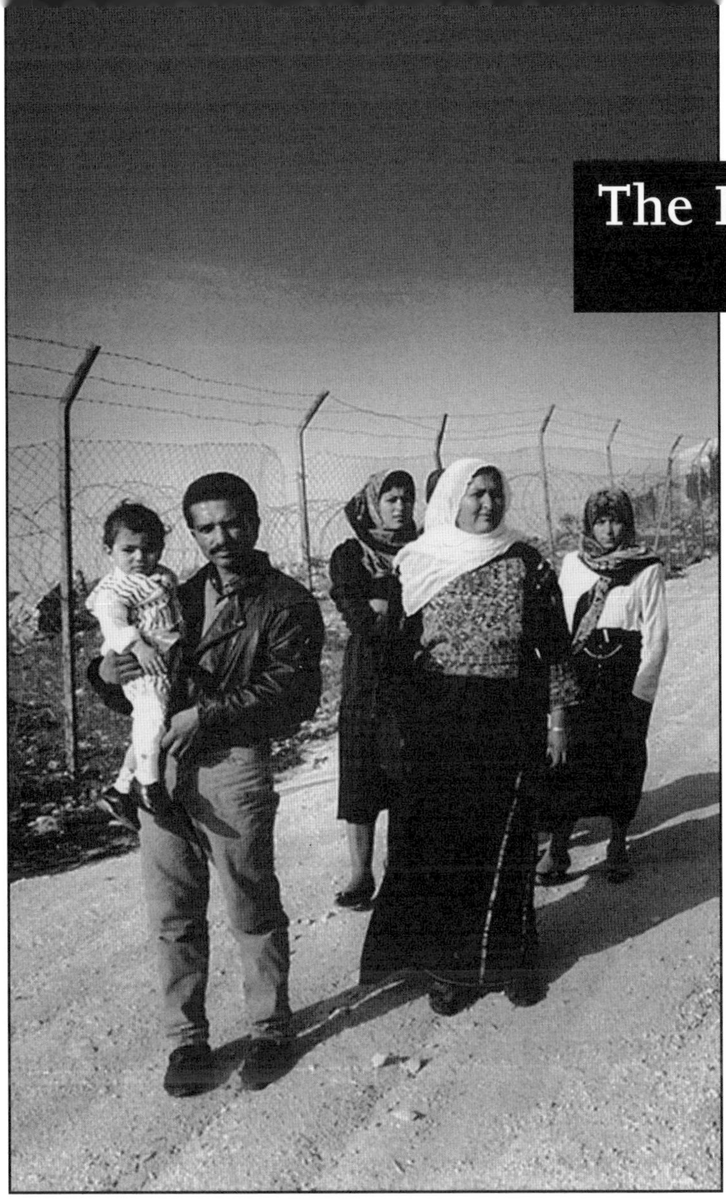

Over 6,194,000 Palestinians live in many different countries. Some Palestinians have been refugees for 45 years. The Oslo Peace Agreement signed in 1993 should provide for the Palestinian refugees of 1948 and 1967.

Palestinian family whose land has been taken by a new Israeli settlement *Howard Davies*

Where the Palestinians live
900,000 in the West Bank
1,100,000 in the Gaza Strip
1,850,000 in Jordan
890,000 in Israel, including East Jerusalem
350,000 in Europe, USA and South America
450,000 in Lebanon
344,000 in Syria
135,000 in Saudi Arabia
100,000 in other Gulf States
70,000 in Iraq
105,000 in Egypt

Some 2,800,000 Palestinians are registered with the United Nations Relief and Works Agency for Palestine Refugees in the Near East (UNRWA). This UN organisation provides education, health and relief services to Palestinian refugees who are living in the Gaza Strip, West Bank, Jordan, Syria and Lebanon. Not all Palestinians who are living in these countries are registered as refugees with UNRWA.

Events

200 BC The land that now forms Israel is occupied by several different ethnic groups including Jews and Philistines. The Philistines give their name to the land of Palestine.

63 BC The Romans colonise Palestine. In 70AD the Romans destroy the Temple of Solomon in Jerusalem. Many Jews flee to north Africa, Spain, Turkey, Greece and other parts of the Middle East. During the next 1,500 years descendants of these Jews move to France, Germany, Poland, Russia and other European countries.

1516 The Ottoman Turks capture Palestine. The Arabic-speaking population numbers about 600,000 people. The majority are Muslims but some are Christians. Palestine becomes part of the Ottoman Empire.

Late 19th century Nationalist political

movements begin to develop throughout the Arab world. The population of Palestine begins to identify itself as being 'Palestinian'.

1881–1917 There is increased persecution of Jews living in the Russian Empire. Millions of Jews flee from eastern Europe to western Europe and north America. A small number arrive in Palestine including members of an organisation called *Hovevei Zion*.

1897 Theodor Herzl, an Hungarian Jewish journalist, founds the World Zionist Organisation in Switzerland. Herzl believes that Jewish people can only be safe in a Jewish homeland. Herzl meets with political leaders in order to find this homeland; possibilities include Uganda and Palestine.

1917–1919 The Ottoman Turks fight against the British during the First World War. In 1917 the British capture Palestine. Some 640,000 Palestinian Arabs and 56,000 Jews live in Palestine. The Jewish community makes up eight per cent of the total population.

After the British gain control of Palestine, Lord Balfour, the British Foreign Secretary, promises British support for a Jewish homeland in the Middle East. His promise becomes known as the 'Balfour Declaration'.

'His Majesty's government view with favour the establishment in Palestine of a National Home for the Jewish People, and will use their best endeavours to facilitate the achievement of this object, it being clearly understood that nothing shall be done to prejudice the civil and religious rights of existing non-Jewish communities in Palestine...' (Extract *from the Balfour Declaration*).

At the end of the First World War, the Ottoman Empire is dismantled, and Palestine is administered by the British under a League of Nations Mandate.

1920–1930 The Jewish Agency buys land titles from absent Palestinian landlords. Palestinian farmers, who have farmed their land for centuries, have no idea that the land titles exist, but as a consequence of the sale, are evicted from their land.

The 1920s also see growing opposition to Jewish immigration by the Palestinian Arab community. This opposition ends in a violent demonstration in 1929.

1930s Jewish guerrilla groups such as Irgun and the Stern Gang are formed to fight for independence from the British. Many of those active in these guerrilla groups become future leaders of Israel including Menachim Begin and Itzhak Shamir.

1933–1945 The Nazi persecution of Jews in Europe: Jewish people are desperate to leave Nazi-occupied Europe, but are refused entry to the USA, UK and her colonies. Many Jewish refugees enter Palestine illegally.

1936 A revolt by the Palestinian Arabs against British policies. The revolt ends when Britain sets up a Royal Commission under Lord Peel to investigate the problem. It rules in favour of the partition of Palestine, dividing Arab and Jewish communities.

1937–38 The Arab Revolt against the British. Some Palestinians, worried about their future in a country that is becoming more and more Jewish, turn to violent protest. Britain brings in more troops and many people are killed.

1939 The British try and stop Jewish immigration to Palestine.

1945 The end of the Second World War. The horrors of the Nazi Holocaust are seen by the world. Many of the remaining Jewish communities in eastern Europe feel they have no future there, and seek to emigrate to Palestine.

1946 Irgun blows up the King David Hotel in Jerusalem. Some 98 people are killed, including 41 Palestinians and 28 British.

1947 Britain gives notice that it wishes to leave Palestine. The UN Partition Plan proposes that Palestine be divided. Most Jews accept the plan, but Palestinians reject it because it gives 54 per cent of the land - mostly in fertile areas - to the Jews.

1948 The violence worsens. The Stern

Gang assassinate Count Bernadotte, a UN mediator. Many Palestinians leave their homes, some are driven from their homes by force, including those who live near the village of Deir Yassin. Here 254 men, women and children are murdered by Irgun. By mid-1948 300,000 Palestinians are refugees.

On 14 May 1948 the State of Israel is proclaimed, with David Ben-Gurion as its first Prime Minister.

1948–49 The First Arab-Israeli War. Arab armies from Lebanon, Syria, Jordan, Egypt and Iraq invade Israel. Although Israel suffers heavy losses, it wins and captures new territory. Some 725,000 Palestinians flee as refugees in *al Kakba* (the catastrophe). Israel now controls 73 per cent of the land that was Palestine.

held
ael
he
g of
949
tice

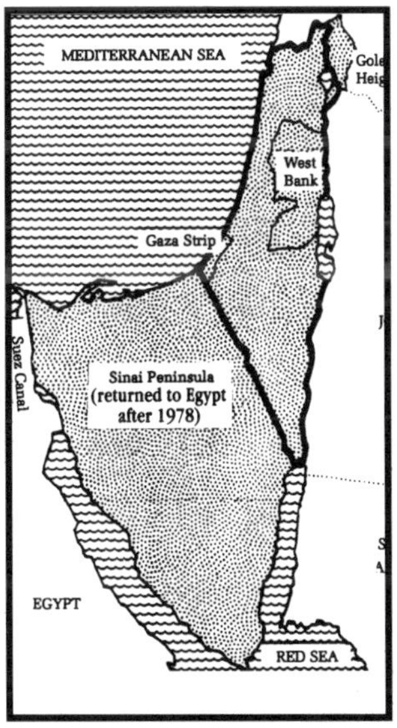

1948 onwards Many Jewish people arrive in Israel from Europe, North and South America, North Africa and the Middle East. Some arrive as refugees, others migrate for economic, religious or political reasons. All Jewish people and their close relatives have the right to live in Israel under the 'Law of Return'. But Palestinian refugees who fled from their homes in 1948 and after, are not allowed back.

1956 The Second Arab-Israeli War. The Egyptians nationalise the Suez Canal, which threatens British and French interests. They give Israel military support and encourage it to attack Egypt. The Gaza Strip and Sinai desert are captured by Israel, but handed back after protests from the UN.

1964 Founding of the Palestine Liberation Organisation (PLO). This is an umbrella organisation to which many Palestinian political groups belong. The PLO lobbies governments for support. Its member organisations also have military wings which launch attacks on Israeli targets.

1967 The Six Day War. Israel captures Gaza, the West Bank, the Golan Heights and the Sinai desert, and annexes East Jerusalem. Some 260,000 Palestinian refugees flee to Jordan. The Palestinian population of Jordan then numbers 1,100,000 people.

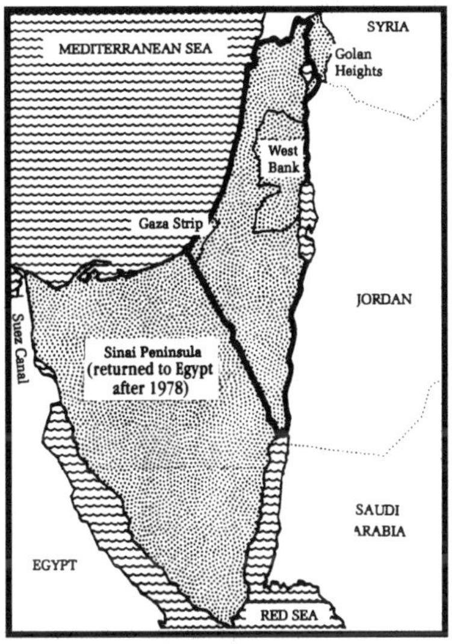

Land held by Israel after the 1967 war

In November 1967 the UN passes Resolution 242. This states that the 1949 armistice line should form the borders of Israel, that Israel should withdraw from the territories that it captured in the Six Day War, and that there should be a settlement to the refugee problem.

1970–71 Black September. There is fighting between Palestinian guerrillas and Jordanians. Most Palestinian fighters are forced to leave Jordan, and move to Lebanon.

1972 Palestinian guerrillas kill Israeli athletes at the Munich Olympic Games.

1973 The Yom Kippur War (known in the Arab World as the October War). Syria and Egypt attack in an attempt to win back land. After initial success, the Syrian and Egyptian armies are pushed back, and lose more territory.

1974 Yassir Arafat, the PLO leader, offers a choice between 'a gun and an olive branch' at the UN. Arab countries recognise the PLO as the sole legitimate representative of the Palestinian people.

1975 PLO guerrillas, based in Lebanon,

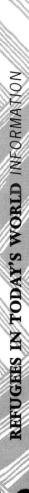

Arab A person whose first language is Arabic. Until the growth of Palestinian nationalism in the late 19th century, the Palestinians considered themselves to be Arabs. Now they call themselves Palestinians. Many Jewish Israelis still call the Palestinians 'Arabs'. The reasons for this are complex, but basically it is a rejection of the Palestinian claim to a country called Palestine.

Israeli Someone who is a citizen of the State of Israel. Israeli citizens include Jews, Palestinian Arabs, Bedouin Arabs, Druze and other minorities. But Israeli citizens who are Palestinian Arabs face discrimination in housing, employment and social security. Most Israeli Palestinians do not serve in the army, but many job advertisements call for army service.

Jew Someone whose mother is Jewish or has been converted to the religion of Judaism.

Palestinian Someone whose family originates from what was called Palestine before 1948. The majority of Palestinians are Muslim but some are Christian.

launch raids on northern Israel.

1977 Jewish settlements in the West Bank are built in increasing numbers.

1978 Israel invades southern Lebanon, but withdraws after pressure from the UN and the USA. Israel and Egypt sign a peace agreement at Camp David in the USA. The Sinai desert is to be handed back to Egypt. But President Sadat of Egypt is denounced by other Arab nations for betraying the Palestinians and making a separate peace with Israel.

1979 A crackdown on the occupied West Bank by the Israeli army is met by strikes and protests. Inside Israel a group of 27 high school students refuse to do their army service in the occupied West Bank and Gaza Strip.

1982 Israel invades Lebanon in 'Operation Peace for Galilee', to destroy the bases of Palestinian guerrillas. The guerrillas are forced to flee, but over 19,000 ordinary Palestinians and Lebanese are killed. Others are injured or have their homes destroyed. Over 600 Israeli soldiers lose their lives; as a result the Lebanese War is opposed by many Israelis.

In the summer of 1982 the PLO are forced to leave Beirut, supervised by UN peacekeeping soldiers. As soon as the PLO guerrillas leave, the UN also goes. In September 1982 the Israeli army watches as Lebanese Maronite soldiers massacre Palestinians living in Sabra and Chatilla refugee camps in Beirut. Over 2,000 Palestinians are murdered. Over 12 per cent of the Israeli population protest about Israel's role in the massacre. The demonstration, plus international pressure, force the Israeli army to withdraw from Beirut.

1983 The Israeli army is forced to withdraw to southern Lebanon. Here it arms and trains another force called the South Lebanese Army. The South Lebanese Army fights Palestinians and other guerrilla groups.

1987 There are riots in Gaza after an Israeli settler's truck hits a car containing four Palestinians. This is the start of the Palestinian uprising or *intifada*. Palestinian activists hold demonstrations and throw stones at Israeli soldiers in the West Bank and Gaza Strip. The resistance to Israeli occupation is well-organised. Within Israel there is increased tension between Israeli hardliners and 'doves' as to how to respond to the Palestinian *intifada*. The Israeli Labour Party calls for withdrawal from the West Bank and Gaza Strip negotiated with non-PLO Palestinians. Hardliners call for tough military action to suppress the uprising. A few right-wing extremists believe that Israel should annexe the West Bank and Gaza Strip and expel the Palestinians to other Arab states.

1989 The Palestinian *intifada* enters its third year. Over 700 Palestinians have been killed and 80,000 injured by the Israeli army in the West Bank and Gaza Strip. Some 8,000 Palestinians have been imprisoned without being charged with any crime. Nearly 900 houses have been demolished or sealed, and schools and universities have been closed for most of the time.

1990 The Palestinian *intifada* continues and there are more deaths and injuries. A resurgence of anti-Semitism in the Soviet Union and economic collapse causes increasing numbers of Soviet Jews to arrive in Israel. There is pressure for them to settle in the West Bank.

1992 The Israeli Labour Party wins a narrow majority in the general election. Yitzhak Rabin becomes Prime Minister and Shimon Peres becomes Foreign Minister. The US government puts pressure on the Israeli government to negotiate a peace settlement with the Palestinians and other Arab nations.

International peace talks are started but there is little progress. But at the same time as peace talks are running, Israeli officials are having secret meetings with PLO officials.

The building of settlements in the West Bank is stopped, although private contractors are still allowed to build.

In the Gaza Strip and West Bank a greater number of Palestinians give their support to Hamas and other Islamic fundamentalist organisations. Hamas has a military wing which launches terrorist attacks on Jewish targets.

1993 The secret meetings between the Israeli government and the PLO continue in Oslo, Norway. In August 1993 the Israeli government and the PLO announce a breakthrough. On 13 September 1993 Yassir Arafat, Shimon Peres and Yitzhak Rabin sign a peace agreement. The peace agreement is made of three parts:

1. The PLO agrees to recognise the State of Israel. The Israeli government recognises the PLO as the representative of the Palestinian people. The Palestinians will be granted self-rule in phases starting with Gaza and Jericho.

2. Palestinian self-rule will be extended to another six West Bank towns and 450 villages.

3. Final negotiations will start to discuss the future of Jerusalem, the return of Palestinian refugees and the future of Jewish settlements in the West Bank. The final negotiations are meant to start by May 1996.

1994 Palestinian self-rule begins in Gaza, and Yassir Arafat returns. But the Palestinians face many social problems, particularly in the impoverished Gaza Strip. Here unemployment is very high.

Some 140,000 Israelis are living in settlements in the West Bank and Gaza Strip. Most of the settlers oppose the peace process. In February 1994, Baruch Goldstein, an extreme settler from Hebron, shoots and kills 29 Palestinians at the Tomb of the Patriachs, a Jewish and Muslim holy place in Hebron.

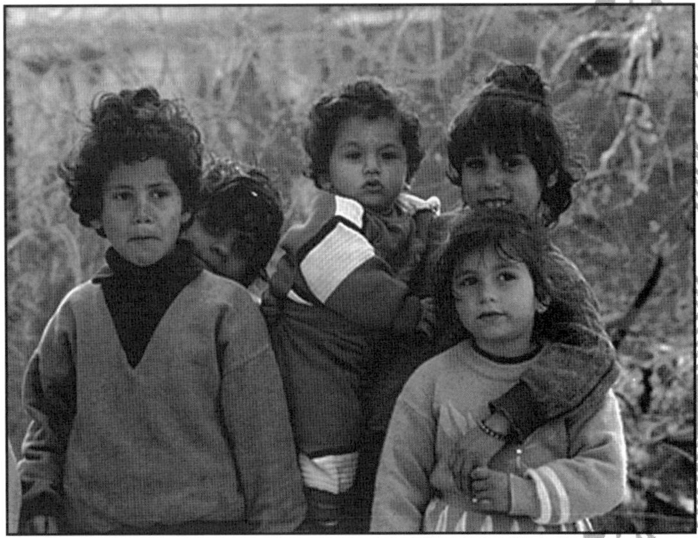

A peace agreement is signed with Jordan. Yassir Arafat, Yitzhak Rabin and Shimon Peres win the Nobel Peace Prize.

1995 Jewish and Arab opposition to the Oslo Peace Agreement increases. Some 17 Israelis are killed by a suicide bomber who boards a bus in Tel-Aviv. The bomber belongs to Hamas, the Islamic fundamentalist group.

The Palestinian Self Rule Authority and the Israeli Government sign the Oslo Two agreement. This means that the Israelis will give military, police and civil powers to the Palestinians in six West Bank cities and 450 surrounding villages. The Israelis will also partially withdraw from Hebron. But the Israelis still hold 70 per cent of the land in the West Bank, including all settlements, military bases and uncultivated land.

In November 1995 Prime Minister Yitzhak Rabin is assassinated at a peace rally in Tel-Aviv. His murderer is a Jewish law student who belongs to an extreme right-wing religious group opposed to the peace process. There is a great deal of revulsion in Israel at the assassination of Prime Minister Rabin. Shimon Peres becomes Prime Minister. He is determined to carry on with the peace process.

Children, Gaza Strip *Howard Davies*

*

Palestine Liberation Organisation (PLO) The PLO is an umbrella organisation founded in 1964. It represents different Palestinian groups. The PLO is recognised as the representative of the Palestinian people by the United Nations. The largest group within the PLO is Fatah, led by Yassir Arafat.

Zionism This is a political idea developed by Theodor Herzl, an Hungarian Jew, in the 1890s. Before the founding of the State of Israel, Zionism meant that Jewish people had a right to a nation. Today Zionist political parties support Israel as a state for Jewish people.

Afif Safieh's story

At the time he was interviewed Afif Safieh was a diplomat and working in London as the Palestinian Delegate to the UK. He has lived in exile for nearly 30 years. Afif Safieh's application to return home was blocked by the Israeli government.

'I was born in 1950 in East Jerusalem but I came from a family who has lived in West Jerusalem before 1948. My family was a Christian family. In May 1948 my family moved from West Jerusalem to East Jerusalem. They spent three months living as refugees in a school classroom. After this they spent some months as refugees in Lebanon and Syria before returning to East Jerusalem at the end of 1949. East Jerusalem and the West Bank of the Jordan were then part of Jordan. My father was a member of the Jordanian Parliament from 1963-66.

I lived in Jerusalem from my birth until 1966. After I finished High School in 1966 I left Jerusalem to go to Belgium to study at the Catholic University of Louvain. So when the 1967 War took place I was abroad, as was my brother. East Jerusalem was occupied during the war and then afterwards annexed by Israel. After the Israelis annexed East Jerusalem they conducted a census. I was not included as a resident of Jerusalem because I was abroad. I ceased to exist from the point of view of the Israeli government, as did a whole generation of Palestinian students. We were not allowed to return to Jerusalem because we were not considered as residents. My father used to say, "In 1967 we lost our country and in 1967 we lost our children." I have lived in exile since then, for nearly 30 years.

At University in Belgium, and then later in France, I was President of the General Union of Palestinian Students. In 1976 I started work for the Palestine Liberation Organisation's Observer Mission to the UN. Then from 1978-81 I worked for Chairman Arafat's office in Beirut.

When the Oslo Peace Agreement was announced I was interviewed by the BBC. I was asked how I felt about the peace agreement. I said I felt euphoric. I told all my colleagues and friends that I wanted to spend Christmas in Jerusalem. I wanted to take my family with me and to celebrate my daughter's first communion in Jerusalem. The dream became a reality. On 18th December 1993 I returned to Jerusalem. On 19th December 1993 we celebrated my daughter's first communion. The ceremony was officiated by the Patriarch of Jerusalem. The ceremony was meant to be a private affair, but over 800 people ended up coming, including all the mayors of West Bank towns and even Shulamit Aloni, a member of the Israeli government.

Returning to Jerusalem also meant that I could visit my father's grave. He died in 1983 but I was not allowed to be with him during his last days.

My feelings during that visit was that the Palestinians were living in a state of limbo, waiting for an end to occupation and waiting for a Palestinian state. Arab East Jerusalem was a sad place, it seemed to be in decline. This was when I thought of returning to Jerusalem to start an English language weekly magazine. I wanted to call the magazine 'The Palestinian'. I was told that I needed to apply for family reunion for this. My mother filled in the forms. These were delivered to the Israeli Ministry of the Interior in November 1994. The people who dealt with me in the Ministry were a Tunisian Jew and an Ethiopian Jew who had only arrived in Israel recently. My family had always lived in Jerusalem yet I had to apply to them to request family reunion.

The answer from the Ministry of the Interior was no.'

Conflict resolution

The Israeli government and the Palestinian Self Rule Authority have many issues to resolve before there can be long lasting peace in the Middle East. Conflicts that must be resolved include:

◆ **Independence or self rule?** Will an independent Palestinian state be formed or not?

◆ **Borders** Where will the final borders of a Palestinian state or autonomous area be?

◆ **Jerusalem** Will the Palestinians be given control over any part of Jerusalem? The Palestinians want to base their capital city in East Jerusalem. The Israeli government believes that Jerusalem should be the undivided capital of Israel.

◆ **Refugees** How many Palestinian refugees from 1948 and 1967 will be able to return? The Palestinian Self Rule Authority believe that 800,000 Palestinian refugees should be allowed to return. The Israeli government states that 200,000 people should be allowed to return.

◆ **Compensation** Will Israel grant compensation to Palestinian refugees who lost their property in 1948?

◆ **Settlers** The Palestinian Self Rule Authority would like to see the dismantling of Jewish settlements in the West Bank and Gaza Strip. Will the settlers be forced to move?

◆ **Military bases** There are many Israeli military bases in the West Bank. Will these be dismantled after a final peace agreement?

These issues are resolved in negotiations between Israeli and Palestinian officials.

But the 50 year conflict in the Middle East has had a enormous effect on the lives of ordinary Israelis and Palestinians. Many people have died, others have been wounded or lost their homes. There is still a lot of hatred and prejudice on both sides of the conflict. As well as governmental peace talks, there is a need for ordinary Israeli and Palestinian people to come together to resolve conflicts. There are now a small number of conflict resolution projects in the Middle East where Israelis and Palestinians meet, discuss their differences and try and move forward.

One conflict resolution project is *Neve Shalom/Wahat al-Salam*. The name means 'oasis of peace' in Hebrew and Arabic.

Neve Shalom/Wahat al-Salam is located in the countryside between Jerusalem and Tel-Aviv. It consists of a village and educational centre.

Neve Shalom/Wahat al-Salam is the only village in Israel where Jews and Palestinian Arabs of Israeli citizenship have chosen to live together. In the village there is a bilingual nursery and primary school attended by Jewish and Arab children. This is very unusual in Israel, as most Arab and Jewish children are educated separately.

Within *Neve Shalom/Wahat al-Salam* is the School for Peace. This is an educational centre which runs workshops and courses on the Jewish-Palestinian conflict. The courses are attended by both Jews and Palestinians. Some of the most important courses are with young people and teachers. *Neve Shalom/Wahat al-Salam* organises a Youth Encounter Programme. In Israel, Jewish and Palestinian young people rarely get the chance to meet each other. To overcome this problem some schools encourage students to attend *Neve Shalom/Wahat al-Salam's* Youth Encounter Programme. Some 30 Jewish and 30 Palestinian young people meet each other for a four-day workshop. The participants get the chance to talk to people from 'the other side'.

Neve Shalom/Wahat al-Salam trains teachers. By doing this it hopes that school teachers will be better equipped to promote conflict resolution within their schools. *Neve Shalom/Wahat al-Salam* also offers training to people working in other areas of ethnic conflict throughout the world.

What is conflict resolution?

The activities that are carried out at *Neve Shalom/Wahat al-Salam* are intended to help resolve a long standing conflict in the Middle East. Conflict resolution is all about creating a peaceful alternative to a situation of despair. Conflict resolution is a process, not a set of easy answers.

There are five different stages in conflict resolution.

1. Agreeing that there is a need to get together to resolve a conflict.

2. Affirmation - getting together, and recognising that people on the 'other side' are human beings and have good qualities too.

3. Communication - talking to people on the 'other side' of the conflict, about beliefs and needs.

4. Cooperation - working together.

5. Problem solving - coming up with solutions to the conflict that everyone supports.

The workshops that take place at *Neve Shalom/Wahat al-Salam* help young Jews and Palestinians progress through the five stages, and resolve conflicts.

Conflict resolution

Aims

The activities below are used in conflict resolution work throughout the world. Students may like to use them to resolve conflicts within their schools or groups. Alternatively they can be used to give students a feel of what conflict resolution involves.

Affirmation activity

Big sheets of paper and marker pens are needed. Each participant is asked to write their name in block capitals on the sheet of paper. He/she then tells the group about how he/she got the name, whether he/she likes it and so on. If the person is known by a nickname get them to write it down too, and to talk about it.

Building bridges

This is an activity to encourage communication, cooperation and problem solving. At least two hours are needed for this activity.

1. The group should be divided into pairs. Each pair should list several controversial issues relevant to their lives that they thought would divide the group.

2. The group should then come together and make a list of the issues. Participants should be asked to state their position on each issue. Those issues that do not divide the group should be struck off the list.

3. The group should select the two most important issues. The participants then have the opportunity to practise coalition building skills. Two volunteers should present the case for choosing one or other of the issues. They should do this in such a way that the whole group does not know what positiion they took on the issue they were presenting as being important.

4. Participants should then vote on the most important issue to be tackled.

5. Two members of the group who feel strongly about the issues, but saw it from opposite points of view should then be asked to come to the front.

Person A should be asked to state their case. Person B has to listen carefully and then verbally summarise the points made by Person A. Person A then has to say whether Person B has understood and repeated all the main points that he/she made. The process should then be reversed, with Person B stating their case. This part of the exercise encourages people to listen to each other.

6. Finally the group should identify areas of common ground between the two different opinions. The group should be broken down into pairs, to brainstorm areas of common ground. After this the whole group should come together for a plenary session.

Conflict resolution in the Middle East

Instructions

Time needed: 30 minutes

All students need a copy of the following information. Lots of small pieces of paper or post-its are also needed.

The students should be divided into pairs. Each pair needs to decide what is needed to make peace in the Middle East. The students should then write down all the things they believe will help create peace in the Middle East on the paper or post-its. (These are all the things they have answered with a 'yes'. One item should be written on each post-it.

Students should then try and rank the items in their list, into the ones most likely to help create peace and the ones least likely to create peace.

Students

Conflicts cause the large scale movements of refugees, as has been seen in the Middle East. If you think of peace as a state in which the possibility of conflict is reduced, which of these would help to create peace in the Middle East.

To have peace you need:

A strong Israeli army Yes/No

A ban on extremist political parties on both sides Yes/No

Freedom of speech Yes/No

The death sentence for terrorists Yes/No

The fair distribution of wealth between Israelis and Palestinians Yes/No

An end to the Israeli occupation of the West Bank Yes/No

Israeli settlers to give back land in Palestine Yes/No

An Israeli withdrawal from East Jersusalem Yes/No

The Israelis to keep East Jerusalem Yes/No

Israelis and Palestinians to be able to share Jerusalem Yes/No

A strong Palestinian police force Yes/No

A strong Israeli police force Yes/No

Full independence for Palestinian areas Yes/No

Democratic elections in Palestinian areas Yes/No

More jobs in Palestine Yes/No

Palestine children, West Bank
Jenny Matthews

Somewhere to live for everybody **Yes/No**

Improved schools, roads and hospitals in the West Bank and Gaza Strip **Yes/No**

Palestinian refugees in Syria, Lebanon and Jordan to be able to return to their original homes **Yes/No**

Palestinian refugees to be able to return to the West Bank and Gaza Strip **Yes/No**

Palestinian refugees to be given compensation for the homes they lost **Yes/No**

Ordinary Israelis and Palestinians to be able to talk to each other **Yes/No**

Palestinians to be forced to leave the West Bank and go and live in Jordan **Yes/No**

You can add some ideas of your own to the list.

◆ Taking the items you have answered with a 'yes', what things are most likely to create peace in the Middle East?

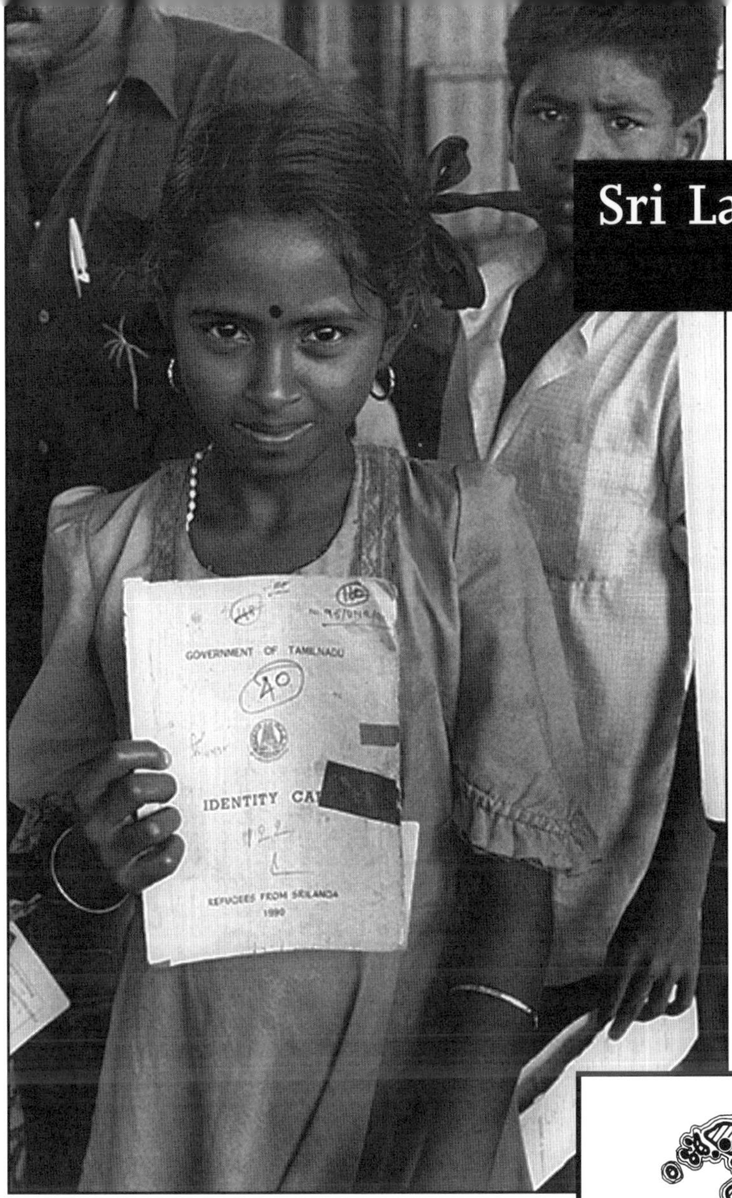

Sri Lanka

A civil war between Tamil guerrillas and the Sri Lankan government has caused over one million people to flee their homes. There are also serious human rights abuses in Sri Lanka.

Sri Lanka was known as Ceylon until 1972.

Population
17 million

Capital
Colombo

Economy
About 45 per cent of the population is employed in agriculture. The agricultural workforce is employed on small farms or plantations. Tea is Sri Lanka's main export crop and is grown on tea plantations in central Sri Lanka. There is very little economic activity in the Jaffna peninsula because of the war.

Ethnic groups
Some 74 per cent of the population are Sinhalese. They speak Sinhala as a first language and are mostly Buddhist. Another 18 per cent of people are Tamils. They speak Tamil as a first language. Most Tamils are Hindu although a small number are Christian.

Muslims make up 7 per cent of the population. They are known as Moors because some people believe that they are the descendants of Moroccan Arabs. The Moors speak Tamil as their first language. There are also small numbers of the descendants of Portuguese and Dutch settlers.

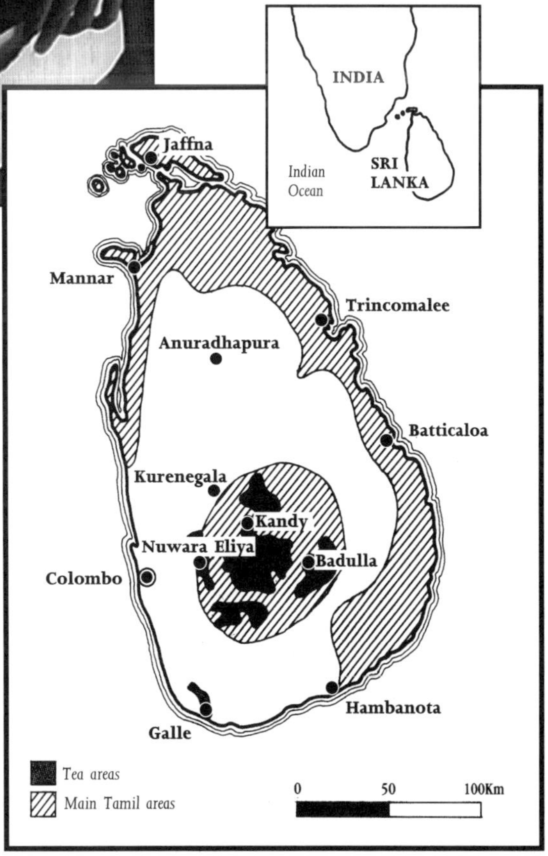

Returning refugee, Sri Lanka *UNHCR*

Events

During prehistoric times Sri Lanka was joined by land to India. Veddahs (indigenous people) lived in Sri Lanka at this time; today a small number of Veddahs still live in southern Sri Lanka.

In the 5th century BC, ancestors of the Tamils arrived in Sri Lanka after migrating from southern India. The ancestors of the Sinhalese people migrated from northern India at about the same time. Many Sri Lankans converted to Buddhism in the 2nd century BC.

In the 11th and 12th century AD there was a Tamil kingdom in the northern part of the island. Between the 14th and 16th century three kingdoms existed: a Tamil kingdom in northern Sri Lanka, the Sinhalese Kingdom of Kotte and the Sinhalese Kingdom of Kandy.

1505 The Portuguese arrive in Ceylon attracted by the spices grown on the island. Over the next 20 years they capture the Kingdom of Kotte.

1621 The Portuguese capture the Tamil kingdom.

1656 The Dutch conquer Portuguese Ceylon. The Dutch introduce plantation agriculture to Ceylon, growing coffee, sugar cane, spices and tobacco. Like the Portuguese before them, the Dutch colonists are unable to capture the Kingdom of Kandy in central Ceylon.

1796 The British make an agreement with the Dutch to give Ceylon to the British East India Company. This company makes profits from the plantations and the spice trade.

1802 The Tamil and Kotte Kingdoms become a British colony. In 1815 the Kingdom of Kandy is brought under British rule.

1833 The former Tamil and Sinhalese kingdoms are administered together as one country.

1840 The British pass a new law called the 'Waste Lands Ordinance'. This allows the British to claim any land where ownership cannot be proved. As many farmers do not have legal documents that show they own their land, the British colonial administration is able to claim many farms. The land is then sold very cheaply to British plantation owners. Coffee, coconuts and rubber are grown on the plantations. Over 200,000 Indian Tamils are brought from India to work on the coffee plantations in central Ceylon.

1870 The coffee crop is killed by a fungal disease. Tea bushes are planted in their place and tea becomes Ceylon's main export.

By the end of the 19th century Ceylonese Tamils begin to obtain jobs in the British colonial administration.

1911 There are now more Plantation Tamils (recently migrated from India) than Ceylonese Tamils. The Plantation Tamils mostly work in the plantations of central Sri Lanka and are generally poorer than Ceylonese Tamils.

1944 The Soulbury Commission arrives from London to prepare Ceylon for independence. Tamil leaders ask the Soulbury Commission for safeguards to protect minorities. Sinhalese politicians assure the Tamil population that they will be safe after independence.

1948 Ceylon gains independence from the British. One of the first acts of the new government was the passing of the Citizenship Act. This effectively makes Plantation Tamils stateless. They later lose their right to vote.

1956 Sinhala becomes Sri Lanka's official language. It replaces English as the language of government. Many Tamils protest as they are now at risk of losing their government jobs. Twelve Tamil MPs and their supporters stage a peaceful demonstration outside parliament about the change in the official language. A Sinhalese crowd stones the protesters and the police take no action. Rioting spreads in Colombo and over 150 Tamils are killed.

1958 Protests about the language issue continue. In May 1958 Sinhalese crowds attack Tamils. The rioting worsens and over 1,000 people are killed. British and French ships have to rescue 12,000 Tamil refugees from Colombo.

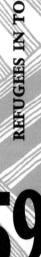

1964 An agreement is signed by India and Ceylon which will allow 525,000 Plantation Tamils to be given Indian citizenship over the next 15 years. Some 300,000 Plantation Tamils will be given Ceylonese citizenship and allowed to remain. But the citizenship process is very slow.

1972 Ceylon is renamed Sri Lanka and Buddhism is declared a state religion. There are no longer any legal safeguards to protect the rights of minorities.

1976 Tamil leaders meet and call for a separate state of Tamil Eelam, located in northern and eastern Sri Lanka. This move is supported by the majority of Sri Lankan Tamils as they feel that their rights are not being protected.

In the same year some young Tamils found an organisation called the Liberation Tigers of Tamil Eelam (LTTE). This organisation soon resorts to armed struggle.

1977 Over 500 Tamils are killed in anti-Tamil violence. The army and police do nothing to protect Tamils who are being attacked.

1978 Tamil becomes a 'national language', but in practice this does not mean there are any changes.

1981 After the LTTE kill a policeman and a politician, there are more riots.

1983 Violence against Tamils worsens. In July 1983 a week of riots leaves 2,000 people dead and 150,000 Tamils in refugee camps. Over 23,000 homes and businesses are destroyed. Tamils living in Colombo are the worst affected. Many of this group leave Colombo for northern and eastern Sri Lanka where they are not in a minority. Some Tamils also flee to India, Europe and North America.

1985 The Indian government arranges peace talks between the Sri Lankan government and Tamil political parties and guerrilla groups. The talks soon break down as the Sri Lankan government is unable to make proposals that satisfy the Tamils.

1986 The violence between the Sinhalese

Displaced child's drawing, northern Sri Lanka

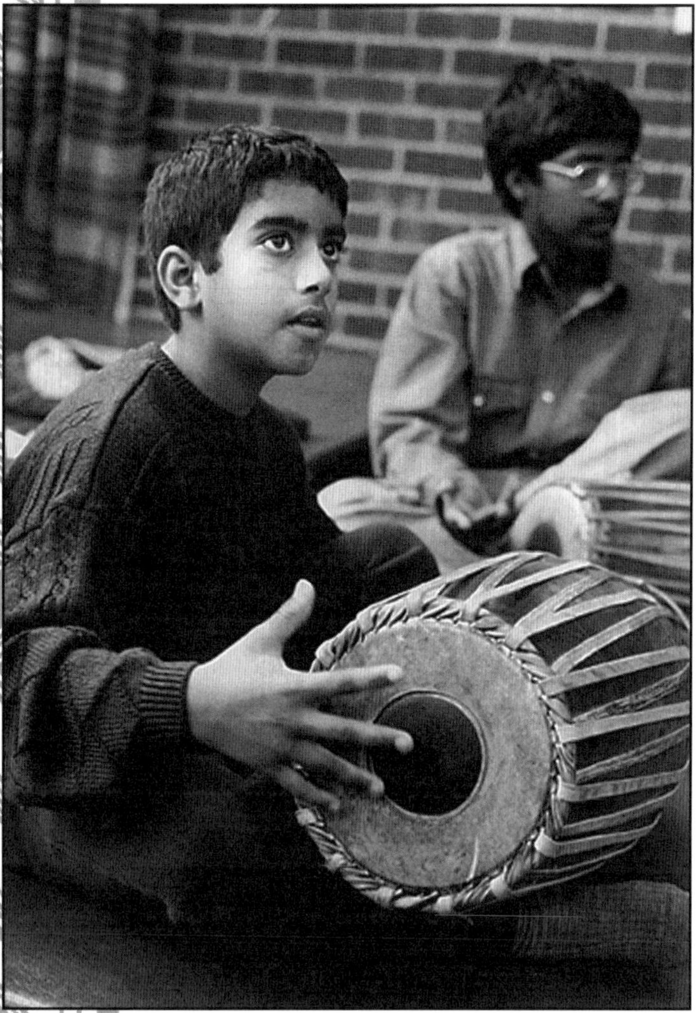

and Tamil communities worsens. The Sri Lankan government is condemned by Amnesty International for the torture of Tamil prisoners and the extrajudicial execution of Tamils. There is also fighting between some Tamil guerrilla groups. By the end of 1986 over 85,000 Tamils have fled to India where many live in poverty.

1987 India arranges further peace talks and then sends the Indian Peace Keeping Force to northern Sri Lanka. Indian soldiers are soon accused of human rights abuses, particularly extrajudicial executions.

The Sri Lankan army launches a major attack on Jaffna where Tamil guerrillas get most of their support. There is also violence in southern Sri Lanka. The JVP, a Sinhalese political party, begins a guerrilla war. This organisation has a combination of Marxist and Sinhalese nationalist politics. It assassinates politicians. In response, the Sri Lankan army and police arrest and kill many young men they suspect of supporting the JVP.

Tamil refugee boy at supplementary school, London
Howard Davies

1989 Human rights organisations estimate that at least 3,000 people are killed in Sri Lanka in 1989, by the Sri Lankan army and police, the Indian Peace Keeping Force, Tamil guerrillas and the JVP. After the violent start to the year there are some peace talks between the Tamil guerrillas and the Sri Lankan government.

1990 In June 1990 the Liberation Tigers of Tamil Eelam attack 17 police stations and kill 110 police officers. The Sri Lankan army responds violently. Within two weeks over 1,000 people are killed and 200,000 left homeless. The government also stops food, medicines and many other essential goods from reaching the Jaffna peninsula. There is no electricity in Jaffna and people have very little to eat.

1991 The blockade and bombing of the Jaffna peninsula continues. Over 1,000,000 people are internally displaced in Sri Lanka. Some 620,000 people have fled as refugees to India, Europe and North America.

At the end of 1991 the governments of India and Sri Lanka announce that they are planning to return refugees from India to Sri Lanka. Human rights organisations oppose this as they believe Sri Lanka to be unsafe.

1992–93 The war and blockade continues. India returns 25,000 refugees, some of them against their will. Those who do return find their houses destroyed or looted and they receive very little assistance to help them rebuild their homes. European countries announce that they will also be returning some Tamil asylum-seekers.

1994–95 Elections in Sri Lanka bring a new government to power. A ceasefire is called and there are some peace talks.

1995 In early 1995 the ceasefire is broken and the war resumes. Within a few weeks hundreds of people are killed, including 120 refugees who were sheltering in a church. In November 1995 the Sri Lankan army launches a military offensive on Jaffna. Another 400,000 people flee as refugees.

Markandu Gnanapandithan's story

Andrew North

'My name is Markandu Gnanapandithan and I was born on 26th November 1959 in a village near Jaffna in northern Sri Lanka. My father is a retired civil servant and also has a farm in our village. My mother comes from Jaffna.

I went to school and then was admitted to the University of Jaffna. I won a scholarship and then entered the University of Peradeniya in 1983.

I was politically active at school and university. The rights of Tamil people were being eroded by successive Sinhala governments. The Tamil workers on tea and rubber plantations had been made stateless and denied their basic rights. Tamils also suffer discrimination in education.

I joined a Tamil youth organisation in 1976 when I was at school. I also did voluntary work with an organisation helping Tamil refugees who had fled from southern Sri Lanka during the riots of 1977. This organisation was given funds by Oxfam in Britain. But as it was working with Tamil refugees it was a target. Its offices were eventually destroyed by Sinhalese racists, and the workers and volunteers arrested and tortured.

In 1983 I was at the University of Peradeniya. We had student elections and the Tamil undergraduates supported and worked for progressive Sinhalese candidates and they won. After this the Sinhalese candidates who had lost began to make life difficult for the Tamil students. They were stripped naked, dragged out of their rooms and paraded on the streets. As a result of this the university had to close.

In the riots of July 1983 the house where I was living was burnt down. My books and other belongings were destroyed. I was forced to abandon my studies and return home.

On 8th January 1994 about 30 police officers came to my house to arrest me. I was kept in Vavuniya police station on 8th and 9th January 1994. On 9th January 1994 I was taken to Kandy. On the way to Kandy the police stopped the jeep opposite a Sinhalese Buddhist temple. The crowd outside the temple shouted abuse at me.

I was kept in another police station from 9th to 11th January. Here I was locked up with Sinhalese remand prisoners who also attacked and abused me. On 11th January 1984 I was taken to Norwood police station and kept there for 15 days. During the time I was detained there I was removed to another police station and tortured.

I was forced to lie down on a bench. My hands and feet were tied up and the soles of my feet were hit with clubs. I was burned with lighted cigarette ends. I was beaten on the head and also hung upside down from a bar and assaulted.

On 26th January 1984 I was taken to Iratperiyakulum army camp and questioned by Ronny Wikramsinghe, an Assistant Superintendent of Police. He got the soldiers to torture me. They inserted a wire into my penis and drove pins under my fingernails.

On 1st February 1984 I was taken to another army camp and kept alone in a dark cell for 15 days. I was then taken back to Iratperiyakulum army camp with 12 other young men. Here we were tortured and sexually assaulted.

On 22nd March 1984 I was taken to Wellikade prison in Colombo. It was in this prison that Tamil political prisoners were murdered by Sinhalese prisoners during the riots of 1983. The prison officers did nothing to stop the riots.

On 9th April 1984 I was taken to Tagalle prison with 90 other Tamils. We were denied medical treatment and water for washing. Here we went on hunger strike, demanding that we should either be put before a court of law or released.

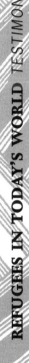

In December 1984 I was taken to an army camp in southern Sri Lanka. I was given very little food here and when I asked for more I was beaten. In January 1985 I was taken back to Tagalle prison. In September 1985 I became ill. In all my time in Tagalle we were abused and beaten by prison officers. A Tamil prisoner was murdered by one of the prison guards.

In October 1985 with the help of friends I managed to pay a bribe of about £75 to police officers and I was released. I returned home to my village. But soon after my return I was summoned to Mankulum army camp. I did not answer the summons but went into hiding. I had no alternative other than to flee the country as I feared for my life. I paid an agent to help me leave Sri Lanka and left by boat to India on 3rd October 1986.

I travelled on my own passport without knowing the the visa stamp on it was forged. When I arrived at Heathrow airport on 19th October 1986 I was told that the visa stamp was false. I asked for asylum and was granted temporary admission to Britain and was told to report to the immigration office when they called me for interview.

My asylum application was refused on 7th March 1987. The Home Office's immigration department told me that even though my life was in danger in Sri Lanka, it was not the only country in which I could live. I think they wanted to send me to India.

The lives of Tamils in Sri Lanka are in danger from the Sri Lankan government's military attacks. We are compelled to leave our homelands. I ask the British government to consider our plight and give us asylum in Britain, so we can remain here until there is peace in Sri Lanka.'

Markandu Gnanapandithan was eventually given 'exceptional leave to remain' in Britain. The interview is reproduced with thanks to the Tamil Refugee Action Group.

Torture

Sri Lanka is one of nearly 100 countries which use torture on detainees and prisoners. In 1993 Amnesty International reported that torture had been used in 96 countries in the previous year. Some people believe that as torture is not used on prisoners and detainees in Britain it should not be examined in educational material. But perhaps torture - a deliberate way of inflicting pain on another person - forces us to ask questions about ourselves. Read the information about the Milgram experiment and decide what you think.

The Milgram experiment

For many years it was thought that torture was something that was carried out by monstrous people who suffer from personality disorders. Psychologists believed that 'normal' people could never be torturers. But in the early 1960s this notion began to be questioned. This was prompted by the trial of Adolf Eichmann, a Nazi war criminal. Those who witnessed the trial which was held in Jerusalem noted how ordinary Eichmann appeared to be.

A psychologist called Stanley Milgram was one person who started to examine what makes ordinary people commit crimes such as torture. He set up a psychological experiment to examine how far people will go when given orders to hurt other people.

Stanley Milgram recruited some actors who trained to act as 'learners' in his experiment. At the same time he placed an advertisement in a local newspaper asking for volunteers to help in a study of memory and learning methods. The volunteers were told that they would act as 'teachers'.

The 'teachers' were told that their job was to punish the 'learners' when the latter made a mistake in their memory tests. Every time the 'learner' made a mistake the 'teacher' was to give them an electric shock. The teachers were told by Stanley Milgram that the experiment was to test the theory that people who were punished for their mistakes learnt things more quickly.

Stanley Milgram built a special machine to give the electric shocks. The machine had many levers. Each lever increased the strength of the electric shock. For each mistake that the 'learner' made the teacher had to use an extra lever to give a bigger shock. Some of the levers were also marked with the words 'extremely dangerous'. The levers were graduated up to 450 volts.

The machine did not really give the 'learner' electric shocks. The 'learner', who was an actor, simulated the pain of a shock and made many protests about his treatment. The 'learner' also made many mistakes.

At 150 volts the 'learner' was screaming with pain and asked for the experiment to be ended. Stanley Milgram and his colleagues ordered the 'teacher' to carry on. Most of them did. Some 65 per cent of all the 'teachers' administered shocks at 450 volts. The 'teachers', however, were very tense when they were giving the electric shocks.

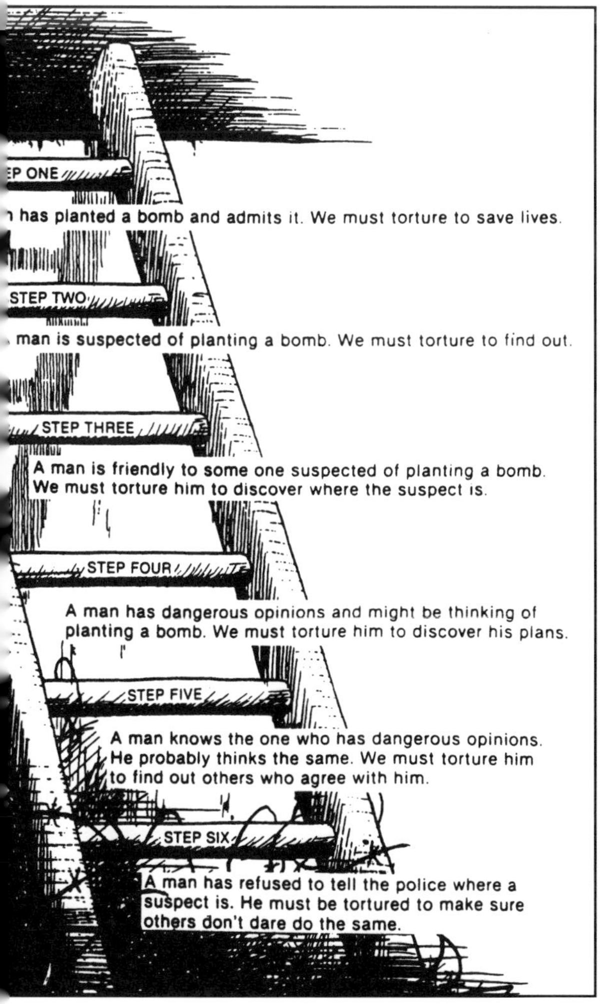

EP ONE
has planted a bomb and admits it. We must torture to save lives.
STEP TWO
man is suspected of planting a bomb. We must torture to find out.
STEP THREE
A man is friendly to some one suspected of planting a bomb. We must torture him to discover where the suspect is.
STEP FOUR
A man has dangerous opinions and might be thinking of planting a bomb. We must torture him to discover his plans.
STEP FIVE
A man knows the one who has dangerous opinions. He probably thinks the same. We must torture him to find out others who agree with him.
STEP SIX
A man has refused to tell the police where a suspect is. He must be tortured to make sure others don't dare do the same.

Before the experiment, Milgram discussed with fellow psychologists what proportion of 'teachers' would be giving 450 volt electric shocks. They believed that less than one per cent of all the 'teachers' would administer electric shocks at 450 volts. Stanley Milgram and his colleagues were very surprised that 65 per cent of all 'teachers' administered 450 volt shocks.

There has been further research on torture since the Milgram experiment. In the 1970s research was carried out in Greece on those who had perpetrated torture under the military governments of 1967-1974. Psychologists found that there were no personality differences between torturers and the general population; indeed many of the torturers were young national service conscripts. In their training, however, the torturers had been taught to think that they were defending good values.

Read the passages above. Discuss what the Milgram experiment and the research in Greece tells us about people who are torturers. What can people who are concerned about human rights learn from this research?

What is torture?

Torture can be used to extract information out of prisoners or those in detention. But more often torture has another aim: political control and the control of dissent. An individual who has been tortured may flee his or her country after torture or cease to be involved in political opposition. If many people involved in political opposition are tortured this will cause a much larger number of people to be fearful of any political involvement.

Torture can include:

◆ the ill-treatment of prisoners and detainees, such as starvation, the use of leg irons and hand cuffs in a way that causes pain, beatings and solitary confinement

◆ forms of punishment such as electric shocks, beating the feet and hanging a person for a prolonged period

◆ the misuse of drugs, for example injecting people with drugs that paralyse them for a period of time

◆ sexual torture such as the rape of women in prison

◆ psychological torture such as making threats against family and friends

Britain's links with torture

Britain has in the recent past exported torture equipment to several countries that regularly torture prisoners and detainees. As controls on such exports are inadequate it is possible that British business could continue to export torture equipment.

The exports include:

1983 The export of leg irons by Hiatts & Co, a company based in the West Midlands. As a result of a campaign by Amnesty International, British government export licences were refused for future exports.

1991 Hiatts & Co were discovered promoting the sale of leg irons through a US-based associate company.

1991 Electronic Intelligence, a British based company, was discovered to have installed a torture chamber in Dubai. The torture chamber used sound and high intensity lighting, causing the person inside to scream in agony within moments.

Work with people who survive torture

Most people who are tortured do not survive. A small number of refugees who have been tortured flee to Britain. Here they may need help to enable them to recover from past experiences. This is given by a a charity called the Medical Foundation for the Care of Victims of Torture.

The Medical Foundation was founded in 1985 by members of Amnesty International's Medical Group. From small beginnings it has grown to be an organisation that sees over 2,000 people a year. It sees clients from many different countries including survivors of the Nazi Holocaust. At present most of the Medical Foundation's clients come from Iran and Turkey.

The Medical Foundation employs 20 staff, but a large part of its work is done by volunteers. The staff and volunteers include social workers, psychiatrists, psychotherapists, GPs, physiotherapists, art therapists, nurses, a careers adviser and an information officer. The Medical Foundation offers a wide range of services to people who have survived torture and their families. These services include:

◆ making reports to help asylum-seekers who have been tortured apply for political asylum in Britain

◆ psychotherapy, art therapy and music therapy to help survivors of torture come to terms with their experience

◆ medical treatment and physiotherapy for people who have physical injuries as a result of their torture

◆ advice and support for clients who are having other problems in their lives such as not being able to find housing

◆ training for doctors, nurses, teachers, social workers and other workers who may encounter survivors of torture during their work.

Refugees in the Caucasus

The Caucasus is a multi-ethnic region. Increasing nationalism since the break-up of the Soviet Union in 1989 has led to ethnic conflict and the movement of large numbers of refugees. Today there are over 700,000 refugees in the Caucasus and 1,200,000 internally displaced people.

Azeri refugees
UNHCR

Armenia

Population
3,500,000

Capital
Yerevan

Ethnic groups
Armenians make up 95% of the population, but there are small numbers of Azeris, Russians and Kurds.

The Armenians are an ethnic group whose home is in the Caucasus and eastern Turkey. The Armenians were converted to Christianity around 300AD. They speak Armenian.

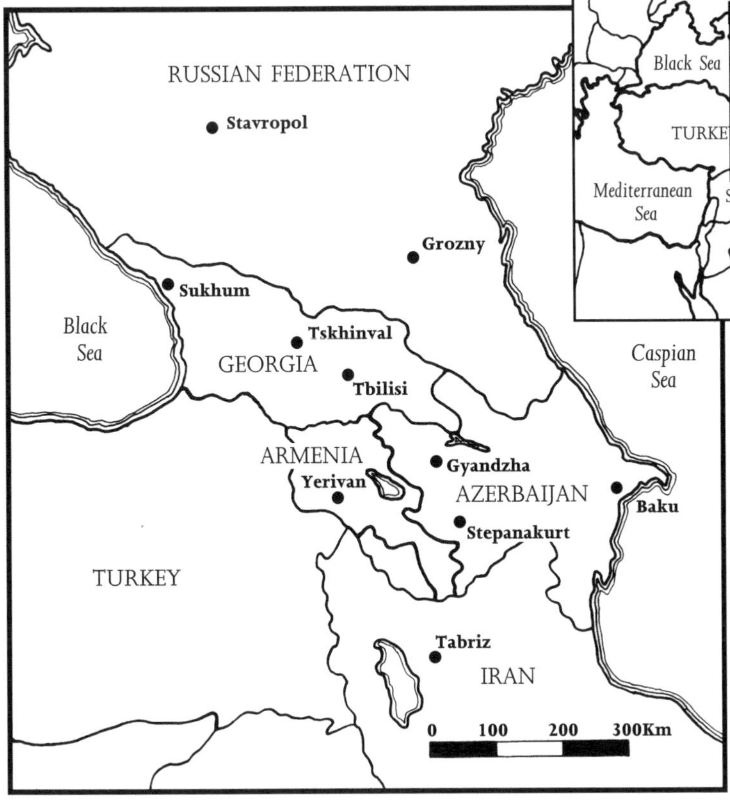

The Armenian homeland has never experienced peace. Over the centuries the Armenians have found themselves ruled by many different empires. In the 15th century a large part of Armenia became part of the

Ottoman Empire. By 1827, after the Russian conquest of the Caucasus, large numbers of Armenians found themselves living in the Russian Empire.

But the most tragic event of Armenian history was the genocide of 1915. In 1908 there was a revolution in Turkey. The Sultan was removed and replaced by a more democratic government. The revolution was led by the 'Young Turks', but it brought few benefits to minority groups such as the Armenians and Kurds. The Young Turks were very nationalistic, and the Armenians represented a non-Turkish minority, suspected of being sympathetic to Turkey's enemies. After military setbacks in the First World War, the Young Turks used the Armenian community as a scapegoat to blame for Turkey's problems. Starting in the summer of 1915, some 1,500,000 Armenians were killed, or died of starvation or disease. Thousands of Armenians were forced to leave their villages, and died as they were forcibly marched through the deserts. One third of all Armenians died in 1915. Those who were responsible were never brought to justice. Adolf Hitler was later to praise the killing of Armenians, and ordered his troops to behave to Jews as the Young Turks did to the Armenians.

After this genocide many Armenians fled to countries such as Iran, Lebanon, Cyprus and Palestine. In the 1970s and 1980s civil wars in Lebanon and Cyprus, and human rights abuses in Iran forced Armenians to become refugees again.

There are over five million Armenians in today's world. They live in Armenia (3 million), the USA (500,000), France (250,000), Lebanon, Turkey, Syria and Iran (500,000).

Azerbaijan

Population 7,100,000

Capital Baku

Ethnic groups
Azeris (81%), Armenians (5%), Russians (5%)

Religion
Mostly Shi'a Muslim

Georgia

Population 5,500,000

Capital Tbilisi

Ethnic groups
Georgian (70%), Armenian (8%), Russian (6%), Azeri (5%), Ossetian (3%), Greek (1.8%), Abhazian (1.8%), also Ukrainian, Kurdish, Georgian Jewish and 17 other groups.

Refugees and internally displaced people
290,000 ethnic Armenians refugees have fled Azerbaijan and the disputed territory of Nagorno-Karabakh since 1989.

230,000 ethnic Azeris have fled from Armenia. Another 800,000 Azeris have been internally displaced in the fighting between Armenia and Azerbaijan.

130,000 South Ossetians and Russians have fled from South Ossetia (Georgia) to Russia. Another 25,000 people have been internally displaced in Georgia.

65,000 Ingush have fled North Ossetia and are internally displaced in other parts of Russia.

64,000 refugees have fled the conflict in Abkhazia and fled to Russia.

150,000 Chechens and Russians have been internally displaced by the conflict in Chechnya.

The Armenia/Azerbaijan conflict

Persecution of Armenians by the Turkish government from 1908-1918 led many Armenians to fear Muslim groups in the Caucasus. This fear and suspicion continues to the present day. The Azeris are Muslims and live in close proximity to the Armenians. In Armenia, the minority Azeri community became the target of suspicion. In Azerbaijan, the Armenian community also suffered.

Nagorno-Karabakh is part of Azerbaijan which is surrounded by Armenia. Its population is made up of Armenian and Azeri people. In Nagorno-Karabakh many Armenians felt they suffered discrimination at the hands of the larger Azeri community.

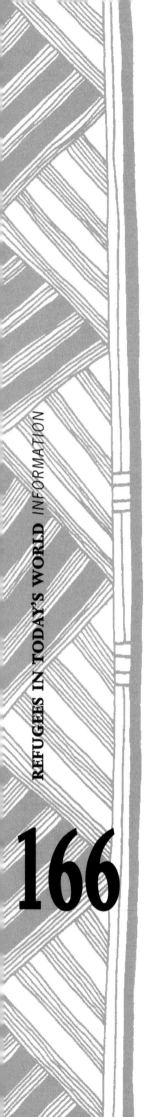

In 1988 Armenians, supported by some Russian politicians, requested that Nagorno-Karabakh be transferred to Armenia. This was resisted by the Azerbaijan government. In 1989, fighting broke out between Armenia and Azerbaijan, over control of Nagorno-Karabakh.

Ordinary Armenians and Azeris have been caught up in this conflict. The governments of Armenia and Azerbaijan have become increasing nationalistic. This has led to attacks on minority communities in Armenia and Azerbaijan. Thousands of Armenians fled from Baku, in Azerbaijan after they suffered attacks.

The war over Nagorno-Karabakh, and attacks on minority communities have caused 290,000 Armenians to flee from Azerbaijan. Over 230,000 Azeris have fled from Armenia. The war has left over 800,000 Azeris as internally displaced people.

South Ossetia

The Ossetes are a minority group who live in the northern Caucasus. They speak Ossetian and are Christian or Muslim. The Ossetes now find themselves divided between two countries: Georgia and the Russian Federation. Ossetes now live in the Georgian region of South Ossetia and the Russian republic of North Ossetia.

From 1920-1989 relations between Georgia and the Soviet government in Moscow were poor, but Ossetes remained loyal to the Soviet Union. After the collapse of the Soviet Union in 1989 most South Ossetians wished that their region be reunited with North Ossetia. This proposal was welcomed by the Russian government but totally rejected by the Georgian government. The Georgian government believes that South Ossetia is historically part of Georgia and should remain so.

Georgia declared itself independent of the Soviet Union in 1989. Ruled by nationalist politicians, Georgian became the official language. But in South Ossetia, very few people spoke Georgian and this measure was strongly opposed. In 1990 South Ossetia declared itself to be an independent republic within the Russian Federation. In response to this, the Georgian army entered South Ossetia. Fighting followed, and 130,000 Ossetian and Russian people fled as refugees to Russia. Georgians were also internally displaced in the fighting.

Although the Georgian army has since withdrawn many of its soldiers from South Ossetia, fighting and human rights abuses still continue. Ossetian people are the target of nationalist Georgian militia. The militia do not appear to be under the control of the Georgian government. The Georgian militia are trying to terrorise the Ossetes into leaving for North Ossetia.

North Ossetia

North Ossetia is an autonomous republic within Russia. It borders Ingushia. Like most of the neighbouring republics, it is a multi-ethnic state. Its population is made up of Ossetians, Russians and Ingush people. One person in seven is a refugee from South Ossetia, and most of the refugees live in very poor conditions.

During the 1940s, Stalin forcibly moved large numbers of Ingush to central Asia, and altered the borders of North Ossetia and Ingushia. After the collapse of the Soviet Union many Ingush who lived in the eastern part of North Ossetia hoped that their land would be transferred to the autonomous republic of Ingushia. This was not to be. In 1992 fighting broke out between Ingush and North Ossetia militia. Over 65,000 Ingush refugees fled North Ossetia.

Abkhazia

The Abkhaz are a minority group living in Georgia. They speak their own language. Some Abkhaz are Muslim, others are Christian. Their culture is different to the Georgians. The Abkhaz live in Abkhazia, in western Georgia, by the side of the Black Sea. But even in Abkhazia the Georgians are a majority.

During the late 1980s Georgian nationalists organised violent demonstrations against Abkhazians who wanted more autonomy. Violence in Sukhumi and Tbilisi led the Soviet Red Army to intervene. In 1990, when Georgia became an independent state, Abkhazias declared their own independ-ence from Georgia. Georgian army tanks then entered Sukhumi. The conflict has now developed into a guerrilla war fought between Abkhaz militias and the Georgian army and Georgian militias. Some 64,000 refugees have fled Abkhazia.

Chechnya
Chechnya is an autonomous republic with the Russian Federation. Some 57 per cent of the inhabitants of Chechnya are Chechens and 23 per cent are Russians. The Chechens speak their own language and most of them are Muslims. Many Chechens are herdsmen or farmers, and their culture is different from the Russian population. Many Chechens feel that they suffered discrimation at the hands of the Russian community, particularly in education and employment. High unemployment among the Chechen community has forced many Chechen to migrate for work.

As a result of this discrimination, many Chechens supported the idea of independence from Russia. Chechnya declared itself an independent state in 1991. The Chechens organised their own army and government. In early 1995 the Russian army marched into Chechnya, to try and put an end to the independence movement. Thousands of Chechens and Russians were killed in the fighting. Over 150,000 Chechens and Russians have been internally displaced. The Chechen army, led by President Dudaev, has now retreated to the mountains, and is fighting a guerrilla war against the Russian army.

UNHCR

Arseni's story

Arseni is from South Ossetia. She has been forced to flee as a refugee and is now living in North Ossetia.

‘Georgians came many times and burned Ossetian houses in our village. I do not remember how many houses were burned. I heard recently that all the Ossetian houses were burned. There were five or six houses on my street that were set on fire.

After this we fled to the forest. Every night we went to sleep in the forest, as we felt that it was safer to be there as the Georgians only came to burn houses when it was dark. We had gone to the forest every night at midnight. But my husband's mother was old and ill. My husband said it would be better to go home. On the way back to out house we passed a group of Ossetian watchmen on the street. They did not have any weapons. Later that night my husband heard many cars near our house. He went outside, although I tried to stop him. When he stepped outside they started to shoot and he was wounded in the leg.

There was heavy shooting. Everyone in the house got down on to the floor, my neighbour, me and my husband's mother. Bullets went through all the windows.

An ambulance came next day to take people who had been wounded to the hospital. But we were afraid to leave the house because we knew that the Georgian militia were still watching. After the ambulance went the militia came and arrested us all. There were six men in civilian clothes all of them armed. They accused me of cooking food for Ossetian fighters. I do not cook, because I never have any spare food. But they blamed me all the same. I was very frightened.

One of the Georgian militia was our neighbour. He questioned me again and let me go. After this we left out village for good. My husband joined us after he had left the hospital.’

Nationalism

Nationalism is a political or cultural movement the priority of which is the future of a particular national group. Many sociologists believe that European countries and the former Soviet Union are experiencing a rise in nationalism. In the Caucasus and former Yugoslavia increased nationalism has led to war between different communities and the movement of refugees.

To understand nationalism we have to examine what we mean by a 'nation' and 'nation-state'. A nation is a community of people of mainly common descent, history and language who inhabit a certain area. A nation-state is a nation which governs itself. The nation-state is the dominant form of political organisation today.

Some historians believe that nation-states are a modern political trend. During the Middle Ages, ordinary people had personal allegiances to their locality and region, but not to a 'nation'. There was also little central government in most countries and ordinary people had no democratic rights. But in the 18th century nation-states and nationalism began to develop. French nationalism grew from the French Revolution of 1789; German nationalism grew after the unification of Germany. Turkish and Arab nationalism developed at the end of the 19th century.

Other historians believe that nationalism and the nation-state evolved slowly and are not unique to the modern world. And today, some political scientists believe that the nation-state is becoming less important. Nations are organising themselves into trading blocs like the European Union. Multinational companies have much more power over governments than ever before.

In the past nationalism has led to self-determination for colonised people. For example, the growth of Indian nationalism in the 1920s and 1930s eventually led to Indian independence in 1947. But nationalism can also lead to racism and the exclusion of minority groups. At its extreme, nationalism can lead to civil war. This is what is happening in the Caucasus and in the former Yugoslavia. At times of economic crisis nationalism can be very appealing to people; everybody likes to belong to a group, and feel proud of it. Nationalism may grow at times when other political ideas have been discredited. Nationalism, too, may grow at times of war as it is used by politicians as a way of mobilising soldiers to fight for their nation.

Today politicians in countries such as Armenia, Croatia and Serbia have used nationalism as a way of maintaining their power, and as a way of mobilising soldiers. They have:

◆ used heroes from folk stories to create a national identity

◆ linked the idea of 'nation' with membership of the majority ethnic group, thus excluding people who belong to ethnic minority communities

◆ linked the idea of nation to membership of a particular religious group

◆ linked the idea of nation to the use of a particular language or dialect

◆ restricted the civil rights of some minority groups

◆ created scapegoats and promoted the idea that minority groups or foreign nations are acting against the interests of their nation

◆ used newspaper and television to promote nationalist ideas.

Discussion points

◆ Find out about the growth of nationalism in Nazi Germany. What methods did Nazi propagandists use to gain support?

◆ Find out about the growth of nationalism in Serbia and Croatia. What methods did politicians use to gain support?

◆ What are the links between nationalism and racism?

◆ Find out what the word 'patriotism' means. Do you think patriotism is always a good thing?

A good source for finding out more information is the BBC book 'The Death of Yugoslavia'.

Armenian refugees, London
UNHCR

Insiders & outsiders

Aims

To help students think about the formation of groups.

Instructions

Time needed: one hour.

The ideal group size is about 20 people. Stickers, paper, marker pens and chalk are needed.

Divide up the group and give about a third of them stickers. Send the students with stickers into another room. They are the 'outsiders'.

The rest of the group are 'insiders'. Sit with them and explain that they are going to work out some rules for break time in school. They will be able to make up five rules that will govern the lives of insiders and outsiders. Any rule that gets a majority vote will be passed.

Rules could include:

◆ outsiders may not enter chalk circles unless invited.

◆ outsiders may only use toilets marked with a sticker.

After five rules have been decided, they should be written on a large sheet of paper. The outsiders should then be invited back into the room. They should be told that it is an ordinary break time, but they must follow the rules decided by the insiders.

After ten minutes of the 'break' stop the simulation. Ask the students to discuss and write down answers to the following points.

Discussion points

◆ Do you think that the rules were fair?

◆ What was the worst thing about having a sticker?

◆ Were there any disadvantages about being an insider?

◆ Did any of the outsiders try to do something that was forbidden to them? If so, how did the insiders react?

◆ How did the insiders feel about the outsiders? Did they feel sorry for them or hostile towards them?

Belonging

Aims

This activity aims to explore the many different groups to which students belong. It aims to help students recognise that difference and diversity are positive.

Instructions

Time needed: 45 minutes

Old newspaper and magazines, large sheets of paper and coloured pens are needed.

Divide the class into pairs. Each pair should use their own ideas, newspapers and magazines to make a list of as many social groups that people can belong to. Examples of social groups include religions, gender (male or female), type of job, ethnic group, hobbies and interest groups, political beliefs, home language, sexuality and football team supported.

After 20 minutes, come together. Make one big list of all the groups to which people can belong. Pin up the list. The pairs should then examine the discussion points.

Discussion points

◆ How many different groups do you belong to?

◆ Diversity and difference among people is positive. Do you agree or disagree with this statement? Why?

fluences on ır identity

Aim

The activity aims to help students think about their own identity.

Instructions

Time needed: about 45 minutes and homework time.

Marker pens and large sheets of paper are needed.

Students will be working in pairs.

The activity should be introduced. The students are going to imagine that they are living in China. They have been asked by teachers at their new school to give a five minute talk about life in Britain. Each pair should choose seven things that they think are typical of life in Britain. They should make a list of their choices on a large sheet of paper.

The group should come together. Each pair should pin up the list. The class should discuss the following points.

For homework, the students should take away their lists, and find out more about the origins of the items on their lists.

Discussion points

◆ What items were common to most of the lists?

◆ Were there any major differences between the lists made by different groups?

The media & nationalism

Aims?

Instructions

Time needed: one hour

Old tabloid newspapers are needed for this activity; students could be asked to collect them. Students will also need a highlighting pen. Introduce the activity and divide the group into pairs. Each pair should have two copies of tabloid newspapers.

Students should examine the newspapers and look for stories which they believe may promote nationalism. Such stories could include:

◆ negative references to foreign nations and the European Community

◆ negative references to minority group

◆ stories about national heroes or the royal family

◆ exaggerated stories about sporting success.

They should mark each story with a highlighting pen. The class should then come together and look at the discussion points.

Discussion points

How did the students decide whether a newspaper story promoted nationalism or not?

How many of such stories did they find in each newspaper?

From where do you think these stories came?

How do newspapers and television influence what we think of as being British?

Former Yugoslavia

Since June 1991 some 3,720,000 people have become refugees in the countries that make up former Yugoslavia. Most of them are Bosnians but some Croats, Serbs and Kosovo Albanians have also become refugees.

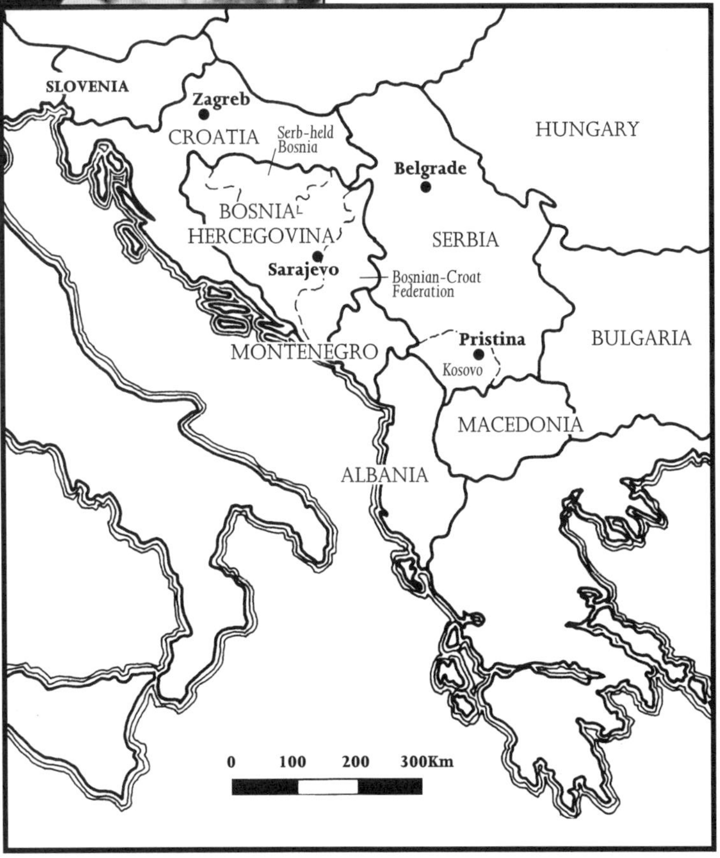

Populations
Slovenia 1.8 million
Serbia 9.3 million
Croatia 4.6 million
Bosnia 4.1 million
Macedonia 1.9 million
Montenegro 600,000

Ethnic and religious groups
The Serbs are the largest ethnic group in former Yugoslavia. They make up 65 per cent of the population of Serbia. There are also large numbers of Serbs living outside the borders of Serbia. At present about 10 per cent of Croatia's population are Serbs. Some 30 per cent of the population of Bosnia-Hercegovina are Serbs. Most Serbs who are religious are Eastern Orthodox Christians.

The Croats mostly live in Croatia and in Bosnia-Hercegovina. Some 18 per cent of

Bosnian refugee in Croatia *Billi Rafaeli*

the population of Bosnia-Hercegovina are Croats. Most Croats who are religious are Roman Catholic.

The Muslims mostly live in Bosnia-Hercegovina where they form 40 per cent of the population. They were converted to Islam during Turkish rule. Although most Bosnian Muslims have a relaxed attitude towards religion, it is a part of their identity.

Some 14 per cent of the population of Montenegro are Muslim. Muslims also live in a part of Serbia called the Sandzak. Here they make up 55 per cent of the population.

There is a lot of debate about the origins of Macedonian people. The Macedonians speak a language which has Serbo-Croat and Bulgarian roots. Nationalist Serbs regard the Macedonians as Serbian people. The Bulgarian government believes that the Macedonains are a Bulgarian people. Alexander the Great - a hero to many Greek people - was a Macedonian. Greek nationalists state that the Macedonians are Greeks who happen to speak a Slavic language. Macedonia also has a large Albanian minority. It is a very tense country which could easily be dragged into a war.

Many ethnic Albanians have their homes in Serbia and Macedonia. Most ethnic Albanians live in the Serbian province of Kosovo. Here they make up 90 per cent of the population. There are serious human rights abuses in Kosovo and some Albanians have fled as refugees. Ethnic Albanians are Muslim or Christian.

There are other minority groups in Serbia including Hungarians and Roma (Gypsies).

Refugees
Over 3,700,000 people have become refugees or are internally displaced.

Bosnia-Hercegovina 2,400,000 internally displaced
Croatia 300,000 refugees and internally displaced
UN protected areas 100,000 refugees and internally displaced
Serbia 405,000 refugees
Montenegro 44,000 refugees
Macedonia 15,000 refugees
Slovenia 29,000 refugees

Other European countries 570,000 refugees
Austria 75,000 refugees
Germany 300,000 refugees
Sweden 50,000 refugees
Denmark 17,000 refugees
Italy 32,000
UK 12,000

Events

The civil war in former Yugoslavia has its roots in history, in long-standing disputes between different ethnic groups. There is no simple explanation for the conflict.

Many people believe that the collapse of communism played an important part in starting the conflict. In the late 1980s communist governments fell throughout eastern Europe. People felt very uncertain about their future. They blamed other ethnic groups for causing them problems, and became more nationalistic. Politicians in former Yugoslavia used nationalism as a way of keeping power.

In Yugoslavia economic factors also played a part: the richer republics of northern Yugoslavia sought to separate themselves from the poorer south. There is also tension between the richer urban areas, and the poorer and more conservative countryside. Nationalist leaders have found it easier to gain support from the rural population, while in towns there is less concern for a person's ethnic origins.

Yugoslavia's weapons industry, concentrated in Bosnia and Serbia, has ensured that Serbian soldiers have easy access to weapons.

Historical divide The legacy of history is an important factor in today's conflict. For many centuries Yugoslavia was divided between two great empires which cut across Europe. To the north Slovenia and Croatia were part of the Western Roman Empire and, subsequently, the Austro-Hungarian Empire. In the south, Serbia was part of the Eastern Roman Empire and later the

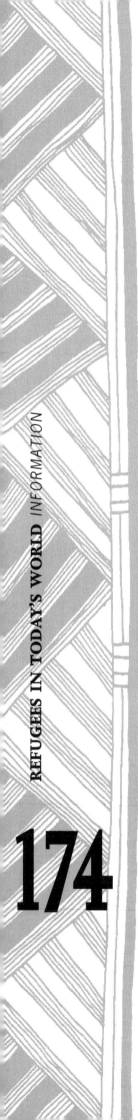

Ottoman Empire. Yugoslavia was not a united country until the end of the First World War.

1918-1945 Yugoslavia becomes a country in December 1918 under the name of the Kingdom of Serbs, Croats and Slovenes. From the start there are serious tensions between the different ethnic groups. Croats and Slovenes are fearful of Serbian domination, and there are continual disputes between the three groups.

The conflict between Serbs and Croats reaches a climax during the Second World War. The Nazis invade Yugoslavia in 1941 and create a puppet state in Croatia, with the support of the *Ustashe*, Croatian fascists. This state includes parts of Bosnia-Hercegovina and Serbia. Hundreds of thousands of Serbs, Croatian democrats, Jews and Roma are murdered by the *Ustashe*.

The *Ustashe* has opposition in the form of the Serbian nationalist Chetniks, and Josep Broz Tito's communist partisans. The Chetniks and communist partisans also fight each other with great brutality. Over 1,700,000 people - one tenth of Yugoslavia's population - are killed between 1941 and 1945, most of them by fellow Yugoslavs. The memories of the Second World War play a part in maintaining future hostilities.

1945-1990 Tito emerges victorious in 1945 and rules the country until his death in 1980. He chooses to sweep ethnic conflict under the carpet and attempts to unite the population of Yugoslavia.

Tito creates a socialist government which stands outside the Soviet bloc. Yugoslavia becomes a relatively liberal society with some privatised industry. It is more prosperous than other eastern European nations. But President Tito does not succeed in solving the great regional differences in the country. Slovenia is a richer, central European country, while the south is much poorer.

Obsessed with the threat of Soviet invasion, Tito builds up the largest army in Europe - virtually all men over the age of 20 complete military service. The Yugoslav weapons industry is also large. President Tito dies in 1980.

1990 Yugoslavia remains a united country until 1990. But with the collapse of eastern European communism, the last thin threads holding the country together are broken. In the summer and autumn of 1990 Kosovo Albanians take to the streets demanding more rights. These demonstrations are brutally put down. Kosovo is put under martial law. Albanian teachers, doctors and civil servants are dismissed from their jobs. Albanian schools are closed. Serbian nationalists claim that Kosovo is an ancestral part of Serbia and the Albanians have no right to live there.

In 1990 Slovenia holds multi-party elections. Other republics follow them, and everywhere nationalist parties are victorious. Even in Serbia and Montenegro, where former communists win elections, they do so by appealing to nationalist feelings.

After the elections the new Governments of Slovenia and Croatia wish to turn Yugoslavia into a looser grouping of states. The republics of Serbia and Montenegro want to retain a central government and a central army.

1991 On 25 June 1991 Croatia and Slovenia declare their independence. The Yugoslav People's Army is brought into action firstly in Slovenia. After a ten day war, Slovenia wins its independence and the conflict moves to Croatia. Here a Serb minority rebels against the moves towards Croatian independence. The Serbs are frightened of Croatian nationalists.

Thousands of people are killed in Croatia, and towns such as Osijek, Dubrovnik and Vukovar suffer extensive damage. The Croatian war creates thousands of refugees, both Croatian and Serbian. Parts of Croatia are occupied by Serb forces.

The UN brings in 14,000 peace-keeping soldiers to Croatia. Under the UN Peace Plan, Croatia is set to regain its occupied areas, despite statements of no surrender by Serbian leaders. The UN Mandate in Croatia has to be renewed at intervals.

1992 After the ceasefire in Croatia the

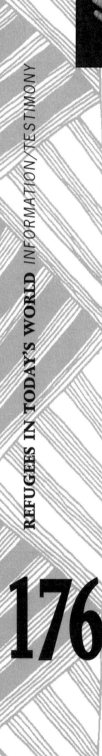

Suada's story

Suada is 13 years old. She is living in a reception centre run by the Refugee Council.

'It was a nice morning in May. I was in my house in my home village, Cejreci, near Prijedor, Bosnia. I was about to have breakfast. I often heard people talking about the war going on around us, but I could not imagine it happening to me. That morning it did, and it turned my life upside down. First I heard the sounds of shooting. They were not distant at all.

Then I heard our neighbour crying. "They are taking the men away" she said. My father came out to see what was happening. I came out as well. I saw a lot of soldiers coming towards us, screaming and using indecent words. Soldiers, tanks, the smell of shooting everywhere.

I was afraid as I had never been in my life. The soldiers made us children and our mothers gather under a tree. They were shooting over our heads and threatening that they were going to slaughter us. I saw them take my daddy away together with the other men. They were beating them all the time. I was crying. The a dirty soldier took my first cousin Nermin and killed him in front of my eyes. I was too afraid even to cry.

Many houses in the village were burned down - ours as well. We were taken to Trnoplje camp. We stayed there for two weeks. We thought that we would never get out.

Two weeks later they let us go to our home village. Most of the houses were burned down so we stayed in those that were less damaged. Two or three families stayed in a house. My mummy and I lived with my aunt and her daughter.

Soldiers would come every night bumping the door. They had socks over their faces and guns. They were so scary. One night they broke into the house. They demanded money and gold. One of them grabbed me and put a dagger under my chin. The other one shot his gun around us threatening he was going to kill us all. I thought I would never see my dad again. My cousin Naida stood up and said "Shoot". I admired her for being so brave. Luckily they just took money and gold from my mum and my aunt and left. They told us not to go out when they left, or they would shoot us. We kept still for a while and then my cousin and I went out to our neighbour. He was a Croat and helped us go to Croatia the next day.'

Suada, her mother and aunt made the dangerous journey through battlefields to reach Croatia. Life in the camp was very hard, but for the children, after all the horrors they had seen, it seemed like heaven. Suada was eventually united with her father. Her family was then told they were going to Britain.

'I am very happy now being in London with my parents and my cousin and her parents. But I often think of my friends and my toys I left in Bosnia. Sometimes I have nightmares and I think that the soldiers with socks over their faces are coming to get me again. I wish that they could never frighten and kill children and their parents again.'

conflict moves further south. In Bosnia-Hercegovina Muslims make up 40 per cent of the population, Serbs constitute 30 per cent and Croats about 18 per cent. By 1992 Bosnia-Hercegovina has a hung parliament representing different ethnic groups, and a Bosnian Muslim President. The Bosnian Parliament attempts to maintain a multi-ethnic state initially within Yugoslavia. But in

February 1992 nationalist pressures cause the Government of Bosnia-Hercegovina to declare independence. Bosnian Serbs then proclaim their own state and soon after Serbian forces attacked Sarajevo and other Bosnian cities.

By the end of 1992 the Bosnian Serb army has gained control of 70 per cent of Bosnia-Hercegovina. The Bosnian Croat army has seized control of most of western Hercegovina and central Bosnia, and also proclaimed their own state. The Bosnian army, made up mostly of Muslims has been driven out of large parts of Bosnia-Hercegovina.

Serbs, Croats and Muslims have been accused of using methods reminiscent of the Nazis to drive people from their homes. In some areas race regulations are made. Muslims are put under curfew, or forbidden to visit certain areas. Other towns have tried to organise population transfers through advertisements and posters: a Croat in the Serb-controlled town of Banja-Luka may exchange a house with a Serb from the Croatian town of Split.

But 'ethnic cleansing' is rarely so peaceful. Often people have been forced to leave their homes after signing a document renouncing all claims to their property. If people refuse to sign away their homes they are subject to campaigns of terror. Amnesty International has reported rapes, torture, beatings and murders being part of the process of 'ethnic cleansing'. The Serbian forces are accused of committing the largest numbers of human rights violations, but Serbs too are victims of 'ethnic cleansing'.

1993–94 Ceasefires have come and gone, and all peace talks have failed. The UN and EC have appointed mediators. A ceasefire, followed by a plan to divide Bosnia-Hercegovian into ten provinces, failed. In 1994 a UN peace plan created a Bosnian-Croat federation and a separate area for Bosnian Serbs.

1995 The US government decides to intervene. The Bosnian, Serbian and Croatian governments are called to peace talks in the USA. A ceasefire is declared. It is agreed that Bosnia be divided into two regions. A Bosnian-Croat federated government is to control 51 per cent of Bosnia. Bosnian Serbs are to control the rest. British, French and US soldiers, supervised by NATO are to ensure that land is handed over and peace is kept.

nderstanding the uses of the conflict

Aims

The activity aims to help participants understand the causes of the conflict in former Yugoslavia. It also aims to improve their communication skills.

Instructions

Time needed: Two hours

Some big sheets of white paper, coloured paper and felt pens are needed. The information on former Yugoslavia needs to be photocopied so that everyone has this material. Articles in quality newspapers and books about former Yugoslavia may also be used.

Divide the group up into threes and fours. Each group is going to make a strip cartoon or collage to show the causes of the conflict in former Yugoslavia.

Discussion points

- **What factors have led to the conflict in former Yugoslavia?**

- **What can ordinary people in Yugoslavia do to work for peace?**

Conflict

Since the beginning of the 20th century there have been hundreds of wars throughout the world. These wars have been fought for many different reasons. Often a conflict has many different causes. The reasons for conflict include:

◆ conflicts between countries over disputed territory

◆ wars of independence

◆ conflicts over who holds political power within a country

◆ conflicts over control of economic resources within a country

◆ conflicts between different ethnic groups within a state

◆ conflicts between different religious groups within a state.

Some conflicts are between nations and others are civil wars, fought within a nation. Some conflicts produce large numbers of refugees, other wars produce fewer refugees.

Many academics who study wars and their causes believe that the patterns of warfare are now changing. Fewer wars are between different countries and a larger number of today's wars are civil wars. Today's wars also produce a larger number of civilian casualties. In the First World War only 10 per cent of the casualties were civilians. Today 85 per cent of all casualties are among civilians.

There are also a larger number of countries where civil war has led to the collapse of the government of that country. In Sierra Leone, Somalia, Afghanistan and Georgia, civil war has ended the power of those countries' governments.

> Some academics say that a war must kill over 1,000 people per year to be counted as a war. If a conflict kills less than 1,000 people in a year it is usually called **'low intensity war'** or **'human rights abuse'**. What do you think about the use of these terms?

Finding out about conflicts

Instructions

Time needed: 30-45 minutes

About ten copies of recent broadsheet newspapers and about ten atlases are needed. Every student also needs a blank world map with the countries drawn in.

Divide the students up into groups of three or four and give everyone a map. Each group should have some newspapers and an atlas.

Using the students' general knowledge and the information in the broadsheet newspaper, the students are going to produce a list of countries where there are wars being fought. After they have produced the list, they should use the atlas to mark the countries on a map.

This activity can be taken further; students can find out the causes of conflicts in different countries.

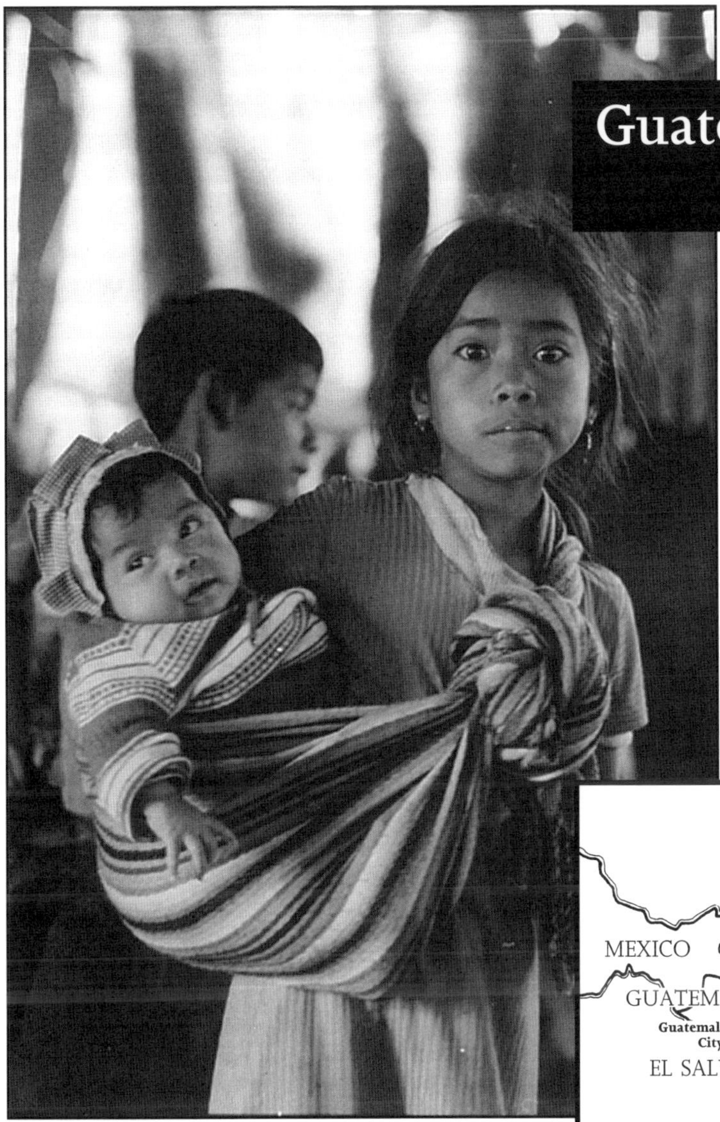

Guatemala

Longstanding discrimination and poverty in Guatemala have led to unrest. Refugees have fled to Mexico.

Population
10 million

Capital
Guatemala City

Economy
The majority of people in Guatemala work on the land as peasant farmers or plantation workers. Agricultural exports include bananas, cotton, coffee and sugar, mostly grown on plantations. Some 2 per cent of Guatemala's population owns 72 per cent of the land; access to farm land is the cause of today's conflict.

Some 86 per cent of Guatemala's population lives in poverty, including almost all of the indigenous Mayan Indians.

Ethnic groups
In the area which is now Guatemala, about 50 per cent of the population are Mayan Indians, 40 per cent are of mixed Spanish and Indian descent and about 10 per cent of the population are of European descent.

Mayan Indians are mostly poorer. Most farm in the high plateau of central Guatemala. They speak their own languages and many Indian women still wear traditional dress. Mayan Indians suffer racist abuse and discrimination in Guatemala. There are fewer schools and clinics in the rural areas where they live. As a consequence Mayan Indians have a shorter life expectancy than Guatemalans of mixed race.

Languages
Spanish is the official language; some 23 Mayan languages are also spoken.

Guatemalan refugee in Mexico *Howard Davies*

Events

Mayan Indians lived in Central America before the Spanish conquest. The cities they built and their works of art have survived and give evidence of a highly sophisticated civilisation.

1523 Pedro de Alvarado, a Spanish conquistador, makes an expedition to Central America. Over the next 250 years Spain takes control of the whole of the region. Spanish colonists marry local people.

1821 Central America gains independence from Spain and Guatemala becomes one province in the new Central American nation.

1838 Central America splits into five countries after Rafael Carrera seizes power in Guatemala.

1873 Justo Barrios becomes president of Guatemala. He is determined to modernise the country and introduces plantation agriculture to Guatemala. Mayan Indians are forced to give up their land to the new plantation owners, sometimes at gunpoint. Plantation owners become rich growing bananas, coffee, cotton and sugar. Mayan farmers try to grow food crops on smaller and smaller farms, or they become plantation workers.

1885 The United Fruit Company, a US company, buys up large amounts of land on which to grow bananas. The Guatemalan economy becomes very dependent on bananas and the United Fruit Company. Over the next 60 years the US is able to exert great power over Guatemala, through the United Fruit Company.

1898 Manuel Estrada Cabrero takes power in a military coup. He is the first in a series of fascist dictators who rule Guatemala until 1944.

1944 There is a revolution, and Guatemala becomes a democracy. In 1945, Juan Jose Arevalo becomes president of Guatemala. Under him, and his successor, Jacobo Arbenz, the Guatemalan government begins programmes to improve the lives of poorer people.

Land owned by the United Fruit Company and large landowners is confiscated and given to over 100,000 families without land. Schools are improved and racial barriers begin to break down.

1954 The US government accuses Jacobo Arbenz of being a communist, and gives money to those that oppose him. There is a military coup, supported by the US, and Colonel Castillo becomes the new president. The land taken from large landowners in 1944 is given back. From 1954 to 1986 Guatemala is mainly ruled by fascist dictators.

1970 Without democracy, many Guatemalans come to believe that the only way to change the country is through revolution. From 1970 onwards guerrillas start to organise among poor people.

The Guatemalan government reacts violently to the guerrillas. People who are thought to be sympathetic to the them are imprisoned or killed by death squads. The victims include trade unionists, community workers and politicians who call for democracy.

1974 There are elections, but the new president is accused of cheating in order to win his election.

1978 This is a year of protests and a general strike. During the general strike, 30 people are killed and over 1,000 people arrested.

1980 Mayan Indian farmers occupy the Spanish Embassy protesting about human rights violations. The Guatemalan army attack the Spanish Embassy and many people are killed. The Guatemalan government adopts a harsher policy towards the guerrillas. As the guerillas get more support from poorer people, the army destroys hundreds of Mayan Indian villages. There are widespread human rights abuses and over the next six years at least 150,000 people are murdered by the army or death squads.

1982 General Rios Montt comes to power in a military coup. The destruction of Mayan Indian villages continues. The government then tries to move the homeless Mayan Indians to 'development villages', which are little more than prisons. Rather than live in

Maria's story

Maria is living with her brother Antonio, her husband and two small children in a refugee camp in Mexico. They are Mayan Indian refugees from Guatemala.

'I am 24 years old and Antonio is my youngest brother. Originally there were seven of us and I am the eldest. I got married when Antonio was five years old and we all lived in the same house.

Our father, mother and two older brothers were in church one Sunday when soldiers surrounded the village square. All the men were killed and only a few of the women survived. Our mother was one of them. The soldiers dumped her outside our house. That evening the soldiers came back to murder her. We heard the tramping of their boots. The soldiers burst in through the door, but the back door was open and two of my brothers got away. Now they live in hiding in Guatemala, I think.

Antonio was too little to run away. He was sleeping in my mother's arms. When the soldiers came she didn't get up but remained lying on the bed. They shot her right there and she was killed instantly.

Morten Arnfred

I ran to my mother-in-law and started crying. My mother-in-law told me that there was nothing to do but to leave the village, because if we stayed we would also be killed.

So I left for the mountains with Antonio, my children and my husband. We crossed the border into Mexico and came to this camp. All the people in the camp come from Guatemala. But there are not many who come from the same region as us, so we don't all speak the same language. Our language is called Mam and there are only a few people here who speak it. But Antonio learns Spanish at school so we can all talk together.

My husband works on a coffee plantation owned by Mexicans. I work in a small clinic we have in the camp and Antonio looks after my children when I am working. The local people and the church here in Mexico have given us a lot of help. I hope that we are allowed to stay here until it is safe to return to Guatemala.'

development villages many of those who lose their homes go into hiding or flee to Mexico.

In the first five months of General Rios Montt's rule over 2,600 people are murdered by death squads. The US continues to give support to the Guatemalan army. By the end of the year about 200,000 people are refugees in camps in the Mexican jungle. Although helped by the churches and ordinary Mexican people most of the refugees live in poverty. The Mexican government only recognises a few of them as refugees.

1983 The Guatemalan army attacks refugee settlements in Mexico. The Mexican government decides to move some of the refugees away from the border to camps in the Yucatan peninsula. Most of the refugees do not want to move; the Mexican army uses force to evict some of them.

1986 Vinicio Cerezo becomes president of Guatemala after general elections are held. Of the 200,000 refugees in Mexico, only 53,000 have refugee status. There are smaller numbers of refugees in Belize and Honduras and about 350,000 Guatemalans living in the US and Canada.

Some refugees try to return to their home villages in Guatemala, but they are prevented from doing so. Instead they are told to go to the new development villages.

1989 There is a failed military coup in

Guatemala. The human rights situation and the civil war worsen, becoming as bad as the early 1980s. Trade unionists, human rights workers, teachers and peasant leaders are murdered. But there are talks between political leaders and representatives of the guerrillas.

1992 There are peace negotiations between representatives of refugees living in Mexico and the Guatemalan government. In 1992 they sign an agreement to allow for the return of Guatemalan refugees living in Mexico. This is the first time that refugees themselves have been involved in negotiations about their return (usually it is left to governments and the UN High Commissioner for Refugees). The agreement is meant to ensure that those returning will be safe and have access to farm land.

Rigoberta Menchu, a Mayan Indian woman living as a refugee in Mexico, wins the Nobel Peace Prize for her human rights work.

1993 The first Guatemalan refugees return home.

1994 There is a peace agreement between Guatemalan guerrillas and the government.

1995 Small numbers of refugees continue to return home from Mexico. But there are concerns about their safety. The Guatemalan army kills 10 returning refugees, and there are widespread human rights abuses. And there is still great poverty and inequality in Guatemala; this is the root cause of the conflict.

At the end of 1995 some 40,000 refugees remain in Mexican camps and another 200,000 Guatemalan refugees are living in Mexican towns and cities.

Designing a project partner leaflet

Aims

This activity aims to develop students's written communication skills.

Instructions

Time needed: at least two hours.

Students need access to coloured pens, paper and a computer with a desk top publishing programme. All students should have a copy of the information about the aid project in Maya Tecun. The class may also want to view the Refugee Council's video 'Refugee Children' which tells the story of a Guatemalan refugee child living in Mexico.

Many charities working in poor countries use the 'project partner' approach when raising money. The potential donor is given information about a particular project in a country. The donor (the person who donates money) gives a commitment to keep giving money for use in the project. In return he or she receives information about the project and the conditions in that area.

The class should be divided into pairs. Each pair should write and design a project partner leaflet designed to raise money for the project at Maya Tecun. The following information might be included in the leaflet:

- **location of the project**
- **the people it helps**
- **what the project does**
- **how the money will be used**
- **a short testimony of one of the refugees.**

Maya Tecun refugee camp, Mexico

Maya Tecun is located in southern Mexico, in the Yucatan peninsula. This area is home to a large number of Guatemalan refugees. Most are living in refugee camps.

When the refugees first arrived at Maya Tecun, the Mexican authorities did not allow them to leave the camp. The refugees, who numbered about 3,000 people, were entirely dependent on food aid supplied by the Mexican government. In exchange, all adult male refugees had to work to clear the land, and to build houses, schools, clinics and roads. Many of the refugees were very proud of the building work that they did.

But after this period the refugees began to face problems. The Mexican government ordered that the refugees become self-sufficient. Some refugees earned money by working as labourers on Mexican farms and plantations. Others cleared land in the forest to grow crops for the refugee camp. But the Maya Tecun area has very poor soil and little rainfall. Many crops did not grow well. There were many disagreements among the refugees. They were unused to working together to grow food. There were arguments between those who worked hard and those who did not. The refugees were not well-organised. Many of the refugees could not communicate with each other because they did not speak the same language.

There is now an aid project to help the Guatemalan refugees become more self-sufficient. Refugees were encouraged to cultivate some land together, but also have small vegetable gardens where they grow food for their own families. Refugees have been allowed to rent land outside the refugee camp. Here they can make their own decision about what they can grow.

As many of the refugee could not read and write, adult literacy classes were set up to help them learn. They also learned to speak Spanish in these classes, so that there was a common language in the refugee camp.

Refugees were given help to set up workshops to make shoes and clothing. The workshops were run by a group of 10 families. Although the things they made were mainly for use in the camp, some were sold outside.

Since the aid project started, the Maya Tecun refugee camp has become more self-sufficient. It is intended that this will continue.

Reforestation project, Maya Tecun *Howard Davies*

Finding out more

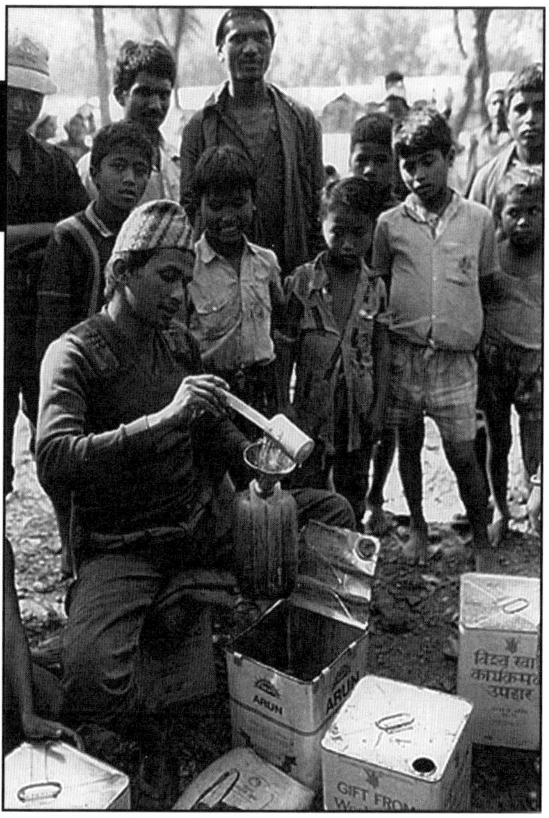

Aims

This activity aims to help students develop research skills. Students will be finding out additional information about refugee-producing countries not featured in this section.

Instructions

The time needed for this activity depends on how much detail goes into the students' presentations.

Apart from the 17 case studies in this book there are many more refugee-producing countries in the world, albeit in smaller numbers. These countries are listed in the table. There may be refugee students from these countries in British schools.

Students should chose one of these countries and engage in a small research project. They can collect information from various sources: their school library, their local library, by writing to the Refugee Council or Amnesty International (UK) or perhaps by interviewing appropriate local community organisations.

When the students have completed their research they should present it as a piece of written work. They could follow the layout of the information in this chapter, or present it in another way.

Countries producing small numbers of refugees

Algeria	Iran
Bangladesh (Chittagong Hill Tracts)	Ivory Coast
Bhutan	Mali
Colombia	Mauritania
Cuba	Nigeria
Djibouti	Senegal
Haiti	Tajikistan
Honduras	Tibet
Kenya	Togo
India	Uganda
Indonesia	Vietnam

Your research project could have the following sections:

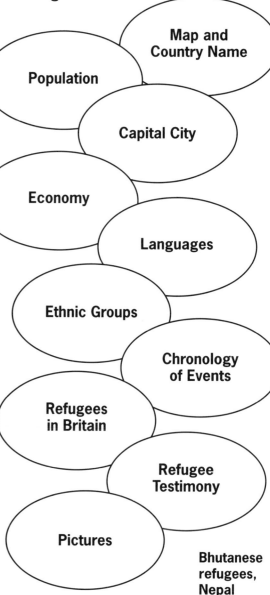

- **Map and Country Name**
- **Population**
- **Capital City**
- **Economy**
- **Languages**
- **Ethnic Groups**
- **Chronology of Events**
- **Refugees in Britain**
- **Refugee Testimony**
- **Pictures**

Bhutanese refugees, Nepal
UNHCR

CHAPTER FOUR

Kurdish refugee family
Howard Davies

ARRIVING IN BRITAIN

In 1995 over 41,000 asylum-seekers arrived in Britain ◆ This chapter looks at what happens to asylum-seekers when they arrive.

Refugees in Britain

Country of origin	Main dates of entry	Number of Asylum Seekers
Huguenots	1685-1700	100,000
Jews from Poland, Russia, Austria & Romania	1880-1914	200,000
Belgians	1914-18	250,000
Germany, Austria & Czechoslovakia	1933-39	56,000
Other European refugees from the Nazis	1940-45	100,000
Poland	1939-50	250,000
Czechoslovakia, Hungary & Romania	1945-50	50,000
Hungary	1956	17,000
Czechoslovakia	1968	5,000
Uganda	1972-	36,000
Chile	1973-79	3,000
Ethiopia & Eritrea	1973-	16,000
Cyprus	1974	24,000
Viet Nam	1975-92	24,000
Iran	1978-	21,000
Iraq	1980-	12,000
Poland	1981	1,000
Ghana	1982-	11,000
Sri Lanka (Tamils)	1983-	24,000
Pakistan	1984-	4,000
Somalia	1988-	27,000
Turkey (Kurds)	1989-	22,000
Zaire	1989-	15,000
Sudan	1989-	4,000
Angola	1989-	10,000
Former Yugoslavia	1992-96	12,000
Sierra Leone	1993-	3,000
Kenya	1994-	2,500
Nigeria	1994-	4,000

Throughout history many refugees have returned home once the situation became safe in their home country. Other refugees have moved from Britain to new countries. For example about 40 per cent of Polish refugees arriving in Britain from 1939-45 returned to their home country or were resettled in another country. This table does not take into account repatriation or the resettlement of refugees in a new country.

Source: Refugee Council, 1995.

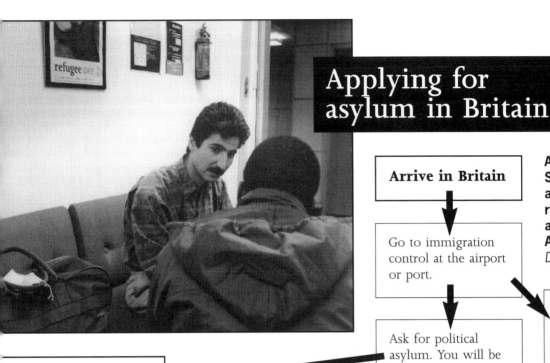

Applying for asylum in Britain

A newly-arrived Sierra Leonean asylum-seeker receives advice at Heathrow Airport *Howard Davies*

Arrive in Britain

Go to immigration control at the airport or port.

Ask for political asylum. You will be given a short interview. At this interview immigration officers ask questions about your journey to Britain. You may be fingerprinted, and have to prove your identity.

Go through immigration control. You may decide to apply for asylum after you have been in Britain a few days. Some people who may be studying or working in Britain apply for asylum if the situation in their home country suddenly changes. Now people who apply for asylum after arriving in Britain are no longer entitled to income support or help to pay their rent.

You can be told that your application for political asylum is 'without foundation'. If this happens you are likely to be detained in an immigration detention centre. You have a limited right to appeal. Your appeal will be dealt with very quickly, often within eight days. You are likely to be sent back to the last country you passed through on your way to Britain.

You are given a form called a Political Asylum Questionnaire. You have to fill this in, explaining how you and your family were persecuted in your home country. You may have to fill in this form at the airport, but it is more usual for asylum-seekers to take it away with them.

Go to see immigration officers, and tell them you wish to apply for asylum.

You may be asked to attend another interview to find out more information.

Attend interview to prove your identity. You will also be fingerprinted.

This is a simplified flow chart to show how people apply for asylum in Britain. For some refugees the procedures are more complicated.

Immigration officers at the Home Office make a decision about your case. This can be quick or it can take many months.

You can be refused refugee status or exceptional leave to remain.

You can appeal against your refusal.

OR

You may decide to leave Britain.

OR

You may be removed from Britain.

You can be given full refugee status. This gives you the right to stay in Britain, to work, to study and to bring your family here.

You can be given 'exceptional leave to remain'. This allows you to stay in Britain for one year, then you have to ask for an extension to stay. If you have exceptional leave to remain your family cannot join you for four years after the decision has been made. You can work, but it is more difficult to study at college or university.

What happens to asylum-seekers in Britain?

Look at the statistics that shows the decisions that are made on asylum applications. What are the main trends shown in the statistics?

◆ What might be the reasons for these changes?

Decisions on applications for asylum in Britain, 1982–1995

Year	Refugee Status (%)	ELR* (%)	Refusal (%)
1982	59	12	31
1983	40	32	28
1984	33	39	28
1985	24	57	19
1986	14	68	18
1987	13	64	23
1988	25	60	15
1989	31	59	10
1990	26	63	11
1991	9	40	51
1992	3	44	53
1993	7	48	46
1994	5	19	76
1995	5	18	77

* Exceptional leave to remain

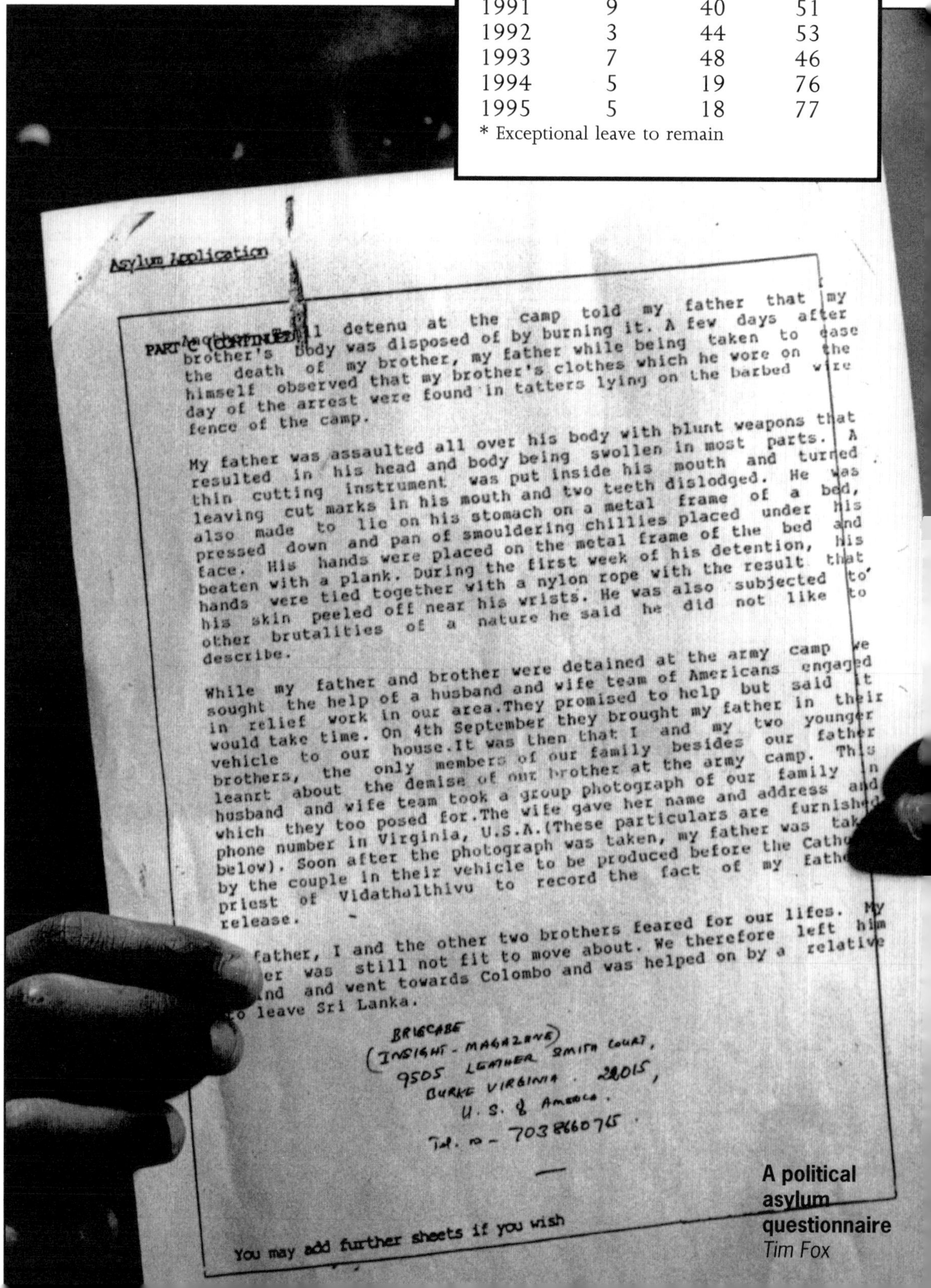

Asylum Application
PART C (CONTINUED)
detenu at the camp told my father that my brother's body was disposed of by burning it. A few days after the death of my brother, my father while being taken to ease himself observed that my brother's clothes which he wore on the day of the arrest were found in tatters lying on the barbed wire fence of the camp.
My father was assaulted all over his body with blunt weapons that resulted in his head and body being swollen in most parts. A thin cutting instrument was put inside his mouth and turned leaving cut marks in his mouth and two teeth dislodged. He was also made to lie on his stomach on a metal frame of a bed, pressed down and pan of smouldering chillies placed under his face. His hands were placed on the metal frame of the bed and beaten with a plank. During the first week of his detention, his hands were tied together with a nylon rope with the result that his skin peeled off near his wrists. He was also subjected to other brutalities of a nature he said he did not like to describe.
While my father and brother were detained at the army camp we sought the help of a husband and wife team of Americans engaged in relief work in our area. They promised to help but said it would take time. On 4th September they brought my father in their vehicle to our house. It was then that I and my two younger brothers, the only members of our family besides our father leanrt about the demise of our brother at the army camp. This husband and wife team took a group photograph of our family in which they too posed for. The wife gave her name and address and phone number in Virginia, U.S.A. (These particulars are furnished below). Soon after the photograph was taken, my father was taken by the couple in their vehicle to be produced before the Catholic priest of Vidathalthivu to record the fact of my father's release.
My father, I and the other two brothers feared for our lifes. My father was still not fit to move about. We therefore left him behind and went towards Colombo and was helped on by a relative to leave Sri Lanka.
BRIEFCASE
(INSIGHT - MAGAZINE)
9505 LEATHER SMITH COURT,
BURKE VIRGINIA . 22015,
U. S. & America.
Tel. no - 703 8660765 .
You may add further sheets if you wish

A political asylum questionnaire
Tim Fox

Defining persecution

Aims

To be given refugee status in Britain the Home Office has to decide that a particular asylum-seeker has a 'well founded fear of being persecuted'. But the idea of persecution is subjective - it depends upon the interpretation of the government. This activity aims to get students thinking about what 'persecution' means.

Instructions

Time needed: 30 minutes

Copy the sheet of speech bubbles. Discuss with the students the importance of a definition of the word 'persecution' in the context of the 1951 UN Convention Relating to the Status of Refugees.

The students should work in pairs and come up with their own definition for the word persecution. They should use the ideas in the bubbles, and write a paragraph about what they believe constitutes persecution.

The students should then mark the quotations where they believe the speaker is being persecuted.

When each pair has finished the students should compare their answers.

*

A **refugee** is someone who has fled from his/her home country or is unable to return to it 'owing to a well-founded fear of being persecuted for reasons of race, religion, nationality, membership of a particular social group or political opinion'.

(From the 1951 UN Convention Relating to the Status of Refugees.)

'It is illegal for me to practice my religion and I wish to do so.'

'I want to leave my country, but it is illegal for me to do this.'

'I fear I may be killed. I am active in my trade union. In my town other people from my union have disappeared and then been found murdered.'

'My parents are going to force me to marry someone I do not want to marry.'

'Military service is compulsory in my country and I do not want to serve in the army. I believe what the army is doing in my country is wrong.'

'I am a gay man and in my country it is illegal to have a partner of the same sex. You can go to gaol for homosexual sex. And if anyone from my village knew I was gay I am sure that my house would be burned and I would be forced to move.'

'I cannot get a better job because my papers show that I belong to a certain religious group.'

'I want to buy more land and expand my farm, but it is illegal for me to own more than 25 hectares of land.'

'I have been attacked because I belong to a certain ethnic group. I fear being attacked again.'

'My political party has been made illegal.'

'My brother has been put in prison because he held views that our government did not like.'

'I am in danger of being arrested because of my political beliefs and torture is often used in my country.'

'It is illegal for me to speak my language in public or call my child a name in our language.'

'I have already spent seven years in prison for criticising the government in a public meeting. I am worried that I will be imprisoned again.'

Arriving in a new country

Instructions

Time needed: 15-20 minutes for the initial part of the activity, then about an hour for the diary.

Divide the students up into pairs and give them the scenario below. When the students have produced their list of needs the group can come together for a short discussion.

Students

Applying for political asylum is not the only difficulty that faces asylum-seekers when they arrive in Britain. Housing, a job and schools for children have to be found. Many newly-arrived refugees also have to learn a new language and find out about their rights in a new country. As a result, the first few months in Britain for refugees are often very difficult.

Try putting yourself in the shoes of a newly-arrived refugee. Imagine that civil war has broken out where you live. You arrive home from school and find your house has been destroyed. Most people have left your home town and you have been told that your parents have fled.

You walk to a port town. By chance there is a cargo ship in the port. You manage to persuade a sailor on the ship to take you on board (after you have paid him £50). The boat sails to Malmo, Sweden. Here the journey ends and you are made to get off the boat. You are taken to see the Swedish immigration officials. What will happen to you?

In your pairs make a list of the things that you will need in the new country:

- ◆ immediately
- ◆ during the next six months.

Then write a diary describing what it was like during your first month in Sweden. You should describe what you need, how you spend your time and how you might feel.

Discussion point

◆ What did you learn about the life of a newly-arrived refugee from this activity?

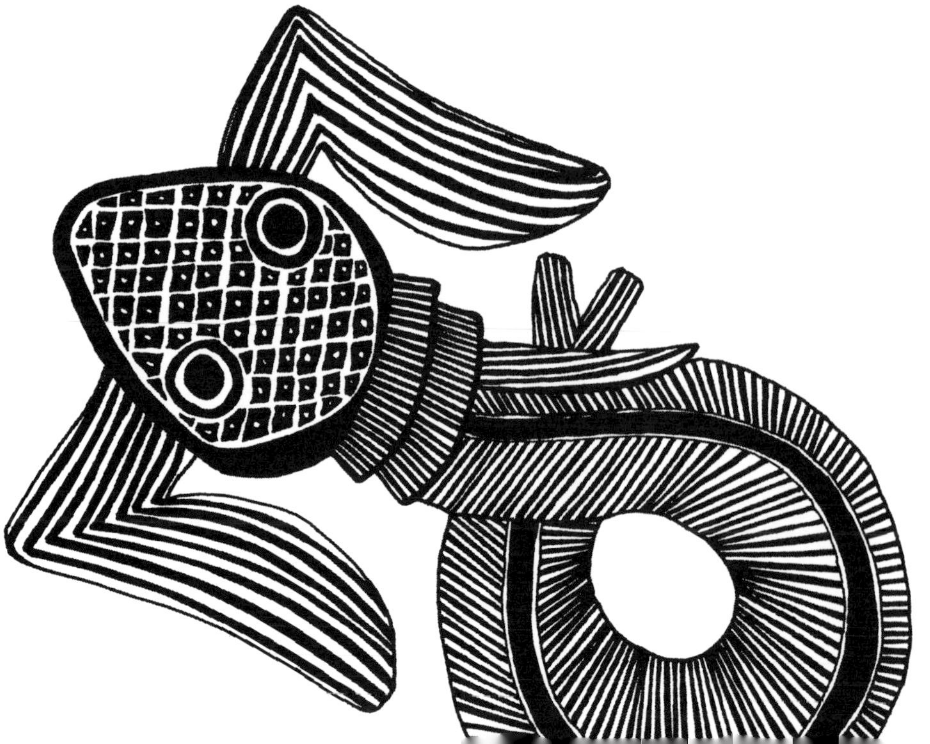

Finding a home

Refugees in a hostel, London
Karen Robinson

Very few people can get along without the peace and security of a home. For many refugees who have experienced war, torture or the death of close relatives, good housing is needed to recover from such experiences. Yet flight from danger often heads to homelessness and bad housing in Britain.

Nearly 90 per cent of Britain's asylum-seekers and refugees live in Greater London where the housing shortage is worst. Some refugees are lucky and find housing quickly. They may rent homes from local authorities, housing associations or private landlords.

Other asylum-seekers and refugees are not so lucky. If housed by a local authority they may spend a long period of time in temporary accommodation before finding somewhere permanent to live. Some refugees who rent rooms from private landlords find themselves living in very bad conditions. Rooms may be damp and cooking facilities limited. Some refugees face racial harassment in their new homes.

Asylum-seekers & housing

Before 1993 asylum-seekers had the same right to be housed by a local authority as anyone else in Britain. If people have school-aged children or are old or sick, a local authority will take responsibility for housing them. The rights of people to council housing are outlined in the 1985 Housing Act.

But in 1993 asylum-seekers' rights to council housing were changed by the Asylum and Immigration (Appeals) Act. Now all asylum-seekers who are housed by local authorities have to stay in 'temporary accommodation' while they wait for the Home Office to decide whether they can stay in Britain. Temporary accommodation usually means a bed and breakfast hotel or a privately rented home. Children who live in temporary accommodation face particular problems. It can be difficult to do homework in an overcrowded room in a bed and breakfast hotel. Children who live in temporary accommodation have to move homes - and schools - many times.

Social Security changes, introduced in 1996, mean that the majority of asylum seekers no longer receive benefits. Many asylum seekers have become homeless since then, because they cannot afford to pay rent.

Housing for refugees with special needs

Some organisations provide housing for refugees. The Refugee Council runs hostels for refugees with special needs. It has a children's home for unaccompanied refugee children and some reception centres for newly-arrived Bosnian refugees. The Refugee Council also runs an old people's home for elderly refugees from eastern Europe, a day centre and night shelter for homeless refugees.

Refugee Housing is another organisation that offers housing to refugees. One of its hostels, Basle Court in Brixton, provides short-term housing for newly-arrived refugees. Basle Court is a 32-roomed hostel; eight staff are employed to help residents. The demand for housing at places like Basle Court far exceeds the number of places. The hostel workers can only house the most vulnerable refugees. Examples of vulnerable groups include rape and torture victims, the disabled and refugees suffering from physical or mental illnesses.

Near Basle Court are some small houses also managed by staff of Refugee Housing. About five refugees live in each house. For them it is the first step towards an independent life in Britain.

Homelessness & refugees

Students

Homelessness can generate a lot of strong feelings. Here is an extract from a letter which appeared in a local paper in south London. It was published at the same time that some refugees on a council housing estate were abused by some local residents.

'People who have been born in this area are not getting council housing. My own daughter who has just had her second child is still living in a one-roomed flat. At the same time refugees are given houses on the best estates. These people have made themselves homeless when they left their own countries. They should not expect to go to the top of the queue for council homes. Council housing should be for local people.'

Try and answer the questions below:

◆ What are the main points that the author is making?

◆ Why might she write a letter like this?

◆ Do you feel that the refugees are to blame for her daughter's situation?

◆ What do you feel about what she is saying?

Using the information about housing write a reply to the newspaper.

Fact Sales of council homes has led to a reduction of 1,300,000 council homes since 1981.

Fact Councils are not allowed to replace most housing that is sold off because of government restrictions on council spending. At the beginning of the 1980s, councils were building new homes at the rate of about 23,000 a year. During 1993 about 1,000 council homes were built.

Fact The London Research Centre found that asylum-seekers and refugees have to wait longer to be found permanent housing by councils.

*

Scapegoat A person or a group of people who are blamed for things that go wrong. Refugees can easily be made into scapegoats: when societies are experiencing poverty and unemployment it is easy to blame a scapegoat like refugees for taking jobs and houses. Blaming outsiders is a simple explanation for things like shortages of jobs and homes, but it ignores the real causes of homelessness and unemployment.

Finding a job

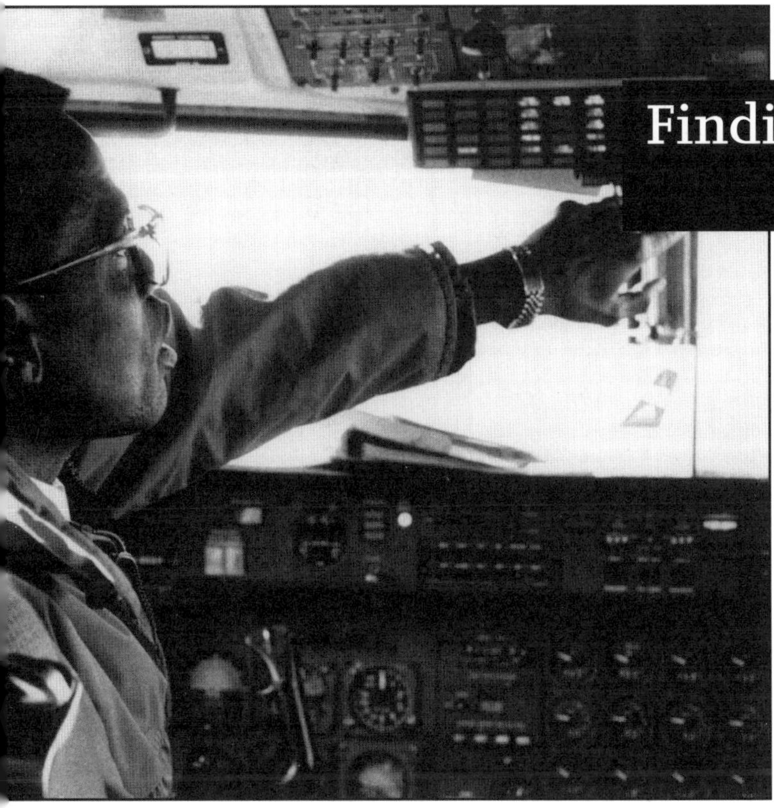

A Ugandan refugee who found a job as an air traffic controller
Howard Davies

Asylum-seekers are allowed to work in Britain after they have lived here for six months. People with refugee status can also work, but finding a job is not always easy. Refugees are often highly qualified people but find it difficult to obtain a job which is as good as the one that they left.

The Refugee Council and the Government have both carried out research on refugees' work experiences. Here are some of the results:

Economic activity of refugees & asylum-seekers

	Males %	Females %
Employed	29	23
Unemployed	42	21
Student	13	11
On training scheme	4	0
Looking after family	4	39
Retired	3	3
Sick or disabled	6	3

Source: Home Office, 1995

English language ability at time of arrival

I could speak no English	35.5%
I could speak a few words	18.3%
I could speak enough English to get by	15.9%
I could speak conversational English	12.6%
My English was fluent	17.2%

Source Refugee Council, 1989

Discussion points

◆ **What do the statistics show you?**

◆ **The unemployment rate for adult men in Britain is about 14 per cent. Why do you think that asylum-seekers and refugees are more likely to be unemployed than the 'average' person?**

◆ **What does the cartoon (on page 194) tell you about refugees' experiences of work?**

◆ **How might refugees be helped to get work?**

One day while at my work . . .

. . . disaster struck! The giant Rotalith came to a shuddering halt.

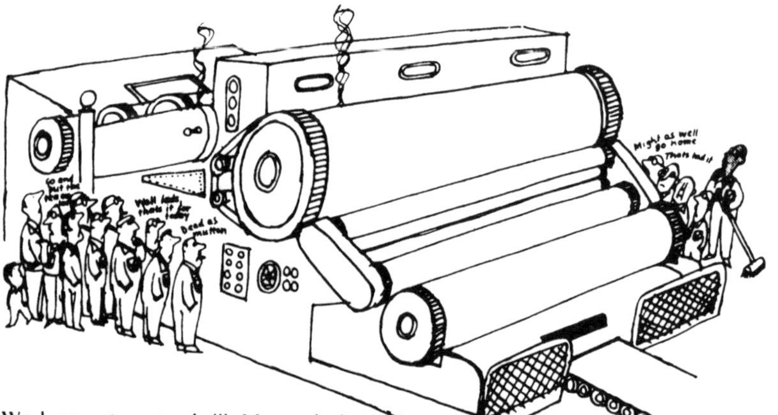

Work came to a standstill. Men rushed to the machine, trying desperately to get it started. But all in vain. The men stood there, grim and silent, thinking of the money they would lose. (Some of them had houses, wives and children to think about.)

I could stand the suffering of my comrades no longer. "I know what's wrong," I cried, rushing forward.

I worked in a silence broken only by the encouraging shouts of my workmates. A few minutes later, the mighty machine started. The day's production was saved!

Yes, it's certainly an exciting life as a factory sweeper—especially when occasionally you get a chance to use your higher degrees in science and engineering.

New Internationalist

Unaccompanied refugee children

Unaccompanied Vietnamese girl
Howard Davies

Every year about 350 unaccompanied refugee children arrive in Britain without their parents. At present most unaccompanied refugee children who come to Britain have fled from Angola, Ethiopia, Eritrea, Sierra Leone, Somalia, Afghanistan, Sri Lanka, Turkey and former Yugoslavia. In the past Britain has received unaccompanied refugee children from Vietnam. Between 1938 and 1939 nearly 10,000 children came from Germany, Austria and Czechoslovakia on the *Kindertransporte* (the children's transport).

Some children who come to Britain by themselves have seen their family killed or disappear. Other unaccompanied refugee children have become separated from their parents in the chaos of war. Yet others have been sent away by their parents when the situation in their home countries becomes very dangerous. In this group are boys and young men who have been sent away to avoid conscription into the army or a guerrilla organisation.

Sometimes unaccompanied refugee children are brought into Britain by a family friend or relative and are cared for by the people that brought them here. Other children come to Britain by themselves or are abandoned by those who brought them into Britain.

The right kind of help

Unaccompanied refugee children need care and support - just like any other children. They may be cared for by family friends or relatives. Other unaccompanied children are found foster parents or live in children's homes.

It is very important that unaccompanied refugee children receive the right kind of help when they arrive in Britain. Some unaccompanied children find it difficult to get over distressing events in their past - they may have seen their parents killed or witnessed other terrifying events. Those who still have parents will naturally miss them or may be very worried about them. The children will have left friends and familiar things behind. Many unaccompanied refugee children also have to learn a new language after they arrive in Britain.

The Refugee Council has a home for unaccompanied refugee children. It is called Korczak House and is named after Dr Janusz Korczak, a doctor who worked with orphaned children in the Warsaw Ghetto. Experienced social workers are able to help the children start a new life. At Korczak House children are cared for by social workers who speak their own language and can cook familiar food.

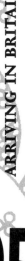

Abeda's story

Abeda is a 15 year old girl who is living in a home for refugee children in London. She came to London in 1990. Here she describes her life:

'I've been here for a year now. There were five of us Eritrean children in the home when we arrived. Now there are more than 20. We are rather crowded, but we are all like a family.

I lived with my uncle and aunt because my dad died and we don't know what happened to my mum. She disappeared. But my uncle was put in prison for political reasons and my aunt decided we had to escape.

When my aunt decided to send me here I understood why. She said the fighting around Addis Ababa made it too dangerous for me. The soldiers behaved very badly to girls and I had reached the age when they notice us. When they see an Eritrean girl they want to sleep with her. Girls who say 'no' are sometimes killed. It happened to a girl I met; she was only 15.

My aunt made sure that two cousins, my sister and me escaped. Then she fled herself - to Saudi Arabia. I miss my friends and my aunt and worry about my uncle in jail. I don't know what's happened to them all.

All I can do now is study hard and hope to go back. I'm waiting for peace and no more fighting. Then when I am older I want to be a chemist and do what I can to help.'

Saturday schools

An Iranian Saturday School *Howard Davies*

Every Saturday about 10,000 refugee children can be found learning their first language in living rooms, church halls and schools throughout Britain. They are students in Saturday Schools run by refugee communities. One Saturday School is the Iranian Community Centre's school in London.

There are over 21,000 Iranian refugees in Britain. Most of them arrived after 1978 when there was a revolution in Iran. Farsi is the language spoken by most people in Iran. Farsi lessons are the main activity of the Iranian Community Centre's Saturday School.

Over 70 children attend the school. They meet in a school building which is empty on Saturdays. There are three different Farsi classes and also Iranian music, dance and drama classes and an English class.

The teachers at the school are all volunteers. Parents help run the school, helping in class and in the library.

Discussion point

- **Going to school on a Saturday may sound like a bad idea, but can you think of some reasons why refugee children may want to attend Saturday schools?**

Choman's story

Refugees write about their experiences

Choman is 18 years old. She is Kurdish and was born in Iraqi Kurdistan. Here she describes how it feels to arrive in Britain as a refugee.

'It was war again and running away from your land, marching through the mountains to reach a peaceful place and getting separated from your parents.

Two years ago, on a misty evening in September I arrived at Heathrow airport, alone and scared, but full of hope. I was happy as I was going to be with my parents again after being away from them for over a year.

So I arrived in England. Before I came I thought of England as a country where all doors are open to you, where you are safe and free, where you can get anything you want. I thought of England as a green land, full of rain. English people, respectful and friendly. This is what I was thinking about during my journey. I was thinking about starting again, being happy, seeking knowledge so that maybe someday I can help my country. England to me was a mysterious land where I was going to fulfil my dreams. England was also the place where my parents lived. The minute that my mother hugged me crying, I thought that all my sorrows had ended and life was going to be sweet and happy again.

I was so enthusiastic about starting school and learning English. I had been away from school for two years because we were travelling and did not have a permanent place to live. I promised myself not to miss school again and not to waste more time. I had to be serious and work hard, there was no time for being lazy. So, ten days after my arrival I started going to a school close to my house, called Hampstead School.

The problem was that at my age I should have been doing A-Levels, but because I didn't speak any English they put me in year ten with students who were three years younger than me. The teachers didn't believe that I would be able to do GCSEs with so little English. I was told that the best thing for me was to stay in year ten until my English was better and maybe in two years I could attempt GCSEs.

Being with younger people is not a problem if they are mature. But when you are a teenager a three year difference is quite a big gap, especially if you don't speak the language and you are new to the culture. It is at this time that you need friends the most. But I was shocked to find out that in the lunch queue they used to laugh at me and say that I never had decent food in my country. They said I had always been hungry that's why I ran away from my home. Some people treated me like a fool because I couldn't speak English well, some just ignored me as if I didn't exist.

Nobody wanted to sit next to me in lessons and no-one wanted to have me as their partner in PE. I was all alone in the corner and did not understand the jokes during the lessons. I couldn't understand the subjects we studied because of my English and could never express myself during any simple discussion. I was too scared to talk because I knew that if I made a mistake some of them would laugh at me. Once I even got beaten up by a group of students who used to bully everyone. They beat me one evening when I was walking home alone. They said they couldn't stand me because I was a refugee who lived on the Government's money (which they considered to be their own money). After this I lost all my confidence and began to think that I was the most unwanted person on earth. I used to cry on my own and thought about leaving school. I started to believe that what other people thought about me was true.

I almost gave up. The reason that I didn't was because of my mother's help, the support I got from my teachers and the school charity called 'the Children of the Storm' which helped me to learn English. The charity helped me to socialise with others. Miss Demitriades who runs the charity was someone who always listened, gave us advice and had time to give us a hug on the depressing days. So there was still hope. There were people who cared and helped, so I carried on. I had to anyway because I believe life is a fight. I managed to do three GCSEs eight months after my arrival which I counted as a big success. Now I am doing three A-Levels in maths, physics and art. I speak English quite well and sometimes I write poetry in English, other times I translate my poems from my language. I have some published work and I have made a few nice friends who can accept me as I am.

I am planning to study philosophy at university. The love of my life is poetry and writing and I always dream of the day when I can go home.

Now I take care of my parents who don't speak English. I hate the letters which tell me about changes in income support, paying council tax, decrease in housing benefit, surgery appointments and so on. There is always a form to fill in, a letter to reply to, proof of being a student, proof of receiving income support, of not being entitled to some things and being entitled to others. Sometimes I miss a few lessons to get these things straight.

The other side of the story is living in two completely different cultures. There is the British culture which I live in from morning until evening, and my Kurdish culture as I get home. The British culture which breaks all the rules, uncovers all the secrets and has a great sense of adventure. The Kurdish culture where every little thing is forbidden, all the feeling repressed and is really hard for a girl like me to say or do what she wants. I am divided between the two cultures and sometimes I think I don't belong to any of them. There are strong and weak points about both cultures, and I can't totally accept or refuse either, so now
I don't fit in any of them perfectly. Sometimes I feel I need to change my character or lie to avoid serious clashes.

At other times I feel so depressed because I can't get in touch with my family back home. I only get to hear about my brothers and sisters when someone travels back home. Often I feel I can't fulfil the expectations of my parents, my brothers and sisters back home, Kurdish society and myself. I always feel left behind, and I want to read and read to conquer my depression. I will carry on as long as there is someone I can share my sorrows with. I shall not stop. If I feel lonely and depressed I sing, and I try and remember that only honest words can stay.'

Poems about exile

Opposite are two poems written by refugees at different points in their lives.

Students

◆ Read the poems by Maria Bravo and Gerda Mayer. Maria Bravo's poem was written soon after she arrived in Britain. Gerda Mayer wrote her poem after she had lived in Britain for many years and had been able to return to her home town for a visit.

◆ What were the two writers feeling when they wrote their poems?

◆ What do these two poems teach us about how refugees sometimes feel when they come to Britain?

On Exiles & Defeats

No. It was not the bad time in Chena,
nor the sudden grim prosecutions
in improvised war councils.
No. The blind gun that hits me on the
shoulder
didn't defeat me,
nor the investigator's black hood of
horror
nor the grey hell of the stadiums
with their roars of terror.

No. Neither was it the iron bars at
the window
cutting us in pieces from life,
nor the watch kept on our house
nor the stealthy tread,
nor the slide into the deep maw
of hunger.

No. What defeated me was the street
that was not mine,
the borrowed language learned in
hastily set up courses.
What defeated me was the lonely,
uncertain figure
in longitudes that did not belong
to us.
It was Greenwich
longitude zero
close to nothing.
What defeated me was the alien rain,
forgetting words
the groping memory,
friends far away
and the atrocious ocean between us,
wetting the letters I waited for
which did not come.

What defeated me was yearning
day after day
at Jerningham Road
agonising under the fog
at Elephant and Castle
sobbing on London Bridge.

And I was defeated step by step
by the harsh calendar
and between Lunes-Monday
and Martes-Tuesday
I had shrivelled into a stranger.
What defeated me was the absence
of your tenderness, my country.

Maria Eugenia Bravo Calderara

Translated by Cicely Herbert and taken from 'Prayers in the National Stadium' Katabarsif Press, 1992.

Maria Bravo is Chilean and works for the Refugee Council. She was imprisoned and tortured in Chile in 1973. After she was released she came to Britain as a refugee.

The Town (Karlsbad/ Karlovy Vary)

It is an irony that I return
with a heart so trembling,
I who was ever its stepchild?
It begrudged shelter to my ancestors.
It spat me out.
It welcomes me now
cautiously
as a guest
who comes
and goes again.
It has changed its language;
it calls itself
by a new name.
It speaks neither my mother tongue
nor the language of my enemies
(which is the same);
Its voice will be
foreign and strangely
neutral and that too
will be difficult
to endure.
It is an irony that I return
like its hailed, like its hallowed
like its own true love;
I shall fall at its green feet.

Gerda Mayer

Gerda Mayer was a Jewish woman who was born in Karlsbad, a town in a German-speaking area in Czechoslovakia. This part of Czechoslovakia was annexed by Nazi Germany in 1938. After the Second World War Karlsbad was renamed Karlovy Vary.

Understanding how refugees might feel

Aims

To develop some of the issues raised in Choman's story and in the poems on pages 197-199. The activities aim to help young people understand how refugees might feel at different points in their lives. Only people who have been refugees can really know what it is like, but it is important for people involved with refugees to have greater understanding and sympathy with how refugees may be feeling.

How did you feel after a bad experience?

Instructions

Time needed: 30 minutes

Large pieces of paper and coloured pens are needed.

The students should be divided into pairs. The pairs should be asked to think back to a time when they had a bad experience. This could include events such as having an accident, losing a pet, being lost or in danger or the death of family member or friend.

The pairs should write down the emotions that they felt during the experience and afterwards. The group should come together. The teacher or group leader should use the ideas from the group to make a list of different emotions.

NB This activity should only be done by a group of students who know each other well and have good relationships with each other.

Discussion points

◆ How long did it take you to get over the experience, or do you think that it is still affecting you?

◆ Do you think that refugees might feel similar emotions?

What does home mean to me?

Aims

To explore different understandings of what a home is.

Instructions

Time needed: 30 minutes

The students should be divided into threes or fours. Each group should think about words which say something about home to them. For example they could mention certain people, places, objects, feelings and memories. Each group should make a list of their words on a piece of paper.

The students should then come together. Each group should read out their words to the rest of the class.

Discussion point

◆ What kind of feelings about your home would you have if you had to move to another country?

Vhat does a refugee eave behind?

Refugees leave their homes in fear and some have to leave very quickly. They have to leave many things behind. Obviously many material possessions are left, but also family and friends.

Put yourself in the position of having 30 minutes to pack your bags. Make a list of all the things you would take with you. You will have to carry all these items. Then make a list of all the things that you value that you would have to leave behind.

How does it feel to be new?

Instructions

Time needed: 45 minutes

The students should be divided into threes and fours. In their groups the students should discuss how it would feel to arrive in Britain from another country. They can decide from which country they have come. The groups should talk about arriving in Britain, their new home, food, their first day at school and other new experiences.

They should then write a letter to a imaginary friend they left in their home country, to tell them about their new home.

London
4th May 1990

Dear Juan,

Today I started my new School in London. It is so large, nearly 1500 pupils. There is one other Colombian boy in the school, but he is much older Than me.

CHAPTER FIVE

HOW WE RECEIVE REFUGEES

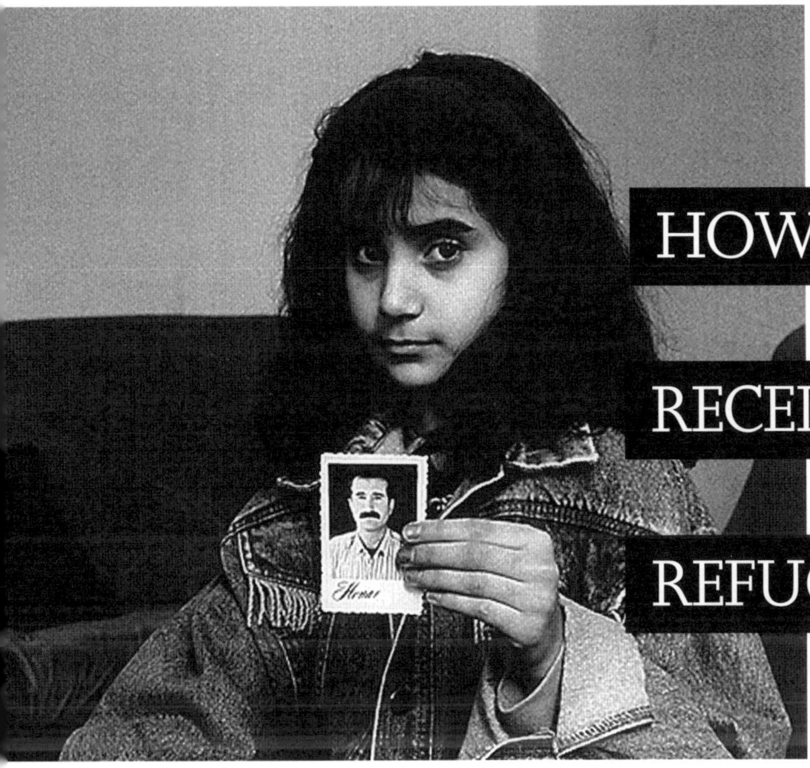

Kurdish girl, living in London, who has been denied family reunion with her father *Tim Fox*

Many refugees are made to feel welcome in Britain. But during the last ten years hostility to refugees in western Europe has increased ◆ This chapter looks at our perceptions of refugees ◆ how we form ideas about other people ◆ the influence of the media ◆ what we mean by racism ◆ discriminatory legislation in Britain

Who influences our opinions?

Aims

The activity aims to help participants understand who influences their opinions.

Instructions

Time needed: 45 minutes

Some large sheets of paper, thick pens, ball point pens and 'post-its' are needed.

Explain to the group that many different things influence our political opinions, whether these opinions are about refugees, the environment or any other issue. The group is going to examine who influences their opinions.

Divide the students up into groups of three or four. Give each group a large sheet of paper, pens and 'post-its'. Everyone should draw a circle in the middle of each sheet of paper and write 'me' in the circle. Then using the 'post-its' each group should make a list of who influences their opinions. (The list can include things like parents, teachers and television). They should write each factor on an individual 'post-it' and stick them on the sheets of paper.

Using the 'post-its' on the other side of the paper the groups should then rank the factors starting with the most important. The groups should then come together for a discussion.

Discussion points

◆ Who influences your opinions?

◆ What are the most important influences on your opinions?

◆ Who do you think influences your opinions about other people such as refugees?

Conducting an opinion poll about refugees

Aims

The activity aims to help participants assess and understand prejudices about refugees.

Instructions

Preparation time, time in a lesson and homework periods are needed for this.

Copies of the following opinion polls need to be made so that each participant has ten of them. You will also need some large sheets of paper, graph paper, pens, pencils and rulers.

Explain the aims of the activity, and that the group is carrying out an opinion poll in your school to find out about young people's attitudes to refugees. Give each participant ten copies of the opinion polls. They should interview students from other classes. Everyone should try and make sure that they get an even balance of male and females in their interviews, as well as people from different ethnic groups.

After the opinion polls are filled in the group should come together to analyse them. The participants can draw graphs to illustrate some of the results. The graphs should be used as a basis for discussion.

Discussion points

◆ What proportion of people interviewed gave a good definition of who are refugees?

◆ How many people thought that Britain accepted too many refugees?

◆ Did any of the results of the opinion polls surprise you?

◆ If you worked for an organisation such as the Refugee Council would you be happy about the results of such an opinion poll? How would it influence your work?

◆ How many people who were interviewed recognised the wealth of skills refugees bring to Britain?

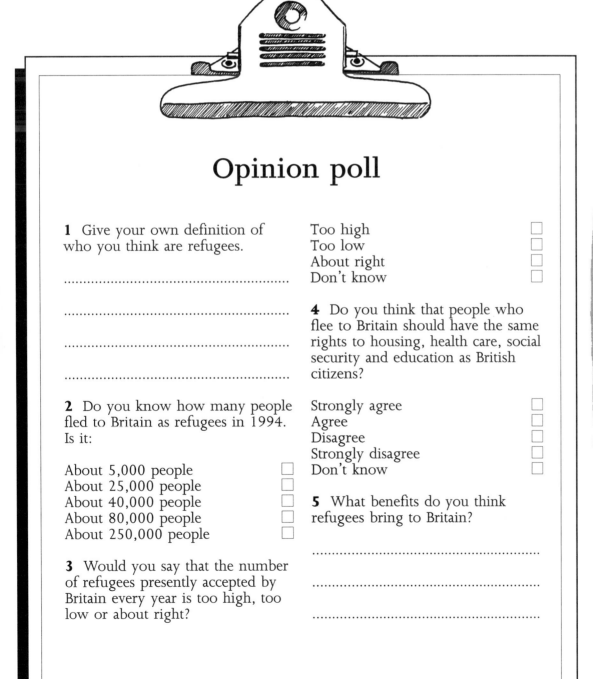

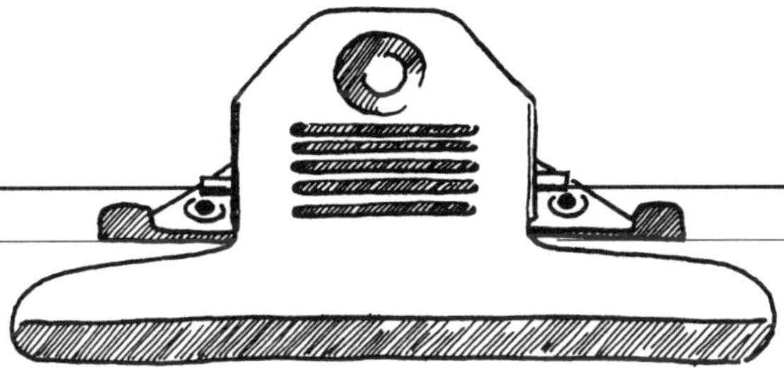

Opinion poll

1 Give your own definition of who you think are refugees.

....

....

....

....

2 Do you know how many people fled to Britain as refugees in 1994. Is it:

About 5,000 people ☐
About 25,000 people ☐
About 40,000 people ☐
About 80,000 people ☐
About 250,000 people ☐

3 Would you say that the number of refugees presently accepted by Britain every year is too high, too low or about right?

Too high ☐
Too low ☐
About right ☐
Don't know ☐

4 Do you think that people who flee to Britain should have the same rights to housing, health care, social security and education as British citizens?

Strongly agree ☐
Agree ☐
Disagree ☐
Strongly disagree ☐
Don't know ☐

5 What benefits do you think refugees bring to Britain?

....

....

....

Refugees & the media

A disaster that caused thousands of people to become refugees would receive a lot of newspaper coverage if it was near home. But how much coverage does the press give to refugees in poor countries?

And is the media coverage of refugees in Britain always fair? Is it biased? Does it cause ordinary people to develop stereotypes about refugees? How does the media coverage of refugees in Britain influence how we behave towards refugees in our community? The following section examines the issue of how stories about refugees are covered in the media.

Read the following information and then think about the discussion points.

*

Bias is the one-sided coverage of events or issues, so that only one set of views are put forward. Newspapers and television may be guilty of media bias. There are many ways in which a newspaper articles can be biased. These include:

◆ putting forward only one viewpoint

◆ quoting or interviewing a limited group of people

◆ not telling the whole story, just a small part

◆ using emotive language to discredit people who have opposing views

◆ using photographs that add to bias or do not tell the whole story.

A **stereotype** is an oversimplified and inaccurate idea about a particular group, race or sex. Stereotypes are not based on fact, and are often insulting. Stereotypes are dangerous because they can lead to people developing fixed ideas about a particular minority group. Poor quality newspaper and television coverage can lead to some groups being stereotyped.

One example of media bias ... All the following expressions were used in the British press during one week of the 1991 Gulf War:

We have ...	**They have ...**
Army, Navy and Air Force	A war machine
Reporting guidelines	Censorship
Press briefings	Propaganda
We ...	**They ...**
Take out	Destroy
Eliminate	Kill
Neutralise	Kill
We launch ...	**They launch ...**
First strikes	Sneak missile attacks
Pre-emptively	Without provocation
Our boys are ...	**Theirs are ...**
Professional	Brainwashed
Dare devils	Cannon fodder
Young knights of the skies	Bastards of Baghdad
Loyal	Blindly obedient
Desert rats	Mad dogs
Our boys are motivated by ...	**Their boys are motivated by ...**
An old fashioned sense of duty	Fear of Saddam
We ...	**They ...**
Precision bomb	Fire wildly at anything in the skies

Source: *The Guardian*.

Discussion points

◆ **Why do you think that the Allied Forces and the Iraqi Forces were described so differently in the British press during the Gulf War?**

◆ **How might the media coverage of the Gulf War affect Iraqi refugees living in Britain?**

Refugees & media monitoring

Aims

The activity aims to help students look at the way newspapers cover stories about refugees.

Instructions

Time needed: two hours

A week's supply of broadsheet and tabloid newspapers and some rulers are needed. The instruction sheets need to be copied so that every student has one.

Divide the students into groups and give each group an instruction sheet, two tabloid newspapers and two broadsheet newspapers.

Students

Newspapers are very important in helping us form opinions on many issues, including refugees. Just as two people will tell a story differently, two newspapers will describe events in a different way.

Some newspapers may have a lot of coverage of overseas stories. Others rarely cover overseas stories.

Front page news stories are more important. One newspaper may put a refugee story on the front page, another will put a similar story inside the newspaper.

You are going to survey how different newspapers cover refugee stories. You will need a ruler and a week's supply of four newspapers.

Read each newspaper for stories about refugees then fill in a table for each story like the one below.

Name of newspaper	The Guardian
Date	Monday 1st Sept.
Refugee story on	Vietnamese refugees in Hong Kong
Is this an overseas or home story?	Overseas
Position in newspaper	Front page
Size of story*	150 cm^2

** How to measure the size of a newspaper story:*

Pinochet hint

Santiago (AFP) – A senior adviser to Chile's army chief, General Augusto Pinochet, said the former dictator was considering stepping down before his mandate expired in 1998, to help improve the image of the military, a cabinet minister said yesterday.

Enrique Correa, Secretary-General of the government, said General Jorge Ballerino, head of the army chief's advisory committee, had told him "the army and the commander-in-chief himself were willing or inclined to talk about shortening his mandate".

$4 \times 6 = 24\ cm^2$

Discussion points

- **Which newspaper gave most coverage to refugee stories?**
- **What differences did you notice between the newspapers?**

Comparing two accounts of the same event

Aims

The activity helps students understand media bias.

Instructions

Time needed: one hour.

A selection of newspapers is needed. They can be purchased in advance,

GUARDIAN

£40m goes to 627 of 4,500 applicants ● Success rate even lower for 10,800 remaining

Lottery refuses 9 in 10 charities

David Brindle on the first awards

ALMOST nine in 10 charities that have sought National Lottery funding will be refused, the lottery charities board said yesterday as it announced its first grants totalling £40 million.

The warning prompted calls for the board to be given a larger share of the lottery's proceeds by cutting the Treasury's take, squeezing the other "good cause" boards, or reducing the profits taken by Camelot, the game's operator.

Stuart Etherington, chief executive of the National Council for Voluntary Organisations, said: "The charities board has turned the tide and demonstrated that the lottery can help good charities very effectively. What the Government should do is look again at the proportion of money that goes to the board — and increase it."

David Sieff, the board's chairman, said it was up to ministers to decide if more cash should go to charities. But he added: "I certainly know how to spend it."

Controversy continued to dog the board as it announced that the £40 million would be split among 627 groups — fewer than 14 per cent of the 4,500 applications so far decided upon. The success rate is expected to be even lower among the 10,800 remaining bids for cash under the board's first programme, aimed at relieving poverty and disadvantage. After advance criticism of grants going to groups helping refugees and other "politically correct" causes, the board went out of its way to stress the breadth of its awards.

Call for needy to have larger share of take

Timothy Hornsby, the board's chief executive, said: "Less than 1 per cent go to refugees — and they need it. Less than 3 per cent go to charities dealing with drug and alcohol addiction — and they need it. About 6 per cent go to ethnic minority groups — and they need it."

About a quarter of grants were going to groups working with children, and household names among recipients included citizen's advice bureaux (£1.9 million), the Royal National Institute for the Blind (£188,500), and Scope, formerly the Spastics Society (£315,000).

Some commentators had dwelled on a grant of £91,000 to the London-based Eritrean Advice and Information Centre, Mr Hornsby said. "So much play has been made about one refugee group, but it's a jolly good scheme."

About 44 per cent of yesterday's grants money is going to groups in Scotland. The board says that this is because its Scottish arm has made faster progress in assessing bids and that further awards over the next two months — the first programme is worth a total £162 million — will favour England.

The board has purposely concentrated on helping smaller, community-based groups, with almost half of yesterday's grants going to organisations with annual income of less than £20,000.

Typical recipients include the 19th Swindon Scout group (£1,480 for a minibus and equipment); the Hull Council of Disabled People (£59,000 for a transport scheme); and the Dundee Cyrenians Night Shelter (£39,000 for a new hostel for homeless people).

Some charity experts are calling on the charities board to cut the average size of its grants and spread its limited funds further. There are concerns, too, about the impact on smaller groups of a large, one-off injection of cash — although the £64,000 mean average award yesterday disguises the fact half of all awards are less than £50,000. The board says it vets applicants to ensure they would not be destabilised and be able to continue smoothly in future.

The board receives 5.6 per cent of lottery proceeds — as do the heritage, millennium, sports and arts boards. The Treasury keeps 12 per cent, ticket agents receive 5 per cent, and Camelot takes 5 per cent in costs and profit. Lottery winnings account for 50 per cent.

preferably at time when there is a major event that receives coverage in a large number of newspapers. Divide the class into small groups. Give each different group two different newspapers, for example, a tabloid and a broadsheet, or two politically different newspapers.

The class should be told which story to select. Each group should cut out the report of the same event. They should then write a comparison of the two articles, examining factual content.

Discussion point

◆ Why were there differences in the accounts of the same event/issue?

hese two tories ppeared on ne same day, 2.10.95

Thousands to be given to immigrant groups

NEW LOTTERY CASH SCANDAL

By Christopher Leake
Consumer Affairs Editor

THE National Lottery is facing a major new row this week over handouts to obscure ethnic minority organisations.

About £90,000 will go to a group which helps Eritrean immigrants claim benefits in Britain, The Mail on Sunday has learned.

The Eritrean Advice and Information Centre, based in a cramped room above a parade of shops in Stockwell Road, South London, advises some of the 7,000 Eritreans in the UK about their rights and Social Security claims.

Mohammed Adam, secretary of the Eritrean Community Organisation, said the one-year-old centre gave advice on housing, immigration and Social Security matters, including helping people fill in application forms.

Handout

The board in charge of the awards to be announced tomorrow – the first Lottery cash for charities – is expected to justify the payout on the grounds that it is helping victims of poverty. But critics will argue that medical charities which help the entire country should have been given preference over minority groups.

There will also be anger that cash will go to an advice centre for the parents of drug addicts in Glasgow, and that £170,000 will go to the Scottish Council on Alcohol and grants of £70,000 to other drug-related projects.

Handouts averaging £64,000 will be given to groups such as the Vietnamese Mental Health Project, the Liverpool Accessible Sensory Environment Resource and the Topyard Afro-

Continued on Page 2

Lottery

From Page One

Caribbean Association. A Chinese Women's Group in Gloucestershire is expected to get £7,000, part of which will go on an interpreter to help with tasks such as shopping.

Heritage Secretary Virginia Bottomley is set to come under renewed attack in the Commons on Wednesday over the way the Lottery's £1.1 billion is being distributed.

Fifteen thousand organisations made applications worth £2.4 billion for the first round of cash for charities in tomorrow's handout of just £40 million.

In the Lottery's first year, organisers have already faced fury over decisions to give £78.5 million to the Royal Opera House, £30 million to Sadler's Wells ballet, and £13.25 million to buy Sir Winston Churchill's papers.

Diana Garnham, secretary of the Association of Medical Research Charities, said: 'The awards are going to be very disappointing for a large number of charities.'

Timothy Hornsby, chief executive of the National Lottery Charities Board, denied that medical charities had been overlooked.

He said: 'The first round has concentrated on poverty. Many groups which will get awards will be small, self-help community-based organisations where relatively small amounts of money do a lot of good.'

(The Daily Mail)

Emotion & fact in newspaper reports

Instructions

Time needed: 40 minutes

The activity aims to examine media representation of a refugee issue or conflict situation. Some newspaper cuttings of a refugee issue or conflict situation are needed; the cuttings on this page could be photocopied. The students will also need two highlighting pens of a different colour (two pens will be needed per pair of students).

The class should be divided into pairs. Each pair should be given highlighting pens and copies of the press cuttings. Each pair should mark in one colour all the facts they can find in the articles. All students should use the same colour. Then ask the students to mark in another colour all the emotive or biased words that are used.

Pin the sheets on the wall. This will give graphic representation of the relation between fact and emotion in each article.

THE SUNDAY EXPRESS October 27 1991 — *News*

Go back home!

Government acts fast to kick out the illegal aliens

by Anthony Smith
Foreign Editor

BOGUS refugees arriving in Britain will be kicked out within six months under tough new immigration laws being drafted by the Government.

The new limit on clearing thousands of phoney asylum seekers will be introduced shortly following the Sunday Express exposure into the way Britain's immigration rules are being exploited.

Four out of five asylum seekers coming into the UK are bogus — but it still takes around two years to assess each case.

With the number of "refugees" entering Britain set to soar to 55,000 this year — almost double the number of a year ago — the scandal is costing taxpayers hundreds of millions of pounds in board and lodgings.

Now Home Secretary Kenneth Baker has given instructions on a new fast track appeals procedure to his senior immigration officials.

He has promised that legislation to be unveiled in this week's Queen Speech will help clear the massive backlog of illegal immigrants that has built up in the past 18 months.

Whitehall officials have disclosed that under the legislation, the Home Office intends to take a maximum of three months to assess suspect cases — which covers the vast majority of applicants.

Unless there is clear evidence that refugees are genuinely in fear, the cases will then go to an independent adjudicator who will be expected to deliver a final ruling within three months.

The plan is not as draconian as proposals drawn up in Germany where bogus refugees are to be herded into camps and expelled in just six weeks.

But senior Home Office sources said Mr Baker would put the asylum seekers on the same basis as overseas visitors, who were allowed to stay in the UK for a maximum of six months.

One official said: "The legislation is intended to send out an extremely tough message — it will be a case of saying goodbye within six months of a bogus applicant arriving in the UK.

Maximum

"We very much hope that we can clear some new arrivals in a few weeks, but for all those trying to exploit the system the maximum period they should be here is 24 weeks. That should give enough time for a fair and reasonable assessment, and yet minimise the present appalling drain on the taxpayer."

SCANDAL OF THE BOGUS REFUGEES

From last week's Sunday Express

Last week the Sunday Express revealed how a tidal wave of immigration has swamped the Home Office, with around 50,000 cases under investigation.

Mr Baker pledged quicker procedures to tackle the backlog as well as extra staff to process applications.

However, many Tory MPs are preparing to give a rough ride to the new legislation.

John Carlisle, MP for Luton North, said: "Bogus refugees should be kicked out in six hours not six months.

"The sad truth is that the immigration system is in total chaos. We should hav[e] a total ban on immigratio[n] until the mess is sorted o[ut] because at the momen[t] many illegal immigrants ju[st] vanish into the system an[d] they are not tracked dow[n] for years."

Letters: Page 18

THE INDEPENDENT

UN anger over cut in aid to refugees

JAMES CUSICK

The Government is facing renewed criticism from the United Nations over its plans to remove social security payments for most asylum seekers.

Although a judicial review in the High Court today will challenge the planned new regulations, the London office of the United Nations High Commissioner for Refugees has privately told Peter Lilley, the Secretary of State for Social Security, that the law changes will cause "undue hardship". Central to the UNHCR's criticisms is that the UK will fail to honour its treaty obligations under the 1989 Convention on the Rights of the Child if the welfare withdrawal changes are made.

In today's judicial review the Joint Council for the Welfare of Immigrants is challenging the legality of plans to withdraw benefits from about 70 per cent of asylum seekers. The changes may take £200m off the annual welfare budget. Immigrants who fail to make an application for asylum immediately on arrival will be no longer entitled to claim state support and those applicants rejected will be unable to claim benefits while their appeal is being heard.

As part of an internal UNHCR report delivered to the Social Security Advisory Committee, Mr Lilley was made aware of the concerns about children of asylum seekers who, according to the report, would be "adversely affected by the proposed changes"

THE TIMES

Gangs attack Bosnian refugees over housing

By Michael Horsnell

POLICE have drafted in special patrols to protect a community of Bosnian refugees who have been threatened and attacked by gangs on an Essex council estate.

Officers have been taken off other duties to tackle the assaults and damage to property in South Ockendon where the grim estates have produced racial hostility to 68 Bosnian Muslims given housing priority by the local authority.

Police are also planning a scheme in which mobile telephones programmed for emergency calls are issued to the victims and alarms installed in their homes.

Yesterday, Bejdo Sabahudin, 39, who had fled the small town of Kozarac where 28,000 Bosnians were "ethnically cleansed" by Serbs, explained the refugees' predicament. "In England we have problems now. Everyone wants to go home. But it is too dangerous and I don't know how long we will have to stay," he said.

Mr Sabahudin, unemployed, was among the first former concentration camp inmates to arrive in 1992 with his wife and their elder son, who had been wounded and needed hospital treatment.

With his younger son, Kenjar, interpreting, Mr Sabahudin said: "No one in our family has been assaulted, though others have. But last week I found my car had been sprayed with black paint. One of our problems is that we arrived here without speaking any English. Some people do not like us, but not everyone is like that."

Another Bosnian, who did not want to give his name, said: "We are being baited by a small group of people and it is not nice. But we do not want to sound ungrateful, because England has taken us in."

Police, who are investigating window-breakings, daubings and harassment, have charged four people with assault. Papers in another case have been sent to the Crown Prosecution Service. Officers are hopeful of arrests in other incidents.

Superintendant Michael Holyoak said: "These people are living in difficult circumstances in a less than easy area. We are being very supportive because they need help. It is only a small minority who are causing the difficulties."

Inspector Bob Palmer said the police were in touch with the Refugee Council, which is caring for the 1,600 Bosnian refugees currently in Britain.

The Bosnians are a target of resentment in South Ockendon partly because they were allocated council flats while others had to wait.

Margaret Aberdein, who served on Thurrock housing committee when the allocations were made, said: "They are very quiet people who bother no one and they have fitted well into the community. But they have been victimised. You get the same old thing from some people: 'Why should they get a house before my son does?' I told those who have been complaining that the Bosnians are here by the grace of God. They should remember that the majority of those who came here were in concentration camps. As far as most people are concerned, they are most welcome."

Bejdo Sabahudin, a Bosnian refugee now living in South Ockendon, with his vandalised car

Writing to a newspaper editor

Aims

Newspapers do not always cover stories in the way that a person or group might like to see the story told. Writing to a newspaper editor is a way of putting across a different opinion. Students are going to compose letters to the editor of the Daily Star.

Instructions

Time needed: 45 minutes

Copies of the Daily Star article (on page 212) and the information sheet about Sierra Leone (taken from Chapter Three of this book) need to be photocopied in advance, so that every student has a copy. Divide the class into groups of three or four. Get them to write to the editor to comment on the article.

DAILY STAR 21 October 1994

WE'RE A SOFT TOUCH

THEY KILL BOREDOM by filling out the benefit forms they were given on arrival to help them milk our state.

The refugees camping out at Heathrow airport yesterday relieved their boredom by filling out benefit and income support forms.

The paperwork was handed to them on arrival so that they can begin milking the State.

The men admit that they do not know anyone in the country but are confident Britain will find them a home.

One of them who refused to give his name said: "We will be rescued very soon and given places to sleep and food to eat."

Another, Sabr Goorie, said: "We are confident we will be looked after in this country. We had to get away from our home country and follow our friends to Britain. We believe it was the best place to come."

PENNILESS

And his friend Mohammad Kamar added: "We have no food and no money. No family and no friends, but we believe we will be looked after. We expect we will get somewhere to stay until we can be looked after properly."

One of the men, Abu Bakerrkamara, 21, said: "Many of us have no families left because of the fighting. We have no homes, nothing. We have come here with nothing and claimed political asylum. We were told this was the best place to come to be looked after."

Abu, whose father, mother and two sisters were killed at their home said that they had scraped together their remaining possessions and money to pay their way to Britain.

He added: "We came here seeking asylum. We didn't know where else to go.

The refugees flew into Terminal Four from Amsterdam on a KLM flight, after transferring on another plane from Freetown to Holland.

The refugee hostel that is meant to house them is swamped with immigrants.

The Refugee Arrivals Project is intended to serve 65 people but is dealing with FIVE times that number.

The Sierra Leone refugees have been given a room of their own and promised shower facilities at Heathrow.

Manager of the Refugee Arrivals Project, Mr Taata Ofusu, said: "There is nothing we can do.

We are already five times oversubscribed and cannot offer the refugees a place to stay."

The project is dealing with more than 300 refugees.

FULL

Mr Ofusu added: "We have to give the more vulnerable - people in wheelchairs and pregnant women - priority.

At present there is not enough space for us to offer these refugees somewhere to stay. We have contacted hotels and bed and breakfasts who normally help us out in times like this but they are also fully booked and have not got a bed or room to spare.

The refugees are coming here in such numbers that a project like ours cannot cope with the amount of space and funding we receive." Mr Ofusu admitted that the Heathrow Airport immigration detention centre was also full.

He went on: "That takes about 100 people who are normally being detained but there isn't even any space there to accommodate them for the time being."

As the Sierra Leone refugees settled down to another night at Terminal Four, they were told they would be accommodated as soon as space became available.

Mr Ofusu said it would mean that the party was likely to be split up into smaller groups.

Yesterday airport immigration officials began interviewing the refugees as part of an assessment to decide if they had a case for staying in the country after claiming political asylum.

A Heathrow spokesman said: "We are aware of the situation which is being handled by immigration officials."

An airport police spokesman said: "It is far from an ideal security situation to have refugees wandering around an airport terminal and sleeping rough for days. We have kept an eye on them but they have caused us no trouble or concern whatsoever."

Sierra Leone has been racked by civil war since 1991. Almost 200 people from Sierra Leone flew to Britain last month, double the July figure, and 47 arrived together on September 1.

The latest batch - aged 18 to 32 - have been bedding down in the Terminal Four arrivals hall.

The penniless men, many of whom speak fluent English, arrived with nothing more than a few possessions stuffed in backpacks.

Immigration officials have treated them to free meals in their staff canteen and allowed them to use showers.

Yesterday 18 of them were picked up by the Arrivals Project refugee charity and taken to hostels near the airport.

A spokesman blamed lack of funds for the delay in collecting them. He said: "The project just can't cope with the large number of refugees all arriving at once." They have run out of money.

HANDOUTS

A Home Office spokesman said: "Exceptionally large numbers of asylum-seekers have been arriving at Heathrow in the last few weeks. The Refugee Arrivals Project are working hard to make suitable arrangements for these people's immediate needs."

It could be four months before hard-pressed immigration officials rule on whether they can stay. Many could be kicked out. But while they are here the men are entitled to 90 per cent of the normal state handouts.

A Refugee Council spokesman said: "We help them with housing and claiming welfare benefits. If they are with families they will be considered for local authority housing. If not, we help them find somewhere to live and give assistance for flats. They are entitled to housing benefit."

46,000 PLAY WAITING GAME

The number of immigrants in Britain applying for political asylum has soared to a staggering 46,000. That includes 22,000 who arrived last year.

Each application takes between three and four months on average to process.

And illegal asylum seekers cost taxpayers £200 million in benefit claims.

DAILY STAR SAYS

They land here day after day and say the magic words: "Political asylum," closely followed by "social security."

The 34 men from Sierra Leone filling in their benefit forms at Heathrow are just the latest wavelet of a flood.

We are playing host to 46,000 refugees who are eating us out of house and home.

The bill is £200 million a year, on top of millions we dole out in aid to the very countries they are fleeing.

Even if these clamouring hordes really are in fear of torture and death, our little country has no room for them. But if they were genuinely living under tyranny they would never be allowed to get on a plane out. They'd be imprisoned or shot.

The vast majority are not political refugees at all. They just know that Britain is a soft-touch escape route from poverty.

Under the Geneva Convention we have absolutely no duty to take them in.

The Government says that it will no longer admit immigrants unless they have visas.

But we have heard Home Secretary Michael Howard say many times before that he's going to get tough.

Let's see him match his words with action. Send them packing.

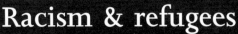

Racism & refugees

Funeral of Ruhallah Aramesh, a young Afghan refugee who was murdered in London in 1992. He was one of eight refugees murdered since 1990. Every year another 140,000 people suffer racial attacks in Britain. But few incidents of racial violence are reported to the police.
Billi Rafaeli

Refugee organisations believe that hostile media coverage of refugees in Britain, plus hostile remarks of some politicians have led to an increase in public hostility towards refugees. In a hostile climate refugees are more likely to become victims of racial discrimination and racial attacks. In a hostile climate governments are more likely to pass laws that restrict the rights of refugees.

If we are to challenge racism facing refugees (and other groups) it is important to understand how our opinions of different ethnic groups are formed.

The word **race** is often misused. Sociologists tend to use the words ethnic group or ethnic minority to distinguish people from each other. An ethnic group is a group of people who share a distinctive culture. Where such a group forms a minority of the population in a certain country they are know as an **ethnic minority group**.

Racial prejudice means negative and unfavourable feelings about a particular ethnic group, not based on knowledge or fact.

Racism is where people are treated differently because they belong to a particular ethnic group. Racism can take many forms. People can be victims of violent attacks. They can also be treated differently by employers and by other institutions in society.

Institutional racism happens when ethnic groups are treated differently by the institutions in society. Schools, colleges, work places, local and central government have great power over people's lives. Sometimes such institutions can discriminate against ethnic groups, intentionally or unintentionally.

Psychologists and sociologists have come up with four explanations for racism:

The Individual Explanation Some people are unable to express their feelings and frustrations with life. They find an outlet for their frustrations by being hostile to easily identifiable groups such as people with black skin.

The Group Explanation All people like to identify with a group or a number of groups. The group can be something innocent such as people who support a certain football club. Or it can be all people who belong to a certain ethnic group. All groups are exclusive and must exclude certain people. What happens to those who are excluded from membership of a 'group'? They may face isolation, discrimination or worse.

The Cultural Explanation Prejudice about certain ethnic groups is part of the culture of most countries. People are taught to think in racial terms, in their families, at school, and through newspapers and books. Ethnic minorities are stereotyped. This means that people have fixed ideas about ethnic groups. These ideas have usually developed without a basis of fact.

The Economic Explanation When societies are experiencing poverty or unemployment it is easy to blame an outsider or scapegoat for taking jobs or housing. Scapegoating goes hand in hand with racism. Blaming other ethnic groups for taking jobs or housing is a simple explanation for things like unemployment and poverty, but it ignores the real causes. Jews were economic scapegoats in Nazi Germany in the 1930s. Today racist parties in many European countries are blaming immigrants and refugees for unemployment, poverty and homelessness. Refugees may suffer as a result of individual people's hostility. Many refugee and human rights organisations also argue that much recent refugee legislation is racist.

What do we mean by racism?

Aims

The activity aims to get participants thinking about the meaning of the word 'racism'. It should only be carried out by a group that knows each other well.

Instructions

Time needed: 45 minutes

Large sheets of paper and marker pens are needed. The information sheets on racism are also needed.

Divide the students up into groups of three or four. Give each group a large sheet of paper and ask them to write down what they mean by the word 'racism'. They should spend about 15 minutes doing this, then come together. Pin up the sheets of paper and discuss the participants' definitions. Then introduce the information sheet and continue the discussion.

Discussion points

- **What do you think racism means?**
- **How did your definitions differ from those on the information sheet?**
- **Do you know the names of ethnic groups who have had to become refugees because of racism in their home countries?**

Difficulties at the youth club

Aims

The activity aims to help students understand how to deal with racist incidents.

Instructions

Time needed: 45 minutes

Students will need copies of the role cards. Divide the class into fours. (Any extra people can be members of the youth club). Read the scenario to the class, and give out role cards. Each person should take a role. The groups should act out the role play for 20 minutes and then come together to discuss the points below.

Discussion points

- **How do you think Hamid felt when he was told he was not welcome?**

- **Why do you think Roland acted in the way that he did?**

- **How did each group resolve the argument?**

- **Do you think that anything like this could happen in your youth club or school?**

The scenario

Sarah and Hamid enter the building where the group is meeting. Roland asks other members who Hamid is. The youth club members then help themselves to drinks and biscuits. Roland greets Sarah but ignores Hamid. He is heard to mutter "when did we start letting Blacks in then?" The remark is obviously targeted at Hamid. Sarah starts to argue with Roland. Jane is forced to try and mediate ...

---

rah belongs to Oak Wood Youth Club. e is 16 years old. Her friend Hamid is ying with her and she decides to take m to her youth club.

Hamid is 16 years old. He lives in London. He was born in the Sudan. Sarah's parents worked in the Sudan in the 1960s and were close friends with Hamid's parents. Hamid's father was a university lecturer but the family had to flee from the Sudan in 1990. They came to Britain. Hamid has been to stay with Sarah many times.

---

land is 16 years old. He is a member Oak Wood Youth Club.

Jane is 17 years old. She is a friend of both Sarah and Roland.

Immigration law & refugees

During the last 100 years many immigration laws have been passed. All western European countries have slowly stopped immigration. In Britain the first major restrictions placed on post-war immigrants came with the passage of the 1962 Commonwealth Immigrants Act. But it was not until 1985 that asylum-seekers faced restrictions. Since then they have been viewed as another group of immigrants, and hence people that the British government believes should be kept out.

New laws have been introduced since 1985 to try and prevent the entry of asylum-seekers. Such laws have sought to do three things:

◆ build barriers to stop asylum-seekers from entering Britain.

◆ reduce the social rights of those asylum-seekers who do enter Britain, in the hope of deterring others.

◆ cut down on the proportion of asylum-seekers who are given refugee status or exceptional leave to remain, and increase the proportions of asylum-seekers who are refused permission to remain in Britain.

Barriers

Did you know! The nationals of most refugee producing countries need visas to come to Britain. This makes such a journey very difficult for people fleeing persecution. To obtain a visa, a person needs a valid passport, which many endangered people do not have. To obtain a visa to come to Britain, a person needs to travel to a British embassy to collect the visa. If there is war in a refugee producing country, or if the British embassy is being watched by security forces, it can be too dangerous to travel to obtain a visa.

Did you know! The British government fines airlines and shipping companies £2,000 for every person they carry who lacks the correct travel documents. Many asylum-seekers do not have the required passports and visas. An airline company such as British Airways has two options when an asylum-seeker tries to board a plane without the correct documents. That person can be stopped from boarding the plane. Or the airline can let the asylum-seeker on to the plane, but pay the fine. What do you think airlines do?

Did you know! Asylum-seekers can be stopped when they arrive in Britain, and told that they do not have a strong claim to asylum. This might be because they have come from a certain country which the British government does not believe persecutes its citizens. Asylum-seekers who are stopped are not usually allowed to fill in forms which allow them to claim asylum and can be removed from Britain within a few days.

Deterrents

Did you know! About eight per cent of all asylum-seekers are held in detention when they arrive in Britain.

Did you know! Asylum-seekers are not allowed to work during their first six months in Britain.

Did you know! In Britain most new asylum-seekers are not allowed to collect income support and other social security benefits. Those asylum-seekers who do qualify for benefits are only allowed to claim 90 per cent of the levels that others collect.

Did you know! Most new asylum-seekers cannot be given local authority (council) housing.

Cutting down on the proportions of people allowed to stay in Britain

Did you know! In 1990 some 89 per cent of all asylum-seekers were given refugee status or exceptional leave to remain in Britain. Only 11 per cent were refused. In 1995 some 23 per cent of all asylum-seekers were given refugee status or exceptional leave to remain in Britain. Some 77 per cent of all asylum-seekers were refused. The Medical Foundation, a charity working with people who have survived torture examined 92 Zairean asylum-seekers in 1993 and 1994. All of them had been tortured at the hands of the security forces and most of them had scars on their bodies as a result. But by 1995 18 of these Zaireans had been refused permission to stay in Britain. Two of them had been sent back to Zaire.

mmigration laws 905-1996

Immigration and asylum laws are the responsibility of the Home Office and the Home Secretary in Britain.

1905 Aliens Act This stopped immigrants and refugees entering Britain without the permission of an immigration officer at the port. Sick or 'undesirable' people were prevented from entering, but those escaping persecution were meant to be allowed to enter. Some Jewish refugees were sent back to Russia and Poland. This law was passed as a result of anti-immigrant pressure.

1914 Aliens Restriction Act This gave the Home Secretary the power to refuse entry or to deport any non-British citizen. Refugees were meant to be allowed entry to Britain.

1919 Aliens Restriction Act This confirmed the Home Secretary's power to refuse entry or deport non-British citizens. It made no allowance for the entry of refugees, unlike the 1905 and 1914 Acts. Many Jewish refugees, fleeing persecution in eastern Europe, were prevented from coming to Britain by this law. Irish immigration law is still based on the 1919 Aliens Restriction Act.

1935 Visa and Work Permit Requirements German refugees, escaping the Nazis, were told that they needed visas to come to Britain. Visas were often conditional on having a job in Britain.

1948 British Nationality Act This gave all citizens of Commonwealth countries full rights as British subjects, including the right to settle in Britain and to vote. This act was passed when Britain was short of workers and needed people for vital industries and services. Men and women from the West Indies, India, Pakistan, Bangladesh and other former British colonies came to settle in Britain.

*

A **visa** is a stamp put into a person's passport. It allows them to enter a certain country.

1951 UN Convention Relating to the Status of Refugees Britain signed this international law which is meant to govern how we treat asylum-seekers and refugees.

1962 Commonwealth Immigrants Act This restricted the entry of Commonwealth citizens. Only those who had work vouchers could come to Britain. This act was passed as a result of racist campaigns against Black workers already in Britain.

1971 Immigration Act This law gave the Home Secretary the right to make and change 'immigration rules' without needing to change British law. Immigration rules determine whether a person can enter or stay in Britain. The 1971 Immigration Act is the most important recent immigration law. It also gave the Home Secretary the right to detain immigrants and asylum-seekers in prisons, police cells and immigration detention centres.

1981 British Nationality Act This changed the rights of some people to British citizenship. Children born in Britain but who do not have British parents may no longer have the right to British citizenship. Hong Kong Chinese and East African Asians who held British passports were also prevented from settling in Britain.

1985–1995 Visas The nationals of more countries required visas to come to Britain, specifically to keep out asylum-seekers. Visas were introduced for Sri Lankans in 1985 after Tamil asylum-seekers came to Britain, for Ghanaians in 1986, for Turkish citizens in 1989, for Ugandans in 1990, for Bosnians in 1992 and for Sierra Leoneans in 1994.

1987 Immigration (Carriers Liability) Act This law fined airlines and other carriers £2,000 for every person brought

A Nigerian asylum-seeker in Britain. At present 99 per cent of all Nigerian asylum-seekers are being refused permission to stay, despite the fact that many of them have survived imprisonment and torture. *Patrick Barth.*

to Britain without the correct passport and visa.

1988 Changes in social security regulations Asylum-seekers were only allowed 90 per cent income support.

1990 Dublin Convention on Asylum Britain and 11 other European Union countries signed an agreement which only allowed asylum-seekers to apply for refugee status in one EU country.

1993 Asylum and Immigration (Appeals) Act All asylum-seekers, including children, have to be finger-printed when they apply for asylum. A new system was introduced at the ports of entry where some asylum-seekers are not allowed to make a full claim for political asylum because their cases are judged to be unfounded. Asylum-seekers also face restricted rights to council housing.

1993 Immigration Rules change This made it more difficult to gain refugee status. Since 1993 more and more asylum-seekers have been refused the right to stay in Britain, in particular those who make a stop in another country before arriving in Britain.

1996 Changes to Social Security Regulations Two groups of asylum-seekers were denied all access to benefits, even though most of them have no money and are not allowed to work in Britain. The two groups that lost access to benefits are those asylum-seekers who apply for asylum after they have entered Britain, and those who have been refused asylum in Britain (even though they may wish to appeal). Refugee organisations estimate that 46,000 asylum-seekers may be destitute, and homeless by the end of 1996.

1996 The Asylum and Immigration Bill This introduces a system where some countries are listed as 'safe' by the Home Office. If an asylum-seeker comes from one of these countries he/she may be denied the opportunity of making a full claim for political asylum. Most asylum-seekers also lose their right to be housed by a local authority (council).

Immigration law

Aims

The activity aims to help students understand how immigration law affects people.

Instructions

Time needed: 50 minutes

All students will need copies of the information sheets on immigration law and refugees. The students should be divided into groups of four or five. As a group they should hold a discussion on the points below. Students should pay particular attention to listening to each other and allowing opinions to be expressed. Each group might like to elect a chair and someone to present their ideas.

After 20 minutes the students should come together as a whole group. Each small group should present the results of their discussions.

Discussion points

◆ What do you think about the changes in immigration law? Do you think they are fair?

◆ Which do you think were the most significant changes?

◆ What do you think about using visas to keep asylum-seekers out of Britain?

◆ What do you think about preventing asylum-seekers (who usually do not have savings) from claiming benefits when they come to Britain?

Making a board game

Aims

The activity aims to get participants to think about the hurdles that refugees face when they try to flee to Britain.

Instructions

Time needed: at least two hours, depending on the creative skills of the group.

You will need to collect some board games; snakes and ladders and monopoly are ideal. You will need counters, felt pens, dice, card, scissors, scrap paper and some large sheets of paper. You will also need to photocopy the flow chart on page 187 to give to each group.

Divide the class into fours, and explain the purpose of the task. After each group has made their board games, they should swap them around, so that everyone gets the chance to play the game of other groups. Then participants can then come together for a discussion.

Discussion points

◆ What kind of hurdles to people face if they want to flee to another country?

◆ Do you think these hurdles discriminate against refugees?

Detention

Detainees protest at Campsfield House, Oxford 1995 *Migrant Media*

An increasing number of asylum-seekers are being held in detention centres when they arrive in Britain. Refugee and human rights organisations are very concerned about the increasing use of detention.

A detainee's story

'Julius Dontoh fled from Ghana where he had been imprisoned and tortured. He arrived in Britain on a false passport. Julius was arrested after driving a friend to Heathrow, and held in detention in a police cell. He was then transferred to Haslar Detention Centre and remained there for five months. The Joint Council for the Welfare of Immigrants (JCWI), an advice and campaigning organisation, visited him in Haslar. Its workers found that he was so disturbed and ill that he could not remember what had happened to him. JCWI helped Julius fill in an application for asylum in Britain. The Home Office refused to release Julius, and stated that it would refuse him refugee status in Britain.

JCWI then asked for a doctor to examine Julius. The medical report showed 'findings consistent with his history of being badly tortured....this young man is too disturbed to be in a detention centre....he needs expert psychiatric help and should be in hospital'. On receiving the report the Home Office wanted to release Julius immediately, even though he was too ill to travel into London alone. One month later Julius was granted full refugee status.

The use of detention for asylum-seekers and refugees has a long history in Britain. During the Second World War over 27,000 refugees were detained in army camps in Britain. At this time 56,000 refugees had escaped from Nazi-occupied Europe. Newspapers, and some politicians, feared that the refugees would not be loyal to Britain and it would be easy for spies to live among the refugee community. Conditions in the camps were very hard. Some refugees were also deported to Canada and Australia.

Asylum-seekers continued to be detained after the Second World War. In 1987, a ship called the Earl William was used to detain asylum-seekers. The ship was moored off the port of Harwich. There were many complaints about conditions on the ship. Since 1992 about 3,000 asylum-seekers have been detained every year in detention centres like Harmondsworth, Middlesex, Campsfield House, Oxford and in police cells and even in prisons. The average length of time spent in detention is 30 days.

For those kept in detention, normal rules of justice do not apply. Unlike convicted criminals, no court is required to give permission for the detention of an asylum-seeker. Most people in detention centres do not know when they will be released. They have little contact, if any, with lawyers. If they are to be released, a detained asylum-seeker may have to find two British residents who can each stand bail. Usually a court will ask a for £2,000 - £4,000 bail.

Asylum-seekers may be detained because the immigration officer thinks they might disappear or go into hiding. They can also be detained because they have no address to go to, they have forged documents or they have no documents at all.

Refugee organisations believe that the Home Office has an additional reason for detaining people. If large numbers of refugees from one country are detained, this will act as a deterrent, and stop more people coming to Britain.

◆ **How would it feel to be an asylum-seeker detained on arrival in Britain?**

◆ **Do you think detention is fair or unfair?**

Detention: fair or unfair?

Aims

Students will make a short radio documentary about detention. The activity aims to get participants thinking about justice and the way Britain treats asylum-seekers.

Instructions

Time needed: two hours, plus homework

The class should be divided into groups of six. Each group should have access to a cassette recorder with a microphone and blank tape. Each student should also have a copy of the typed information about detention.

The students are going to make a 20 minute radio documentary which will explore issues surrounding the detention of asylum-seekers. The theme of the documentary will be the exploration of whether detention is fair or not.

Students will take on different roles during the production of the documentary. The roles are:

Journalist He/she asks the questions and provides the commentary on the tape. The journalist works with the editor to write the journalist's script.

Editor He/she works with the journalist to write the script, and makes the final decision about the content of the documentary.

Producer He/she takes charge of technical matters, such as finding a quiet place to record, and operating the cassette recorder.

Detainee 'Abdul' He has recently been detained and tells radio journalist of his experience.

Detainee 'Mary' She has recently been detained and tells the radio journalist of her experience.

Director, Refugee Council He/she represents a refugee organisation that believes that detention is unjust. The director of the Refugee Council gives the radio journalist his/her opinions, and tries to answer some of the points made by the Home Office Minister.

Minister, Home Office He/she supports the detention of some asylum-seekers, particularly those who do not have the correct identity documents.

Fortress Europe?

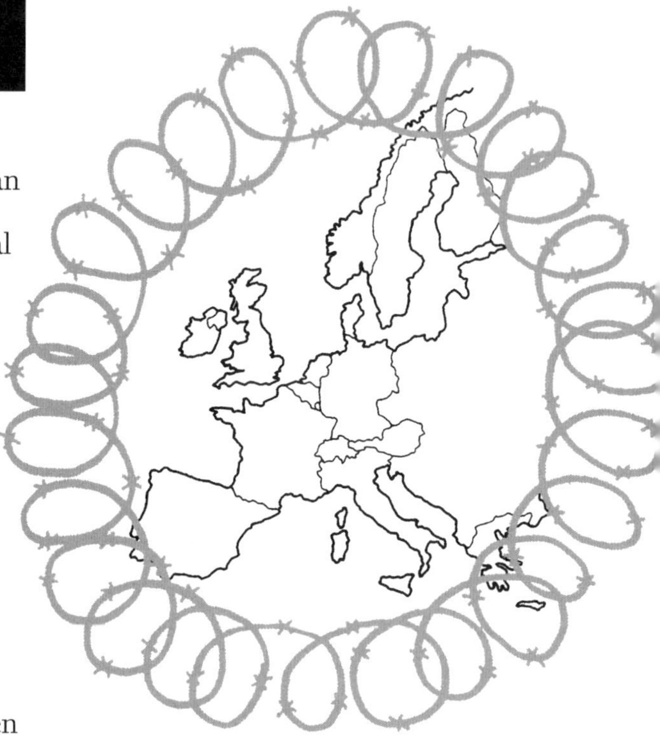

There have been changes in refugee and immigration laws in all European Union (EU) countries since 1985. As well as legal changes made by individual governments, there have been changes made at a European level.

Britain has been a member of the EU since 1972. In 1987 the British government passed an Act of Parliament called the Single European Act. Similar acts were passed in the parliaments of the other member countries of the EU.

The Single European Act stated that all EU countries should have borders that allow for the free movement of goods, people and investment. There would be fewer customs checks at borders between EU countries.

The governments of some EU countries became worried that terrorists and drug smugglers would be able to travel between EU countries more easily. They also believed that asylum-seekers would find it easier to enter the EU. During the last ten years ministers and civil servants have been meeting to try and find ways of strengthening the borders around the outside of the 15 EU countries. In their meetings they have discussed border security, terrorism, drug smuggling, immigration, asylum-seekers and refugees.

Recently ministers and civil servants have formed a special group to discuss immigration and asylum-seekers. It is called the Steering Group on Immigration and Asylum. It meets in secret and does not give reports about the meetings to parliaments. The Steering Group on Immigration and Asylum is also independent of the European Community and does not report to the European Parliament.

The Refugee Council and other organisations that work with refugees are very concerned about the effects of trying to strengthen the borders around the 15 EU countries. The Refugee Council is concerned because:

◆ Asylum-seekers are only allowed one chance to apply for asylum in an EU country. Mistakes can be made, and asylum-seekers refused unjustly. Such people are now barred from all other EU countries.

◆ By the mid-1990s there will be a common list of countries whose nationals need visas to come to the EU.

◆ There will be a common system of fining airlines and other transport companies who carry asylum-seekers who lack the correct travel documents.

◆ There will be a common EU system of refusing asylum-seekers who are judged to have a weak case. Many more asylum-seekers will be refused at the EU's external borders.

◆ There will be a computerised exchange of information between EU countries, giving information about individual asylum-seekers and the routes they use to travel to Europe.

◆ How might these European changes affect the safety of asylum-seekers?

Instructions

Time needed: 45 minutes

All students will need the information sheet on Fortress Europe and a copy of the sample newspaper editorial.

Explain to the class that the editorial column of a newspaper is a place for the editor to give his or her personal opinion about an event or an issue. Using the information about Fortress Europe students should write their own newspaper editorial about changes in the treatment of asylum-seekers in Europe.

Writing a newspaper editorial

An example of a newspaper editorial

THE GUARDIAN 2 JAN. 1996

Soup kitchen asylum

Turning refugees on to the streets is wrong

CLOSURE of the Crisis at Christmas emergency shelters for the homeless rightly caused concern at the weekend as sub-zero temperatures continued across much of Britain. Yet a much bigger crisis involving thousands — rather than hundreds — of people looms. Three months ago in the fevered atmosphere of a Conservative Party conference, withdrawing welfare benefits from 13,000 asylum seekers (plus their children) seemed a good way to ministers to appease rightwing demands for tighter asylum control and wooing the racist vote. Three months on as ministers desperately deny their lurch to the right, the spectre of thousands of refugees being turned out of rented rooms and forced to use soup kitchens, shelters and even street doorways takes on a different hue.

Only a last minute decision before Christmas by ministers to allow a parliamentary debate on the issue before implementing the cuts has saved the Government from a public relations disaster. The benefits were due to be withdrawn on January 8. For refugees the new regulations are much more serious than just bad PR. Both income support and housing benefit are to be withdrawn from those who apply for asylum *after* entering the UK. Only those who apply immediately upon arrival will retain entitlement. But even those applicants will no longer be provided with support if they are initially rejected by the Home Office and wish to appeal. One more crucial safeguard — the right of appeal — is being taken from thousands of refugees when the UN Convention on Refugees requires Britain to protect them.

There is no sign yet of ministers reversing their decision. All they have promised is a debate, not a change of policy. Yet the debate will be a useful way of exposing the injustices and inefficiencies of the office over which Michael Howard presides. The emergence of a "culture of disbelief" in the Home Office's asylum division has been well documented by Amnesty International in its report on UK asylum procedures published six weeks ago. Just five years ago 23 per cent of all applicants were granted asylum and 60 per cent given exceptional leave to remain (ELR). This year the relevant figures have shrunk to four and 18 per cent. Amnesty has documented the emergence of an undisclosed quota system which has operated since July 1993. Previously, ELRs varied enormously but no longer. Since 1993 they have never gone higher than 23 per cent.

It is only two years since ministers passed the last Asylum Act. Then they were promising the new procedures would remove delays by providing for "prompt and fair" decisions. Ministers claimed initial decisions would be taken within four weeks and appeals within three months. That was the rhetoric: the reality is that initial decisions are now taking eight months and appeals a further 10 months. That is the reason why the social security bill for refugees has risen so dramatically. There is a solution: recruit more appeal adjudicators and make the initial decision-takers more efficient. Instead, ministers have removed further safeguards which are essential if those fleeing from persecution are to be protected.

Bishops, peers and refugee agencies have all been speaking out against the new regulation. They are a powerful alliance. Pictures of soup kitchens and emergency shelters will be even more powerful. The churches and charities which are setting up emergency support services should maintain their pressure on ministers. John "One Nation" Major is reported to be wooing the Tory left. He could make no better start than by scrapping this racist and regressive measure.

Writing a manifesto

Aims

The activity aims to enable students to summarise their own ideas about the just treatment of asylum-seekers and refugees.

Instructions

Time needed: one hour

All students need copies of the information about immigration law and refugees and about detention. Additional information in Chapter Four and Five can be supplied. Explain to the class that they are going to write a ten point manifesto to demand the fair treatment of asylum-seekers and ref-ugees in Britain. A manifesto is a statement of aims or beliefs. Many political and campaigning organisations publish manifestos that state the things they would like to happen. A refugee manifesto might include statements such as 'no asylum-seeker or refugee should be held in detention.'

The class should be divided into groups of three or four. Each group is going to produce their own manifesto. Students can illustrate their manifestos, or use desk top publishing programmes to design them.

After each group has written a manifesto, the class should come together. The manifestos can be pinned up and used as a basis for discussion.

Discussion points

◆ What items were common to most manifestos?

◆ How could you use the manifestos if you were organising a campaign to support the rights of refugees?

◆ The Refugee Council published a ten point manifesto in 1989 for European elections. How is this manifesto similar to yours?

REFUGEE MANIFESTO

"Everyone has the right to seek and to enjoy in other countries asylum from persecution."

Article 14(1) of the United Nations Universal Declaration of Human Rights.

To respect the basic human rights of asylum-seekers and refugees, we demand that the British and other European governments adopt asylum and settlement policies to effect the following ten principles.

1. People seeking asylum should not be prevented from reaching Britain by restrictions such as visas and fines on airlines
2. Immigration officers should be specially trained to deal with asylum seekers, as well as in international human rights issues. Asylum-seekers should be given clear information about their rights and entitlements in English and their mother-tongue
3. No asylum-seeker should be held in detention
4. Every asylum-seeker should have the right to legal advice and representation when applying for refugee status
5. Every asylum-seeker should have a right of appeal before deportation or removal
6. Applications for refugee status should be dealt with quickly, normally within three months
7. Asylum seekers and refugees should have the right to be joined by their immediate family
8. People seeking asylum should be entitled to full welfare benefits, and have the right to education, training, employment, housing and health-care
9. Every refugee in the European Community should enjoy the same rights of movement, work, political, social and religious activity as EC nationals
10. Governments and the EC should help long-term settlement by funding refugee community groups and agencies working with refugees. Governments should consult such groups about asylum and refugee policy

Press conference

Instructions

Time needed: 30 minutes for preparation, 30 minutes for presentations and at least 60 minutes to write newspaper articles or make taped radio reports.

Paper and pens are needed to make newspaper reports. If any of the students are preparing radio reports they will need a cassette recorder and tapes. Students will also need copies of instructions, role cards and background material about immigration law and detention, and their own or the Refugee Council's manifesto.

Members of a panel will present to a group of journalists their criticisms of Britain's treatment of asylum-seekers and refugees. The press conference will also launch a refugee manifesto stating a fair way of treating asylum-seekers. Explain the aim of the activity and choose three people who will take the role of the panel in the press conference. The other members of the class will take the roles of journalists. The three panel members should receive role cards.

Explain to the class how a press conference works. Give the panel members and the journalists 30 minutes to prepare their presentations and questions. The panel members should then make short presentations (not more than five minutes each) explaining their concerns, and giving support to the manifesto. The journalists should then ask the panel questions for about 15 minutes.

The journalists should then write newspaper articles about Britain's treatment of asylum-seekers and refugees. The newspaper articles can be written in a variety of styles. Examples of news-paper articles can be provided to give the class some ideas.

Students

A press conference is where a person or group of people want to tell newspapers, television and the radio an important story. Journalists are invited to the press conference, they listen to the information and then have the chance to ask questions.

Rights for Refugees is an organisation that campaigns about human rights issues and refugees. They are presently trying to make the British public more informed about the needs of asylum-seekers and refugees. Rights for Refugees is very concerned about recent changes in the way that asylum-seekers are treated in Britain. It is concerned about the detention of asylum-seekers and that many asylum-seekers have now lost their right to social security.

Rights for Refugees have called a press conference. Three speakers will explain to journalists their concerns about Britain's treatment of asylum-seekers. Each speaker will use the manifesto to suggest ways that asylum-seekers and refugees could receive better and more just treatment.

Lord Rees-Martin, aged 59.
Lord Rees-Martin sits in the House of Lords. He has always been interested in human rights and has visited Guatemala and Sri Lanka to find out about the human rights situation in those countries.
He is concerned about Britain's treatment of refugees. In particular, he feels it is wrong to detain asylum-seekers in prisons and detention centres.

Elvira Delgado, aged 43.
Elvira is from Peru. She ran a woman's training centre in a shanty town in Lima. In 1986 many of the women from the training centre joined a demonstration to protest against rising food prices. Elvira was photographed and identified by the police at the demonstration. She was later arrested and wrongly accused of being a terrorist.

Elvira was held in prison for four months. During this time she was tortured. Human rights organisations took up her case, and as a result of their work, Elvira was suddenly released.

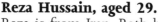

Elvira felt her life would be in danger if she remained in Peru. She bought an air ticket to London. She had a passport but she had to buy a forged visa, as many asylum-seekers are forced to do. She flew to London and asked for political asylum at Heathrow airport. She was allowed to enter Britain, and after ten months was given 'exceptional leave to remain'.

Elvira now works for 'Rights for Refugees'. She feels that a civilised society is one that treats newcomers as human beings. She feels that refugees have a lot to contribute to their new homelands. She wishes to outline to the press conference how she thinks asylum-seekers and refugees should be treated in Britain.

Reza Hussain, aged 29.
Reza is from Iran. Both his parents were active in the Communist Party in Iran. His father was in prison when the Shah of Iran ruled the country. When the Ayatollah Khomenei came to power in 1978, life did not improve for his family.

Reza was lucky and was accepted for a university place in London. He decided he did not want to return to Iran, and was given refugee status in Britain. He now works for 'Rights for Refugees'. He is concerned that most newly-arrived asylum-seekers can no longer claim social security. He fears that many young asylum-seekers will be forced to beg and live on the streets.

CHAPTER SIX

WHAT YOU CAN DO

Demonstration to support Bosnian refugees, London *Tim Fox*

This chapter looks at what young people can do to support refugees ◆ It will examine what can be done at an international, national and local level.

Supporting refugees

The wars and human rights abuses that cause the movement of refugees may seem distant or overwhelming. But there are many things that people here can do. You can help refugees in different parts of the world.

Internationally
You can do things to prevent people becoming refugees and to support refugees living in other countries.

Nationally
You can do things to help refugees who come to Britain.

Locally
You can do things to help refugees living in the local community.

You can support refugees in many different ways.

You can raise funds for projects that help refugees, in Britain and abroad.

You can inform your friends and family about the needs of refugees, in Britain and abroad. You can organise an event to raise awareness about refugees and invite speakers to your school, college or youth group. You can get in touch with the Refugee Council to find out more about refugees. It is important that the public is informed about refugees and why they need to flee from their homes. Well-informed people are more likely to be sympathetic to refugees, and to be able to campaign effectively.

You can join campaigns that try to uphold the human rights of refugees in Britain.

You can also join campaigns that try to prevent refugee movements, for example by campaigning against the sale of weapons to unstable parts of the world, or by campaigning against human rights abuses in countries that produce refugees.

You can meet refugees who live in your local community, and try and support them. You can befriend newly-arrived refugee students who go to your school, and ensure that their needs are not forgotten.

Discussion point

◆ **What you think is the most important activity that you can do to support refugees?**

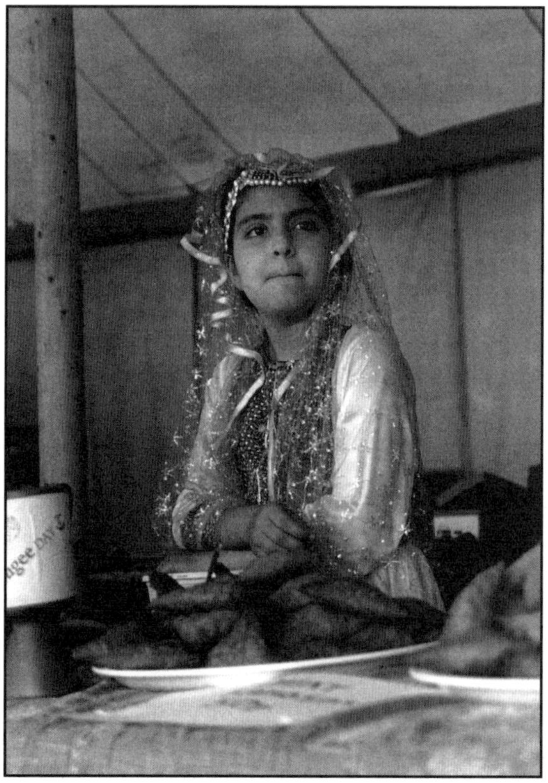

Afghan girl at refugee festival, London *Pat Marsden*

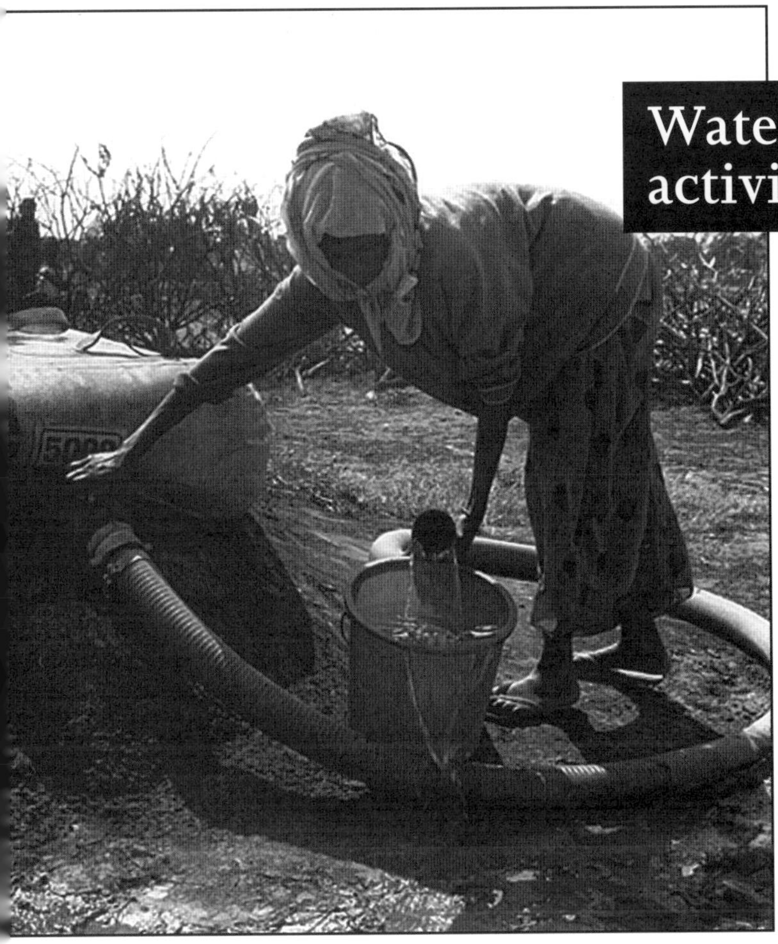

Water! A fundraising activity

Somalia refugee woman collecting water, Ethiopia
UNHCR

Aims

To help students develop their organisational and communication skills.

Instructions

Refugee girls and women living in the camps in Sudan, Somalia and Kenya walk an average of 4.5 kilometres every day to collect water for their families. The group is going to walk 4.5 kilometres carrying a bucket of water, to raise money for work with refugees. Students will need to chose a charity to support. They can write away to some of the groups listed at the end of this book.

They will need paper to design sponsorship forms, and some buckets for the activity.

The group of students will need to set a day for the walk and to plan the route that participants will follow. They could walk around a football pitch, for example. It should be safe, and away from roads. The group may have to get permission for the walk if they are going to use a football pitch.

The group will need to meet to design sponsorship forms. They must have a contact name and address on them, and give a brief explanation of the uses of the money.

The group may like to publicise their fundraising activity in the local paper or on local radio. They can draw attention to the problems faced by many refugees in poor countries, and also the way that organisations are working to support them.

Participants should collect sponsorship from family and friends. On the day of the walk they will need buckets and access to a tap.

Someone should be appointed to be responsible for collecting the money.

After the walk the group can discuss how they felt, and what they learned from the activity.

Designing leaflets

The Refugee Council and many other campaigning organisations have public information departments. One of the jobs of people who work in public information departments is to produce leaflets and books for the general public.

The Refugee Council's public information department has produced many leaflets about refugees. Some of the leaflets are for young people, others are for the general public or for people who have a particular interest in certain issues.

When writing a leaflet, it is important to consider certain points. It is important to think about the purpose of the leaflet and who will read it. Here are some guidelines that may help you when designing your leaflets:

◆ What is the purpose of your leaflet? What do you want to achieve?

◆ Is it to raise the profile of your organisation?

◆ Is it to sell a particular product?

◆ Is it a campaign leaflet to raise public awareness about a particular issue?

◆ Is it to suggest specific actions?

◆ Who is the target audience? The target audience will influence the writing and design of your leaflet.

◆ You should use language appropriate to your target audience.

◆ What message do you want to communicate?

◆ What kind of pictures or images do you want to use?

◆ Are the images negative or positive?

◆ Do the images reinforce stereotypes?

◆ It is important to put over the message that refugees are ordinary people, just like yourselves.

Designing a leaflet about refugees

Aims

To develop students' communication skills.

Instructions

Time needed: one hour or longer. Students may want to spend time researching the leaflet and designing it using desk top publishing programmes.

The students are to design an information leaflet on refugees. They will need to decide their target audience; one suggestion is to produce the leaflet for other young people. The leaflet should be about 500 words in length.

Students should be given freedom to decide their own content and design. For those who need for guidance, a question and answer format can be used. Question and answer leaflets are often produced by those who write public information leaflets. In this case the leaflet attempts to answer common questions about refugees.

The students can devise their own questions or use some of the suggestions below. They should research their own answers.

◆ Who are refugees?

◆ What causes people to become

refugees?

◆ How many refugees are there today?

◆ How many refugees come to Britain every year?

◆ Are all refugees genuine? Don't people come to Britain because they want a better life?

◆ Homelessness and unemployment is already bad in Britain. Won't refugees make the situation worse?

◆ Is it our responsibility to help refugees?

◆ What can I do to support refugees?

Raising awareness about refugees in your school

Aims

Students are going to produce a display about refugees. The display aims to raise awareness about refugees within the school. This activity can be extended with students organising a school event about refugees. The activity will develop students' organisational and communication skills.

Instructions

The time needed for this activity depends on the complexity of the display and whether an event is also organised. Display boards, tables for literature, pens, large sheets of paper, and pins are needed. Students may also want to have access to a computer. Books for research and copies of world maps should also be supplied.

The students should be divided into groups to prepare material for the display. One group of students should also be given the responsibility for finding a suitable place within the school and for assembling the display boards.

The display material should explain who are refugees. It could also include information about where refugees live. Students may also want to gather refugees' stories and information about local organisations that support refugees. If students have produced leaflets about refugees, these, too, can be displayed.

Students may also want to organise an event to support their display. A suggested event might be a school assembly or an evening of food and international music. Students will need to think about the following things if they are organising an evening event:

What type of event are you going to hold?
When? Set a date.
Do you need permission to do this?
How many people will be coming?
Who do you want to invite?
Who will send out invitations?
How much money will you spend on organising your event?
Who will make a budget?
Are you going to charge people?
Will you have food?
What will you cook?
Who will do the cooking?
Who will buy refreshments?
Who will organise the music?
Who will take charge of putting up displays?
Will you get anyone to speak at your event?
Who will clear up afterwards?

School projects to raise awareness

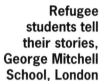

Refugee students tell their stories, George Mitchell School, London

Students at George Mitchell School in London recently produced a play and a video about refugees in Britain. The drama and video project raised awareness about refugees, both for the class involved in the two projects, and the rest of the school.

George Mitchell School is a secondary school in east London. Like many schools in London it has young refugees among its pupils - mostly from Somalia and Turkish Kurdistan. It was the presence of young refugees in the school that provided the inspiration for the two projects. Both teachers and students wanted to find out more about refugees.

The students used their humanities classes to produce the drama and video. The class was divided into two groups. One group worked with a drama teacher to produce a 15-minute play about refugees in Britain. The play traces the journey of a group of refugees from Turkish Kurdistan to London.

The other group of students worked on a video. The video is titled 'Why?' and it examines what happens to refugees when they arrive in Britain. As well as looking at what faces refugees when they arrive in a new country and a new school, it examines whether refugees are treated fairly in Britain. In particular the students look at the detention of refugees.

The students who made the video interviewed two MPs. They also filmed a protest outside Harmondsworth detention centre and one of them managed to visit detainees inside. The students interviewed refugees living near their school and visited other schools in London to look at ways that schools can support refugee students.

The students who were involved in the project researched the issue for themselves. They decided on the form and content of the play and video. With the support of teachers, the students were the actors, directors, photographers and video editors. The play and video were shown to other students in the school as well as invited members of the public.

George Mitchell School is not unique in organising such a project. Other schools have made displays about refugees for their schools. George Orwell School, also in London, recently made a video and CD-Rom giving information about refugees. The video is called 'Safe in Another Country'. A group of refugee students from Bolivia, Turkish Kurdistan, Somalia and Ethiopia worked with a video producer to make a 20-minute video. The video is now for sale and has been bought by other schools.

Campaigning

To campaign means to work to change laws or practices in a way that benefits a target group or person. For example the Central America Committee for Human Rights is a British-based campaigning group. It works to improve human rights conditions in Central America. Its target group is all people who live in Central America.

Campaigns can be carried out by individuals or small groups of people. More usually, however, pressure groups organise campaigns. A pressure group is an organisation that works to defend the interests of its members, or to campaign for a certain cause.

Pressure groups use many different methods to campaign. These are described below. Some pressure groups concentrate on lobbying. Other pressure groups may put more effort into organising protests and building large scale public support.

Working with Members of Parliament and other people who hold power The decisions made by MPs have a large amount of influence over people's lives, in Britain and also abroad. Most pressure groups work to influence MPs' opinions, to try and get them to change laws and practices in ways that benefit the pressure group's target.

Pressure groups may also try and influence the opinions of other people who hold power. Such people might include Members of the House of Lords, Members of the European Parliament, civil servants and local councillors. Working to change the opinion of people who hold power is called lobbying.

Building support with the public
Many pressure groups also encourage members of the public to support their cause. Pressure groups may ask members of the public to write to their MPs, to join demonstrations or to give money to the pressure group.

Organising protests and public events
Some pressure groups organise demonstrations or publicity stunts - to give publicity to the their cause. Pressure groups may also organise public meetings to discuss issues.

Getting the interest of the media
Newspapers, radio and television influence the opinion of members of the public. Pressure groups feel that it is important to ensure that their cause is covered in the media in a positive way. For this reason a pressure group may employ a press officer, to supply information to journalists.

Refugee Council

The Refugee Council acts as a pressure group. It campaigns for asylum-seekers, refugees and internally displaced people throughout the world. Some of its recent campaigning activities include:

- attending the annual party conferences of the Conservative, Labour and Liberal Democratic Parties, to raise concerns about refugees with MPs;
- sending information to MPs about refugees;
- giving information about refugees to Members of the European parliament;
- mailing information to members of the public, asking them to write to their MPs about the rights of refugees in Britain;
- writing letters about refugees to newspapers;
- sending press releases to newspapers about refugees in Britain, and in other countries.

Fiinding out how different organisations campaign

Students can collect more information about organisations that campaign for refugees or related issues. The following are a list of campaigning organisations to which students may wish to write to collect more information (some of the organisations are also involved in other types of work):

Amnesty International
Campaign Against the Arms Trade
Catholic Fund for Overseas Development
Central America Committee for Human Rights
Minority Rights Group
Oxfam
Refugee Council
Survival International
World Development Movement

Students may want to consider the following issues after they have collected information:

- On what issues does the organisation campaign?
- Who is their target group?
- What methods do they use?

Organising a campaign for refugee rights

Aims

The activity aims to develop participants' communication skills. Students are expected to devise a campaign strategy to promote refugees' rights.

Instructions

Time needed: 45 minutes.

Paper and pens are needed. All students will need a copy of the information about campaigning and a copy of the Refugee Manifesto. Students can use the Refugee Council Refugee Manifesto (see page 224) or they can devise their own.

The students should be divided into groups of three or four. Each group has to devise a campaign strategy, using the Refugee Manifesto. Students should think about to whom they might want to write about the Refugee Manifesto. They should also think about how they want to publicise the Refugee Manifesto and how they might work with the media.

Students should spend about 30 minutes devising and writing up their campaigning strategy. The class should then come together and different groups should present their ideas. The students may wish to take the campaign further, and make press releases, newspaper articles or a radio documentary about the campaign.

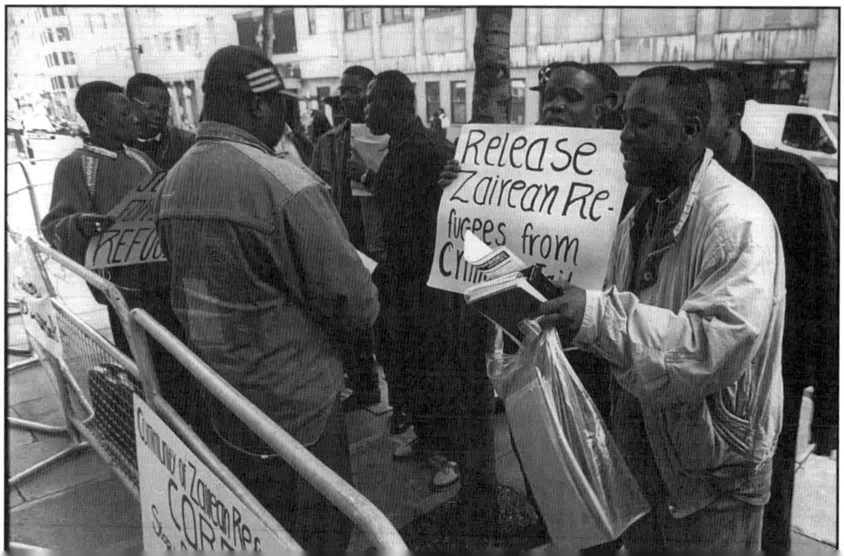

Zairean refugees picket the Home Office
Jon Walter

Amnesty International & Amnesty International Youth Action

Amnesty International is a pressure group which campaigns for human rights. Using information supplied by Amnesty International's Headquarters, ordinary people in many countries write protest letters to governments and other groups that abuse human rights. Amnesty International Youth Action groups bring together young people. Together they campaign for human rights.

How Amnesty began

In November 1960, Peter Benenson, a 40-year old lawyer who lived in London, read a newspaper article about two Portuguese students. The two students were living in Portugal, and their government was a fascist dictatorship. The two students had been arrested and sentenced to seven years' imprisonment for raising their glasses in a public toast to freedom.

Angered by this injustice, Peter Benenson thought about ways that the Portuguese government - and other repressive governments - could be persuaded to release such victims. His idea was to send thousands of letters of protest to those governments who were detaining prisoners of conscience.

Together with Eric Baker, a Quaker, and Louis Blom-Cooper, a lawyer, and others, Peter Benenson launched a one year campaign. It was called 'Appeal for Amnesty, 1961', and highlighted the fate of prisoners of conscience. The campaign was launched with an article in the Observer newspaper. It focused on eight prisoners of conscience. The article received a tremendous response. Many people sent letters of support and money. Other people volunteered to work for the campaign. And very importantly, more information about other prisoners of conscience was collected. Amnesty International had begun.

In the next 12 months Amnesty International sent delegations to four countries to lobby on behalf of prisoners of conscience, and promoted a further 210 cases. Members had organised national bodies in seven countries.

Amnesty International now has over one million members in 150 different countries. There are national sections of Amnesty International in 55 countries. Amnesty International's headquarters, known as the International Secretariat, is based in London. Here information about human rights violations is collected and analysed. Individuals and national sections are then mailed with 'actions'. The 'actions' contain information about human rights abuses to help individuals and groups write protest letters to those authorities that are committing these crimes.

The work of Amnesty International

Amnesty International has a mandate which outlines the type of work that the organisation should do. Amnesty International seeks:

The release of all prisoners of conscience Prisoners of conscience are people detained for their beliefs, colour, sex, ethnic origin, language or religion. Prisoners of conscience must not have used or supported violence.

Fair and prompt trials for all political prisoners.

Abolition of the death penalty and an end to extrajudicial executions Amnesty International opposes all executions. It campaigns against killings inside the law - the death penalty. Amnesty International also opposes killings outside the legal system. These are extrajudicial executions, killings carried out on the orders of governments.

An end to torture and other cruel, inhuman or degrading treatment of prisoners.

An end to 'disappearances' Amnesty International opposes the 'disappearance' of individuals. Disappearances are when individuals are detained by governments or security forces, but their detention is never admitted. People who have 'disappeared' may be prisoners of conscience, or be facing torture or death.

An end to human rights violations by opposition groups Amnesty International opposes killings, torture and hostage taking by opposition groups but believes that the upholding of human rights to be a matter primarily for governments. This is because only governments are bound by international law.

An end to the forcible return of refugees Amnesty International opposes the forcible return of refugees to their home countries in situations where they would face imprisonment for their beliefs, or are likely to face torture, execution or cruel, inhuman or degrading treatment. Amnesty International collects information about the risks that refugees would face if returned to their home countries.

It is very important that Amnesty International is seen as an independent and impartial organisation. For this reason Amnesty International does not accept funds from governments. And Amnesty International members are not usually involved in campaigning on individual cases in their own country.

Amnesty Youth Action

Amnesty Youth Action is for young people under 18 years old. It was started in 1988 and now has over 8,000 members in Britain. Amnesty Youth Action members are active as individuals, or in Amnesty Youth Action Groups. The groups exist in schools, colleges, faith groups and scouting groups. Every year members of Amnesty Youth Action meet at an annual conference.

Amnesty Youth Action Groups are involved in:

- letter writing
- fundraising
- information campaigns
- contacting MPs and MEPs
- issuing press releases

For more information contact Youth Officer, Amnesty International (UK), 99-119 Rosebery Avenue, London EC1R 4RE.

Supporting refugees in your local community

Aims

The group will examine ways they can support refugees who live in their local community, particularly young refugees. The activity aims to improve participants' organisational skills.

Instructions

Large sheets of paper and pens. You also need to find out about refugees who live locally or attend the school.

The students should be kept together. Explain that they are going to think of ways of supporting refugees who live locally, particularly young refugees. Get the group to list the practical things that they can do. If the group get stuck they can be prompted.

Some of the things that young people have done before include helping young refugees learn English (see Lunchtime Link), befriending new students and making sure that their first days in school are not difficult. Other students have made a guide for their school or have shown newly-arrived refugees the best places for shopping.

The group should decide what they will do, then make plans to carry this out. They will have to think about practical details, such as those described below for the Lunchtime Link project.

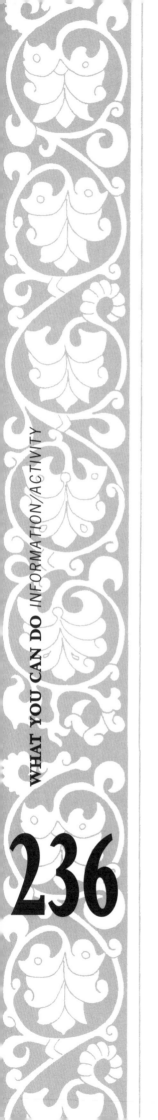

Lunchtime Link

Lunchtime Link is a scheme which has been operated by Community Service Volunteers in London. Groups of sixth form students receive some appropriate training, then help a small group of students who speak little English. They commit one lunchtime a week to the scheme.

The training consists of four lunchtime sessions held once a week at the beginning of term. After that, the lunchtime sessions are held once a week. Students who have helped on the scheme said that volunteering did not interfere with their school work.

The volunteers do not give formal English lessons. Instead, through the use of specially chosen games, the volunteers provide assistance with spoken or written English. For example, volunteers play Scrabble with the younger students during a lunchtime session. Scrabble helps students improve their vocabulary, spelling and conversational skills.

Teachers are present for a few trial sessions, but after this the scheme is led by older students, without the presence of members of staff. But there are members of staff involved in the project. They arrange the training and also some feedback sessions where volunteers discuss how they are getting on.

Community Service Volunteers produced a check list to help volunteers organise their sessions. Points that should be considered include:

Keys Who has the keys to the door of the room you are using? Have you made an arrangement to collect the key at a particular time? Do you have any backup procedure in case you or the teacher is away on a particular day? All these details need to be sorted out.

Register Teachers should be able to provide you with a list of names and tutor groups of the younger students who will attend the scheme. A register should be taken at each session, but this does not need to be called formally. If a students is absent for a few sessions the link teacher should find out if he or she still wants to come to Lunchtime Link. The teacher can also find out why the student has decided not to attend. In some cases it may be that things have been going wrong with the scheme, so getting feedback from the younger students will enable problems to be corrected.

Storage There must be a safe place to store the register, games and dictionaries. Again there needs to be a procedure for unlocking cupboards.

Notebooks Each of the younger students should be given a notebook by the school. They should be encouraged to bring them as writing down new words reinforces the learning that takes places through the games.

Lunch Passes Link teachers should arrange for all those attending a lunchtime link to have early lunch passes.

Some of the games include Boggle and Scrabble. Information about Lunchtime Link and the games involved can be obtained from Community Service Volunteers, 237 Pentonville Road, London N1 9NJ, telephone 0171-278-6601.

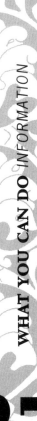

WORD LIST

Annexe - to take a piece of land as a new possession.

Anti-semitism - discrimination and/or violence against Jewish people. It is a form of racism.

Appeal - a legal challenge to a refusal of refugee status.

Armed struggle - where political organisations decide that they will use violent means to achieve their political aims.

Asylum-seeker - someone who has fled from his or her home country, and is seeking refugee status in another country.

Bias - the one-sided coverage of events or issues, so that only one set of views are put forward.

Census - a survey carried out every ten years, to count the population and find out other facts.

Civilian government - a government that is not run by the army and is usually a democracy.

Civil war - a war between two or more groups of people within a country.

Colonisation - conquering and ruling other countries.

Communist government - a government whose policies are based on the economic ideas of Marx and Lenin. There is no private ownership of factories and large farms. Communist governments usually provide good educational and health services.

Conflict resolution - talks or activities that help people solve disagreements or conflicts.

Death squad - a group of people who kill their political opponents.

Democracy - a country with a fairly elected government, and with respect for human rights.

Deportation - sending people to live in another place against their will.

Destabilisation - making a government less stable or popular, with a view to overthrowing that government.

Detention - imprisoning people who have not been charged or convicted of an offence. Asylum-seekers are sometimes held in detention in Britain.

Disappearance - when a person is detained by a government or security forces but his or her detention is not admitted. Some people who disappear may later be killed.

Economic migrant - someone who has left his or her home to look for better work and a higher standard of living in another place.

Ethnic minority - a group of people who share a distinctive culture, usually different from the culture of the majority of people.

Exceptional leave to remain (ELR) - an immigration status given by the British government which enables a person to remain in Britain for one year before it is renewed. People with exceptional leave to remain may work, but they cannot bring in members of their family for four years.

Extrajudicial execution - this is where a person is murdered by a country's armed forces or police outside the legal processes of that country.

Family tracing - a search for a lost member of a family, who may have been separated during war.

Fascist government - a government which practices policies which are authoritarian and nationalistic. Under such governments there are many restrictions on individual freedom. Fascist governments are rarely elected.

Genocide - the deliberate murder of an ethnic, religious, political or national group.

Ghetto - an area of a town or city to

which Jews were confined during the Middle Ages and also in Nazi-occupied Europe.

Guerrilla - someone belongs to an organisation that takes part in small scale attacks.

Home Office - the section of the British government which is responsible for asylum-seekers and refugees. The Immigration and Nationality Department is part of the Home Office and is responsible for examining the applications of asylum-seekers.

Huguenot - a French Protestant. Some 100,000 Huguenot refugees fled to Britain and Ireland in the 17th century.

Human right - a universal right to which everyone is entitled, for example the right to clean water, shelter and free speech.

Human rights abuse - an incident where someone has lost a human right, such as the right to life or freedom of speech. Human rights abuses cause refugees to flee.

Immigrant - someone who has entered a new country to settle.

Internally displaced person - someone who has fled from his or her home but has not crossed an international border.

International Monetary Fund (IMF) - an international bank that lends money to countries which face debts. The IMF may make an indebted country cut its public spending.

Landmine - an explosive device placed in the ground and designed to explode when a person steps on it.

Land reform - a change in the ownership of land so that many people can own land, and not just a few.

Lobby - working to change the opinion of people who hold power.

Manifesto - a statement of aims or beliefs.

Migration - the permanent movement of people from one place to another.

Military dictatorship - rule by a government made up of members of the armed forces. Military dictatorships are not elected.

Militia - people who are trained like soldiers but are not part of an official army.

Nationalism - a political movement whose priority is national identity and the future of a particular national group.

Non-governmental organisation - an organisation that is not run by central or local government.

Persecution - being unjustly harassed, threatened with death or imprisonment, usually for political or religious reasons, or ethnic identity.

Political asylum - the process of applying for refugee status in another country.

Prejudice - negative and unfavourable feelings about a group of people, not based on knowledge or fact.

Pressure group - an organisation that works to defend the interests of its members, or to campaign for a certain cause, for example, human rights.

Propaganda - the use of the media to create certain actions or beliefs.

Racism - when people are treated differently because they belong to a particular ethnic group.

Reconstruction - rebuilding; before refugees are to return home there may be a need for reconstruction, to mend homes and public buildings destroyed by war.

Referendum - when a government gives voters the opportunity of voting 'yes' or 'no' to a particular question.

Refoulement - where an asylum-seeker or refugee is forcibly returned to the country from which he or she has fled.

Refugee - a person who has left his or her home country or is unable to return to it 'owing to a well-founded fear of being persecuted for reasons of race, religion, nationality, membership of a particular social group or political opinion.'

Religious fundamentalism - where people believe that religious teachings and books like the Koran and the Bible are absolutely true. At times of crisis many people may turn towards religious fundamentalism, believing that religious governments will solve their country's problems.

Repatriation - returning a person to

his or her home country. People can be forced to go against their will; this is 'forcible repatriation', or they can go voluntarily.

Scapegoat - a person or group of people who are blamed for a problem they have not directly caused.

Self-determination - allowing a national group to decide its own political future.

Self help group - an organisation founded by people to help themselves and others who are faced with the same problems.

Socialist - a person who believes that all people should have equal access to education, health-care and other resources.

Stereotype - an oversimplified and inaccurate idea about a particular group. Stereotypes are not based on fact and are often insulting.

Torture - a deliberate way of inflicting pain on another person.

Trade union - an organisation that defends the rights of workers who are its members.

Travel documents - passports and visas.

UN - the United Nations, an international organisation that works to promote peace and security. Almost all of the world's countries are members of the UN. It comprises a Security Council, the General Assembly and many international organisations such as UNHCR.

UNHCR - the United Nations High Commissioner for Refugees. The United Nations organisation that has responsibility for protecting asylum-seekers and refugees and ensuring they receive adequate food, water, shelter and other necessities.

Unaccompanied refugee child - a refugee child who has lost his or her parents or usual carers or has become separated from them.

Visa - a stamp on a passport that allows a person to enter a particular country.

Zionism - a political idea developed by Theodor Herzl, meaning Jewish people have a right to a nation of their own.

FURTHER RESOURCES

General issues/human rights

Amnesty International (1995) *Report 1994*
This is an annual report which gives summaries of human rights conditions in all parts of the world.

Amnesty International (1993)
Working for Freedom.
An action video pack on human rights. Highly recommended.

CAFOD (1994) *Run for Your Life*
A simulation game for students aged 14+. Highly recommended.
Available from CAFOD, price £5.

George Orwell School (1994) *Safe in Another Country*
A video made by refugee students in a London school. Available from George Orwell School, Turle Road, London N4.

International Broadcasting Trust (1992) *Refugees in Today's Europe: an action video pack*
Available from Academy TV, 104 Kirkstall Road, Leeds LS3 1JS.

Peace Pledge Union (1994) *Peace and War: A resource for teaching and learning*
An excellent resource containing background information and activities for use in schools. Available from the Peace Pledge Union.

Refugee Council (1988) *Africa, Asia, Central America and Refugee Children.*
A set of four videos of refugees' testimonies. Available for hire from the Refugee Council.

Rutter, Jill (1994) *Refugee Children in the Classroom.* Trentham Books
A background book for teachers and others who are working with refugee students.

Rutter, Jill (1992) *Refugees: A Resource Book for 8-13 Year Olds*. Refugee Council
A teacher's resource book.

Save the Children Fund (1993) *Children: a right to refuge*. SCF, London.
A free leaflet about refugee children.

Save the Children (1995) *Children at War* SCF, London.
A free leaflet giving useful background information.

Selby, David (1987) *Human Rights* Cambridge University Press
An informative reading book on human rights.

Selby, David (1998) *Human Rights*. Mary Glasgow.
Teaching pack with many activities to encourage human rights education.

UNHCR (1994) *Refugee Children* UNHCR, London.
A free leaflet for students.

UNHCR (1995) *The State of the World's Refugees*. Penguin
A background book about current refugee issues.

Watson, James (1983) *Talking in Whispers* Gollancz.
The story of a 16 year old living under the junta in Chile.

Refugees in history

Cesarani, David *A History of the Holocaust* Holocaust Educational Trust.
The booklet contains maps by Martin Gilbert.

Cohn, Frederick (1990) *Signals: A Young Refugee's Flight from Germany in 1930s* United Writers Publications.
An exploration of the feelings of two young refugees as they travel to Britain

Ethnic Communities Oral History Project *Passport to Exile: the Polish Way to London*
Polish people tell their experiences; suitable for students. Available from the Ethnic Communities Oral History Project.

Ethnic Communities Oral History Project *Ship of Hope*.
The story of 4,000 Basque children evacuated to London in 1936.

Geras, Adele (1989) *Voyage*. Hamish Hamilton.
The story of refugees fleeing Eastern Europe at the beginning of the 20th century.

Gwynne, Robin (1985) *Huguenot Heritage* Routledge and Kegan Paul

Kent Arts and Libraries *Anne Frank in the World Teacher's Pack*
Available from the Anne Frank Educational Trust.

Landau, Ronnie (1992) *The Jewish Holocaust: A Universal Experience*. IB Tauris, London.
A book of background information, of great use to teachers.

Levy, Herbert *Voices from the Past*
The testimony of a child who came on the Kindertransporte. Available from the Anne Frank Educational Trust

Rutter, Jill (1994) *Jewish Migrations* Wayland.
A book for students aged 11-15.

Serraillier, Ian (1956) *The Silver Sword* Puffin.
A story of four refugee children, suitable for 11-15 year olds.

Supple, Carrie (1993) *From Prejudice to Genocide: Learning about the Holocaust* Trentham Books.
A background book for teachers.

Supple, Carrie and Hudson, Nick (1991) *Where Shall We Go?*
A 56-minute video in which Holocaust survivors tell of their experiences. Available from Swingbridge Videos, Norden House, 41 Stowell Street, Newcastle NE1 4YB.

White, Irene *I Came As A Stranger*
The story of a young refugee who fled to escape Nazi persecution. Available from the Anne Frank Educational Trust.

White, Irene *And So We Shall Gather* Further memoirs of a young refugee. Available from the Anne Frank Educational Trust.

Afghanistan

Arney, George (1989) *Afghanistan* Mandarin Books.
A background book for teachers.

Dupree, Louis (1980) *Afghanistan* Princeton.
A background book for teachers.

Hiro, Dilip (1988) *Islamic Fundamentalism* Paladin.
A concise non-partisan account of events in the Middle East and Asia.

Minority Rights Group (1995) *Afghanistan: a nation of minorities*
Available from MRG. Useful background reading.

Angola

Christian Aid (1995) *Angola: Highlight Sheet*
A useful fact sheet for students and teachers.

Jamba, Sousa (1993)*A Lonely Devil*. Fourth Estate.
A novel that examines issues surrounding torture.

Jamba, Sousa, (1990) *Patriots*. Penguin.
A novel about an Angolan refugee who flees to Zambia as a child then returns to fight in Angola's civil war.

Vines, Alex (1995) *What Went Right and What Went Wrong? Angola and Mozambique* Catholic Institute for International Relations.
Background information for teachers.

Warner, Rachel (Ed) (1995) *Voices from Angola*. Minority Rights Group.
A collection of testimonies of refugee children.

Burundi & Rwanda

Minority Rights Group (1995) *Burundi: Breaking the Cycle of Violence*
A 28-page report; background information for teachers.

Oxfam (1994) *Rwanda: Caught in Conflict*
Leaflet for students and teachers.

Waller, David (1993) *Rwanda: Which Way Now?* Oxfam Country Profile.

The Caucasus

Lang, D. and Walker, C (1991) *The Armenians*. Minority Rights Group.

Minority Rights Group *The Northern Caucasus*. MRG Report, providing useful background information.

Eritrea

Keneally, Thomas (1989) *Towards Asmara* Hodder and Stoughton. A novel about political events in Eritrea.

Warner, Rachel (Ed) (1991) *Voices from Eritrea*. Minority Rights Group.
A collection of testimonies of refugee children.

Guatemala

Burr, Margaret (1992) *We Have Always Lived Here; the Maya of Guatemala*. Minority Rights Group.
A teaching resource.

Minority Rights Group (1995) *The Maya of Guatemala*. MRG report.
Useful background information.

The Kurds

Hicyilimaz, Gaye (1990) *Against the Storm* Viking.
A novel about rural life in Turkey.

Izady, Mehrdad (1992) *The Kurds: a concise history and fact book*. Taylor and Francis.
Useful background information.

King, John (1992) *The Kurds*. Wayland Publishers.
A reading book for 11-16 year olds.

Laird, Elizabeth (1991) *Kiss the Dust* Heinemann.
A story about an Iraqi Kurdish girl forced to flee from her home to London.

Laizer, Sheri (1991) *Into Kurdistan: Frontiers Under Fire*. Zed Press.

Warner, Rachel, (Ed) (1991) *Voices from Kurdistan*. Minority Rights Group
A collection of testimonies of refugee children.

Iran

Ethnic Communities Oral History Project (1990) *In Exile - Iranian Recollections*
A collection of bilingual testimonies of Iranian refugees.

Hiro, Dilip (1985) *Iran under the Ayatollahs* Routledge and Kegan Paul.
Useful background information for teachers.

The Palestinians

McDowall, David (1995) *The Palestinians* Minority Rights Group.
Excellent background information.

Somalia

Lewis, I.M. (1993) *Understanding Somalia* HAAN Associates.
An invaluable teacher background to Somalia.

Sulieman, Anita (1991) *Somali Studies: Land of the People, Early History, Stories from the Land of Punt, Somali Nomads, Food and Somali People of the Horn of Africa*. HAAN Associates.
Six booklets plus teaching notes.

Warner, Rachel (Ed) (1991) *Voices from Somalia*. Minority Rights Group.
A collection of testimonies of refugee children.

Wilkes, Sybella (1994) *One Day We Had to Run*. Evans Brothers.
A book for children aged 11-15, with the stories of refugee children from Somalia, Sudan and Ethiopia. Highly recommended.

Sri Lanka

Hensman, Rohini (1993) *Journey without a Destination*. Refugee Council.
The story of Sri Lanka's civil war as told by those displaced by the fighting.
Suitable for teachers or older students.

Refugee Council *The Sri Lanka Monitor*
Monthly journal about events in Sri Lanka.

Sudan

Oxfam (1993)*Egypt, Sudan and Ethiopia: Turbulence along the Nile*
A booklet for students available from Oxfam.

Oxfam (1995)
Sudan: An Oxfam Country Profile
A background for teachers, available from Oxfam.

Warner, Rachel (Ed) (1995) *Voices from Sudan*. Minority Rights Group.
A collection of testimonies of refugee children.

Wilkes, Sybella (1994) *One Day We Had to Run* (See under **Somalia**).

Uganda

Warner, Rachel (Ed) (1995) *Voices from Uganda*. Minority Rights Group.
A collection of testimonies of refugee children.

Viet Nam

Maclear, Michael (1981) *The Ten Thousand Day War: Viet Nam 1945-75*. Eyre Methuen

Strachan, Ian (1980) *Journey of a Thousand Miles*. Methuen.
A novel about the journey of a Vietnamese refugee.

Former Yugoslavia

Centre for Education in World Citizenship (1993) *The Disintegration of Yugoslavia*. CEWC.
A leaflet for 14-18 year olds.

Filipovic, Zlata (1994) *Zlata's Diary* Methuen.
The diary of a girl growing up in Sarajevo.

Rady, Martyn (1994) *The Break Up of Yugoslavia*. Wayland.
A book for students aged 12-16.

Silver, N (1995) *The Death of Yugoslavia* BBC Books.
An excellent background book for teachers.

Zaire

Biddlecombe, Peter (1994) *French Lessons in Africa*. Abacus.
Useful background information about francophone Africa.

Warner, Rachel (Ed) (1995) *Voices from Zaire*. Minority Rights Group.
A collection of testimonies of refugee children.

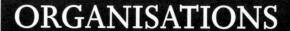

ORGANISATIONS

P = organisations which provide publications on refugee related issues.

E = organisations which have educational programmes working with young people.

Action Aid Collaboration Learning Project
Hamlyn House
London N19 5PG
Tel: 0171-281-4101
P E

Africa Centre
38 King Street
London WC2E 8JT
Tel: 0171-836-1973
Bookshop and an extensive programme of cultural and educational events.

AIMER
(Access to Information in Multicultural Education Resources)
Bulmershe College of Education
Woodlands Avenue
Reading RG6 1HY
Tel: 01734-663387

Amnesty International – UK
99-119 Rosebery Avenue
London EC1R 4RE
Tel: 0171-814-6200
P E A worldwide human rights organisation. Amnesty International produces a wide range of published material and is engaged in human rights education. It has youth and student groups.

Anne Frank Educational Trust
PO Box 432
Bushey
Herts WD2 1QU
P E

British Red Cross Society
9 Grosvenor Crescent
London SW1X 7EJ
Tel: 0171-235-5454
E

Campaign Against the Arms Trade
11 Goodwin Street
London N4 3HQ
Tel: 0171-281-0297
P

Catholic Fund for Overseas Development
2 Romero Close
Stockwell Road
London SW9 9TY
Tel: 0171-739 7900
P E CAFOD has recently run a refugee campaign. It has regional offices and a team of education and youth workers.

Catholic Institute for International Relations
Unit 3, Canonbury Yard
190a New North Road
London N1 7BJ
Tel: 0171-354-0883
P

Central America Committee for Human Rights
83 Margaret Street
London W1N 7HB
Tel: 0171-631-4200
P E

Children of the Storm
Hampstead School
Westbere Road
London NW2 3RT
0171-435-4880
A charity to support refugees organised by students in Hampstead School.

Christian Aid
P.O. Box 100
London SE1 7RT
Tel: 0171-620-4444
P E Christian Aid has regional offices and works with schools and youth groups.

Commission for Racial Equality
Elliot House
10 Allington Street
London SW1 5EH
Tel: 0171-828-7022
P E The Commission for Racial Equality runs a youth campaign.

CAABU
(Council for the Advancement of Arab-British Understanding)
21 Collingham Road
London SW5 0NU
Tel: 0171-373-8414
P E

Council for Education in World Citizenship
13 West Smithfield
London EC1A 9HY
Tel: 0171-329-1711
P E

Development Education Association
3rd Floor
29-31 Cowper Street
London EC1R 4AP
Tel: 0171-490-8108
The DEA is the umbrella group of British development education centres. The DEA will give you the adress of your nearest development education centre if needed.

Development education centres
Development education centres are often a good source of educational materials about refugees and related issues. Many of them have libraries and will lend teachers educational materials. The Development Education Association (0171-490-8108) will put you in touch with your local development education centre.

At present development education centres operate in Aberdeen, Ambleside/Cumbria, Aylesbury, Bangor, Belfast, Birmingham, Bournemouth, Brighton, Bristol, Camarthen, Cambridge, Canterbury, Chelmsford, Clitheroe, Colne, Craven Dales, Derry, Dudley, Dundee, Edinburgh, Glasgow, Guildford, Hull, Leamington Spa, Leeds, Leicester, Llandidloes/North Wales, London, Malvern, Marlborough, Middlesborough, Milton Keynes, Neath/South Wales, Newcastle, Norwich, Nottingham, Oxford, Preston, Reading, Rochdale, Saffron Walden, Sheffield and Winchester, Yeovil.

Ethnic Communities Oral History Project
The Little Husset
191 Talgarth Road
London W6 8BJ
0181-741-4076
P

Haan Associates
PO Box 607
London SW16 1EB
0171-737-4747
P Publishes educational material about Somalia.

International Broadcasting Trust
2 Ferdinand Place
London NW1 8HE
Tel: 0171-482-2847
P E

Iranian Community Centre
266 Holloway Road
London N7 6NE
Tel: 0171-700-0477
A larger self-help group, working with the Iranian community.

Irish Refugee Council
Arran House
35 Arran Quay
Dublin 7
Tel: 01-724433
P E

Jewish Council for Racial Equality
33 Seymour Place
London W1N 6AT
Tel: 0181-455-0896
P E

Jewish Museum (Finchley)
The Sternberg Centre
80 East End Road
London N3 2SY
Tel: 0181-346-2288
P E

Joint Council for the Welfare of Immigrants
115 Old Street
London EC1V 9JR
Tel: 0171-251-8706
P

Kurdish Information Centre
10 Glasshouse Yard
London EC1A 4JN
Tel: 0171-250-1315

Refugee community organisations
There are over 250 active refugee organisations in Britain. They are self help groups working with refugees from many different regions and countries, including

Afghanistan
Algeria
Angola
Bosnia
Chile
China
(Kosovo)
Colombia
Czechoslovakia
Eritrea
(Bravanese)
Ethiopia
Ethiopia (Tigrayans and Oromo)
Ghana
Iran
Iran (Armenians)
Iraq
Iraq (Assyrians)
Iraq (Kurds)
Ivory Coast
Nigeria
Poland
Rwanda
Serbia
Sierra Leone
Somalia
Somalia
Sri Lanka
Sudan
Turkey
Turkey (Kurds)
Uganda
Togo
Viet Nam
Zaire

The Refugee Council will provide addresses of these organisations and can put teachers in contact with refugee speakers.

Latin America Bureau
1 Amwell Street
London EC1R 1UL
Tel: 0171-278-2829
P E

Liberty
21 Tabard Street
London SE1 4LA
Tel: 0171-403-3888
P

Medical Foundation for the Care of Victims of Torture
96 Grafton Road
London NW5 3EJ
Tel: 0171-813-7777
P

Midlands Refugee Council
201a The Argent Centre
60 Frederick Street
Hockley
Birmingham
Tel: 0121-212-1435

Minority Rights Group
379 Brixton Road
London SW9 7DE
Tel: 0171-978-9498
P E

National Association of Race Equality Councils
8/16 Coronet Street
London N1 9LZ
Tel: 0171-739-6658
There are 110 race equality councils in Britain. They will often provide speakers on race issues.

National Committee for Development Education
16-20 South Cumberland Street
Dublin 2
Tel: 01-662-0866
Coordinates development education work in Ireland.

North East Refugee Service
19 Bigg Market
Newcastle upon Tyne NE1 1UN
Tel: 0191-222-0406

Northern Refugee Centre
Jew Lane
off Fitzalan Square
Sheffield S1 2BE
Tel: 01742-701429
This organisation has a resource centre.

Ockenden Venture
Guildford Road
Woking
Surrey GU22 7UU
Tel: 014862-772-012
E

Oxfam
274 Banbury Road
Oxford 0X2 7DZ
Tel: 01865-311311
P E Oxfam has a youth and education department and also regional offices carrying out educational work in Brighton, Bristol, Cardiff, Glasgow, London, Southampton and Manchester.

Peace Pledge Union
6 Endsleigh Street
London WC1 0DX
Tel: 0171-387-5501
P E

Quaker Peace and Service
Friends House
Euston Road
London NW1 2BJ
0171-387-3601
P E

Reading/Berkshire Refugee Support Group
102 London Street
Reading RG1 4SJ
Tel: 01734-505356

Refugee Action
The Cedars
Oakwood
Derby DE2 4FY
Tel: 01332-833310
Refugee Action has regional offices in Birmingham, Bristol, Leeds, London and Manchester.
P

Refugee Studies Programme
Queen Elizabeth House
St Giles
Oxford OX1 3LA
Tel: 01865-270722
P This research body will provide speakers.

Refugee Council
3 Bondway
London SW8 1SJ
Tel: 0171-582-6922
P E The Refugee Council supports asylum-seekers and refugees in Britain and campaigns on refugee issues throughout the world. It publishes a wide range of information and there is a specialist service for schools, including

- answering individual requests for information from students and teachers
- producing publications for use in the classroom, by youth groups and for teachers
- providing in-service training about refugees and educational provision for refugee students
- giving advice and curriculum support to teachers
- speaking to school students
- running workshops for voluntary agencies.

The Runnymede Trust
11 Princelet Street
London E1 6QH
Tel: 0171-375-1496
P This organisation publishes booklets on race issues and will provide speakers.

Save the Children Fund
Mary Datchelor House
17 Grove Lane
London SE5 8RD
P E
The Save the Children Fund has an education department and regional offices.

Scottish Refugee Council
2nd Floor, 73 Robertson Street
Glasgow G2 8QD
Tel: 0141-221-8793

and 43 Broughton Street
Edinburgh EH1 3JU
Tel: 0131-557-8083

Survival International
11-15 Emerald Street
London WC1N 3QL
Tel: 0171-242-1441
P

Tamil Information Centre
720 Romford Road
London E12 4BY
Tel: 0181-514-6390
P

Uganda Community Relief Association
Selby Centre
Selby Road
London N17 8AD
Tel: 0181-808-6221

UNICEF UK
55 Lincon's Inn Fields
London WC2A 3NB
Tel: 0171-405-5592
P E

UNHCR, UK Branch Office
21st Floor, Millbank Tower
21-24 Millbank
London SW1P 4QP
Tel: 0171-828-9191
P

Welsh Refugee Council
Unit 8, Williams Court
Trade Street
Cardiff CF1 5DQ
Tel: 01222-666250

Western Sahara Campaign
47 Moreton Road
Buckingham MK18 1JZ

Wiener Library
4 Devonshire Street
London W1
Tel: 0171-636-7247
A library of material on German Jewish refugees.

Woodcraft Folk
13 Ritherdon Road
London SW17
Tel: 0181-672-6031
P E

World Aware
1 Catton Street
London WC1R 4AB
Tel: 0171-831-3844
0A distribution service for development education materials.

World Development Movement
25 Beehive Place
London SW9 7QR
Tel: 0171-737-6215
P

World University Service
20 Compton Terrace
London N1 2UN
Tel: 0171-288-4601
P